STOLEN LIFE

THE JOURNEY

Stolen

OF A CREE WOMAN

Life

Rudy Wiebe and Yvonne Johnson

SWALLOW PRESS
OHIO UNIVERSITY PRESS
Athens

FIRST SWALLOW PRESS/OHIO UNIVERSITY PRESS EDITION, 2000.

Swallow Press/Ohio University Press,
Athens, Ohio 45701

Swallow Press/Ohio University Press books are printed on acid-free paper ∞ ™
09 08 07 06 05 04 03 02 01 00   5 4 3 2 1

Library of Congress Cataloging-in-Publication Data

Wiebe, Rudy Henry, 1934-
Stolen life : the journey of a Cree woman / Rudy Wiebe
and Yvonne Johnson.
    p. cm.

ISBN 0-8040-1030-7 (paper : alk. paper)

1. Johnson, Yvonne, 1961– . 2. Cree women—Biography.
3. Women murderers—Biography. 4. Child abuse—Canada.
5. Justifiable homicide—Canada.
I. Johnson, Yvonne, 1961– .   II. Title.

E99.C88 J648 2000
364.15'23'092–dc21
[B]   00-033844

Cover design: C.S. Richardson

To my children, whom I love endlessly;
to all survivors and those who help them;
and, with the greatest respect, to Rudy

YVONNE JOHNSON

———

To the memory of Mistahi Muskwa (Big Bear),
1825–1888

RUDY WIEBE

The sentence has changed.
Once I could not remember.
Now I cannot forget.

ELLY DANICA
Don't: A Woman's Word

———

But crushing truths perish from being acknowledged.

ALBERT CAMUS
The Myth of Sisyphus

———

We pray at best for the open wound
to grow a scar.

PETER FALLON
"A Part of Ourselves"

CONTENTS

PREFATORY NOTE

This book is based on what Yvonne Johnson holds to be her own truths about the life she has lived. However, since there is never only one way to tell a story, other persons involved in this one may well have experienced and remember differently the events and actions here portrayed. The book is also based on my research into the circumstances of Yvonne's life. Besides over five years of dialogue with her, this research involved travel to various places crucial to the story; interviews wherever possible; attendance at trials; and the gathering of data from court, police, government, school, and newspaper records in both Canada and the United States.

I have gathered together Yvonne's words, as given in the present text, as she and I agreed, from various sources: largely her seventeen black prison notebooks, her letters to me, her comments on official records and documents, her statements to police, my notes of our conversations in person or on the telephone, numerous audiotapes. She has a natural gift of language, which at any moment will follow a detail and widen into incident, story, often humour. This was at first sometimes confusing, even disorienting, until I recognized that her thinking was often circular, revolving around a given subject, and her writing almost oral in the sense that I had to catch the tone of her inflection to understand exactly how the incidents she was remembering connected; where the expanding images or even parables with which she tried to explain herself were leading. These qualities can only be fully appreciated when talking with Yvonne face to face, but I hope this book will give its readers a good flavour of such a conversation.

What is remarkable and enlightening is how Yvonne's powers of writing have expanded during her time in prison. Her first letter to me (November, 1992, quoted at length in the first chapter) was as chatty as her talk still is; her formal education could, at best, barely be called erratic and ended in Grade Eight, but even in the earliest of her writing that I have seen she had a profound ability to capture an astute perception with words. For example, during her trial in March, 1991, she handed to her lawyer a long analysis of a relative, which included this comment:

> "She is a woman of many faces. . . . You know, the only feelings you get from her is one of her faces. One of her strong feelings is fear, anger. And she has a tongue like a knife in your heart."

Reading has helped her think and write. By 1998, after years of reading widely and deeply—including the works of Carl Jung, some of whose books she read and re-read while making copious notes—and thousands of pages of writing—by pen, typewriter, computer—Yvonne's imagistic insights have widened into longer, much more coherent explorations and descriptions. The written language of her perceptions and her natural oral story-telling ability have grown immensely, to become acute, distinctive, and often beautiful.

The selection, compiling, and arrangement of events and details in this book were done in a manner the two authors believe to be honest and accurate. Public documents are quoted selectively, but with every attempt at fairness and accuracy.

The actual names of people are used when their identities are a matter of public record; for others, and in the case of all persons at present minors, the names are pseudonyms. Also, the spelling, punctuation, and grammar in Yvonne's letters and notebooks have been standardized.

– Rudy Wiebe,
Edmonton, April 1998

O Creator of all, I pray you, look at me, for I am weak and
pitiful.

I pray,
        help me to make amends to all those I have harmed;
        grant them love and peace, so that they may under-
           stand I am sorry;
        help me to share my shame and pain, so that others
        will do the same, and so awaken to themselves
        and to all the peoples of the world.

Hai hai

Yvonne Johnson,
Okimaw Ohci Healing Lodge, April 1998

1

Blood Runs Thick and Long and For Ever

Nothing just happens, my friend, unless it was meant to be. . . . If we are guided under the Bear, then even our futures can be changed. . . . You and I may have been chosen long ago to meet, and our past has given us each a gift of understanding.

— Yvonne Johnson to Rudy Wiebe, 24 December 1992

TO BEGIN A STORY, someone in some way must break a particular silence. On Wednesday, 18 November 1992, in Edmonton, Alberta, I received an envelope from Box 515, Kingston, Ontario. Inside, folded into quarters, was a long sheet of paper typed from top to bottom, edge to edge, solid with words on both sides. It began:

Howdy Howdy Stranger

My name is Yvonne Johnson. I am currently an inmate at the Prison for Women in Kingston, Ontario. I am thirty-one years old. I am a Cree from Saskatchewan, that is where my ancestors come from. We were accepted back into my grandmother's rez after my mother was kicked out for marrying my father, who is a White from Great Falls, Montana. My grandmother Flora was a Baptiste, my grandfather was called John Bear, I lost him a few years back now; and my grandfather's grandfather was the Cree chief Big Bear.

On either side of the straight Saskatchewan road, the lines of barbed-wire fence try to square the land into right angles on the curving earth. The land is white here in January 1996, prairie-snow flat, and on this morning frigid fog hides the world; I can see nothing of sun beyond the fence. At the road crossing, where I feel the pavement end, I stop, turn right, and drive south—the Cree direction of the Law of Order, which is the natural order of Creation, the order of how things will happen. I need that today: order.

The road disappears ahead into limitless mist, slopes down a little and east, then straight south again, with all the land now rising about me. Gravel clatters, swerves. White-tailed deer feed above brush on the bare shoulders of a ravine; they will look up only if I stop, probably scatter if I get out, so I continue moving, very slowly. The temperature is twenty-two below, but the deer are spaced delicately at ease, heads bowed to their feeding scrawls in the snowy earth, and when the ravine hides them again I continue my watch into the grey mist, into its brightening; waiting. And then, imperceptibly, the high hills begin to emerge.

They are very nearly upon me, their folded shapes covered with hoar-frosted trees, the mass of the Cypress Hills like immense, furry animals kneeling down tight together, brilliant as spun glass against the sudden blue sky.

The road ahead vanishes again down into mist, then reappears once more, higher, like a question mark up into the hills.

The Stoney people called them *pa-ha-toonga*, the Thunder-Breeding Hills.

———

The "Howdy Stranger" letter continued:

> I was accepted by the Red Pheasant Reserve south of Battleford, but I do not know where I truly belong. As you may be aware, in 1885 my family and band were spread all over this continent after the imprisonment of Big Bear. I don't know where to start, or where to go from here, but I have a will and hopefully you can help to guide me somehow. I have been through a lot in the last few years. I don't have that much education, just what I've learned or I think I've learned over the years. I try to fake it a lot; sometimes it works, sometimes it doesn't [. . .].
>
> Well, once again, I am thirty-one and mother of three children and a stepson. I was born in a place called Kalispell, Montana, and raised in Butte, Montana. My brother was killed by the cops there when I was nine and my family, or what of it we had, went all to hell. My mom went on the AIM [American Indian Movement] march from Wounded Knee to Washington

in 1972 to see if she could get anything done about my brother's death, but came back empty and soon filed for divorce and said she was going back to her people. I stayed with my father, as no one else would and I could not leave him alone like that. All the other kids, minus the one brother who was in prison, went with my mom to Canada. Me, I was pulled back and forth a lot, as I am born with a cleft palate and lip and only in the United States would the Crippled Children's Fund pay for the repair I needed. I had a hard life and it keeps getting harder. I think it's a deep sense of true justice and understanding and of true knowledge I search for that keeps me going.

And believe me, death seems a lot easier and a lot less painful at times, but I guess I truly am a sucker for punishment. What can I say? I still hang in. Well, I just wish my life would change for the better at some point. I don't want to die this way, with nothing settled or overcome. I need to fight, I need to know where I come from and why our race suffers so from the hands of my White brothers. Just because I went through my first thirty years in silence does not mean I went through it blind and deaf as well. If anything, my silence enhanced my keen sense of observation — had to get the dictionary out for that one. All my luck, I probably copied it wrong! . . .

My mom's a Cree from a residential school in Sask.; my father is a ex–U.S. Marine of the Norwegian race. My dad was out of the war for a short time when he met my mom, who had also just got out of a hell of her own, the Indian school. Quite a combo, hey? There were seven kids in my family. Anyways, I don't hold it against them; they tried as best as they knew how. And I love them. I just hate reality, it's so cruel and unkind. But I hold history responsible for that as well. You see, I've spent the last thirty years running from it, but due to imprisonment I was forced to stop running, and that's so hard.

The car shudders over a cattle guard and I have entered the land of the Nekaneet Cree Nation. The road splits, one branch skirting right around an open slope towards the band office, but the one I want continues up into a fold of hills between the thick-rimed poplars. An occasional, isolated family house is visible behind trees or in a clearing, and then a large driveway breaks away at right angles, left. This must be it. Around a bend a standard wire double gate appears, its two halves swung back wide open, its two posts set into the shoulders of the road and connecting to nothing; no fence, no barbed wire, no warning sign, no suggestion of barrier or clearing, simply the snow and brush and white poplar forest which covers the Cypress Hills, vanishing into itself.

On these slopes that forest has never been touched by either axe or saw, and the Okimaw Ohci Healing Lodge for Federally Sentenced Aboriginal Women, Correctional Services Canada, Prairie Region, has been built in a narrow space cleared and levelled especially for it. When I get out of the car on the upper level of the parking lot, it seems I am above the entire world. I look north over the flat centre and wings of a low building, past the swallowtail crossings of what must be the poles of a huge wooden teepee rising behind it, and beyond, over the frosted trees and bare white slopes and shoulders of hills, down to prairie. The level land disappears everywhere into horizonless silver under the blue, brightening sun, disappears everywhere north, which is the direction of the Bear and Honesty and the Law of Harmony that subsumes within itself all four of the sacred laws—the control, order, balance, and harmony within Creation.

The double set of entrance doors (this is, after all, a winter country) pull open into a lobby which faces the building's round inner courtyard, open to sky. The four colours in the floor tiles—yellow, red, blue, white—orient me in the four directions.

The young woman seated at the reception desk knows I am coming, and for whom; I sign the register, name and time, and in a moment Yvonne is there. Smiling, as happy to see me as I am to see her, here, for the first time away from the oppressive stone-and-old-painted-steel monstrosity of the Prison for Women (p4w) in Kingston, where we last saw each other and from where she first wrote to me; tall and slender in sweater, jeans, moccasins. We hug, quick and loose because for her the arms of men have mostly been dangerous, often terrible.

We circle through the building, talking. She introduces me to everyone we meet, all women, almost all apparently Native, and since everyone wears casual working clothes I have no idea from either her introductions or their insignia, if any, what their status is. Inmates here are called "residents," guards "older sisters," administrators "aunts," the warden "Mother." A circle of young women in the windowed bay of the dining room/lounge is assembling a 1,000-piece Italian landscape puzzle, and an older woman is introduced to me as one of the local Elders—there is one present all the time. She nods and smiles gently, warmly, at me, saying nothing.

"This place is a circle," Yvonne tells me as we walk the curving corridors. "See, offices inside and outside, and then the extensions on either side are like the spread wings of an eagle. From above it looks just like a flying eagle. With four exit doors, opening to the four directions."

I hadn't recognized the eagle shape from above in the parking lot: I have to learn how to look. "It's amazing," I say. "So much light, and delicate, beautiful wood. I've never seen a building like this."

"A lot of cedar," she points out, "the wood of protection. We are all safe inside cedar. It's an architectural marvel. The Elders said how it should be, and they chose this place. When the government decided to go ahead with the plan that the band here suggested for a new kind of prison, the Elders went looking on this land. No one had ever even hunted here; this hill and trees were sacred. And when they walked here, the tobacco they carried was pulled down, so they laid it on the ground and said, 'This is the place, build it here, a house for healing our people. Where Elders shall lead.' "

If I close my eyes and stare into memory, I can see the massive grey façade of the Prison for Women, stones cut square and mortared together high and straight and thick as irrefutable sin. Yvonne was in there from April 1991 until September 1995; I visited her there four times. But now her quiet voice continues, telling me the new story of this place:

"Once the site for the Healing Lodge was chosen, the Elders tied four ceremonial flags to the trees on the limits of the land at the four directions, to let the Creator and the Spirit World acknowledge the place. So the spiritual boundaries were set, and now no bars or fencing is needed here because if you cross the boundaries of the four colours you defy the Creator and the Spirits, the ultimate disrespect, and who would do that?"

We are standing on the open balcony off the dining room in the bristling cold, leaning on the railing and against the huge wooden posts that support the rafters. The living units where the residents share apartments are separate, built along a short road to the west. Before us, shingled in cedar, is the great teepee-like structure Yvonne calls the Spirit Lodge, and beyond it the frosted poplar forest folds down ravines into the prairie.

"There are beavers here." Yvonne gestures with her cigarette into the trees below us. And through brush, between poplar trunks, I can see the flatness of white ice that curves sharply at a possible dam, the white hump of a lodge with dark logs sticking out. The only animal that architecturally alters its environment—except human beings, of course.

———

Yvonne's first letter to me from Box 515, Kingston, concluded:

But I have read your book The Temptations of Big Bear. *And I must admit I have seen it many times before but did not wish to even pick it up, as I figured, yeah, what do any of those White people or history really know of my family [. . .]. But now I am glad I read your book. I was slapped in the face by how much you really knew or could understand. And I wondered if you had talked to my relatives. Or how you did your research. Where did you get it all? [. . .] Lately more and more Natives are interested in Big Bear, for reasons too numerous to mention. Land claims would be my guess. My grandpa John was a self-proclaimed chief by blood to Big Bear, and he went to Hobbema and other places to get them to fight for his birthright, and now many people are looking into him. And in my own research I find everyone shutting up on me [. . .]. I run into special difficulties because of where I am, and I don't have great contact with my family, so I cannot get at all the info I need to get a better understanding which is in the minds of the old folks that are left alive on the rez. And I fear I lose one every day I am in here. The old people tried to tell me before, but I was not ready for it. I've lost too many already. I feel as if I'm the last in my family who can get it back, as the others just don't care. I fear it will all be lost. I'm scared of the great loss that will be; I can't let it die.*

Please help me share what it is you know, and how you got it. How is it you came to know as much as you do? Were you led? What was the force behind you? Who are you? Why did you choose Big Bear to write about? What sparked your interest in this powerful man of long ago? I wish to clear his name and to recover his medicine bundle as I try to find my lost family, and only under our Bear Spirit will it ever be true. We have not guarded it as we should have, and now we have suffered long enough; now is the time to heal and to return to the land and reclaim our rightful place and to meet my family that has been sent all over the four winds. We need to come together as Big Bear wished.

[signed] *Yvonne Johnson*

On 14 January 1996, wherever Yvonne and I look from the balcony of the Okimaw Ohci Healing Lodge on the eastern massif of the Cypress Hills, everything we see, and beyond, was her great-great-grandfather's country. Mistahi Muskwa—Big Bear—and his Plains Cree people lived and hunted buffalo and antelope and deer and moose north to the Great Sand Hills and the Eagle Hills and Sounding Lake and the North Saskatchewan River and Fort Pitt and Jackfish Lake, where he was born about 1825, and all the way south to the Milk and Missouri rivers, country they walked and rode and hunted, old people, children, women, men, this immense land as familiar to them and the soles of their feet as the terrain of their own hands. Land which Big Bear refused to surrender to the Canadian government when Lieutenant-Governor Alexander Morris and all his officialdom dragged themselves painfully through the country during the long summer of 1876, carrying many little presents of food and ceremonial clothing, and the paper which would become the Cree's eternal sentence, Treaty Number Six:

The tract [of land] embracing an area of one hundred and twenty thousand square miles, be the same more or less; to have and to hold the same to Her Majesty the Queen and her successors forever.

A land area a third larger than the entire United Kingdom.

The Canadian government first officially appeared on the prairie to Big Bear and his band in 1875, in the form of a Methodist minister, the Reverend George McDougall. It was McDougall's official assignment to "tranquillize" the prairie Indians so they would "await in full confidence the coming of the Treaty Commissioners." But Chief Big Bear refused a quick tranquillization; he told McDougall with absolute clarity:

"We want none of the Queen's presents. When we set a fox-trap we scatter pieces of meat all around, but when the fox gets into the trap, we knock him on the head."

As a result of that statement and McDougall's report of it, Big Bear officially became known as "a troublesome fellow"; to his own people, he was a great leader with powerful medicine who received dreams and saw visions, but, for the churchmen advising the government, he was an evil conjuror. So he was not notified to attend any signing for Treaty Number Six the following summer. But he appeared in September 1876 at the Fort Pitt treaty ceremonies anyway and badly interrupted what until then had been mostly expansive, agreeable speeches. Facing Lieutenant-Governor Morris, Big Bear made the second of his profound, imagistic statements about Native–White relations:

"There is one thing that I dread: to feel the rope around my neck."

At first Morris understood this on a simple, literal level: it must refer to the White legal practice of hanging criminals, and since Big Bear was now definitely confirmed as "troublesome," no doubt he feared that fate if he signed. But Big Bear persisted, and at a certain point in the debate, which Morris himself recorded in his memoirs in 1880, the governor seemed to grasp the larger meaning of the statement: Big Bear was speaking for his people then alive and their children yet to be born in an all-inclusive image, and suddenly Morris made a radical concession in his interpretation of what the treaty meant:

"I wish the Bear . . . to understand fully, and tell the others [those people who are not here]. . . . The Government will not interfere with the Indian's daily life, they will not bind him."

Clearly, Morris understood what Big Bear was saying, and he responded with a transparent, official lie. Taking the Cree's immense land and forcing them to live in a reserve system was such an enormous "interference" and "binding" of their daily life—many Native people now speak of their reserves as "prisons of grass"—that it seems the chiefs listening to this debate in 1876 could not even imagine how enormous a lie it truly was. They all "touched the pen," and so signed. But Big Bear refused; he and his people followed the buffalo south into Montana.

Of course, Big Bear did eventually sign as well. He had to, when the death of the last buffalo between the Missouri and Milk rivers in Montana forced him and the 1,200 Cree then in his band into starvation. When they arrived at the Medicine Line between U.S. and Canadian territory, they found that the North-West Mounted Police had very clear orders: no food for non-treaty Indians. After holding out for a better treaty for over six years, after debating strategy with his family and council all fall, on a cold December day in 1882 Big Bear signed his adhesion to Treaty Number Six so that his starving people would have something to eat during the hard winter.

Big Bear signed at Fort Walsh in the Cypress Hills—as the raven flies, less than fifty kilometres from where Yvonne and I now stand, talking.

"I'm just happy to talk," Yvonne says; "it's really new for me. I spent my life listening and dreaming as other people spoke, to feel what they were saying."

"You talk well enough now," I tell her with a grin. "You've sent me fifteen notebooks already, most of them over three hundred pages!"

"But I can never write fast enough, I can't keep up, feelings aren't words, if I could speak things all the time you'd have even more!"

She's smiling at me; she has sent me tapes and videos as well, but they are so difficult to organize, her memories are so interwoven and intersnarled, that I've begged her to write only, however it comes and she remembers, but write it down; write, please.

She continues, "I guess when I talk I express myself like I listened, story form. It's actually an easy way to understand if you yourself can listen. But not many people are good listeners and that doesn't matter to me. I tell little stories so you can see, live, feel what I am trying to explain to you. Like I'm figuring it out, out loud. I'm always all over the place. People say I can't stay on one topic; sometimes when I just say things head-on, point blank, it drives them crazy to have to listen to me. Some of the girls in P4W used to tease me; they said they were going to paint a T-shirt with words on the front, 'Ask me a question . . . ,' and on the back '. . . and I'll tell you a story!' "

She laughs white clouds into the cold air; her cigarette is finished and we're freezing.

"But the Elders say that storytelling is a gift too. If a person with a story can go deep, where people are angry, sad, where they're hiding thoughts and emotions, raise the past they've maybe forgotten and can't really recognize any more, push them to spirit-walk into themselves — to do that with a story is a gift."

We go back into the open dining/social area and find a private space.

I nudge Yvonne back to her ancestry. "You've never told me exactly how you're related to Big Bear."

"Yeah," she says. "Maybe some of my aunts or uncles know, but my mother will not tell me now. Perhaps for some reason she's afraid to break the silence about my family, but I need to know my heritage. My grandma Flora wouldn't speak about Grandpa John's family, and he never did either. Maybe because they were both related to Big Bear, somehow, and in the Cree way that isn't right, they shouldn't marry, but they never would say. Big Bear had several wives who had many children, so it's possible. I don't know, and no one tells me now. In Natives, blood runs thick and long and for ever."

"So what was your grandma Flora's mother's name, the great-grandma you knew, your dad showed me a picture of her in her coffin, she died in the seventies and over a hundred?"

"They said she was a hundred and sixteen, and I don't know her name. Mom just called her 'Kohkom,' 'Grandma' in Cree. Mom just always said, 'You're Native, you be proud of it.' And I did have such pride being Native that I never thought to justify it by finding out my bloodline."

"And you never asked her the Cree names of ancestors?"

"No, not really. You're careful with Cree names — brother, daughter, okay, but not names. When I was little I heard that Grandpa John's father was Big Bear's son, and the story was that people came to call him a bad medicine man because they feared Big Bear. It had something to do with submitting to the Whites, with turning against Big Bear's advice during the rebellion in 1885, because in doing that they had also turned against his Bear Spirit. So they feared Big Bear, and that was made worse by their shame at having given in rather than stand up for their rights and spiritual beliefs, as he wanted them to. So they called his son 'a bad medicine man,' and they said he made some sort of pact with bad spirits because he was mad at the government, and forfeited all his boys to the evil—all except John, who was the youngest. The story was that John and his father stood on the shore of a lake and watched all the other sons walk into the lake and drown. They say that as the last bubble of their breath broke on the surface, John's father screamed and jerked a handful of hair out of John's head, threw it on the ground and spit on it, and swore that never again would there be anything like this in our family, never. I don't remember—know— what the deal was my great-grandfather had made; it had something to do with government, but he renounced it then, and I think Grandpa John knew this from when he was a small boy."

Yvonne looks up past the wide, laminated rafters of the room, away into distance; her long, black hair falls in a thick braid to her waist and her long slant of body sits still as a shadow, but I have watched her talk for hours and I know she is deeply troubled. She searches her way into sound, slowly. "I don't know . . . maybe, when Grandpa died, the curse had run its course . . . I just don't know. Sometimes I pray for direct guidance, from Big Bear's spirit. I've written many, many letters to archives, but they won't look up anything for me. I wish I could go to those places, and poke around, to get any information hiding in papers, in pictures. Even if I don't know what I'm looking for, I know I would know if I saw it."

But she won't be able to go "there," to Ottawa or Washington or Montana or Regina or wherever the archives are that might help inform her. She is sentenced to life in prison for first-degree murder, and not until she has served twenty-five years—15 September 2014—will she be eligible for parole. If that is granted, she will be released, but nevertheless remain on parole until she dies. The "faint hope" clause of a parole hearing at fifteen years is truly that: so faint as to be, for her, almost indiscernible.

"If I even live that long."

———

Who is Yvonne Johnson, and what was she accused of doing to become the only Native woman in Canada with such an immovable sentence of first-degree murder?

Why is she serving the heaviest possible sentence in the Canadian Criminal Code, but nevertheless was the fifth woman to be accepted in this minimum-security prison, this new Healing Lodge in *mi-na-ti-kak*, "the beautiful high lands" as the Cree call them, of southern Saskatchewan?

Early on Friday morning, 15 September 1989, the body of Charles Skwarok was found in the Wetaskiwin, Alberta, city dump. Within hours Yvonne, her common-law husband, Dwayne Wenger, and her acquaintance Ernest Jensen were arrested, charged with murdering Skwarok in the basement of Yvonne and Dwayne's Wetaskiwin house. Three days later Yvonne's maternal first cousin, Shirley Anne Salmon, was arrested for the same crime. In the various trials that followed, Shirley Anne pleaded guilty to aggravated assault and was sentenced to one year in jail; Dwayne pleaded guilty to second-degree murder and was sentenced to life, ten years; Ernie was convicted of second-degree murder and sentenced to life, ten years; Yvonne was convicted of first-degree murder and sentenced to life, twenty-five years.

Did Yvonne, of all the four acknowledged participants, deserve the heaviest sentence? Did she get justice, or simply a full, overwhelming measure of law?

And the larger question: why was she involved in murder at all? When I answered Yvonne's first letter, I had no idea of what crime she was convicted; I was powerfully intrigued by this self-aware, storytelling descendant of the historical Big Bear who had been living, growing, in my imagination for over three decades and who himself died in 1888 from the effects of what was surely an unjust imprisonment. But as Yvonne's and my letters, phone calls, and finally our personal visits grew, her life became as vital and irrefutable to me as that of her magnificent ancestor.

———

Seven months after my first meeting with Yvonne at the Healing Lodge, on 22 August 1996, I will be lying on my back in a high-hill glade nearby, staring up into a blue sky running with mare's tails. Yvonne's cousin Rose has organized a cycle of four sweats to help Yvonne on her spiritual walk, and she has invited me to join.

Like the other men visitors lying around me, breathing hard, I wear only shorts and my body pours sweat: the body cleansing itself of wastes and pollutants—the mirror of the spirit cleansing itself in prayer to find balance, wholeness, self-awareness. We have completed the third round of the forty-stone sweat, and soon we will crawl back into the sweat lodge beside us for the fourth and final round. The Elder's helper will have carried the last grandfather stones from the fire into the centre pit and he will close us in, cover us over with complete, absolute darkness—sight and taste gone, but hearing and smell and touch and spirit intensified. Then the ancient, spiritual songs, the Cree prayers, will begin to rise with the steam rising from the white-hot rocks as the Elder sprinkles water on them by shaking his spray of leafy wet poplar branches. And again I will try to pray.

Resting on the ground, I look across the clearing. In the shade of nearby trees sit the women who are praying this sweat also. They wear long, belted robes; we will all soon re-enter the round sweat lodge together, and the women will sit in the darkness on their side across the fire pit from the men. Rose and Yvonne are there; even without my glasses I can see Yvonne's blue robe among the women resting silent on the grass, blurry as bright flowers that have burst out of the green earth suddenly.

Then Yvonne gets up, walks away into the open glade. Against the trees and the grassy shoulders of the hills she moves down the slope; disappears.

Later she writes to me: "I lay down in the field and cried, staring into the sky with such anger mingled with pain, all I could do was shed tears at my lostness. I was so angry I wanted to walk away, go, I'm beyond help, just a lost cause, hopeless. . . . But my cousin knows how I am, all the pain, and she had put up four sweats for me. I had to return. Go back into the sweat, pray for help in my pitiful state, all my misplaced pride and honour; asking again how to become a true, proud, Native woman."

For almost four years she has sent me the journals that I urged her to write—get everything, anything, into words, on paper, write it down, every memory, emotion, rage, laugh, pain—all of it, as it comes. And we

have talked, face to face in the Prison for Women and for hours by telephone; we have exchanged letters; she has sent me boxes of notes and
comments on legal documents, on trial transcripts. At the moment I
cannot see her, but I know she will not have broken the spiritual bound-
ary of the Healing Lodge; I know she is looking at the sky, the grass, the
trees and hills and distant prairie, as I am; looking at Creation's brightness through the darkness of the sweat lodge; looking inward. She has
asked me to help her; I have promised her, "Yes"—though, foolishly, I
had no idea what a difficult thing I was promising—and, for these
years, we have struggled to tell her story so that she, so that I, so that
some possible reader will understand. Something.

Why has she lived such a dreadful life, and why has she been so destructive to herself and those she loves? Why have they been so devas-
tatingly destructive to her? How is it she became entangled in murder?
What I already know of her life makes it almost too horrifically repre-
sentative of what has happened to the Native people of North America;
of what her ancestor Big Bear most feared about the ruinous White
invasion that in his time overwhelmed him, that jailed him in Stony
Mountain Prison in 1885 for treason-felony, that is, for "intending to
levy war against the Queen, Her crown and dignity." Sadly enough,
that stone-and-steel fortress on top of its limestone extrusion in flat
Manitoba had been completed in plenty of time to receive him.

That being said, at the same time Yvonne is as much White as
Native. In fact, she and her family tried to live "White" throughout her
childhood in the United States—she remains a born citizen of the
United States, although through the Red Pheasant Reserve she has Indian status in Canada—but in Butte, Montana, she was "called down"
as "Indian," as "a dirty breed," protected by few discernible laws. The
White so-called law-enforcers destroyed her brother and became her
worst abusers, until finally she had to flee to Canada for her life.

"My Native side sometimes hurt me," she writes to me, "but it
never came close to doing to me what the White side did. I became
comfortable with my Native self, so that is where I chose to exist out of.
And yes, I am happy being a 'dirty Indian.'"

Yvonne finds growing strength in nothing the White half of her
heritage gave her in the first fifteen years of her life, but rather in the
spiritual and personal heritage of her Cree ancestors, particularly in

her grandmother Flora Baptiste Bear, and most particularly in her extraordinary progenitor the Plains Cree chief Mistahi Muskwa. Her voice speaking to me echoes his: a sense of heritage, of self-awareness and knowledge, of suffering, of self-deprecating humour, a longing for vision and understanding.

But it is necessary to recognize, to understand that though Yvonne Johnson, in contrast to her historic great-great-grandfather, may be in a beautiful, natural place said by all the official brochures to be built for healing, where no stone walls or barbed-wire fences are anywhere visible, nevertheless she remains in prison.

The astonishing beauty of the Healing Lodge and landscape in which it is built have made me forget that; but I am reminded late in the afternoon of the second day of my visit in January 1996. I've signed out, and Yvonne and I are opposite the entrance desk, near the two sets of outside doors. She stops; I am slightly ahead of her, reaching for the door handle.

"Here," she says. "I can't go farther."

I look at her and she gestures slightly with her hand and turns quickly—she told me the first time I met her in the stone prison in Kingston, "I'm not so good at saying goodbye. I just say 'See you later'"—and I recognize what she means by "here."

And I turn too and go out, fast, out to the snowy huddle of cars near the stark poplars.

She never had to say that in Kingston; there, I was never lulled into comfortable blindness by sitting for two days in a high open lounge, by easy chairs, and laughter from shifting groups of women across a bright room, by loading our trays side by side with food from a buffet and eating and talking with others around a round table. In P4W even I could see the painted and repainted stone walls, the steel bars and doors, and now as I push through snow towards my car it seems suddenly that the whole weight of that oppressive fortress lands on me—despite Saskatchewan cold burning my face—and in my nostrils I am inside it again, the smell and the sound and what I discovered within myself to be the almost unendurable *heft* of it; I'm so happy I'm out, free and out, I sprint to my car. Even as I think of Yvonne having to walk back, I'm euphoric. I crank the engine and wheel around out of there. I will drive, drive!

On the Trans-Canada Highway, near Strathmore, Alberta, the blizzard begins to shiver the car. I ease through it into the edge of Calgary, gas up, make a phone call, and avoid the police patrolling Highway Two north to Edmonton. It's only three hundred kilometres, with four lanes all the way—easy, I could drive it blind. And as I accelerate to cruise speed out of the valley of Nose Creek and up onto the prairie, momentarily the western wind from the mountains seems to wipe the snow away into clear, star-struck darkness. Nothing but darkness, here and there a farmyard light, a huddle of town, the occasional car lights approaching in the on-coming lanes. Then nothing opposite, the car humming, so contained and unperturbed, ominously nothing but darkness. And then slowly, softly it seems, the snow begins again, slanting through my short, narrow light in streaks, skating, swirling over the whitening pavement like the advance and foam of a running sea—boiling gusts, white waves, washing under, splashing over me. Gradually I catch up and become part of a single line of four cars accumulating behind a snowplough as it drags ridges out of the crunching drifts. I am counting stopped and stalled cars, pick-ups and multitrailer trucks caught in strange angles on shoulders and twirled into ditches, folded across medians by the screaming weight of the wind; I am following two red hazard lights blinking into whistling darkness and I am concentrated, intense. I can do this, this beautiful night blizzard; I can drive or stop if I want to, slide with the wind for the ditch and carefully ease, ease out of it, that heart-lurching slide, do anything; I can do it hunched around the steering wheel of my tough little car; and, peering into the shrieking blizzard, I am singing, very, very happy.

The snow slams at me everywhere, this world I was born into, and in the white darkness I see again the Cypress Hills as I left them behind, an immense herd of shot horses crumpled and heaped down dark on the horizon as I drove west, very fast into red sunset, towards the rising wall of storm clouds, into the cold, coming brilliance of prairie snow.

2

My Eyes Became My Voice

I've learned so much about myself, I can't write it all, or fast enough, I can't write it the way it should be said. It is sometimes easier to say thoughts than to write them because saying something is living it, feeling it, connecting with it again. No writing can capture that fully. In a way, speaking is alive, writing makes it become dead. What is written is not really a thought put to memory, as why remember what you can go back to and look up, if need be?

– Yvonne, *Journal 9*, 20 February 1994

T HE FIRST TIME Yvonne Johnson and I meet to talk face to face is on Thursday, 10 June 1993, in a windowless room deep inside the limestone walls of the federal Prison for Women (P4W) in Kingston, Ontario. The Psychology Department's small interview room is crammed with a sofa and chairs, a coffee table, and tall, locked cupboards; Yvonne's counsellor and her Elizabeth Fry Society advisor have arranged that we meet here without direct supervision.

"We can talk here," Yvonne says, and adds lightly, ironically, "I think . . . it's not supposed to be bugged. At least there's nothing posted 'This Area Is Subject to Monitoring,' like everywhere else."

Her words are slightly blurred, drawn out but intense—is it her Montana drawl or the exact physical control of breathing she must maintain in order to speak, the lingering "s's" she cannot say quite precisely because she was born with a bilateral cleft palate and lip?

When the barred door slid aside on the dark, sounding corridors and stairs of P4W and I saw her for the first time, it seemed that, despite our long telephone conversations, she was materializing out of prison blankness, that she was coming towards me contained in a kind of silence that would surely be indecipherable to me. But she strode without hesitation towards me in the small lobby between the electronic doors, a tall, slim woman with her face set in wary expectation, a bandanna holding back black hair hanging to her waist; dark skin; brown, almost black, eyes. And she reached her hand out; our right thumbs locked and our fingers brushed each other's wrists, her right hand holding me at that slight distance of a careful, formal greeting. Then her left arm came up and hugged me almost without touching, a few pats of warmth on my back.

"Hi, I'm Yvonne," she said, "but my family calls me Vonnie. You can call me anything . . ."—and she laughed a little—"except late for supper!"

Prison is a very tough place to meet; a woman and a man who've corresponded intensely but never seen each other, inside this stone place designed for lifetimes of confinement, where blurred shouts boom and echo along grey corridors and barred steel seems to be slamming continuously. Everything is so loud, controlled, balancing—no, teetering on an edge. No glance is merely a glance; it is a body search. The entire building seems to heave, Yvonne will tell me, breathing hard and blowing away the spirits of all the women it has sucked up.

But she makes camaraderie happen immediately between us, despite the female guard at the electronic doors peering at us, despite the two even larger guards who have brought her here from her cell; she starts it with her deliberate Montana drawl and flat, country joke.

Now we are alone, door closed, and we're seated in easy chairs kitty-corner at the coffee table; she opens her bundle and lays out a small sweetgrass ceremony. When we and the room are cleansed, I give her my gift of cigarettes, she gives me a long braid of sweetgrass and three small red cloth pouches of the other sacred medicines—tobacco, cedar, sage—tied together with leather thongs. We sip coffee; at first we chat about easy things to find our balance, about the usual Canadian distances, weather, the long flight from Edmonton and the seemingly even longer highway trip from Toronto.

Then she places three thick notebooks on the low table—her journals—and explains how hard it is for her to write her thoughts; it would be so much easier, she thinks, to talk into a tape recorder. And I am rippling the pages of one hardcover book and then another, my eye running over words, dates, down pages of marvellous words fixed there for as long as paper and ink will endure, and I tell her again, please, as I have so often on the phone, tapes are so hard to order, so hopeless to organize or grasp because to find anything you have to listen to everything all over again, in sequence: if she wants to tell her story, her words must be on paper.

She of course knows this. She says she's kept a journal since early May 1991, two weeks after they brought her to Kingston. And she likes writing in these hard black books, paper feels good, filling every line even if her spelling isn't so hot, and we chuckle, feeling better with each other; though we remain very careful. We don't know this yet, but in the next six years of working together we will never once have an argument.

And I listen to her low, quiet voice become steadily more flat, her warm, expressive face retreating into an apparent calm, almost expressionless. It must be a projection from within, perhaps a shield to protect herself from all I still have no comprehension of, as gradually, steadily she begins to speak with that amazing candour she will always give me about herself and her family, a taut personal quality which I do not yet know will continue without hesitation for hours.

"Everyone in my family is suffering, but we're never responsible, no, never us — somebody else did something horrible, okay, but never us. If anything ever gets said, about what went on between us, it's a slip of the lip when we're drinking, and sure, that can turn into a drunken argument or a fight, no-holds-barred, and maybe even Mom will get pulled into it, if things are yelled and repeated. But we're all partly drunk when it happens, and then we part ways for a while, and a long time later we'll slowly drift together again, but if we do, it means we never speak about what happened, never. Pretend we don't know, never admit anything, never look into anyone's eyes more than a second — nothing happened. We just can't pull it together to try to talk, about anything. My family has stayed together as much as it has by denial, shame, fear . . . all the other good stuff like that."

She laughs without smiling, humourlessly. "Don't talk, just play the duck."

"Duck?"

"Sure, a duck swims on the water, it dives under, water rolls off its feathers. It's never actually wet — so just float, dive and hide, come up, and let the shit roll off with all the rest of the crap that's being thrown at you.

"But me, I'm tired of playing. The truth and reality of my life is in the existence I live now, in this prison with this sentence. I won't be ashamed of what was done to me in my life any more. I accept my faults, I've learned to wear my own shame, but I refuse to wear anyone else's — and I give back to my abusers the shame that is theirs and theirs alone. What I have done, what was done to me, that will never silence me again."

"Yes," I say, "yes—but it'll be hard. There are so many people in your life, no story is ever only yours alone."

She looks at me quick and straight. We are sitting on the Core Can Industries furniture, assembled by the several thousand men who are inmates in all the other federal stone prisons scattered around Kingston. Neither of us yet has a true conception of how difficult it will be to tell her story. After forty years of work at writing, I think I know a bit about making stories, but I don't grasp the impossibilities of this one; not yet.

"Maybe not *only* my story—but it is *mine*. Others maybe won't agree, but I want to tell my life the way I see it." Yvonne continues more quietly, "Brother against sister, sister against sister, we fight, we shift from one clique to another of gossip and unspoken accusations. Once my sister Minnie said to me, 'So you got fucked, huh! So forget it, you'll get fucked again.' But I can't live like that.

"We won't talk. And now that we four sisters all have kids, we just know we have to watch closer over them, protect them from what happened to us. And if anything should happen, well, we'll run away and just act as if nothing happened—it's all right, nothing happened! We all know it's not right, it's no family secret any more, and yet the denial goes on and on. I try to tell my sisters I've made a way for them to follow, I can take it, I've laid myself down like a bridge, all they have to do is walk over me. But their healing can't be done by me; for them, it's still just deny and run, that's all."

Yvonne pauses. For some time I have been staring at, but not really seeing, her beaded moccasins. They look so soft and delicately beautiful, to walk in them must feel like silk feathers.

"That's a mystery to most of the world—why silence? why denial? But it's no mystery to the abused.

"Predators and victims. That's why my family drinks to excess. Drugs and booze suck up hopes, every little dream you have, as easy as opening your mouth and just lift your hand and pour it down. Abuse happens, and down it goes into you, down to hide in the mucky silence of drugs and booze. Living like we do, it'll happen again, and again, and we take it. It just goes with the territory."

She will tell me later, when I ask, that she sewed the moccasins herself, low, Cree-style. And I will see the superb, delicate drawing and sewing she does, the laced-together knee-high Apache boots she makes but does not wear with jeans. They, too, are as lovely as anything I've ever seen flickering on dancing feet in a powwow.

But now she tells me, grimly, "I never had any great plans about what I wanted to be when I grew up. My life got to be so minimal, my only plan . . . I guess, stay alive. Though sometimes I can't think of why I even wanted that. The cop who interviewed me yesterday said, 'I can't recall anything that young.' I knew he was feeling me out, and I told him I can recall things before three, or even two. If I have a visual memory, I don't doubt myself. I don't doubt the houses I lived in, in Butte, Montana."

———

Yvonne: I'm a baby, less than two, and I've been laid down for a nap. I'm looking through the bars of my crib, through the small square panes of the window, and there's a bell-shaped window in the house next door. Years later my sister Kathy and I play hookey from school and we're in an empty lot on busy Montana Street, just weeds wide open to the sky, and I feel it: I've been here; our first brick house stood here once. A sagging garage at the back is all that's left on the lot, and there's the name *L-E-O-N* painted on the door. My brother's name, with the *E* backwards, the way he often wrote it.

I looked up then and yes, there was the bell-shaped window that got hid in my memories. And on the corner the gas station, still there, where the orange balls jumped around on the side of the pump when Dad gassed up. Leon once started a fire there, and another time the gas station had a fire on its own without Leon's help.

That's the first house I remember, red brick on Montana, Butte's main street, coming wide and straight down the mountain through town, with shaft mines and frames sticking up all over between the houses and buildings. Parades come marching, down past the front of our house, and candy wrapped in paper scatters behind the booming bands. If I can get into the street I can pick it up and shove it into my mouth and let it melt, sweeter than sugar. The front steps give me slivers. I have to go down on my hands and knees backwards, I'm so little.

There never was anything but big sky and mountains over our pink house on Butte's east side, 1138 Madison. Now not only that house is gone, the whole street has disappeared. But the summer between two and three I remember short Madison Street and the wooden house painted pink. There is a yard and a fence, and after a rain the dirt cracks into little pieces and curls, and I pick up chunks of curled mud. My dad once said something about mud pies, so I try to bite into the mud he called pies. It's really gritty, worse than peanut butter choking me up. I can't do anything but cry. There is no roof in my mouth, and crying and choking to breathe makes the mud ooze over my lips, out of my nostrils. I can only run to Mom choking, blowing dirt in snotty bubbles, and crying.

The picket fence is white; only the level grade of the railroad separates our yard from the enormous open pit of the Berkeley Mine that's chewing down into the mountain above us. It is never dark in the house because at night the floodlights from the pit blaze over us, the machinery grinds. Twenty-four hours a day huge trucks, their tires higher than our car, growl past; we have to stop and wait for them to cross the street, and the house rumbles like an earthquake. They could squash us flat and not notice. Dad says a blast of their exhaust would fry an egg on the roof of the car. There are even bigger trucks deep down in the pit on the mountain; the noise never stops, hammering, grinding up the earth.

I remember all the shift changes, the miners from both the pit and the shaft mines walking with their food buckets past our picket fence on the street. Suddenly the sirens roar, long, long, and every truck stops moving; there is a kind of calm, and suddenly a blast shakes the earth as if Butte Mountain has shivered, and shaken all the buildings and all the gallows frames of the shaft mines above us loose, and is going to slide them down on top of us. But then a huge cloud of dust from the pit billows into the sky, and the machinery starts again — it was only a dynamite blast in what is the deepest man-made hole in the world, Butte always brags—besides holding the world record of fourteen thousand miles of tunnels under its city limits. Every day the Berkeley Pit is getting bigger and bigger between us and the next line of mountains, chewing its way closer to the railroad and to us.

Beside us there are a few two-storey houses. Mom tries to keep me away from the train, but sometimes I get up the embankment to the track and find the rocks with pretty gold bits— Dad laughs and says it's "fool's gold"—and silver flecks that fall off the ore cars. There are words like pictures on the cars, the curls of PACIFIC, the angles of ANACONDA, and the cars from the smelter where Mom sometimes works when Grandpa Louie babysits us have runnings down their sides as if they were crying from their one giant eye on top, yellow or white, depending on how recently it was overfilled. The engine will whistle as it approaches the street, and I wait and wait for it. I pull my arm up and down, and the engine driver waves at me; his arm goes pump, pump, and the whistle blows again. I love the caboose. I wait the whole train just to see the caboose, and sometimes the conductor throws a candy to me. It's always hard; it lasts a long time because I can't suck anything.

There are black-and-white pictures of us six kids—Perry wasn't born yet—at the Pink House. One in the kitchen with my tall brother Earl standing back almost in shadow, and Grandpa Louie's round, bald head bent over us four sisters all in a row on chairs. Me with my little bare legs parted, sitting on Leon's lap. And the other snap taken in the yard shows only us kids and the Butte landscape. We stand in a tight cluster so you can see the exact size of our ages, with the picket fence behind us, and beyond that the lines of the power poles and drainpipes and railroad disappearing into rows of piled-up dirt. A long conveyor belt sticks up over the tracks. And the bare, grey mountains along the top of the picture far away look like they were shovelled up together too.

We four little Johnson girls in dresses stand at the front, each of us a year apart. Karen, the oldest, between seven and eight, who will be the first of us to be shacked up when she's seventeen. Sharon, who we always call Minnie, grinning all her bright teeth, always Dad's favourite child. Then Kathy, a year older than me, with her black, beautiful hair—she called herself the black sheep of the family—and finally me, the littlest, smiling so desperately, with my arms wrapped tight around my chest, holding myself together.

The boys stand behind us, Leon between Karen and me and shoulder high to a tall boy Dad says lived with us a lot then, his family was broken up; and beside him, tallest of all, my handsome brother Earl. He's going on fifteen, smiling, his heavy hair greased down in a curl on the right side of his face—he spent a lot of time getting the flip in his hair just so before he left for school—leaning forward a little like a Cree peering at you, his hands behind his back, and wearing a white T-shirt with a dark horizontal band. It looks like a wide rope cinched tight around his chest.

———

"I always loved Earl, my big brother," Yvonne told me the first time we met.

She was staring at the blank cupboard door of the interview room. We had been talking for several hours, pausing only to go out and refill our coffee mugs from the machine near the Psychology Supervisor's window. It struck me that, however oppressive a prison might be, it was an excellent place for a long conversation: once arrangements had been officially made that you were to have a private visit, no one would interrupt you.

"The whole family loved him so much," she continued, "though Leon now sometimes says Earl was mean to him, that he beat him. I do know things would have turned out different if he was alive, though for better or worse I can't decide. I promised him that, like him, before I was twenty I'd be dead. Too bad I never kept that promise."

———

Yvonne: At the Pink House on Madison I am in a high chair. There's a creek or some flow of water running outside the kitchen door, I can hear it, and beyond that a rusty fence, willow bushes, the junk of rusted washing machines. The house suddenly shakes after the siren sounds. I'm shorter than the kitchen table and I have to climb up to get onto the living-room couch. The couch and chair have a hard cover, rough with a design like leaves.

The counters in the kitchen were higher than the table, and there was something on the counter I always wanted. I think it was a cookie jar. It's on the tip of my memory, but I can't quite recall it—I always think if I was out and saw one, I would know it and buy it.

Mom could never understand me. I would try and talk, but she was always so busy—so many kids—and she never had time to figure me out. Sometimes she'd just sit and cry, "What do you want? I don't know what you're saying, I can't do anything." So I'd wind up shutting up, or crying. If I got mad and screamed in frustration, I'd get hit.

My basic problem was the way I was born; in the centre of my face, where my nose, top lip, gums, and roof of my mouth should have been, there was only folded tissue that left a gap in my upper mouth. Even my teeth and inner-mouth bones were affected by this severe deformity. I've now had endless reconstructive surgery, but I still wonder what I would look like if I'd been born like my sisters, all so neatly beautiful, and my brothers, so handsome as well. I think our family beauty comes from mixing two different bloods, dark Cree and blond Norwegian, but I'm told I inherited the genetic problem of my mother's family. Grandma Flora had a single cleft palate: she had a split in her nose, lip, and the roof of her mouth, and she never had any skilled surgery. They were reserve Indians, and someone just sewed her top lip and the right flare of her nose together. She had to live with an open palate till she died, over eighty years old, June 1986.

Even if I could, I don't want to remember all the endless operations I've had on my face from birth. O God, how I hate needles—more than all that cutting and patching of reconstructive plastic surgery. And so, as I grew, my mom could not understand me. To make me stop pestering her, she'd give me things, to buy me off sort of, but I was persistent. I'd cry and pull on her dress. I've felt the sting of her frustrations all my life, and I admit it was hard for her. She'd run from one item in the kitchen to the next, pointing. "You want this? This?" She'd open the cupboards. "Is it this?"

I'd shake my head, "Yes," "No," but often it wasn't such a "yes–no" thing and I'd let her buy me off; or I'd be left to cry until I stopped. Walk away with my head down and shoulders sagging, alone. It was like being deaf but still hearing, speaking but speechless—it was there, heaping up inside me. I could not ask questions, just puzzle everything around inside my head, dreaming it, bouncing it back and forth, without any guidance to help me understand. So I learned by instinct, by watching to see and recognize what others don't, to judge myself by taking chances. To depend only on myself. There was no one else.

My mind was my best, really my only, companion. But I think that then, on a deeper level, my spirit already knew and understood how much I was being hurt. The impact I wore in silence, and shed in tears.

———

The P.A. intercom in P4W—Yvonne calls it the "prisoner address" system, always squawking demands about something—has just warned everyone that afternoon count is coming up and she must go to her cell, but Yvonne keeps talking.

"Shouldn't you be in . . . ?" I gesture, not yet knowing how to say "cell" to her, wherever it may be down corridors, beyond bars and guards, behind bullet-proof glass, somewhere a labyrinth away from this room that feels like it's underground, cut down deep into Kingston's famous limestone. I think, that must be why they built all these jails here: for greater security, they bury the prisoners in limestone.

"My house, you mean?" She lights another cigarette. "I call it my 'house'—no, it's okay, Psychology keeps them informed. They know exactly where I am."

"Exactly where I am too, eh?"

"Especially you—no way they can let men roam loose in here."

"I might get lost."

"Yeah, and with all these man-hungry women around, hey . . ."

We laugh. It's not really funny, but there is an ironic tone we instinctively know we must maintain about certain things here if we hope to continue. And Yvonne is talking; truly talking. Sometimes it has to come from behind the black curtain of her hair, but she talks; her amazing, unstoppable, now utterable words trigger one memory after another and she follows that spoor like a track leading deeper and deeper into a dark forest:

"My grandma Flora died with her palate as open as it was at birth. I can't understand how she could live that way for eighty years, and eat. Once she and Mom were drinking and I saw her wearing lipstick. It shocked me. She never wore any make-up that I saw, though Mom once said Grandma had one wish, to wear lipstick, but as a traditional woman she never did.

"But whoever put it on her this one time had not tried to reshape her mouth—when I put make-up on, I make my face appear normal—the lipstick just followed the deformity of her lip. Deep red; she sat there obviously drunk, and it made her look worse, so sad. Perhaps Mom was looking at her mother with pity, as she must look at me, but why put it on like that? I went to Grandma and asked, 'Do you want this on?' but she didn't answer. So I rubbed it off, every bit."

"But sometimes," I say, "you wear it yourself?"

Yvonne's lips twitch in an ironic grin, and with a slight shift her face behind her long hair is more hidden.

"I know all about disguise," she says. "It's a wonder what I can do to myself with some Cover Girl, lip liner, and lipstick. But if you get close, you can see I'm wearing too much make-up. And it all bothers me still—when I saw Grandma like that, with lipstick and . . . there are lots of reasons I don't want people close to me. My lip is only one."

———

Yvonne: My sister Kathy, exactly a year older than me, understood me better than anyone, and she would sometimes talk for me. When Mom was fed up, she'd tell Kathy to play with me, get me out of the way. Or Dad would come in from work or something and she'd yell at me, "There, go to him!" I guess Mom wanted Dad to feel what she had to put up with all the time; he never did anything, she said, he was never around, he was always out, drinking with his miner buddies, and even when he was home he did damn well nothing to help.

Mom felt she had too many kids, us four girls in a row every October from 1958 to 1961. She says now she was pregnant all the twenty years she was with Dad. I don't know how that's possible—there were four years between Earl and Leon, almost five years between me and Perry, who was last. She says she lost kids, but Dad says never; every one she had was born. Though the kind of man Dad is, how would he know? Mom never drank after she was pregnant with Earl until after Perry was born, and her life with Dad was tough. More than once she vowed to leave him, and once it was so bad between them, I remember when we lived in the big White House on Wyoming Street, she started a fire in the woodstove and burnt everything in the house she could; for hours, until after midnight.

She smashed and slashed the furniture. I was sitting quite happily on the floor in the kitchen and handing her breakable stuff from the cupboards—you don't need to say a word to do that—as she smashed it in the sink and shoved what would burn into the stove. Dad had come home drunk, mocking her with "Leave, go ahead, I'm handsome, I can find a nice blonde girl to take your place," and she worked herself into a certain state, she wouldn't leave one stick of furniture for any blonde bitch! She barely paused while she threw stuff into the stove, flames leaping out at her. She could justify anything she did because there was always something Dad had pulled off first.

She met Dad at sixteen: by seventeen she was pregnant and she married Dad, and Earl was born when she was eighteen. She was herself a child, a beautiful one too. Perhaps she married because she was trying to escape being Indian, or because of the pregnancy. Dad was pulled to pieces at seventeen and put together as a U.S. Marine to kill Japanese soldiers, and Mom was reassembled into something else in a Roman Catholic Indian residential school—when two people like that get together, what could they actually know about becoming and *being* a family? My dad did not recognize that he was the standard male chauvinist; for him, men do one thing and women another. His main way of doing things, as he always said, was work hard, pay the bills, put food on the table and clothing on our backs and a roof over our heads, but his place was not with the kids—that was woman's work. The trouble was, there was often too little money because Dad drank so much, and so he and Mom always fought over who should have what responsibility for us. There were times when Mom felt we were burdens on her; often we'd hear her cry in her room at night.

"The reason I was so tough on you kids," she says now, "was because there were so many of you to handle and care for. You had to toe the line, especially you four girls. I had to make sure you all behaved yourselves."

Strangely enough, Dad tells me now that Mom never beat us; that she was always after him to do it. Has he just forgotten, or did neither of them know what the other did with the kids, nor care?

"I kept you girls in line all right," Mom told me. "None of you got pregnant before you were twenty or married."

Mom got along great when Dad wasn't around and she had food for her kids, but when he came home at best he became like another kid, only bigger and with bigger demands. So things became more stressed. Often Dad would go out at night and get drunk, and then, in later years, after all the kids were born, in self-defence, first chance she got, Mom would take off and go do the same. I think at times both saw family as one of them being stuck with the kids while the other played and had fun. Drink became their only time out, and they could not drink together, no matter how they had decided not to fight, because after a few drinks all agreements went up in smoke. Dad might beat her up with his fists, but Mom's pain was deep and alive, she knew how to hit with words. Dad could never keep up with verbal come-backs. She would twist and snake all over until he felt he could do nothing but bulldoze into her, and she'd fight back as best she could. Dad could fight and forget by blocking it out with booze, but Mom would not let things lie, and both were so shoved into drunken violence all their lives that gradually, after years of living together, each new fight became little more than an extension of the last. And I saw us kids as burdens, both of them trying to get away from us, neither wanting us. So we all chose sides, sometimes siding with one and then the other; and, as the littlest, I had to be the most careful.

When I was very little it was still illegal for Indians to drink in Montana bars, and Mom says Dad used that as an excuse for not taking her out. So she was stuck alone in the house unless Dad brought the drinking party home. When birth control became better known, and drinking legal, Mom finally had some control over two parts of her life that were all-important to her. Her kids stopped with Perry at thirty-three, and she began to drink. As she said, "If you can't beat 'em, join 'em."

Until Perry came along in 1966, I was the youngest, and unable to talk. In a way my eyes became my voice. I cried to make someone understand with my tears. But I could not. I would try to look in such a way that someone must pay attention—not just little Kathy, who had no more power to do things than I—but my looking sad rarely helped. Memories ring in my ears, names like "retarded," "dumb shit," "knothead," "zombie." I learned young that no one likes a sniveller, a whining kid. I hear now— Mom said it in a public courtroom—that I was spoiled at birth, given the "special treatment" of being fed with an eyedropper, my parents taking shifts to make sure I didn't choke in my sleep—I had to sleep sitting up—and maybe that was true a bit before I could walk, but mostly I remember having to do what Dad calls "sucking the hind teat." I learned very young to accept what I got; to hang my head, keep quiet, and hide behind my hair. I learned very fast about eye and body language, others' as well as my own. Look, don't talk; move, don't speak.

"We've got a strong Native Sisterhood organized here," Yvonne tells me. "Sometimes a quarter of the women in here are Native," she adds with her edge of grim irony, "so we always have lots of members. They allow us to sing on the drum, and Elders to come. We've even been able to built a sweat lodge in a corner of the grounds. I'm chairperson of the 'Hood right now."

"Do you like to do that?"

"It's got its moments. I support the sisters, especially the ones on B Range, who have tighter security. The prison here tried to keep them out of the Sisterhood because they were very solid together."

"They try to stop them from joining, even if they are Native?"

"Staff said the B girls helped too many kill themselves. I worked long and hard as the chair. At one point, if I ducked out, the 'Hood would have folded. Everyone was hurting and the institution likes it that way."

"But you kept it together?"

"I stayed out of cliques, to be neutral, so I had no friends, but I didn't have enemies either. And we had Elders come in, and that helped. The Elders always talk of patience. I know that's important, but I may begin to hate that word. 'Have patience'—where're you supposed to have it from? Patience mostly too is silent, and now I look for some understanding as I talk and explain what I remember.

"And I am sort of backwards, I guess—in my thirties and trying to grow into the world at last. How do you give birth to yourself at thirty-one? Too much life has already happened to me, and yet I still have to grow up into it. I'm okay with strangers passing through, but with someone day by day by day, I'm often too much."

Yvonne: To this day I can't breathe and talk at the same time. It took years of practice so I could control my breath right to speak easily. And I still can't speak when wind is blowing hard, or raise my voice. I've perfected it now, but if I forget and hyperventilate, I lose my breath as if I'd run a hundred miles and I have to stop talking to retrack my breathing. Then my heart races. I'm so insecure with myself that often when I speak in public I have to fight panic. And then I can't say a word without tears.

Learning to talk took years, the operations continuing even while I went to school. But long before I started school, things were already happening to me, I was suffering in some horrible way. I didn't know what it was. I was often in brutal pain, and I remember once I went to Dad to try and tell him about it. He was sitting in the living room and I tugged at his sleeve and tried to explain how I had been hurt. He listened and I tried harder. He told me to speak up and I did; I could see his frustration and I tried to yell louder because I knew he was getting mad. Then I started to cry, which of course plugged me up. Dad called to Mom but she wouldn't come, so he got up and grabbed me to take me to her in the kitchen. I didn't want to go, I got more upset, I lost all my breath control; soon it came in hiccups, jerking, sucking deep into my throat. I swallowed and choked on gobs of stuff. I was about to puke with Dad dragging me into the kitchen. But Mom had dinner to get ready: Dad was there, let him deal with it.

Kathy and I understood each other, and at least we could cry together. At the Pink House, Leon, who was nine years old to my three, dug a hole in the yard and placed Kathy and me in it, then he got the hose and started filling it with water. We howled and our Big Brother came to the rescue. As usual, Earl beat Leon until he was shrieking—we always called him "Squeaky" because as a baby he never cried, he squeaked. Our family was all cut from the same cloth: survival of the strongest. And me the littlest of the litter.

Then we had to move out of the Pink House, and Leon—Squeaky—was mad. All around us near Madison were deserted houses filled with the broken junk of people who had had to move on, windowless houses disabled by vandals or kids playing at wreckers. Leon was always hunting, and often he brought things home to be used, but Dad would call him down for being a vulture off other people's fall. How did he know they wouldn't come back to get their stuff? When we were packing up in the Pink House, Leon went into one room with a sledgehammer and smashed holes in the walls big enough to crawl through.

I drove around with Mom to look for a place to rent—in 1965 there were lots of houses available in Butte. Mom found the White House on Wyoming, where the bells from the big

Catholic church nearby always tolled at noon. It was the old, rich kind of house you see on TV in a show like *Roots*, built before the First War, all white with blue trimming, and a cement wall above the sidewalk around the front and side. The Pink House was small and cramped, but the White House was so huge we never had enough of anything to fill it, not even with furniture and seven kids. There were thirteen rooms and, when we moved in, furniture from the previous owners was piled in the centres of the rooms and covered by white sheets. We discovered some little nun dolls, which were given to me. I found out later that the house had once been a Catholic nunnery with paintings on the ceiling of every room but now stuccoed over. There were even narrow stairs; they seemed so *secret* to me, leading off the kitchen to the second floor and up under the roof. I remember every room. I loved the way that house was built.

When you entered you saw a wide, winding staircase going up. On the left was a small area; Mom laughed and called it the parlour, where one day our boyfriends could wait for us when they came for dates — as if that ever happened. On the right was the living room and the connecting dining room, with a long chandelier. My parents' room was off this one, its ceiling blue and painted full of stars, with a door to a small porch, and one window facing south.

My father put a woodstove in one big east room, but Mom hated it. She said it messed up the place with wood and smoke, just like any old cabin — perhaps it reminded her of the rez. In the kitchen was my favourite spot: there was a cupboard with a shelf all around it. That was where I played. I'd place all the spices and stuff Mom had there carefully on the floor and then I'd ride round and round the shelf with my cars. Most of the time I got everything put back before she caught me, but sometimes not.

From the kitchen the secret stairs of red hardwood climbed up to the wide hall on the second floor. At the top there you could see the doors to every room. On the immediate left the hall led back past the stair railing to the bathroom, and inside it a small door opened into a mystery room above the back stairs. That room was always scary for me, its slanted roof and the odd noises you could hear there. The big room on the left of the stair landing Kathy and I shared. It was as large as the room underneath it, hardwood flooring and a huge closet to stash all our stuff when we were supposed to clean up. It also had a door that opened out onto the flat roof of the freezer room. There was no railing around the roof, and out there I thought then I could see everything over all the houses and hills of Butte.

Karen and Minnie's room was directly across the hall from us. There was a hall linen closet, then the front stairs, and Leon's room in the front corner, with Earl's room on the other corner, next to ours.

No one was allowed in Earl's room. I would sit on the floor and see the light under his door. His room was full of records, and when he was there my feet could feel his music coming through the floor.

He had a lovely old floor radio–record player with a little cupboard in it. Once I did sneak into his room to look around, but I heard him coming and I hid in that small cupboard. He came in but did not stay long; he was a young man and always moving. I loved how his room was shaped, the ceilings and walls curved to fit around the round window. Perhaps there was a sitting ledge on the window, I can't remember, but his room was mysterious and all the more exciting for me. I looked at the pictures on his album covers; he had a lot, especially of The Beatles. When I was in his room, it was silent and distant, just like he was.

I remember Earl only as a young man. He seemed tall, quiet, gentle to me. He kept himself very neat; he even had a cup only he could drink from. He seemed to be with us and yet not; he seemed never to be at home or, if he was, he did not want to be there. When Dad could no longer work in the mines, and in the summer, when our family came back from logging up in the mountains, he would ride on the load of logs we brought back and, while we were still moving, he'd jump off the truck at the corner of the house and grab the stop sign, whirl himself around it, and race inside to be the first in the tub.

Once Earl found a hurt pigeon and brought it home. He built a perch for it on the clothes-line post, and soon he had lots of pigeons. He attended Butte High School after we moved to the White House, and I would watch him walk away up the street towards it, high on the hill. Then I waited for him to come home. I was only allowed to go to the end of the block to wait.

I was walking to meet him, the sun low in the west on a very hot day, the tall houses shading the sidewalk. I was carrying the most beautiful doll I ever had. My mom bought it at an auction, where I sometimes went with her, the auctioneer just rattling away *gimmme gimme two bits, two bits to the dollar, sold!* This baby doll was even more beautiful than my nun dolls, head and hands and legs made of china, with patent shoes, long hair, and a soft stuffed body under a frilly dress. When Mom brought it home, I cried and cried to have this doll she wanted to keep for herself. I loved it so much I kept after her, I would not give up, never, until she finally made a deal: if I gave my nun dolls to my sisters, I could have the baby doll. Well, that day I was walking up the shaded sidewalk with it when I tripped over a crack, and fell. The doll's head broke, and so did my heart.

Earl came down the hill and bent down beside me as I sat there crying, tears streaming over my face. I tried to make him understand—please, to fix it, these smashed pieces, fix it! Finally he just said, "Vonnie, no one can fix it. It's gone."

He helped me pick up every bit of it, but he was right. The beautiful baby doll was gone. I tried to get the nun dolls back, but they were gone too. I don't know what became of them.

———

Throughout the summer of 1993, Yvonne sends me more journals from the Prison for Women in Kingston, sometimes via counsellors who help me understand how Yvonne is living her imprisonment. They are all deeply concerned: Vonnie is walking a very narrow edge. One counsellor, Janice Robinson of Vancouver, whose family is of the traditional chieftainships of the Tsimshian people, sends me several journals with a note:

"I am sincerely honoured to have Yvonne as a friend. She is unaware of her specialness. I am, and have profound respect for her."

On 22 July, Janice calls me and we talk for almost two hours on the phone. She has just completed teaching a course on substance abuse in P4W, and her voice is close to weeping. "I don't know how long Vonnie can hang in there. . . . She may not be with us much longer."

Yvonne is near physical collapse from pain and infection problems related to her last natural, now decaying, teeth: Kingston is not giving her the proper dental care. But, beyond that, she is remembering so much of her past, and it is disturbing her more and more. Writing it down seems to bring more memories to the surface, but the effect is contradictory: even as writing helps her to utter the past out of herself, it overwhelms and depresses her. There are times when she addresses me directly in the journals:

"Rudy, I cannot dig any deeper! I will go crazy." Or: "Rudy, I don't know what to do, I've got memories that will blow you away." In her very first journal, begun in May 1991, a few weeks after she was taken to Kingston and a year and a half before she contacted me, she states, "I wish I could write my life-story book. Maybe then and only then will my life be revealed, and it might help the next abused and hurting person whom the world judges and condemns as already dead. But this dead person, me, is not beyond help. Maybe in death I'll be of some use."

Janice says to me, "She's not capable of writing a publishable book, and never in P4W. It's such a dreadful place, games inside games, and she's doing 'The Bitch' as they call it—Life Twenty-five. When they come out they're less able to function than when they went in. There's abuse right in prison, between inmates, between guards and inmates—they'll take you to an appointment if you agree to sex, it's . . ."

She explains that Karla Homolka has just been brought into P4W; she is kept in the prison clinic and under such tight security that all inmate appointments have been cancelled indefinitely.

"For one woman they bugger up the health care of two hundred women?"

"Homolka's on every newscast," she says. "When Corrections Canada get paranoid, they can do some really cruel things."

"I find it really hard," I admit to her. "Sometimes, I feel so stupid, but I can't help it, it's tough just to walk into that place. If Vonnie wasn't so incredible I'd—you teach courses; how do you deal with P4W?"

"To tell you the truth," Janice says, "I pray a lot."

And she encourages me, strongly, to keep helping Yvonne write. "In certain ways she doesn't grasp the magnitude of her own story. People who are abused are ashamed of what happened to them. There's never been such a story out of P4W; dozens of women have died going in there, and it's closing soon. A kind of memorial, it needs a book."

I know about writing certain kinds of books, but I know I know nothing about the one this will have to be.

She adds, into my silence, "You can't tell what impact it would have. Vonnie is ready to discount her shame, to do it."

"Look," I say, "I'm an aging, professional man, exactly the kind of 'powerful White' who's so often created problems for her. Isn't there someone else who should work with her, a woman, a Native writer? . . ."

She tells me quietly, "Vonnie trusts you. Honesty is the key for her, no bullshit, no avoiding. When you're in her shoes, maybe a White male is safer to trust than a Native."

Still, I hesitate. But on 12 August 1993 Yvonne phones me, sick and distraught, to inform me she has just heard that the Appeal Court of Alberta has disallowed her appeal of her first-degree-murder charge on all counts. Unanimous negative ruling by all three judges. It seems we must write her story—from her present perspective, in prison.

After the devastating rejection of her appeal, the hardcover notebooks multiply. She can write day or night in the relatively unsearched privacy of her cell in the Wing—which has bars on the outside windows but not on the door. Her handwritten journals have already become several thousand pages of present and memory—"separate, lone memories, individual acts, but seemingly connected, I'm like a conductor, not a human being. Do I really want to know, and what am I to do with them?"—her awareness flowing through time and endless people and places as unstructured as the questing mind flows, journals more crucial than anything she has yet discovered to somehow help her dare recall the details of her tormented life.

Yvonne: Mom liked the White House partly because the Catholic church was so close. Dad would not let her go to mass—he said religion was a just a way to suck money out of you—but there she could sometimes sneak away to talk to the priest.

The first Christmas I remember, the tree in the White House was set up in the beautiful room with the chandelier, next to my parents' bedroom. It had a fireplace of wood, but the fire was actually fake, with only a bulb inside it to turn on. I asked Mom why there was no fire and she said she didn't want to torch Santa when he came down the chimney.

I tried to figure out how Santa would get down the tiny chimney. Mom said, "He puts his finger to his nose and he becomes so small and skinny, he can come right through." I strained my little mind trying to see him. She also put up a manger set, which I stared at a lot, the sheep and the big star. My favourite was the Baby Jesus. Sometimes I would sneak him away when I had to go to bed, but most of the time I'd put him back again because the others would miss him. Like his mom and dad, looking there and suddenly nothing in their manger! I wrapped six pennies for Mom and Dad, but the night before I took the pennies to bed with me one more time. The next morning we kids all got up and I ran down to place my gift under the tree. I think our parents had had a drunk the night before and they had locked their door, so we started opening our stuff. We had all received toy instruments like drums or pipes, and we started to dance and sing, yelling around, beating or blowing our instruments, we didn't know how to play them, until we formed a parade and danced through the big house, up one stairs and down the other, snaking through rooms and under tables, one behind the other. We heard Dad yell far away, but we just giggled and kept on, working ourselves into a frenzy until he was right over us. A lot of yelling, a few side kicks to the ass or a hit and a shove on the back of the head, and we had to clean up the mess; Christmas was over before it got started.

But my penny present was still under the tree, so I took it and gave it to Mom and Dad while they lay in bed. Then Mom got up, went to the kitchen, and started to cook, like always.

One Christmas, Leon got a chemistry set, so he mixed things together at random and made Kathy and me drink it, no matter how terrible it tasted. He said it was like the mad doctor in the movies, and we were his helpers, we had to. He always had some story to fool us into doing what he wanted. The set was soon taken away from him. Another time he got a bow-and-arrow outfit, but Earl broke it when he caught him shooting at us as we tried to run away.

The two boys were the oldest in the family, and for a short while Mom let them babysit; she said no one but our family would babysit us, such wild kids with no manners. When Karen was a bit older she had to do it, and then Karen also got the authority to discipline us. Karen and Minnie would gang up on Kathy and me, and make us keep the house clean and neat. Leon was big by then, and I think that, to protect herself from Leon, Karen forfeited us two smallest girls to him for whatever dangerous games he wanted to play; she only reported him to Mom when he hurt her. Leon would protect us, both from Karen's demands and from Mom and Dad, if we did what he wanted.

It seems to me now Earl hardly ever spoke to me or Kathy. But he helped us, he stopped Leon from rolling us two down the big stairs in a blanket just to see how we'd bump and scream. Another time Earl yelled at us for dropping our pants and racing down the hall to the toilet to see who could pee first. He was coming out as we crashed to get in, and he warned us to always go inside first, then lock the door, before we pulled our pants down.

Did Earl really care much for me? It was Leon who always seems to have been around. He never left me alone. I remember an argument broke out between him and Dad and Earl. I don't know about Earl, but Leon and Dad were fighting horribly. Dad beat Leon. He yelled things like: "I worked since I was fifteen, I joined the Marines at seventeen and defended my country to the death, I sent money home to support my mom, and you useless piece of shit just helling around, always in trouble!"

Dad never gave up on "manliness" as he saw it. He was always the man, the Marine, as tough and mean a son of a bitch as they come. Maybe that particular fight wasn't actually so bad, as some were in our family, but to a little girl it was dreadful: Leon screaming and crying with Mom trying to protect him as usual and Dad yelling, "The best part of you ran down my leg!" and Leon shrieking scared and trying to get away, into our room, with Dad right after him; he flipped over the bed Leon crawled under, then he punched him with his big fist and dropped him on the floor. Leon tried to defend himself, kicking and screaming, "I hate you! Some day I'll kill you, cocksucker!"

Finally Dad stopped and tried to hug Leon, but Leon dodged between his legs and ran out. We girls were up against the wall, scared stupid, Mom screaming at us to get away. Dad came and said he loved us, don't worry, Leon has to stand and take what he's got coming like a man. Let him run, he'll come back and I'll straighten him out. He left us, and later came back up to use the bathroom, and then into Karen and Minnie's room, where we were all lying together, to say good-night. Evenings like that we two smallest girls slept with Karen and Minnie, their beds pulled together. The other girls acted as if they were sound asleep, but I didn't know any better, I was so scared I moved, and he tucked the blanket up tighter, saying very quietly, "Goodnight, goodnight, don't let the bedbugs bite."

I loved my father, and pitied him, and I feared him as well. I learned to watch him like I learned to watch everyone. There was no trusting him or what he might suddenly do, no warning when he'd yank off his belt. Just wham! When he came home drunk, he did it to any one of us. Now he fell asleep on the bed beside us and after a while I heard Leon come back, so I got up carefully and went to tell him, "Dad's in our room."

Mom was with Leon and she told us to be very still, but Dad woke up anyway, furious. Why was everyone tiptoeing around like thieves? And Mom was the worst, he said, teaching his own kids to hate him.

"And you, Mom's suck," he yelled at Leon, "just a thief and a lousy one at that, why don't you get a job instead of stealing bikes!"

"Leave him alone," Mom yelled back. "You call him a black bastard anyways."

At least this time Mom did not have to take the blows intended for Leon. The next day everyone was sober; you could feel everything that had happened in the whole house, but it was very quiet and calm. Dead calm.

———

The kitchen was Mom's room, that's where she was boss even though she didn't want to be cleaning and cooking all the time. She loved those narrow stairs going up at the back.

"Servants' stairs," Mom would say, and she was so proud. Our big, beautiful house had once had everything proper and in order; it had had servants working in it.

The kitchen itself wasn't very large; we never ate in it, though I remember Mom and Earl sitting there together and eating. By then Earl was big enough to beat off Dad when he came at her, drunk. Earl was hardly ever home, either at school or working, and if he was he'd just eat and run. He had lots of friends and at one point he left home completely, bought himself an old Chevy van from a dealer across from the gas station where he worked. But even after he came back home again to go to school, he wouldn't go logging in summer with us any more. He got a better job in Eddy's Bakery, I could smell the bread he made from my school yard. He was becoming a man.

Earl loved driving the foothills; he knew every road over the mountains where we worked logging. Once he drove a blue fintail Caddy convertible—it must have been my auntie Rita's new car, though I don't know how she got it—and I rode in the Caddy with Earl on a mountain stretch of road like a roller-coaster. He would carefully speed up over each hump and we'd throw our hands up into the open sky and lift over the top as if we were flying, all us kids laughing, screaming as we soared. He got the golden eagle from that straight stretch of dirt road off the highway, where it crossed the fields and hit the treeline. Driving there was like vanishing into a new world, cool, dark, so sudden inside the forest.

It was just before the trees we saw it: something hanging, flapping on the barbed-wire fence and crying out. It was a young golden eagle learning to fly; it had broken its wing crashing into the fence. Earl bundled it carefully in his jacket, to protect it and us, and we took it home. He splinted it up and kept it in his room for a while, but then he moved it into the big linen room across the hall.

A few days later Leon locked me in the linen room and banged on the wall to excite the bird into clawing me. At first I was afraid; the eagle raised her massive wings and screeched. The sound was overwhelming in the small room. She blinked her eye at me, turning and tilting her head to follow my movements, but I did not cry out. When she spread her wings, they touched the walls of the room. I slid to the floor, with her eye following me, and I asked her pardon, I didn't want to bug her, but it wasn't my fault. Her long, thin tongue stretched out of her beak as she shrieked again, and blinked her fierce eye at me, sitting on the floor.

I feared her. Leon got tired of banging outside on the wall and so I began to make the same movements she did, spreading my arms. Soon I was laughing. I thought we were laughing together; we became friends and I visited her often after that. She let me touch her claws: she knew I was afraid so she remained very still. The first time I tried to touch her back, she beaked forward and shrieked. I told her I was scared, and she held her head motionless and slowly I touched it. Her eyes seemed to roll in her head when she blinked, but they were always fixed on one place. It seemed to me our actions and thoughts together were telepathic.

In the evening, when Earl came home from school, he'd take the eagle outside and let her sit on a perch he built on the north side of the White House. Then I was posted at Eagle Watch while Mom and Earl ate in the kitchen, especially to keep kids out of the yard, whom she might attack.

It seemed to me we could speak to each other, her one eye looking at me and then the other. She was quiet, watching and waiting to heal. Now, outside, she seemed to look far away, her round head hooked down like a claw. I watched and watched, and then I had a sense and both of us seemed to know. The eagle shook her claw and the binding on her ankle fell off; she was loose on the perch and we both knew. She hopped a little and I moved against the wall to tell Earl because I was bound to him too, I had to let him know, and then she bounced across the grass four times.

Earl came running out, tried to grab her without his gloves, but she flew to the Catholic church statue across the street. She settled on the Baby Jesus held in the arms of the Virgin Mary. Earl climbed up to reach her, and the eagle flew again to perch on the stop sign where he would swing when we came home on the truck with logs. She sat there till she turned to look at me. I could feel our thoughts intertwine, and I said, "Go. Go!"

And the eagle swooped away, low, was gone in a hiss of steam from a stinking tar truck patching the street. And she reappeared again, rising upwards, rising south over the snowy mountains.

Earl was so sad. He always said—and so did everyone in the family—that I let the eagle go. But I didn't. I was just watching when she shook her claw and the binding fell away. I never took my eyes off her on the perch. I knew at any moment she would stretch her wings wide like she touched the walls in the linen room, and fly.

And I'm glad I watched. I was the only one who saw her when she first moved, saw her tilt forward one tiny movement, hop, swoop low, and lift herself into the light high over the roofs.

3

A Killing in the Family

Answer: I lost my son, Earl, in City Jail in Butte, Montana. That was in 1971 when I lost my son . . .

Question: You seem to recall that date quite clearly, is that true?

Answer: It's always on my mind.

– Cecilia Knight (formerly Johnson),
North Battleford courtroom, 20 June 1995

I FIRST STARTED WORKING in Butte when I left the Marines, in 1946," Clarence Johnson tells me. "There was always a job in Butte then, if you were a miner. I worked underground up to a mile down—shaftwork, staking, shovelling, anything miners do. My back didn't bother me in those days."

He laughs, a tall, still slim, old and mellowed man remembering how strong he was then, twenty-two years old and a four-year Marine veteran, survivor of some of the most hideous fighting in the Pacific war against the Japanese. He sits facing the TV set in a chair worn down around his body, the blinds of the entire small house drawn all day, the gatherings, the accidental arrivals, the hoardings of a lifetime piled everywhere on floor and furniture, toppling out of boxes, suspended on walls. He tells me he intended to vacuum his house after we agreed on the phone that I would drive down from Edmonton to talk to him about Yvonne, but he didn't quite get around to it. In fact, he guffaws enormously at his own joke, he hasn't got around to it for three years now! From what I can see, and feel under my feet, it may be a good deal longer than that.

Clarence's long bushy white hair is brushed back over his head; his glasses rest on his large ears. The TV set mutters on while he remembers and remembers.

"I was working on the Cabinet Gorge Dam that summer, 1961, but I got laid off, living in Kalispell by October, and we thought"—he laughs a huge double laugh—"we'll have the baby at home, it costs so much, but at the last minute we thought, Whoa, this won't work, and we chickened out and jumped in the pick-up for the hospital. Kathy was barely a year, she was sitting on the floorboards and Cecilia's water broke while I was driving like crazy and poured over Kathy's head. She was howling, half drowned! At the hospital they come running out with the wheelchair for Cecilia, and I took Kathy into the bathroom to clean up the mess. Yvonne was born easily after all that, but it turned out real lucky we brought her there.

"The doctor came out. I was holding Kathy, all cleaned up, and he said the baby's fine, healthy but there's a problem, it's pretty bad. He wouldn't say what, so finally I yelled at him, 'I don't give a damn if she has two heads, I want to see her! She's my child and I want her!' So he took me in and the nurse showed her to me, and then to Cecilia too. God, it was pretty bad; double cleft lip and palate, the doctor called it. There was just blood in the middle of her face; he had had to clean it out before he could make her breathe."

He finds a box, knowing exactly where in the room's chaos, and shuffles in it until he tilts towards me, one by one, the clinic pictures of Yvonne's tiny face. A month after birth, eyes squeezed shut above the unrecognizable centre of a tiny countenance, labelled on the back, "Uncorrected." Then, six months later, "Beginning Correction," after the first surgery. The long, excruciating "correction" of a "mistake" — made by whom? — the unaware irony of medical terms. Then Clarence offers a pale picture taken July 1964, two and a half years later, of the same deep cleft, though nostrils and lips are beginning to find shape.

"I want you to see what she's gone through," Clarence tells me. I get up, raise the blinds behind the couch so the sunlight streams in, sit down, and take off my glasses. And look more closely. Doctors trying to make a baby's face. It would seem a lifetime of "mistake correcting" will be needed, provided the lifetime is long enough.

"When we took her back to the doctor the first time for a check-up and Cecilia opened the blanket, the nurse just jerked back. But the doctor was very good about it; he talked to us all the time, he said for sure it could be fixed. All our other kids were fine, but it was heredity. Cecilia's mother had it, and now Vonnie's oldest too, when she was born, but with a single cleft lip and palate, not double. Oh, Vonnie...."

Clarence grinds the small cigar he chain-smokes into the heaping ashtray, wipes his blue eyes while staring at the TV screen talking brightly of firefighter camaraderie in the dark room.

"Jesus, I felt sorry for that girl. She had a rough old life. The Crippled Children's Society paid for most of the operations for years, and when she was in her teens an expert come and did plastic surgery with her lips sewed together — she shoved her food through a little hole — to build up her upper lip. Eat stuff and it would come out of her nose. They had to take her thyroid out, she'll be on pills the rest of her life, but after a while the poor kid was terrified of needles. She'd be crying all the way to Helena, three hours. She'd take the operations, just, 'I don't want no needles!' I'd have to talk her down, into it again. Cecilia had a hard time, but she loves all those kids. I love my kids. I think she loved Vonnie even more for the way she was born."

He appears to believe that beyond any possible question; all the confirmations and contradictions of memory, father and daughter. In any case, hard, rough times were about all Clarence and Cecilia and their family ever knew.

———

Yvonne: Every summer in the late sixties, our whole family went logging. Mom was always telling Dad he worked us too hard, but we had to make money because the mines were so bad. Sometimes we camped near the place in the woods where we had a permit to cut poles, and I remember the white canvas so wide over me, moving, the whole tent breathing, mountain air. I was so little I stood on the seat of our small truck, holding onto the top when we bounced down the rutted track. And I'd get my fingers slammed between the seat and the cab on the bounce.

Driving up into the woods was bumpy; coming back down, the road seemed smoothed out by the weight of the load. I'd sit in Mom's lap, and when I was bigger and could stay awake I'd stand on the floor sometimes, or kneel on the seat. I loved to watch the rivers and trees and cliffs all around the crooked road, the world opening up deep for a minute and then shut away like an eye closing, to open again quick over a valley way down. I learned to watch for branches, one might whip my face as it passed and I'd cry. I enjoyed watching tall trees come at me and then do that funny thing of disappearing behind through the mirror ahead.

And when Mom didn't notice, I'd spit. This was really hard because I couldn't pucker my lips or collect air as I would have if there had been a top to my mouth. Usually all I managed was to blow bubbles out of my nose. But I was stubborn even then when I really wanted something, and I practised and practised what would be so easy for any ordinary kid—to hang out of the truck window in the rushing air and try to gather a big gob of spit together into the tip of my mouth behind my lips and let it fly out just right, sail round and full and aimed so exactly to carry on the wind and bounce big off the back duals. And, finally, I did it!

———

Even under a grey March sky, Butte, Montana, seems to me to be greener than a mining town like Sudbury, Ontario, at the height of summer. Perhaps that's because by 1995 small spruce are again sprouting everywhere on the hills. Before coming to talk with Clarence in his small cottage, I had searched for some facts about this place which began as a gold camp in the 1860s, until digging miners discovered something even more valuable than placer gold along the creeks: an immense mountain of copper. One book explained:

> Tough as the town was, the Company was tougher. While some said that Butte *was* the Anaconda Copper Mining Company, everybody knew Anaconda . . . [to be] one of the most massive mining companies in the world: an operation grandiose enough to have a "500 year plan."
>
> . . . The decline of the Butte labor force before 1955 was due as much to mines "playing out" as to mechanization. . . . The miners were digging farther and farther into the ground for lower-grade ore. . . . To avoid turning Butte into another western ghost town, a profitable method of mining had to be used. With low-grade ore that meant strip mining, but in Butte the ore lay immediately below the city.
>
> [So] in 1955, the Berkeley Pit began to consume Butte. . . . By the time it was abandoned in 1982, the pit contained 2,500 miles of road.

———

"Our Pink House on Madison was a good house," Clarence tells me as we drive to look for the different places where the Johnson family once lived. An overnight spring snowfall has transformed all the contours of this strange, half-dead but lively city into a white, almost shocking, beauty. "But we had to move, the pit was digging closer."

"Wasn't the noise bad, round-the-clock shifts? The lights all the time?"

He thinks about that, and answers like the worker he was most of his life, "Yeah . . . it was cheap, really well built."

In 1995 the Berkeley Pit, like much of the rest of Butte, has become a tourist attraction behind high wire fences; and of course the pit's Visitors' Center is not open in March. Clarence and I stare between wires down the low tunnel through the railroad embankment to where the tiny arch of light opens onto that immense excavation which we cannot see; an exhumation of wealth and greed clawed 1,800 feet into the earth, too enormous ever to refill. Above the embankment the gigantic staircase of the pit's northeast wall, veined by snow, is carved to the top of the mountain.

I imagine streets, houses, people displaced, consumed, disappearing into that hole. The pictures I have seen, and the distant view I will soon have from the street leading up to the town of Walkerville above the pit, reveal an irregular, Stygian black lake: when the mine stopped pumping, rain and groundwater began to gather in the bottom of abandoned excavation. That gathering continues unstoppably, and it is now the deepest body of water in Montana, an incomprehensible reservoir of acidic solution rising slowly, steadily, year by year, until it will eventually find its particular level. If it doesn't overflow. And the Pink House where Vonnie's first memories emerge is suspended somewhere in the invisible air over that black lake, an infected space for memory only. But as indelible as poison to her.

At 943 Wyoming, the site of the Johnsons' thirteen-room "White House," is a vacant lot, its debris softly mounded under the winter's snow. "The best house we ever had," Clarence says sadly. "Big, wonderful house, big rooms with chandeliers and fourteen-foot ceilings. The mortgage was only seventy a month, but I couldn't keep it up when I had my back operation and the miners went on strike. Two thousand miners lost their jobs after striking nine months in '68.

Stupid strike really; they closed the last shafts then. By then I'd lost it. It just stood empty for years, then it burned down."

He stares along the dip of the street spotted with occasional houses and warehouse buildings between long gaps white in the grey mountain light. "Lots of places burn down here. All the time. They're empty, they're vandalized, they burn."

South Jackson Street is scraped into the side of a hill, and the house at 410, the Johnsons' next home, a kind of duplex fitted into the slope below, has been torn down. Space, dropping away. Every house Yvonne lived in in Butte is now nothing but space.

Yvonne: I remember the evening in late October we moved out of our lovely White House it rained, thundered and stormed. From Jackson you could see the streets cut around the sloping hills long and shining wet, all strangely yellow, with metal posts gleaming as if they were fluorescent. Cars and trucks passed swishing, the water flowed up over the sidewalk after them, and I was afraid, but oddly I felt safe as well. The heavy rainstorm comforted me. Leaving the White House and everything that happened to me there was like walking away from one world, clean, into the other. Here maybe it would all be different. Here no one knew me, no one talked to me, no one seemed to see me. I was invisible. Safe.

Clarence and I order steaks and fries in the M and M Bar and Cafe at 9 North Main, last of the original old-time (1891) eating places in Butte. In this high cavernous room, the right side is a long counter with stools, where the food you order is prepared on grills four feet from your face; the opposite side is a bar of the same length, and the back half of the building, veiled in smoke, a miasma of machines and tables where you can play live keno or poker machines twenty-four hours a day (a sign warns you: REMEMBER: *all payments are in merchandise only*). Clarence and I have to wait a while for two free stools at the food counter; there is no space whatever at the other bar, where half the crowd drinks standing up; all you need is six inches to lean an elbow and get one boot on the brass rail. And everyone knows Clarence Johnson; he seems to have worked in the mines and logged with most of the ancient, gnarled men there, and he can tell me as many strange stories about them as we have time for, eating huge steaks off thick china and drinking triple refills of coffee.

Clarence admits that, oh yeah, he and Cecilia had "some pretty good fights." Earl got "mixed up" in one, and "they got me down," and Cecilia called the police. He was arrested, convicted, and fined thirty-five dollars for assault.

"But I wasn't giving no judge any money, I said I'd sit it out for two bucks a day in the county jail. Then she got a job at the Anaconda smelter and she came to jail and said she'd pay the fine, I should come home and take care of the kids. I said no, it was me got assaulted, I'd stay my time. So she brought the judge over, he told me he'd go easy on the fine. So I came out."

When we emerge into the sift of evening spring snow under streetlights, he will not go around the corner of Broadway to the abandoned Butte city-hall building. I've seen its refurbished, square clock tower over the roofs from my aged room in the once-majestic Finlen Hotel, and several times I've walked past its granite-arched windows. A trimly preserved four-storey stone building plus tower built (the tourist brochure explains) in 1890 for $37,000. Its upper floors once housed the mayor, the city courtroom, and all other civic offices, including city police headquarters. And the basement—sloping back down the alley below street level—contained the damp stone cells of the Butte City Jail.

Clarence Johnson can only mutter curses. "They've made a restaurant with white tablecloths outa that jail."

At 12:20 p.m. on Wednesday, 5 May 1971, in the windowless prison corridor below the sidewalk at the base of that city-hall tower, twenty-year-old Keith Earl Johnson was found hanging from exposed plumbing pipes, a green garden hose wrapped twice around his neck.

"The cops said it was suicide, but, Je-e-sus, I've never believed that. Not for one fucken minute."

Yvonne: We are at Red Pheasant. I am in Saskatchewan bush helping Grandma Flora's brother gather firewood, and Karen is there too, when I glance up and look into his eyes. He is lifting his axe to chop a log on an old sawhorse, and suddenly, out of nowhere, I am knocked back on my seat, I don't know how. I sit in the brush and early spring grass a little stunned while they both look at me, and I say out loud, "Earl." And I start to cry.

Karen grabs her chest and screams, "Earl! Earl!" and runs screaming towards the house. We pack immediately, all us girls are there, and start for Butte. I lie on the back ledge of the car—I can get into the smallest places—all glass over me and a full moon. I can see deeper than the stars. But after nine hours the car breaks down just past Great Falls, and Mom tries to call Earl at our house on Jackson Street. There is no answer. Then the Montana patrol car spots us, stops, and the cops inside gesture for Dad to come over. He walks along the edge of the highway towards them very slowly.

———

The people and events surrounding the death of Yvonne's oldest brother in the dead-end corner of Butte's city jail are tangled even more than sudden death usually is. What exactly are the facts of what happened? Who did, who saw, what? If someone had been accused and arrested, if a trial had been possible with enough clever lawyers paid huge fees to ask questions, the data would certainly have piled up for months. But of course Clarence Johnson and Cecilia Bear Johnson had no money, and no one was ever brought to trial for anything. Though they tried.

As it was, the further I searched into Earl's death a quarter-century later, the more convoluted the possible story became and the more I had to settle for the barest probable sequence of facts.

The day after Earl's death the front page of Butte's daily newspaper, *The Montana Standard*—"Good Morning, It's Thursday, May 6, 1971"—headlined pictures and articles of three thousand demonstrators in Washington protesting the Vietnam War. But its largest, top headline read: "CITY CLOSING JAIL TODAY." The article began:

The city jail will be closed today until further notice.

Mayor Mike Micone and the city council ordered the closure at a regular council meeting Wednesday night.

All prisoners at the jail will be transferred to the Silver Bow County jail.

The closure apparently stemmed from a suicide which occurred in the city jail Wednesday, although Micone two weeks previously made negotiation attempts . . . to house city prisoners at the county jail.

As it went on to detail other council matters, the newspaper article had an insert: "Related story on page 12." The complete text on that page read:

Young man takes life in jail

Keith Earl Johnson, 20, of Butte, a bakery worker formerly employed with his parents as a timber cutter, was found dead Wednesday in the city jail.

His body was suspended by a watering hose from an overhead pipe.

Acting Police Chief Bob Russell said it was suicide. Coroner Leo Jacobsen, called to the jail, said he will decide later about calling an inquest.

In Johnson's effects held by police for safekeeping was more than $1300, including some $80 in cash. The rest was in large federal checks and two other checks for work for the baking company here. The job checks were dated April 24 and May 1.

The police reports show Johnson came to the police station about 1 a. m. Wednesday. He was booked for intoxication and also for possible mental examination. The report said Johnson claimed he had been using the drug mescaline and had been "out of my mind for five days."

He slept by himself in a cell, officers said, until it came time for him to appear in police court at 10 a.m. on the drunk charge. He pleaded guilty, but with all that money held downstairs, he refused to pay the fine. He told Judge John Selon he would serve out the penalty at the rate of $10 per day.

Meanwhile, the jailer assigned him and another trusty to sloshing down the main corridor of the jail and washing out the cells, one of which contained three men who came to court later in the day.

About 11 a.m., Johnson asked the jailer to send him a military recruiter because he wanted to join the service. A Marine Corps recruiting officer arrived and talked some minutes with Johnson, who was reportedly advised "you get out of this and then we can talk later about enlisting."

Johnson's fellow-trusty missed him for a while after the recruiter left, so he went looking. He found the body, and summoned help. Various officers raced into the jail, and Johnson was lowered to the floor. A three-man resuscitator crew from the fire department could get no response, and the coroner came.

Earl had appeared in the *Standard* before. On 24 May 1963, there was a front-page picture of him as a twelve-year-old, balancing, arms wide, on a wooden Anaconda cable drum. He is laughing open-mouthed. The caption declares:

Rolling Along A rolling cable drum is the fun vehicle for Earl Johnson, 12, of 1328 Madison. It takes the skill of a log-roller, but many boys have mastered the new fad and found it much more exciting than skate boarding, they report.

"He was no suicide kid," Clarence tells me as we examine the papers, the boxes, the hard black strands of his memory in his dark house. Outside I know the old city houses marooned among vacant lots are flaming snow, brilliant in sunlight.

"Earl turned twenty in January 1971. He was big, over six feet, a hundred and sixty-seventy pounds; he was always so steady. Leon's always been crazy, I can't understand why he behaves the way he does, though he's a pretty good worker if you can get him to work—Leon hurts himself, he's nuts, he never hurt nobody as much as himself. At sixteen he'd just steal a car, get in a speed chase with police, finally get forced over by his tires being shot out, and he'd smash the windshield with his fist, slash his arm all to hell, just nuts—sometimes, when

I look Leon in the eye I see nothing. All the way to the back of his head—nothing there.

"But Earl was careful, and real steady. Vietnam was going on then, worse and worse, and they needed men. He wanted to be a Marine. And he'd've been a good one. I named him after my big brother Earl, who was a Marine too, killed when the Japanese run over the Philippines in '42. He was killed on the Bataan Death March."

After a moment he can continue. He explains that early in 1971 Leon was "always getting into trouble." In a junior-high class he and other boys tried to make Molotov cocktails and one boy had got dreadfully burnt when it exploded; then he stole a car at Dillon and, though police charges were dropped when Clarence paid for fixing it, Leon's growing list of misdemeanours finally caught up with him and he was sent to the Swan River, Montana, boys' boot camp. And then, at the end of April, Cecilia and Clarence suddenly decided to go north to the Red Pheasant Reserve.

Clarence offers no reason for this trip to Saskatchewan. Yvonne tells me she still cannot understand why they made that ten- to twelve-hour drive north when there was no school break for the four girls. It must have been a "spur of the moment" decision, but just before they left she remembers Earl was trying to explain something to Clarence and he couldn't—or wouldn't—understand what Earl meant. They argued until Earl got up, furious, and stormed out of the house; within an hour, parents and all four girls were heading for Canada.

They left, and Earl remained behind to cram for his Grade Twelve final exams at Butte High School; his graduation was to be on 6 May. At age eighteen he had dropped out of school and left home, worked at various garage jobs and bought his '55 Chevy panel truck, but in the fall of 1970 he had come back: "Can I live at home and go to school?" So now, besides studying, he worked every day at Eddy's Bakery; his girlfriend at this time was Susan Samuel.

Clarence says he was unemployed because of the closed mines and problems following his drastic back operations: the family was living on Cecilia's part-time work in a restaurant and his small military pension. "I arranged with a bartender at the Montana Bar, when the cheques came in, Earl should go there to cash them right away. And phone me, in Canada, that they were in."

"Well," I say, having puzzled over the newspaper stories and coroner's forty-seven-page "Inquest into the Death of . . ." report half the previous night, "the police say Earl had cheques in his pocket."

"Yeah, he had them."

"And he cashed something at the Montana Bar; he had a receipt."

"He had a bar cash slip for $140, and $86 cash."

"From that cheque?"

"I guess so. He hadn't cashed his own small cheques from Eddy's."

"So why did he go to the police station? Didn't he know you were coming back soon? Why didn't he just call you in Canada?"

"His graduation was May sixth. Cecilia wanted to be back. . . ."

"So why go to the cops, at one o'clock in the morning?"

"I don't know. Maybe he drank a bit and got mixed up. Or maybe they lied, he didn't go to them at all, maybe they just hauled him in."

"They say he wasn't staggering. The coroner says there was no alcohol in his blood."

"Hell, whatever reason, they always need money, City Hall. The cops just do a sweep, pick guys up at the door of a bar, you pay your five-dollar fine and you're free. They'll maybe pick up the same guy five, six times in one night. If you haven't got five bucks, they shove you in a cruiser and throw you in jail overnight for ten, twenty bucks, and costs. Hell, I've seen them shove ten guys into the back seat of a cruiser and as fast as they shoved them in one side they were crawling right out the open door on the other. Just depends how much money they were told to get."

We go through the transcript of the coroner's inquest together. The police despatcher, Dan Lloyd Hollis, testified that shortly after midnight on the morning of 5 May, Earl

> came to the station looking for his mother and father. He wanted to know if they were there. I said they weren't. I didn't really understand what he meant at the time. I asked him if they were booked or if they were in jail. He said, "No . . . they were in Canada." By that time I could tell that he had been drinking and I could smell the alcohol. So I called in a car. Officer Graham took over.

"I always thought Michael Graham was okay, but now I don't know," Clarence says. "I knew him; he brought some of our kids home sometimes. He told me how bad he felt too, at the funeral. But now I don't know."

Graham testified that Earl smelled strongly of alcohol, though he was not staggering. Earl trusted him, Graham said, and had told him he had purchased mescaline in Spokane three weeks earlier and sold it in Butte. He had taken about five hits and now had been drinking for two or three days. Graham also testified Earl started to talk about how he feared someone and that he wanted to join the U.S. military. When Graham suggested he would take him to the hospital, Earl said, "No, I just want to stay in jail. I think that's the best place for me." But could he have something to eat? Graham said Earl showed them how to start his van by hot-wiring it so they could park it in the police garage. He bought Earl several cheeseburgers and then booked him into jail on a drunk charge.

I ask Clarence, "Didn't Earl have a key to his van?"

"Sure he did. It was his pride and joy, that van. I've still got it parked in my garage right here."

"Does it have keys?"

"Not now. I don't know what the cops did to it, or why."

Earl, Police Officer Michael Graham stated under oath, showed no sign of depression. In fact he offered to take care of a noisy drunk, Kenneth Kasolomon, whose cell he had to share. But he had seemed worried about the money he'd spent drinking, "that his dad would be mad at him." Also "that he had some young lady in trouble," and that "someone was in town and he was afraid he was going to kill him." Twice Graham stated: "He wanted to be in jail. [He said] he was better off in jail."

Clarence leans back, away from the yellowing inquest sheets now twenty-four years old. He has relit his small black cigars again and again, whenever he was aware they had died in his mouth, one after the other; he clicked off the TV set long ago. He removes his bent glasses and slowly wipes his eyes.

Beyond his head, the top picture of six hanging on the wall, framed under glass, is a head-and-shoulders photograph of Earl and his maternal grandfather, John Bear. A beautiful picture of young and old, so light, so dark; faces leaning close to each other that seem to exhibit no resemblance whatever.

"If we'd stayed together, as a family," Clarence says bitterly, "we could've done something about Earl, dead like that. That's the reason I stayed here, why I can't leave Butte, why I kept on this case. Not so much now, but I did for a long time. You can't run away from something like that."

———

Yvonne: Mom and Dad never understood family in the same way. Mom always said Dad never really wanted her family members around. But they didn't come just to visit; they'd move in with *their* whole families, the way Cree sometimes do, and stay for a while, and when they did, they expected Mom and Dad to do all sorts of things for them. And Mom wanted to do it—after all, she was proud to have married White, though she didn't want her family to think she was too high and mighty White now—whenever they showed up in Butte without warning, though I know they did things for us as well when we went north to the reserve. They'd talk in Cree to each other, and Dad thought they were talking about him and finally he'd yell, "Jesus H. Christ! At least talk English when you're at my table eating my food in my house!"

They'd sometimes load up with all kinds of things before they left, with or without anyone knowing, least of all Dad. Mom didn't mind; for her it was always elders and grown-ups first, and at times I went hungry while watching my aunts and uncles stuff their faces. Then we were told to be quiet and respect our elders and guests—the Creator would reward us.

Mom just loved to show off her big house to her brothers and sisters. But I guess Dad thought they were freeloaders.

———

"Do you think it's true?" I ask Clarence. "Earl went to the police for protection because he thought someone in Butte wanted to kill him? Why would he think that?"

But Clarence answers his own question, not mine; his voice stiff with hate: "It was those three cops, John Sullivan, Mickey Sullivan, Moon LaBreche—they're the ones."

Checking the inquest transcript, I realize those three provided all the information about what happened to Earl while he was held in jail.

Lieutenant John T. Sullivan "just happened to walk in the [police station] door" when Earl first came in, and after his arrest Sullivan began the questioning about drugs; Detective Mickey Sullivan further questioned Earl about drugs for over an hour next morning before he was sent up to the judge for sentencing at 10 a.m.; Officer Clarence D. "Moon" LaBreche was half a block from the jail and answered the alarm raised about 12:30 p.m. by the trusty Harold Dishman. LaBreche ran down the stairs, along the corridor, and, as he testified under oath later, he "observed [Mr. Johnson] hanging from the hose around the corner of the jail there. He was approximately two and a half feet off the ground. . . . I took out my pocketknife and we cut the hose and he fell to the ground."

"Those three cops," Clarence continues, "were the biggest crooks in Butte. John T. and Mickey set Earl up, questioning him about drugs, then Moon makes sure he gets there first to the body. All three of *them* were involved with drugs themselves, I think they had a whole ring going. That's why they started this talk about mescaline, about Earl being doped out of his mind. Three weeks before, he was at home, we were there, he never took off to Spokane or anywhere, he was cramming, he was trying to pass his Grade Twelve exams! Where would he have time to run all the way to Washington and get drugs? I know it, Earl stayed away from drugs."

"But studying or not," I push him, "it seems after midnight on the Wednesday Earl was drunk. Everybody smelled it. They put him in a cell."

"The autopsy says nothing about drugs or booze in his system."

"That's noon the next day. That could've cleared up by then, eh?"

"The night before it's the cops' word—nothing else, just cops!"

"What about the guy in the cells, Dishman. Didn't he see him drunk?"

"I knew Harold Dishman, he had worked for me logging in summer. In jail a trusty damn well says what the cops tell him or he's toast. Anyways, he told me he never talked to Earl till next morning, just saw him get locked up at night."

"What about the Marine recruiter, Burgess?"

"Burgess only saw Earl the once, after the city judge sentenced him for drunkenness, after eleven o'clock."

"Well"—I'm scanning the report as we talk—"Graham says that, at one in the morning, when he locked him up, Earl offered to watch the guy he was locked in with, who was getting sick—so Earl couldn't have been drunk that bad, eh?"

Clarence sits bent, his chair moulded around him, staring somewhere into that past. "Mostly I don't think he was drunk at all. He was set up."

Nevertheless the events remain confusing, if not contradictory. Clearly Clarence's aging memory has a lot of self-justification to protect, so I push him, as mildly as I can,

"But that Marine, Burgess, wouldn't be in on any cop set-up, and he says Earl insisted he wanted to join the Marines right away, walk out of jail, join up and leave, today. Burgess says Earl was very disappointed when he told him he had to get his conviction for drunkenness cleared up first, okay, maybe waived by Friday—only two days—but definitely cleared up before he can go. So maybe Earl was scared. Maybe not drugs—but what? He'll graduate tomorrow, May 6, sure, but that's just a ceremony and he can't attend anyway if he's in jail, refusing to pay a small fine. And he won't finish his high-school final exams before the end of May—so why does he need protection in his home town? Why all of a sudden does Vietnam look better than Butte?"

When I first came into his house two days before, Clarence guffawed loud and long as he offered me one of his patented throwaways: "I wish I was as smart as I'm good-looking, then I'd have figured all this family stuff out by now!" But it seems to me that, self-justifying or not, in the twenty-four years since Earl's death he must have thought of almost every possible angle, again and again. He answers me now.

"I know Earl always wanted to be a U.S. Marine. He would have made a damn good one. He was no suicidal kid, he was twenty. Sure he was disappointed about something, but no one saw him depressed. You read it: they all say he appeared 'normal, or even in good spirits,' and then half an hour after talking to a Marine who tells him, 'Maybe you can join Friday'—two days later! when he'll have finished his jail sentence!—half an hour and he's hanging by a hose in a blind corner of the jail?"

In the next room I can hear wood crack, burning in the woodstove beside Clarence's bed to fill the entire house with thick, heavy heat. Clarence strikes another match, holds it to his cigar, and abruptly continues.

"I say them three cops blind-sided him."

"What do you mean?"

"Earl was only in law trouble once before. Not with Butte cops, with the FBI."

For transporting stolen cigarettes between states, which is a federal offence. In 1969, Earl and two friends stole some cigarettes in Butte and ran to Sheridan, Wyoming, before Earl's good sense caught up with him and he phoned home. Clarence told him to return to Butte, which he did. He turned himself in, confessed, and was given a suspended sentence for providing the facts of the burglary in court. But that testimony also convicted his best buddy, who thereupon avoided jail only by agreeing to join the Marines. That buddy had had "a very rough" time in Vietnam; in late April 1971, he returned to Butte, vowing, according to rumours floating around the bars, to get even with Earl.

Clarence hints at a further complication, another of the many strands that are, as always, so tangled throughout living stories: "The girl Earl was with, they were living in our house while we were gone, Susan, Cecilia got her on the phone when she called, she was his buddy's girl first. They had a fight over her back then, and now this guy comes home from Vietnam and here Earl's having it on with her. So maybe Earl wanted to calm his old buddy down, 'Look, you had a rough time, but I'll go to Vietnam too, I'll go.' I'm not saying Earl wasn't mixed up, confused, so he goes to the cops, he figures he's better off in jail so no one can get at him till the family gets back—"

It does make some sense.

"—but the cops don't like Earl Johnson, never did, he never takes any bullshit and keeps his nose clean. But Leon! Leon Johnson's always doing something stupid, in court, in jail, he's in Miles City for juvenile auto theft when this thing happened, so what I think is when this cop Mickey Sullivan questioned Earl for over an hour, 8:30 in the morning before his court appearance, Earl maybe said a wrong word. If he mentioned seeing one cop where he shouldn't be, if he got careless and slipped one word about a cop ring doing deals on drugs or sex around the high school—every kid in Butte knew it was going on, at the time it was even in the newspapers. I think they used older kids to get the younger ones involved—shit, one word and he's finished. Because Mickey Sullivan was the crookedest, worst drug dealer in Butte."

He may very well have been. The newspapers Clarence digs out from under his more-or-less buried coffee table detail careers of continuing crime that directly involve three of the four policemen who were the primary witnesses at the inquiry into Earl's death.

In May 1980, Michael John "Mickey" Sullivan, who in 1971 questioned Earl about the drugs he had allegedly sold, was himself caught when in broad daylight he robbed a drugstore at gunpoint. He was a Butte City Police shift commander, though off duty at the time, with his face hidden under a ski mask. Witnesses said he scooped drugs off the shelves into a denim bag, tried to open the cash register, failed, and fled the store. He was noticed by passers-by, who contacted police on citizens' band radio.

"Sullivan got cornered by people on the street." Clarence chuckles grimly. "They pulled his mask off. By the time the cops showed up they couldn't cover for him! It come out they used school kids, too, to rob for them, and then the cops'd clean up all the evidence."

At the time of Sullivan's arrest it was feared he had police accomplices who would try to break him out of jail. He was held without bail, and Sheriff Larry Connors stated in *The Montana Standard*, "We do have a well-trained, honest and professional law enforcement agency in Butte–Silver Bow." Nevertheless, he ordered an "independent" investigation of his department by the FBI.

Mickey Sullivan, age forty, was tried and convicted in 1980, but I discover he never served time; the *Standard* of Friday, 11 August 1989, states that in 1980 he died "of an accidental gunshot wound while awaiting sentencing for robbery." Later, a lifelong resident of Butte tells me it was also rumoured to have been suicide—though the gun was found twenty feet from his body.

The same issue of the *Standard* is dominated by three full front-page stories compiled by Staff Writer Rich Simpson of how a continuing FBI investigation finally "solved a string of Butte crimes, some led by a police crime ring, stretching over 20 years."

The central characters facing a federal court in Helena, Montana, in 1989 are "Louie" Markovich and former Butte policeman Clarence "Moon" LaBreche. Among other things, they had pleaded guilty to complicity

> in a number of burglaries, arsons, bombings, insurance fraud, a shooting, payoffs from whorehouses, shakedowns of whorehouses, threatened murders, robberies and snatch-and-grab thefts and a conspiracy to commit [other] crimes led and orchestrated out of the Butte police department. . . .

A mere listing of all their crimes, in tiny print, fills over one and a half full-length double columns of the newspaper's front page. At one point Markovich is quoted as saying offhandedly that "putting together a group of criminals to rob and rip off a marijauna growing operation was of no concern. . . ." The newspaper summarizes their history of crimes as follows:

> The two became involved in crime together in the late 1960s, when LaBreche and Lt. Mickey Sullivan, both Butte police officers, learned Markovich could crack safes.
> Markovich became involved in burglaries at the direction of and with the protection of police officers Mickey Sullivan, LaBreche and Lt. John T. Sullivan.
> In the early days the group participated in "smash and grab" thefts in which John T. and Mickey would set up scores, LaBreche would line out the jobs and Markovich would break out a store window. . . . Responding police officers would help themselves to the merchandise in the store. . . .
> They planned much larger heists in the early 1970s. . . . By Nov. 25, 1972 . . . cigarettes worth $65,000 were taken from Christie's Warehouse. . . . The three burglars were assisted by officer John T. Sullivan, who disabled the alarm system at the police station. . . .
> Markovich participated in the armed robbery of the Wells Fargo guards at the Metals Bank Building in Butte on Nov. 25, 1973. Participants included Mickey Sullivan, who set up the job,

LaBreche and Markovich with John T. Sullivan as lookout outside the building. The take was $140,000. . . . Butte detectives called the robbery unusally well-planned.

"John T. and Mickey Sullivan weren't arrested with LaBreche because in 1989 they were both dead," Clarence Johnson says, glaring at me. "Those were the crooks who said at the inquest my Earl was a pusher, he was coming off a drug binge. Jesus H. Christ. You think I'd ever believe that?"

"So how did the cops do it? Dishman says he sees nothing, the three guys in the last cell testify they heard 'gagging and vomiting,' but they just think someone's being sick . . . ?"

"Those three drunks were never actually questioned. It's just what LaBreche says they said."

"Okay, okay . . . and it's all around the corner out of sight. But all those people . . . Dishman knew Earl real well . . . how could . . . ?"

I'm flipping through the inquest report, and stop suddenly. On page 22 is the huge asterisk I marked the night before in the margin beside the trusty's answers to questions from the Chief Deputy Attorney of Silver Bow County. Dishman states that he spoke to Earl immediately after he returned to his open cell from speaking to the Marine recruiter, and then he continues:

> They had an inspector here from Washington. The inspector came through and inspected the jail [. . .]. Johnson was standing in the [cell] doorway there and they went back and inspected the jail.

"Uh-huh, that has to be it," Clarence says, reading past my pointing finger. "Those fucken 'inspectors from Washington.'"

───────

Yvonne: Late in August 1989, I was living in Wetaskiwin, Alberta. It was over eighteen years since Earl died. Dad sent me that whole *Montana Standard* with the cop pictures on the front page and the lists of their crimes. I recognized every one of them from when I was a little kid in school without looking at their names. I read the whole newspaper and I could hardly breathe. I didn't know why.

Suddenly I was so confused. My nightmares were suddenly even more dreadful. I got into all kinds of hassles and fights with people. Then out of the blue, I hadn't heard anything about her in months, she was supposed to be happy and married in Ontario, my cousin, Auntie Josephine's daughter Shirley Anne Salmon, came knocking on my door. Tuesday, September 12, 1989. She added to my problems, and then my whole world went absolutely to hell for ever.

———

"'Inspector from Washington,' 'they went back and inspected the jail.' Shit! There were three of them." With his black cigar dead in his hand, Clarence Johnson continues slowly, living through every detail once again. "I tracked Dishman down a year later and he was working near Dillon, on the county sheriff's ranch there—go figure. He told me there were three of them.

"Those 'inspectors' walked past. Earl was standing in the open door of his cell, watching them go farther back into the jail. He and Dishman had just hosed down the corridor, cleaned it up. Then Dishman went into his cell to read and he said a guy he knows, Smokey, came to bring him some tobacco and he read some more and everything seemed real quiet. So he went out, he wasn't locked up, and looked into Earl's cell next to his. It was still open too, and the other drunk was there, sleeping it off. But Earl wasn't there.

"So he goes farther back into the jail, looking for him. There's three guys in the last cell, locked up, and past that the corridor narrrows right down because opposite the last cell there's a old stone dungeon cell they don't use any more, and if you go past it into that narrow part there's a corner, and around that corner, right, is the dead-end space where they used to have showers rigged up. There's no windows anywhere back there, it's all underground, under the sidewalk, no doors, nothing.

"And he sees Earl hanging there. On the hose they just used, wrapped once around the pipes and twice around his neck. The cops said a table was beside him, but all Dishman remembered was a little three-legged stool tipped over."

I ask, "What's that for?"

"I think they put the table in later, for the pictures. He was too high off the ground for the stool. They needed to show something higher."

"They keep talking about pictures——"

"I asked them and asked them, I could never find out a thing about a Washington inspection. There was no report, no one asked about it in the inquiry, nothing—there were no fucken 'inspectors'!"

"But surely——"

"They stonewalled me, no word, nothing!"

"Did you see the inquiry pictures? Was he actually hanged?"

"Oh hell yes, they had the pictures on him. Cecilia took them and a whole bunch of stuff, and other reports. It all ended up in Washington."

"Yvonne said something—Cecilia went to Washington, D.C., about this?'

"With the AIM March in 1972, the Indian 'Trail of Broken Treaties' caravan from Wounded Knee. It was so crazy," he continues in a rush, his memories focused only on Earl's death. "We were already driving home from Canada. We were on the highway that day, the fifth, we always drove it in one real long day. Cecilia had phoned home the night before to tell Earl we were coming, she wanted to go to his graduation, but no one answered, so we left Red Pheasant and just drove for home. We were just past Great Falls, past Ulm, when my car motor blew. We were sitting on the side of the highway with the four girls.

"I couldn't do nothing with the car and all of a sudden this Montana Highway Patrol comes past, then squeals to a stop and backs up. I think they want to help, and the patrolman gets out and I say, 'Good to see you!' and he's just stone-faced. 'Your name Clarence Johnson? You got a son Keith Johnson?'—fucken hell, they always had his name wrong! Nobody called him nothing but Earl—they had it all over their radios. To find us."

Clarence sits rigid, breathing so hard the air in the room seems to shudder. He gets up, goes back past his stove and through his bedroom into the kitchen, and after a time reappears with a pot of coffee. He offers me a cup, black, and then seats himself; drinks slowly, smokes.

"So I have to go to Cecilia, tell her. The girls are in the back seat. And I tell her Earl is dead. But she won't believe me. She's out of the car, we're in the ditch, we're on the shoulder of the railroad tracks, and she's yelling and screaming. I didn't know what to do. I tried to hold her, held her in my arms, and she couldn't stop screaming. All the girls were out of the car crying, and I got down on my knees and held her for a long time, holding her, hugging her, begging her—No! Earl is not dead! Finally she was just crying that, over and over. I picked her up and carried her back to the car.

"The patrolman was a good guy. He drove us to Butte in his patrol car. Cecilia sat in front, I sat in the back with the girls. We never said a word."

After a time he searches through the box on the coffee table, and finds what he is looking for. The picture of Earl in his coffin.

"Hell of a thing," he says. "Have to go and bury a beautiful boy like that."

"Twenty years old," I say.

We sit there together and cry, until we can talk again.

Yvonne: Earl's room in the Jackson Street house was closed. No one went in there. But I visited it every day, though not after dark. A small window from an alcove in the room opened onto the porch outside; they had let Leon come home from Swan River for the funeral and he and I sat there on the porch. The big sky was dark and beautiful, and he played his horn. "Taps," and he said something about the mountains, the sound bounced back from them as if they sang, they cried when he played. At times Leon could be a bright, good person, when he wanted to be. But he couldn't play much on the porch, he was crying because Earl was dead.

One evening I asked Kathy to come with me into Earl's room, and we saw where the light from the porch shone through the window, making a square of light on the alcove wall. Then the silhouette of a head appeared there, right on the wall in profile. It seemed to me it was Earl. I couldn't hear anything, but he was talking to me, I know he was warning me about something. For a moment Kathy and I sat there as if watching a movie on the wall, then the lips of the shadow moved and Kathy jumped up, screaming. And I jumped up too. We both ran out and told Mom. She said, "Forget it, it was just the shadow of someone walking on the porch."

But I still believe it was Earl, because he was with me at various times for years after his death; I know. Even when I was living in Alberta.

After he died I ran to Mom and told her, "Earl peeks at me when we drive to cut poles in the mountains. I hear what he thinks when we're in the woods. When we were cutting firewood at Grandma's on the rez, I felt something happen to him in Butte and it was true," and Mom asks quickly, "Okay then, where do you see him?" So I show her next day, when we pass the place I look for him, but he's not there and I get so excited I jump out of the car, "He's playing hide-and-seek again!" I run through the trees, laughing, I'm so happy. His name is there on the cardboard tags he stuck on the trees so his friends from town could follow his trail to our work camp, he and I are playing tag between the trees and little ravines, and Mom is sitting in the car, yelling for me to come back. But I want her to come play too. "See, he's so fast. See behind the next tree!" Finally she slaps me, "Stop it. Earl is gone and never coming back." But as we drive away I see him and tell her, "You're leaving Earl alone, I want to stay with him." She has to stop and open a barbed-wired gate, and she's crying. "There's too many memories, too many places around Butte." She stomps into the trees and rips off all the cardboard tags Earl made.

"Okay," she says then, "show me where." And we search through the trees and brush. But there's just the smell of pine and stripped bark and sticky gum, nothing. "See," Mom says.

So I point up. "He doesn't want you to find him. He went up to the sky, but he's here and he takes care of me; he always will."

Mom shoved me into the car. "No, you can't see him. He's gone."

4

The Only Good Indian

I have endless memories without faces. Random, separate memories with no story line, but sprinkled with possible truth.

It was over, it was peaceful to lie buried after all I went through. The ground was cool on my body that had been on fire, it was silent. They were yelling at each other as they dug me out. I tried to rebury myself. Begging them to let me be.

I asked for water. He was standing over me with water; he poured it on the ground and offered me gasoline.

– Yvonne, *Journal* 9, 11 April 1994

Yvonne: I have read and made notes on Carl Jung's *Memories, Dreams, Reflections*. In it he talks about the "natural mind". He says such a mind sees and speaks absolutely straight and ruthless things "like a priestess in a bear's cave."

He is speaking about me. I recognize my mind in what he writes. I'm of Cree/Norwegian ancestry, born and raised on Western mountains and plains, and my mind—as Jung describes it—is like a natural spring welling out of the earth, "and brings with it the peculiar wisdom of nature." This "archaic" kind of gift sees and remembers so much that in a group of educated people with their systematic, often formula ways of White learning, I seem to be stupid. I was the youngest girl in the hard-working world of a miner's family, and—not to speak of the racial hatred I felt even before I went to school, Butte society was created and controlled by Whites and one look was enough to see I wasn't White—for years it was physically impossible for me to speak clearly. I was forced to become a watcher and listener, with all my concentration fixed on surviving, and in my present memories of me then, every action was shaped by that absolute need to defend myself, somehow, in a world where I had no words, protect myself from the yellings and punishments of having always—there was never any getting around it—done something wrong.

Was my wordlessness then the reason I remember enduring so much hopeless misery? Did I only get attention when I was somehow in trouble, usually backhanded or slapped or knocked down before I was aware of what I had, or had not, really done? It seems that way. For me to acquire the words with which I could explain myself to all the powerful people around me never seemed more than a vague possibility of endless slowness; it took years for the words with which I could explain or defend myself to be gradually, and with great pain, carved and sewn into my face. I had few communicating sounds. For me, living was a long, silent secret where the very act of breathing already made me guilty of something. I did not like to hear myself breathe; it was so loud, so noticeable.

But born as I was, I had to be aware of my breath moving through the unclosed spaces of my nose and mouth. In fact, breathing became a private thing that boded no good—the low, heavy breathing of another person was a sure sign of pending pain and violence. I knew that if I could hear them breathe, they certainly could hear me—but I had to breathe!—so stay away, keep your distance, never sit with your legs apart, never forget to wear long pants under your dress or they'll see your panties if you forget yourself and play as a child will play, never talk back, never, ever look them in the eye but listen to every sound, watch, be always alert and ready to outmanoeuvre danger before it's close enough to catch you.

But even more difficult, since my abusers were often members of my family or people living with us—Kathy told me once that Dad should never have allowed so many different boys and men to stay at our house while working with us at logging—there was usually no place to really run or hide; eventually a child has to surface in the home where it lives. All I could do was try to know the events of the day in the house, watch if a growing sense of argument or anger or violence was developing, and be ready to make some kind of distance from it for myself; wherever I was in the house, to know where, to know how I could disappear. Try.

This was my childhood: the world even in my home is uncontrollable and can at any moment burst into violence. I can only react. If I do get caught, I was either careless or asking for it. I am always guilty.

When did this happen? How?

I know I was in Earl's room in the White House. Once when something was pulled down over my head. I was forced face-down on the bed. A pillowcase or something so I couldn't see who it was, but I did see: dark hair, a rip in a T-shirt. I was enticed into his room and it happened on the bed, not Earl's bed but the other one in there. I was being kissed, but it wasn't Earl and I couldn't breathe since I breathe through my mouth, and this boy—man—was suffocating me, and then there was a sudden great pain, with wetness on me, running down. My face was shoved down into the bed, I was placed on my hands and knees, and his voice telling me things I could not understand, then movements, pressure, something sliding, then pressure again.

And a terrible ripping pain, and wetness. I tried to scream, to tear myself away, but I was grabbed, twisted back onto my face again, with more ripping. My face was mashed into the mattress, an arm came around my hip and stomach, my body was flying, only my face in the mattress and I could not suck in air to scream, my legs, arms kicking, batting in nothing but air! I would be dead, pain was cutting me in half and I was choking, I would be dead, and he made a long, screaming groan, wet ran all over me. He fell down on top of me on the bed.

Why was he doing this to me, this horrible pain? What was it? I was crushed under him, but I could gasp and breathe, at last, there was blood all over me, and him, even his T-shirt. I tried to scream and he smothered me against himself, began to wipe at the blood, he talked fast, whispering, laid me on my side and rubbed me, told me we shared a deep secret, the secret that we loved each other, I was his love and own.

I cannot see who it was, not quite—a dark-haired boy, a torn T-shirt. I was so little and so terrified of those horrible pains ripping through my body, choking. There was no one to tell. No one was in the White House. I did not know why I hurt so much; I hadn't fallen down and scraped myself to go and show Mom. This boy must have been left to take care of me.

When he was finished he lay down and fondled me, he said the worst was over, I would stop bleeding, and soon I would like this. It was our secret and I would like everything he did, soon. I was his love for ever because he had had me first.

He would teach me how to french-kiss—see, this is how you do it. He stuck his tongue in my mouth. I had no roof there yet, so this happened before Grade Four. I had cried so much and I was crying again, mucous flowed from my nose as if I were bleeding there too.

I remember this. When did it happen?

———

As Yvonne and I struggle together with notebooks, letters, public records, and phone calls to find some order of chronology and fact in her past life, we need to begin again—she sees so much of her life, and consequently memory, as contained in the circle of repetition—we must begin again with her childhood place: Butte, Montana.

Perhaps, better, it should be thought of as Butte, America, the way the Irish workers named it, the hundreds who came there first attracted by the gold and silver along the rivers and then the thousands who arrived to dominate and develop the incredible mountain of copper on which they found themselves. Butte was "American West" only in its location and weather: in reality it was unique to Montana as a mining and industrial island surrounded by trees, a city of mines and smelters sprawling over the top of a 6,400-foot mountain and dominated by industrial tycoons and labour unions and strikes. Historian Joseph Kinsey Howard called it "the black heart of Montana, feared and distrusted"; novelist Ivan Doig found it both marvellous that "in all this wide Montana landscape [there was] a city where shifts of men tunneled like gophers," and at the same time ominous: it made people "apprehensive, actually a little scared about Butte . . . something spooky about a place that lived by eating its own guts."

And eating its own people, as Yvonne found growing up into her silent awareness of Butte in the sixties and seventies, through criminal police networks and largely corrupt government bureaucracies. The copper glory of "the richest hill on earth" had by then been eviscerated, and even the steady drudgery of underground mining that first brought ex-Marine Clarence Johnson there in 1946 was no more. The mines destroyed his back: in 1969 almost two inches of his spine was removed and he was left permanently disabled, though he continued the independent work he had already begun earlier with his family, cutting poles in the mountain forests.

But for Yvonne, growing up in Butte was like living in a time warp: all the feelings of the forties, fifties, even the twenties, remained. Most travel was still done by train, for the highway remained a narrow, twisting track around the mountains; miners continued to answer the sirens that signalled shift changes in the few mines still operating. There were ranchers also, and farmers, a few loggers, the lingering stink of gangsters and snoopy, aggressive cops who were often thought of as—and were—one and the same. There were clusters of city for Irish, Italians, Germans, Chinese—but no place for Natives to claim, like skid row in Winnipeg—with bars for miners, saloons for cowboys, taverns for businessmen on every city block filled with regular drinkers, no bouncers anywhere but plenty of drunks, often old men disfigured and worn by drudgery—and sometimes in the company of battered women—as well as old cowboys still sitting at poker tables, gambling in the wide-open saloons.

Most of these people, she recalls, still thought of themselves as original frontiersmen; for them, Indians remained wagon-burners and wild banshees; for them, the only good Indian was a dead one. Oddly enough, her grandfather "Fightin' Louie" Johnson was among the very oldest of these old-time cowboys. He was born in Minnesota on 15 April 1876, came to Montana when his parents homesteaded near Ulm, and insisted he had ridden for years in Buffalo Bill's Wild West Show—which is possible since that touring "cowboy and Indian" circus continued almost until Bill Cody died in 1917. Grandpa Louie also claimed he had worked for the rancher whose land south of Havre was in 1916 turned over to the refugee Cree from Canada's 1885 war and became the present Rocky Boy's Indian Reservation. The leader of those Cree, who finally got that land for his people after thirty years of negotiations, was Little Bear, better known in history as

Imasees, the oldest living son of the Cree chief Big Bear, Yvonne's great-great-grandfather.

When I tell her this history, Yvonne recalls, "We drove that narrow old highway through Ulm, Great Falls, Box Elder, Havre so often across the plains to Red Pheasant in Saskatchewan. Mom once mentioned having possible relations at Rocky Boy, but I don't remember ever visiting anyone there."

The time warp came from Butte itself and the old people who never left: lots of cheap houses for men, like her father, to live in on tiny war and mining pensions; and also from the town dying: eventually all the mines closed, though their rusting headframes still bristled between houses all over the mountain like the erect skeletons of an extinct form of life. By 1982 even the enormous Berkeley Pit stopped devouring the central business district of Butte and could do no more than slowly collect itself into an acidic lake.

But in a strange way "Fightin' Louie" was proud of his mixed-blood grandchildren growing up in a Butte that never had any Blacks and only one Chinese café, that detested the faintest evidence of Native skin or long, braided hair; where children yelled "You're savages! Your ancestors killed my grandparents and Custer!" across school yards. Yvonne thinks that sometimes Louie's old age loosened his mind into the romantic Wild West notion that they were the Indians who could still, whooping and hollering, knock the shit out of any White cowboy—fists or guns—even though he always considered himself one of the cowboys. When one night a cross was burned in the Johnsons' White House yard, with yells of "Prairie niggers!" his advice was, "You all stick together, you fight together, every kid covers the other kid's back, you can lick 'em."

Grandpa Louie was ninety-five years old when he attended the funeral of the grandson he most admired, his finest "warrior." Earl, just twenty years old, laid out in a coffin with his hands folded over his chest, on Saturday, 8 May 1971, for the Mass of the Resurrection celebrated at nine o'clock in St. Patrick's, the oldest Roman Catholic church in Butte. A warrior who had lost to the cowboys of the city's police. In her despair and rage, Cecilia had Earl's coffin driven from the city in a long procession of vehicles around the shoulder of Big Butte and miles away to the Sunset Memorial Gardens in the fields near the hamlet of Opportunity. Very near Warm Springs, Montana, where she herself would be soon enough, when she committed herself into the psychiatric care of the Montana State Hospital.

———

Yvonne: People call us half-breeds in Butte, but they see Grandpa and Grandma Bear and all our relations together from Canada following the coffin and everyone knows we're really just Indians. When we walk down the street, kids sniff the air and yell to each other, "Indians on the warpath! Redskins coming!" Leon is skinny but tough; he's always our fighter and protector, just threatening someone with his name is enough to get rid of them. Then they cover their nose and run, yelling, "Johnson germs, you'll get contaminated from Johnson germs!" But at least they aren't physically beating us up.

Or they stick out their lips at me, mumbling, talking funny as they run away. I try to yell back at them, but I can't shout words very loudly and they scream at me about my scars, my lips, "Your mom's nothing but a whore, that's why you're deformed, you pud-lip freak." Or, "You got your mouth sucking your brother's cock, you freak of nature."

———

When I visited Clarence Johnson in Butte he showed me a picture of Cecilia sitting on a bed beside him in 1971. Her body and slender legs seeming to hang, hooked onto the edge of the bed, both of them slack and staring down at the floor.

"She would just sit, never talked; she cried and cried. Yeah, your mind wants to forget the bad things." Clarence remembers a fellow Marine saying that to him about the American landing on Tarawa in 1943, where the world ended for 2,700 of their 6,000 buddies and for the 4,500 Japanese soldiers they wiped out; only 17 Japanese survived. "But I can't forget this—us sitting there. It's the mental hospital at Warm Springs."

Cecilia committed herself in the summer of 1971. "A lot of Mom died with Earl," Yvonne says to me, and wonders aloud what the file of the psychiatrist who counselled her would reveal. "Mom never talks about that, or her early school days. As a matter of fact, she hardly talks about any past at all. She always wanted to be perfect for her kids, and she just won't talk about her past. She may get wild when she drinks and then she'll face anyone down, and she'll yell something rough at them, but she's lived her life as if being tough and strong is the essence of all that's needed. And despite everything that's happened, she still has this childlike idea that if she tries to forget, if she hides something long enough, somehow everyone will forget it."

Forget it. That's the main lesson the Delmas Roman Catholic School taught Cecilia and other Native children during the Depression, when the RCMP came on the reserves with the legal right to seize them from their parents and force them into residential schools. And in fact, during the thirties, Cecilia said her parents were so desperately poor they felt they had to give up all their seven kids, from Josephine to Rita, because in school they'd at least get enough food to survive. So their bodies survived their poverty, sometimes abused but somehow alive, but what happened inside their hearts, their heads?

Clarence also shows me a black-and-white snapshot taken of Cecilia in Delmas School. There is a lattice-work wall behind her and she is perhaps eleven or twelve, a slender girl facing slightly away from the camera. A tall woman who may be a nun stands slightly behind and against her. The picture cuts away the left half of the woman's body, and her face, but her arm is draped around Cecilia's neck and over her right shoulder; her clenched hand holds a crucifix tight against Cecilia's chest. It is clear: Roman Catholicism was too deeply fixed in Cecilia for her ever to reject it completely.

At Delmas the Cree children prayed several times a day and worked long hours for their food. They learned the basics of reading and writing—Cecilia said she was at a Grade Two level after seven years of school—and were drilled, often beaten, into good Catholic behaviour. You must be content with whatever happens; forget your pain, you have no pain only sins, pray, confess your dirtiness and sin of being pagan, when you're dead heaven will be wonderful.

"No wonder Native women become barflies." Yvonne speaks sadly, from her own experience. "Where else can you go for momentary relief? In this I see a strange pattern between Mom and myself, me finally running from the United States to Canada—to the Indian streets of Winnipeg—and she, running from residential school in Canada, found an empty rez, went looking for her parents, and got stuck in Great Falls. She learned survival from the really tough Indians in Montana. I was my mother thirty years later."

I try to bring her back to her original subject: Cecilia in psychiatric care after Earl's death. And she shifts instantly, as sharp as all her memories are. In details they can be as precise as a photograph.

"We drove to see her every day. Dad always took a few of us along in the logging truck. She'd just sit there, head hanging, or propped up in her hand as if it might drop on the floor if she didn't, not saying a word to any of us. Sometimes she would suddenly break down, like a dam of tears breaking, but mostly she looked as if she was somewhere far away: her eyes wouldn't focus on us. Dad would say, 'It's hard, it's so hard—but we've got the other kids, they need you,' but even that didn't seem to affect her.

"When I went there," Yvonne says, "I sat and watched her, so different from the mother I knew. She wouldn't look back at me, but I caught something in her eye when she glanced past us, as if we were the cause for something, and sometimes when we walked in she would break down worse. She later had a tiny handgun, a derringer with a shiny pearl handle, that could just fit into a hand. She had that by her bed in the house, we all knew but no one dared go near it. I remember several times when Dad wrestled with her for it. She swore out loud she was going to shoot the Butte cops. Once in a while at the hospital she would hug us, but I didn't think then that she loved me. Looking back, the hardest thing was: Mom and Dad would never talk to us about anything; not even to themselves. They'd cry, but they'd never talk, especially to me. We never tried to talk anything over."

Clarence now says Cecilia was in Warm Springs only a few days, though Yvonne remembers it as much longer. "Then one day," she continues, "we drove to the hospital again along the twisty road around the mountain and up the valley where the Anaconda Smelter smokestacks—where Mom once worked—stick up against the mountains. Mom actually looked at us, and suddenly she stood up and said, 'Let's get outa here.' She got her clothes and went to the desk, checked herself out, and came home with us."

"Just like that?"

"Uh-huh. I think she'd learned whatever she wanted to, there. She never went near that hospital again—except when they sent Leon there, later, for examination—and she was a different person. My mother's body came out of that mental hospital, but I think the better parts of her nature died with Earl; she now wanted action, justice. I don't know, she refuses to speak about this, but I think she denied all personal feelings at that point: what she wanted was to save her remaining six kids. Even before this she'd hauled us to her family on the reserve in Saskatchewan when she thought we were too badly threatened in crooked Butte, and now she knew trying to be accepted in the White world of Montana was useless. There were only two things she wanted: to make her remaining kids more Indian so we'd stay alive, and to seek some form of justice against those who killed Earl."

Through the winter of 1971–72, when Yvonne was in Grade Four after having basically failed Grade Three but received a "Social Promotion" following the trauma of Earl's death, the family was desperately poor. Clarence's veteran's and disability pensions were too meagre for the large family, and Cecilia worked part-time as a cook and dishwasher, but even that wasn't enough; they needed the supplement of State Welfare. And people around the Welfare office—it was upstairs in the courthouse, which made it worse—always had plenty to say about lazy, drunk Indians; attitudes were so ugly that if you weren't careful you could get into a fist fight with the Welfare person you'd have to see to register for assistance. And Cecilia wasn't one to back down from racial confrontation, much less so now than when Clarence first brought her to his apartment in Butte in 1950 and then discovered the landlord refused to accept the next month's rent from him. "'I don't want you in my building' is what the bastard said"—as if money wasn't the same colour for everyone—it was slim, beautiful Cecilia who was the wrong colour. Now, in the winter of 1972, with the original news story of Earl's suicide in jail seemingly confirmed by the coroner's report, it seemed the racist world of Butte was stronger than ever. A drunk Indian whom the police said was a drug pusher: many found it convenient to believe that.

People demanded of Cecilia, "Why don't you work?"

And she'd respond. "I've got *two* jobs on a woman's pay and it still isn't enough for six kids and a husband who broke his back in the mines!"

"So get a better job."

"Get me some training, I'll do it."

"What job you want?" the Welfare people said.

"Anything," and she looked at those smug Whites with their White jobs and she tossed their challenge right back: "I want to drive a truck in the pit."

The best-paying worker job in town. She knew the mine had run an ad for applications and she threw that in their spiteful faces. And the totally unexpected happened: she applied and she was one of eleven people accepted for driver training—the first, and only, woman recruit. With pride Clarence gives me a copy of the 11 June 1972 *Montana Standard*—"I've got two more"—when it ran a half-page feature on her, complete with four pictures: Cecilia in hard hat and horn-rimmed safety glasses standing with her male instructors beside a massive Berkeley Pit truck loaded with one hundred tons of rock, its broad tire half again as tall as she; Cecilia behind the steering wheel, leaning out of the cab.

Her one comment quoted in the paper "was confident and candid. 'There's been nothin' to scare me so far,' she said."

On 1 July 1972, she graduated to a regular shift of pit driving and full pay; Clarence still keeps the certificate she received in his cardboard box of family documents. Yvonne remembers her mother driving a smaller pit truck down the street in one of the Butte Independence Day parades. She had always been proud of her Indian-long, rich black hair, but she cut that in mourning when Earl died; now her short hair fit exactly under her necessary working helmet. It almost seemed as if Cecilia had settled down to become silent and accepting. But no; she was working on her own agenda. Within two months she bought a new full-size 1972 navy sedan, a Cadillac.

When did this happen? How?

Minnie and Kathy get beat up the most—is this after Earl's death?—and Karen is older, she goes to a paid Catholic school; and I'm strong, and they think I'm crazy because of the way I talk and look, and I can run fast. But Kathy is petite and very pretty, skin such a dark tan and hair so black. I am behind the KXLF television and radio station on Montana Street and I've been playing hookey—the school has a hot-lunch program, but I just go without—between the bright steel lines of the railroad and finding glistening stones, but now school time is over and I'm headed home, I'm threading my way behind the buildings on Montana. I never walk on the sidewalk, out in the open is too dangerous. And across the street and between buildings I get a glimpse of Kathy walking down the opposite alley. She's wearing the beautiful dress Mom bought her yesterday and she holds her books close to her chest. She glances over her shoulder as she walks fast. Something is wrong, I know there's trouble when a Johnson walks alone, and then I see boys running up the sidewalk on Montana; and through a missing piece of picket fence I see Kathy run behind an abandoned building, and then another crowd of boys runs across there too, chasing after her.

I dodge around a building to the street and see the first crowd of boys blocking the entrance to the alley. They won't let Kathy get out onto Montana, where a passing adult might stop it, though Butte's full of look-the-other-way people. The second gang is chasing her up the alley towards them, and I have to help her. I run towards her, through and between some old buildings, where the street boys can't see me, but I know they have her cornered: she's blocked between the two gangs in the narrow alley. How can I reach her? I dash across the street and try to scramble through an abandoned house, but I can't make it, it's boarded up, and I see a piece of two-by-four with some long spikes sticking out of it. I grab that and come out and sprint into the alley after the boys.

They've got her surrounded, they've already torn the skirt of her new dress away and they're laughing and screeching; her leotards are stripped down and her panties are ripped and they point and scream about that and then they tear them completely off, laughing and hooting. Kathy disappears, she is shrieking as they beat and grab at her; some of the bigger guys crowding around are opening their pants. They are clawing at her, hands everywhere as she screams, and two of them leap up above the crowd; they are trying to jump on top of her.

They're all so excited, watching and grabbing, I shove in between them and I hit the guy on top of Kathy as hard as I can with the plank. He falls over. Lucky thing I had the spikes backwards or he'd have been paralysed for ever; I hammer his butt and tailbone. I yell at them all around me, Who's next?

They push and shove back, staring at me. The guy I hit squirms around on the ground, groaning. I tell Kathy to get up and stand behind me, backed against a wall, and she does. We're in as good a position as we'll get, and I lift the plank high, spikes pointed out this time. I can nail at least one or two before they get at me.

Come on, come on!

And they scatter. Giving each other shoulder shoves, laughing as if they were brave and couldn't care less, yelling names, trying to swear like men, the stupid little shits.

Kathy sinks down against the wall, sobbing. I help her pull her leotards back on, and her torn panties, but she has to hold the skirt wrapped around her, it's completely ripped apart. It's bright daylight, we have to bend and sneak between houses, down alleys, no one must see us.

When did this happen? We tell Mom we've been jumped and she storms to school. There is a face-off in the principal's office, and the police arrive to escort her out. Or does she hit the principal, clobber him somehow to give him a taste of his own medicine before the police break them up? How did it happen?

———

It seems to me that Cecilia's grandmother, Flora Baptiste Bear's mother, whose name beyond "Kohkum" no one seems to know—or perhaps will not tell me, Cree personal names always being a private and possibly spiritual matter—could well have been Earth Woman, Big Bear's youngest daughter. Historian Hugh Dempsey tells me that certainly her great age would make that possible. Clarence says she was 113 years old when she died, that's what they told him at her funeral at Red

Pheasant in 1976, and from his bottomless box he digs a picture of her lying in her coffin. Yvonne's grandpa John and grandma Flora Bear stand beside it, a regal Cree couple indeed.

No wonder then that when, as Clarence tells me, in 1971 Cecilia contacted Russell Means of the American Indian Movement about the death of her son while in the custody of the Butte police, Means sent an AIM man to Montana to investigate.

Yvonne remembers her great-grandmother, Grandma Flora's mother, a little. She lived with Cecilia's cousin and her family on Red Pheasant and she smoked a pipe, wore a long dress with long sleeves, bound her legs in traditional wrap-arounds over moccasins, and always wore a kerchief, either tied back around her braided hair, or under her chin and hiding her face, whenever anyone visited. She never sat in a chair, always on a blanket on the floor. When a White man arrived, she always disappeared. Sometimes when Yvonne awakes in the morning she finds herself thinking of those two ancient women from her childhood. She knows her great-grandmother told stories about when she first saw a White man, talked about blue eyes, yellow hair, long knives. Apparently she called all Whites "palefaces." But the two spoke only Cree, not a word of English mixed with it, and even then Great-Grandma always seemed frightened, somehow afraid some White person would hear them and understand. Perhaps they both feared the White-supremacy movement, which was always powerful in Butte, whether it exposed itself as the vigilantes or just plain racial hatred in a land where individual violence is easily accepted — Butte rumour had it that no Montana jury would ever convict a person for killing someone who threatened you on your own property — and where the push for individual (read: individual White) rights was especially pronounced after the Kennedy assassination in 1963.

Yvonne wonders now what those two ancient women had experienced, what she might have learned if only she had understood Cree. It was obvious that her maternal grandmothers thought of the world of White power in which they were forced to live as nothing but dangerous.

And Earl's death simply proved them right. Great-Grandma was well over a hundred and could no longer travel, but Grandma Flora came to Butte for the funeral with Grandpa John: she was sixty years old, wearing her usual ground-length black dress that hid even her moccasins, contemplating the dead face of her handsome twenty-year-old grandson. There could be no question for her: Whites—certainly the way of the Whites—had killed him.

In 1971, having lost their thirteen-room "White House" mansion after the nine-month miners' strike in 1968, the Johnsons were living at 410 South Jackson Street. South Jackson was cut into the flank of Butte Mountain, and 410 was on the lower side of the street; on the other side the houses were built above eight-foot walls and could be reached only by narrow stairs cut into the cliff retained by cement or rock walls.

"Those houses towered over us," Yvonne writes to me in a letter, "all the more reason for the Whites up there to look down on us. The Smith family lived across from us, and above. Their father was a cowboy who rode the rodeo circuit, and their two kids were our age. At first we got on all right, until one day my little brother Perry wouldn't do what Shirley Smith wanted and she slapped him so hard she left her handprint on his bare back. Perry showed Leon, who went over and slapped Shirley's face. She yelled, 'Daddy, the Indian hit me!' and the fight was on. It lasted as long as we lived there, and sometimes the cops were called; they'd have their friends over and view us Natives from their high perch. It was mostly yelling. Once Shirley, who was as old as Leon, got us all going, and Auntie Josephine came out and yelled so hard her false teeth came out and she had to push them back in before she could continue. It got worse after Earl died, and one day Dad got into it.

"He was usually pretty laid back about neighbours. 'A bunch of yap traps, let 'em kick up the dust,' he'd say to us, but finally I think he got tired of the racket and of us telling him how we were beat up. Because the attacks on us carried over into the school yard, the cop kids who all knew us said they were glad our brother was a good Indian now, he was a druggie anyway. We started to get scrawled notes at home, threatening; they even got to Mom because now they knew she was not only Indian but also a foreign Canadian one.

"'Go home!' they hollered at her, and she'd yell right back, 'This is my home, and all my ancestors'. You go home, yellow-hair Custers!'

"Which just made it worse for us, because Dad was as blue-eyed and curly-yellow-haired as anyone could be—so us dark kids were obviously bastards or some kind of unnatural freaks. A fat man living on the corner called us 'Speckles!' because we all had different skin tones, and I felt everyone pointed especially at me, my scarred lips and difficult speech.

"That day Dad came home after tying one on and they were up high on their wall across the street, hollering. He got us kids out, lined us all up on the porch straight as Marines from tallest to shortest, and yelled in every direction, 'You want to fight my kids, well, here they are, all of them. If you got any balls, stop yelling and hiding and c'mon out and fight. They're waitin'!'

"He walked around to every neighbour house, banged on doors which didn't open, shouting, if they wanted something from us, come straighten it out once and for all in the middle of the street, just come out! Nobody did. Somebody phoned for the cops and they drove up, so Dad stood on our porch beside us and yelled at the neighbours, but no one would step off their property. So the cops did nothing and finally drove away while we stood there in a row. I was angry and humiliated and proud of my dad and us Marines, and ashamed and laughing and hating my family and excited and hating myself for everything and all at the same time. The Smith kids were up there, yelling, and then their parents came out and slapped them on the side of the head and told them to stop stirring up the Indians."

Yvonne laughs at a lighter memory. "A little later I got a baby doll. It was a clear, hot day and I took it out and danced around in a circle as I'd seen on TV, singing high and thumping the ground. And behold, believe it or not, it poured buckets! The Smith kids were scared, they believed I could curse them—and they behaved even worse to us whenever they could because now they were scared."

Earl's death remains like a mountain divide in the collective memory of the entire family; at any moment of speech or writing Yvonne will swing to that time, detailed incidents leaping into consciousness.

"After Earl got killed my family tried to get whole somehow. So we all drove in Earl's van—he'd decorated it so carefully sixties style and he'd give me two bits to wash it inside and out, right down to the last speck of dust on the floormats before I got the quarter—the whole family drove down to the Bighole River to go fishing. It was spring run-off, the water dropping, everything was still a little flooded and the willow leaves just coming out along the water. The van had a powerful cassette deck and we started playing The Beatles, "Hey, Jude," one of Earl's favourites. Then Dad just stretched out in the back of the van with the tailgate open and cried and cried. When we drove back up to our house there was the Smith girl above us, yelling, 'Indians on the warpath!' They knew we were fighting to find out what had happened to Earl. The whole town knew the cops had killed him."

It would appear that Leon, at fifteen the oldest and seemingly the toughest of the remaining children, was as powerfully affected by his brother's death as was Cecilia. Yvonne still cannot explain why, though she has puzzled about it for years.

"Leon was in custody up north, at Swan River boot camp, or maybe he was at Pine Hills near Miles City when it happened," she writes me. "They brought him home for the funeral. Sometimes I think there might have been some kind of connection between Earl's death and Leon . . . perhaps that would explain why Mom became so obsessed with protecting Leon. Even to the point of selling me out, as it sometimes seemed to me — I don't know — or maybe I already do know and just can't remember enough to understand, but no one now, neither Mom nor Leon nor my sisters, will talk to me about this. Only Kathy says she believes I believe what I'm looking for is true — but then she cries, she won't tell me what she remembers. Dad visits and supports me as he can, but he won't, or just can't, try to explain anything about this either.

"What is to be done? I will remember within myself, and then I will say it. I have to, because as Jung writes, I must within my self 'forge an ego that endures the truth.'

"Here is one thing I remember. Leon made wonderful rope swings. In the woods in summer when we cut poles he'd climb in the tallest tree and tie a rope to a high branch over the ravine. As you swung away, you flew above our camp and out into the wide, deep space between mountains. After Earl's death he always had a white rope hidden somewhere, fashioned in a hangman's noose, and I always knew where it was, though I was never allowed to touch it. After the funeral Leon and I were on the porch at South Jackson. Mom had allowed him to sneak a beer and he was drinking it and crying; he was confused by Earl's death. Then he told me to get the rope, so I ran and brought it.

"Leon had a plan, and I was part of it. Little did I understand. He tied the noose over a two-by-four on the porch roof, then brought a chair from his room and stood on it. He placed his head in the noose, very carefully, testing it out, it seemed, but I did not know what was going on. He told me he was building another swing and I could sit on his feet, use them as a seat and swing on him. So he put himself in the noose with his horn in his hand, then he stepped up on the chair and had me sit on his shoes and wrap my legs tight around his ankles and my arms tight around his legs. He played 'Taps' all the way through, and then he jumped off the chair with me sitting tight on his feet.

"Somehow I fell off. I think Leon shook me loose when he kicked all around. He tried to swing to the porch railing, but he whipped back and smashed the window in the room he and Earl had shared. He could not reach anything in his panic. I stood there, not knowing what was going on. Leon slowed and soon he wasn't kicking, he was grabbing his neck and his face looked really strange, his eyes bulged out scared. I could not get past while he was kicking. I got down on my knees when he slowed down, and belly-crawled under him. I went and told Dad and Mom, 'Leon broke the window.' I couldn't explain to them what was going on, and I ran back to Leon, his arms were now hanging, and just swaying. I tried to put the chair back, I tried to talk to him, and finally Dad was there.

"Dad yelled, he wrapped his arms around Leon and lifted him, and Mom came too. They cut him down. I told them Leon had told me he was making a swing, I should ride on his shoes but he kicked me off and broke the window.

"Leon came round and slashed himself through his wrist tendons with a dog-food lid from the garbage can. He was so angry from that pain he smashed his arm through another window. They took him away then and stitched him up. There was blood splashed on the porch and all over me."

———

When did this happen? How?

I am playing in the sand lot across the alley on Jackson Street. It may be a Saturday or during a long summer. A little girl is with me; she is silently playing in the sand too, making a nice road away from my castle, and so she is a friend. And a teenager, a quiet, black-haired boy, is suddenly there with two pops, the bottles already open, offering us each a cool drink because it's so hot in the sun and we are thirsty, aren't we thirsty?

I don't get many goodies. With seven kids at home we're told to be thankful for food and clothing and a bed to sleep in and a roof over our heads. Everything sweet is rationed. I'll always get a share, sure, but it will be the smallest, even though, if we don't share properly, Mom will adjust the problem fast enough, we'll all get it, or have to kneel on the floor for hours either with our arms folded or held out wide like the crucified Jesus. But here's a bottle all to myself, there's another one for my friend. So I permit myself to take it, and she does too. We sit in the sand lot, pop bubbling sweet into my mouth.

It's hot in the sun, it's nice to drink something strange and cool and sweet, and I'm getting a little sleepy and the buildings swim, sounds flip somersaults, and a man is there, hunching down beside the black-haired boy. The man says, Your mommy wants you; nap, it's time for, and he picks up the little girl's hand and he carries her away. The sun is putting me to sleep too. The sand is warm and there are pieces and bits of what may be pictures passing in front of me — very strange faces, I've never seen them before, a very large room. I cannot make a sound or even move. Faces look distorted and wriggling, changing like TV cartoons and sometimes so close I want to scream. But I can't, I can't hear, I can't move, I've never seen a grown-up body without clothes before. Other children are there, sounds twisting here, and gone, and here again, and somebody is puking over me, bleeding. Where are the clothes? It's so slick and icky I could puke too. I'm being felt all over, terrible hands, pains, this is not a beating, not a slap, but it hurts, I can't run, or move, it hurts.

And I wake up in my own bed, our house. Mom is bent over me. She is pulling off my clothes, they are covered with blood and she is screaming, Where are you hurt?, holding clothes at my face and I can't say anything, or sit up. I fall over limp, I can't hold myself. I hurt as if my legs have been torn apart, my head smashed, but how can I say what I don't know? Now I'm in my bed, I'm home, I want to sleep, it's night time, where did all the day go? My head feels light, like smoke churning over my heavy body, and my mother is screaming. Searching my body for where it has been opened for blood.

———

When I visit Yvonne in Kingston for a second time in September 1993, she says she has arranged for me to see the Prison for Women—"Whatever isn't classified!"—so I'll have some idea of where she must live.

We go out through the Psychology Office into the yard, between stone and wood and metal buildings crowded behind eighteen-foot-high stone walls. There are no gun towers anywhere. "Don't need them for women," Yvonne says. "But all kinds of stuff comes over the wall."

"What!"

"Tossed over, connections outside—drugs, tobacco, booze, tapes, anything. And you better get your times co-ordinated, exactly. If someone inside beats you to it, it's gone!"

"You could hardly complain to the guards!"

Yvonne pulls the peak of her cap lower in the lovely sunlight. If I concentrate on us walking together—as we never yet have—we are simply friends on an afternoon stroll; even the "sugar shacks," as she calls the two small bungalows with their fences and tiny yards where inmates can stay for several days of privacy with visiting husbands and children, might be normal homes—all I need to do is glance past the massive wall leaning over them and consider the blue sky, the bright clouds moving by from where I know Lake Ontario has to be.

And I will especially remember the bent frame of the uncovered sweat lodge in the angle of wall off Sir John A. Macdonald Street—the street where I came walking that morning from my motel. And the large white teepee beside it; the Native Sisterhood holds circles there when Elders come.

Then we're inside buildings, and every corridor and room is packed with people. Often I can recognize by their very posture a person's position in this rigidly ordered world before their clothing confirms my surmise. The laundry room, the gym where assemblies are held, the kitchen and low-ceilinged dining area with cafeteria serving counter and small, round tables. Here Yvonne often sits — she says she eats only three or four times a week, she's never hungry for this food — in an angle of wall and window opening on an enclosure of indirect sunlight between buildings, reading.

"That's my spot. If I'm there, everybody leaves me alone."

Yvonne introduces me to dozens of people, including officials of the prison, who all look at me carefully; she is friendly, laughs and cracks jokes with fellow inmates, and soon I notice what a strain it is for her, all this necessary "easy" camaraderie. There is a cluster of women in the library; they're obviously neither inmates nor officials and they seem large-eyed with incomprehension. Yvonne just shrugs, walks past towards the shelves, and shows me the worn paperback copy of *The Temptations of Big Bear*. That's how she first found out I existed.

And later I will remember one Correctional Services Canada guard at the outside door, when we re-entered the main building. Her face was younger, prettier than those of most of the guards we met, but it too was getting heavy, loose under her styled blonde hair. Yvonne explained that often guard jobs in P4W run in Kingston families, many of whom are related: most have been working there for three or four generations. The city has an excellent university, but the people associated with the many Kingston prisons outnumber the university people two to one. And it seems I remember all the guards as broad, large women, as if their very work produced weight, perhaps demanded a necessity of obvious, oppressive heft.

When we are alone in the counselling room again, we sit in silence, the tape recorder off. Yvonne makes cigarettes — she has a nice little gadget that stuffs tobacco into filtered tubes — and neither of us wants to plunge into anything. So finally I remind her of the Cadillac.

Cecilia bought the brand-new navy Cadillac in the summer of 1972 from Paisley Motors in Butte, so much down and $300 a month. Driving a truck in the Berkeley Pit was guarantee for anything.

"She loved that car." Yvonne is smiling. "Her dream-come-true, right up there, wide and low and sleek with Elvis. She parked it in front of our house on Jackson for the world to see.

"Mom showed us kids all the Caddy's beautiful features, and laid down the rules: no playing with the power doors or windows, no fighting, no food or drink in the car. It was so big no one had to sit on anyone's lap!

There wasn't even a hump in the floor, and I found my place lying flat on the blue carpet. Everyone else fought to sit by the window but I could fit into the smallest space. All the dangling, kicking feet were no problem. I stretched out in the new smell; everything on the thick carpet and under the seat smelled so rich. I could easily lie on the floor stretched along, almost under, the back of the front seat; there were even little skirts to hide me, hidden and safe though in the centre of my family. Or there were padded armrests that pulled down out of the backs of the seats. I could sit there higher between everyone either back or front, watch the highway slip away under us, watch Mom set the cruise control.

"We drove around Butte, down every street, every road in Silver Bow County, showing it. Once Mom stopped in the country for a family pit stop. She disappeared into the woods and suddenly she yelled out; when we got to her she was digging a huge glass tank out from under the leaves. A glass aquarium, she said; it must have held a hundred gallons of water, but it could fit into the trunk easily and we hauled it home. There wasn't a leak in it, the metal corners were sealed perfectly, so we polished it and she put it on a table by the front window and made sure the curtains were open so people walking past could see. Then she bought fish and plants and two turtles. We found interesting rocks and piled them up for the fish to swim through. I think it was the fanciest aquarium in Butte.

"We drove the Caddy east across Montana to Miles City to show Leon. Right out on the flat plains, south. Pine Hills School was a kind of boot camp for the worst teen and repeat offenders. I think it was either drugs or he had stolen a car that time, and we watched them play a baseball game. Bells rang and the boys came marching out like soldiers in white T-shirts and jeans. If they were old enough they could get out by volunteering for Vietnam, but Leon would never volunteer for that anyway, no Marine discipline for him. Driving out, for night we had a mattress folded up in the trunk; Mom and Dad slept on the mattress beside the road and we four girls slept soft and easy in the trunk with the lid open six inches. Little Perry slept inside the car. Mom had a rule: in our family boys and girls don't sleep together no matter what their age.

"We drove to Red Pheasant, Saskatchewan, too, to show the car to all our Canadian relations. Heading through the mountains for Great Falls, we found a stretch of four-lane: Interstate Fifteen had just been finished out of Boulder to Great Falls, and there Mom put the Caddy on cruise. All us Johnson Indians passing every car in sight, even the souped-up specials trying out the wide new concrete looked like they were standing still, whooooo! and us kids yelling, 'Get a horse, look out!' a Caddy slick blue lightning passing in the passing lane."

When did this happen? How?

Why did the Creator give me these intricate memories, this photographic mind, and yet allows me only bits and pieces of my past? So many tiny, exact snapshots branded on me. Why can't I see who the person was?

Somewhere, sometimes, there is the black-haired boy, and also a silver-haired man in a big car. He is often kind and gentle with me. He lives in the big yellow house across from a church. In the front part of his house live his wife and a daughter who both walk around dressed like Shirley Temple. The black-haired boy and Leon—yes . . . it's Leon—take me to the front door, but the man is mad; he orders them never to bring me there, only to the apartment connected at the back. Butte policemen come to that door all the time, wearing their uniforms and bulging guns on their hips. A large camera is set up in the hall of the apartment, and as I stand there alone I smell a funny smell, strange like smoke I have never smelled before.

Kathy is not there. All summer I never travel on the bus with Kathy to her summer classes at the old Washington School, that's where she goes, and every morning Mom takes me to an old woman who is supposed to be my summer school tutor.

But the old woman dresses me like Shirley Temple and leads me out through her back yard to the apartment door. The silver-haired man can do anything he pleases; even big policemen come, or leave, when he glances at them. And he has chosen me, he says he likes me.

The window in his bedroom faces into the sun; it is covered with white fluffy curtains, as is his large bed. The floor is soft white carpet, I am alone in the bedroom with him. He is wearing his white suit and he tells me to dance. But I am shy. I stand and begin to cry and he asks me if I like the pretty room, all the pretty things in it, and I nod my head. He asks if I like the silver hairbrush with all curly engraving. I nod, and he says I have nice hair and I can brush it if I wish. He gets the brush from the dresser and draws it gently down my hair.

He asks, "Why do you cry? Can you talk?"

And I nod, yes, with my back to him as he brushes. He is sitting on the edge of the bed.

"No one will hurt you," he says, "not any more. I won't let them."

He turns me and asks if I like to dance and I nod my head; he puts on music and tells me to dance for him then. I won't look out from under my hair, but he coaxes me to dance. Then he tells me to take off my dress and I am suddenly terrified. I stop, head down. I begin to cry again silently behind my hair.

"You poor thing," he says, and takes me in his arms and pulls me to sit beside him on the bed. "You'll be my little girl now. . . . I won't let . . . anyone hurt you. . . . I've chosen you. . . . I'll take care of you. . . . You're mine."

He lays me back on the bed. I turn to stone.

———

When did this happen? How?

I am standing beside Leon in our living room. He has just brought me back and he gives Mom some money and she is angry. She throws the whole wad of bills into the woodstove, and Leon quickly grabs into the fire and pulls it out again and runs away, crying in his little squeaks. Maybe he burned himself. Mom jerks the presents I hold away from me, a white jacket and hat to keep me warm, and into the stove they go. But she keeps a beautiful plaid skirt and fur muff; she gives them to Karen to wear to the Catholic junior high, where she goes and gets very good marks. I stay in the house, but some days later I hear a noise. I peek out and see older boys carrying Karen. She is wearing the plaid skirt. They bring her into the room, Kathy and I sleep in the bunk bed because we have both started to wet our beds again at night, and they lay Karen on the double bed where she sleeps with Minnie.

She is bleeding. Is she bleeding because she was hurt or because her periods have started?

———

Nineteen seventy-two was a presidential-election year, a good time to exert political pressure. The incumbent president, Richard Nixon, and Senator George McGovern were both running hard. It was while the campaigns heated up in the middle of October that Cecilia, after three and a half months of work, quit her job at the Berkeley Pit. She also gave up a chance to have a movie made about her—the first woman, first Native, mother with six kids and a disabled miner husband, driving a 100-ton pit truck—and turned her Caddy east on Montana Highway Ten, heading for South Dakota. She was responding to the American Indian Movement's call to join their "Trail of Broken Treaties" caravan and move on Washington.

Over a year before that trek took place, Clarence tells me, when several AIM members came to Butte at Cecilia's invitation and heard the details of Earl's death, the leader of the group had told the Johnsons this was exactly what the new Indian movement was about: to seek redress for the continued wanton killing, the persistent, prejudicial violation of the human rights of Indians in the United States. For several days, the leader tried to contact the Butte police and the mayor, but when he identified himself as being from AIM he could never arrange an appointment; instead he received anonymous, threatening calls at his hotel.

"It's like being Black in America," he told the Johnsons. "And the NAACP and Black Panthers are doing something about it. And so will we, for ourselves."

He believed the AIM campaign of focused, public action could be started right here; he would bring five hundred Indians to town and they wouldn't leave until they had some answers about what or who had caused Earl's death. "We'll make a stand right here in Butte," he said. "This case is serious enough."

In his small house, Clarence now sits alone, his upholstered chair shaped around his body, his head in his hands. "I went and sat in Earl's room," he tells me. "I thought and thought about my family, about all this. I love my country, I fought for it for years in one hell of a war, and damn near died half a dozen times. This is the United States of America: you have to do things by law. So I went out and I told him, 'No. There's law in America, we're Americans, we'll get our rights through the law.' "

Clarence stares into blankness, and says what he will tell me several more times over the telephone: "That was probably the worst mistake I ever made."

Because all the structures of "the law" proved as immovable as the mayor of Butte. When Cecilia and Clarence finally got to see Mayor Mike Micone, with Father Finnigan of the Roman Catholic church beside them, the first thing he told them—he didn't speak, he yelled across his cluttered desk—"I won't hear anything said about my police. They're good boys doing a tough job—not one word against my police!"

Cecilia wanted to go with AIM's idea; she and Clarence quarrelled bitterly, but Clarence was adamant and the AIM party left. So Cecilia continued to push the authorities, the law, to find the true cause of Earl's death. She wrote—forget about Butte—to the third most powerful man in the the U.S. government, Montana's senior senator, Majority leader Mike Mansfield; an assistant answered her on 3 September 1971, with the advice that the attorney general of Montana, Robert Woodah, "might be in a position to advise you on a matter of this kind." That was all she ever heard from Mike Mansfield in Washington.

So she took her petition personally to the Capitol in Helena; nothing came of that. She drove to Denver, Colorado, again with Father Finnigan, to speak personally to Hollis Bach, the U.S. regional civil rights director. On 21 October 1971, he wrote her a polite letter saying he had passed her statement about Earl on to the regional attorney for civil rights; nothing came of that. Finally, almost a year later, on 2 October 1972, her Montana district member of Congress, Dick Shoup of the House of Representatives, sent her an answer that completed the futile circle:

Dear Mrs. Johnson:

This will acknowledge your recent letter regarding your son's death.

I am most sympathetic to the situation you outlined, but since this matter is not within my jurisdiction . . . I have forwarded your letter to Mayor Micone for his review. I know he would wish to be apprised of the incidents to which you refer and will do all he can to assist. . . .

"Mom drove away and Aunt Rita went with her," Yvonne tells me. "I don't know if she drove all the way to Washington or not in the Caddy, but Mom was so hyper now, when she wasn't working her shift in the pit she was never home, driving a load of relatives to Idaho to pick potatoes and British Columbia to pick fruit, possibly making political connections. Once she drove to Helena with a box of 'evidence.' I waited outside in a long room while she took the box into an office, and after a long time she came out but never said a word to me of what went on. Later the Montana government said they had seen no evidence, Mom's box did not exist. She drove to federal government offices wherever she could find them, to find the 'inspectors from Washington' or any of the guys in that jail under city hall that day, to the FBI, wherever they had a district office. She was always searching or working on new reports and collecting pictures and making more copies and travelling. I was living my own ugly life and didn't know where she was. And then she was gone completely, away with AIM—South Dakota, Minnesota, Ohio, or Washington, the Caddy could go anywhere. I never knew all the details, but I know she really tried."

Clarence shows me various cards he received from Cecilia.

A postcard dated 15 October 1972, from Custer, South Dakota:

Dear Clarence and children: Be good now as I love you all and pray for me I need it, Love Mom.

An undated card from Wounded Knee, South Dakota:

Be good, you belong to me.

A card dated 24 October 1972, from Mankato, Minnesota:

*Dear Clarence and Kids: . . . I'm A OK hope this finds you all
the same way. Happy birthday to you all [the four girls all have
birthdays in October] hoping and wishing that I was there with
you guys. I'm getting very lonely for home. It was a nice day
today. I guess we'll be here till Friday [She goes on at length
about how expensive everything is : ". . . car wash 2.50 and they
done a piss poor job of it."]*
    So I'll close for now I remain yours, Cecilia

An undated, unplaced card mailed to Clarence, a printed verse
unsigned:

You've seen me at my best
You've seen me at my worst
You've never seen me
when I didn't love you Honey.
Happy Birthday.

Cecilia later told her family that she was "a gunner" for the caravan.
The AIM leaders, who had the trek very well organized—and hoped to
gather together at least 5,000 of the 900,000 Indians in the United
States and the half-million in Canada by the time they arrived in
Washington—intended that the caravan stop at every point where a
treaty had been broken. Cecilia said driving "gunner" meant being at
the end of the long caravan of motor vehicles and assisting any who
broke down, helping them keep on moving to the next stop. Generally
motels refused to rent them space, so they sent individuals ahead and
pinpointed motels they would take over completely: AIM paid all the
bills. The people who stayed home were urged to make memorabilia
for AIM members on the road, mostly beaded medallions, and the
Johnsons in Butte did that too.
    "Dad made more than any of us—necklaces, medallions for jack-
ets, the AIM logo in black and red beads. He still does."
    Cecilia explained that the Trail of Broken Treaties trek to Washing-
ton was to be a spiritual movement, that the caravan really began as a

peace demonstration to make Americans aware of how the traditions and needs of aboriginal people had been destroyed by the Bureau of Indian Affairs, an arm of the Department of the Interior. But as more Indians joined, and they took part in ceremonies held at the sites of massacres and betrayals, their feelings rose higher, especially since many of the travellers were young men.

"Mom was very strong," Yvonne says to me. "She had a powerful need for justice for the death of her son—she had the pictures of Earl in his coffin, the autopsy papers, she told the story—and she helped everyone, she knew things, she made up her mind quickly. She became a true warrior woman for many of those kids."

But at one point the young men tied red bandannas above their knees and moved into the vanguard, as if, like warriors of old, they would lead and were willing to die if they had to. In Ohio, state troopers blocked the highway and an old woman tried to run forward and plead with the police: their men were young and excited, so please, just let them pass through. But troopers surrounded the woman and threw her aside in the ditch, and the young men stormed the roadblock. They rolled several police cars over into the ditch and cleared the road and somehow Cecilia got into the mêlée as well. Calm was soon restored, but not before she grabbed at a cop inside a cruiser and her hand came out with his hat.

The caravan began to arrive in Washington on Monday, 30 October. On 3 November the *Post* reported "at least 500 Indians barricaded themselves inside the Bureau of Indian Affairs building last evening." After that, even during the last days of a presidential election campaign, they created front-page headlines. While "hundreds of young Indians ranged through the government-drab corridors" of the Indian Affairs building, a Cherokee mother, Martha Grass, told *Post* reporter Peter Osnos:

"It's for these youngsters to take us back to Indian ways. They're the ones to say, 'Now we will take care of ourselves.' The older people are just beat. They don't think change is possible."

In the parking lot crowded with Indians' cars, young Len Not-Afraid wiped his nose with an American flag and told Osnos, "We are prisoners in our own country."

The senior chiefs who formed the official National Tribal Chairmen's Association, and who claimed they represented three-quarters of all U.S. Indians, condemned the occupation. There was a flurry of consultations, court orders, and manoeuvrings; rumours flew; young men stated they would die but never leave. On Tuesday evening, 7 November, Richard Nixon was re-elected president in a landslide, and on 9 November the protesters received "binding promises" that the highest officials would deal with their documented grievances. Sixty-six thousand, six hundred dollars in "expense money" was distributed in $100 bills from a black attaché case and eventually everyone scattered back to Canada and the twenty-eight states from which they had come.

Yvonne says, "In their brokenness, they were just bought off."

The week-long occupation had been a misery for the protesters barricaded inside a building with almost no food and nothing but the floor and office furniture to sleep on; where lights and toilets soon ceased to function because the authorities turned off all water and electricity. The women and children had tried to bunk down on the top, fourth, floor, while the men and boys had been on the third floor in case of attack. The newspapers reported they left two million dollars' worth of damage behind; some claimed it surpassed anything federal Washington had experienced since the British burned the city in 1814.

"I guess it's right," Yvonne says sardonically, "that it was Indians did it. But all Mom had when she came home was the Ohio cop's hat and a heavy office-table leg she tore off as a possible weapon one night when they believed the police were set to raid—even perhaps burn them out."

For eighteen months Butte City and Silver Bow County officials had refused to do anything about Earl's death, but finally, Clarence tells me, the sheriff from Boulder in the neighbouring county of Jefferson offered some practical help; he took the information about Earl to the proper authorities in Washington, D.C. In spring 1973, Cecilia finally received two letters from the the the U.S. Department of Justice, Civil Rights Division, Criminal Section. One, dated 2 March, explained to her:

> . . . *an investigation of this matter has previously been conducted by the Federal Bureau of Investigation. After careful analysis of the information . . . and additionally, of the information which you provided . . . we have concluded that this matter does not in-*

volve the violation of a federal civil rights statute. Therefore, this
Department is without authority to take further action.

The second letter was dated 1 May 1973:

Dear Mrs. Lucille [sic] *Johnson:*
    *Your letter of November 15, 1972 to the Director of Civil
Rights, Washington, D.C. has been referred to this office for
reply. Please excuse the delay in responding.*
    *The death of your son . . . has been investigated by the
Department of Justice. No evidence was developed . . . that would
indicate that your son's death was other than . . . self-inflicted
strangulation.*

This letter was signed by the same two men who had signed the one
of 2 March.

———

When Cecilia returned from Washington, the first thing she did was
drive north to see her parents, perhaps for prayer ceremonies. Yvonne
cannot be certain, but one of AIM's purposes was to revive the traditional Native ceremonies, and that encouraged Cecilia. Then she
returned to Butte; after twenty-four years in the United States, a twenty-
two-year marriage to a White American ex-Marine, six children living
and one dead, Cecilia had had enough. She was going to return permanently to her people on the Red Pheasant Reserve in Canada, and
she wanted to take her children with her.

Clarence didn't like either idea one bit. For him, a family was
and remained a family. But Cecilia was "one true warrior woman," as
Yvonne now sees it, and she made her stand: any hope or possibilities
there might have been for her and her White husband were gone; she
was returning to her people. Clarence could not change her mind and
he knew it. She arranged for a lawyer to manage their separation. The
lawyer suggested a compromise concerning the children: why not ask
each child in turn, Do you want to stay with your dad in Butte, or do
you want to go to Canada with your mom?

━━━

When did this happen? How?

The black-haired boy and his friends don't come to get me any more, but I'm at the municipal swimming pool. I'm locked in the house otherwise and not allowed to go out anywhere else, but a boy comes who says he knows Earl, Earl told him to get me, so I go with him. There is construction on the road by the pool, traffic is piled up and I'm in my swimming suit so it must be summer, and I'm in the front seat of a logging truck and I see Earl coming in our logging truck and I shout, Here I am, Earl!

But the boy driving the truck throws me on the floorboards. I'm hauled out under a bridge where there are cars, someone is beating me, shouting. When I'm conscious again I've been placed on a sawmill belt that carries the bark from the logs up to the top of the trash cone that smokes all the time, it's always on fire, but I fall off before I'm carried to the top and crash on hard ground. The burner is rumbling so hard the earth shivers, and I scream and scream. They won't leave me alone, they yank me around, they're fighting among themselves, quarrelling, mad, and then a boy appears at the top of a cliff and yells down at us,

Her brother's coming!

An older man has me in a small black car. He's driving as if he's insane, roaring through town, running corners and red lights. I see Earl in our logging truck right behind us. We shoot into a narrow street. Then I'm on the floor, plastered against the door of the car, as the old man speeds up, tries to hold the car on four wheels going around a big curve, tires squealing, but as the street straightens suddenly the car hits the curb, whips back and forth and smashes into a pole beside a gas station. The attendant comes running out, sees me all bloody, and the driver slumped over the wheel gasping and he jumps in and drives the crumpled car to Silver Bow Hospital; it's just a few blocks away.

At the Emergency entrance, they pull the driver out onto a stretcher fast. Earl arrives in the truck, slams on brakes, and jumps out. He runs straight for the stretcher and starts hammering at the old man while the orderlies try to wrestle him away. Earl's screaming, Where's my sister? What'd you do to my little sister! A nurse looks in the car, sees me, and shrieks,

Here's another one!

They lift me carefully out and onto a gurney. Earl is cursing, trying to tear himself loose from the orderlies to get to me, but they're too many for him. I hear the glass on the emergency door smash. Earl still fighting to reach me.

I am in a green room full of glass shelves. Mom is beside me, and then Dad is there too and he's going crazy at me all bloody, I'm gonna fucken kill the guy that did this! Mom walks around me and grabs him. Be quiet! she says and they're wrestling against the big glass window so hard I can hear his back-support girdle creak; he cries out in pain. We'll take care of it, she tells him, just shut up here, shut up.

Dad stands beside me, crying. A man who looks like a doctor bends over me. He opens my mouth. He says to anybody who is listening, "How do you sew up a tongue?"

5

That's Right, Drive Me to Winter

She does not know how to let anyone love her. Love is just a word someone says to get in your pants.

– Yvonne Johnson to Rudy Wiebe, 14 February 1993

I N THE KINGSTON PRISON FOR WOMEN, Yvonne's memories
have moved inevitably from the Johnsons' brief Cadillac saga to
her parents' permanent split. I listen carefully, take fast notes as
usual, but my mind seems imprinted with the prison tour we have
made, the residue of her February letter, which explained P4W as a
place where "in the span of eighteen months eight women succeeded
in killing themselves, and another is in a coma for trying." Even as I
concentrate, jot words and sequences, the images of the antediluvian
core of this place—the cell blocks—run like a continuous reel in the
back of my mind.

Two and a half years from now a federally appointed judge will
describe this place. Yvonne will introduce me to Brenda Morrison,
one of the eight Native women strip-searched by the all-male Emergency Response Team on 26–27 April 1994; Brenda will send me
a copy of Judge Louise Arbour's *Commission Inquiry into Certain
Events at the Prison for Women in Kingston*, and she will inscribe the
book: "April 3, 1996 / To Rudy Wiebe / I give you this book to read
with understanding. . . ."

Judge Arbour's description of the prison is precise and damning:

. . . an old fashioned, dysfunctional labyrinth of claustrophobic
and inadequate spaces holding 142 prisoners of all security levels,
minimum through maximum. It has been described as "unfit for
bears." It is inadequate for living, working, eating, programming,
recreation, and administration. Spaces are poorly ventilated and
noisy . . . reached through narrow corridors, steep stairwells, and
innumerable locked barriers. . . . Surrounded by an enormous

wall . . . the building has the characteristics of a [male] maximum security institution.

"Unfit for bears"—how unwittingly apt for Yvonne, the great-great-granddaughter of Big Bear, and whose spiritual power comes from the Bear's Spirit. In our tour of P4W, I had one glimpse through bars down one long range of fifty-four cells stacked in two tiers of twenty-seven stone cells, one above the other. Each cell is nine by six feet, and there are two of these tiered stone ranges, A and B, built back to back. Yvonne could take me no closer than a glimpse: there was no way the female guards grouped and staring at us grimly through the entrance bars would slide them open for us.

Yvonne's "house" is in the Wing, which provides relatively better accommodation: fifty small rooms with tiny windowed doors, no bars or mesh except on the outer perimeters. She reached an agreement with the guard in the cubicle at the entrance to her narrow corridor, and then she asked me, "Please, don't look to either side: the doors are open but people don't like to be looked at." So I controlled my curiosity, Yvonne called out, "Man on the floor!", and I walked a step behind her, past doors, with my eyes straight ahead in the glaring bare light.

To her house. At the end of the corridor, just wide enough for a bed placed lengthwise under the small, curtained window. Tightly filled with the little she now has to live with: narrow clothes cupboard, a small table for a "kitchen," another for writing piled with a typewriter and papers, her tape collection and a tiny TV received from an inmate who had served her time.

Yvonne leaves the door open as she points out her things; with both of us inside, there is just space to turn around without bumping into each other. Close outside the barred window is the corner of the stone wall. "I can turn out this light," Yvonne says, "and with the door closed it's a little darker. In prisons the lights are on twenty-four hours."

"But . . . there's so much noise."

"You learn—your pillow is for on top of your head, not under."

———

Whatever order and security existed in the Johnson family, whatever stability might have developed as the children grew into adults, any united family possibilities, however tenuous, disappeared with the split between Cecilia and Clarence. And what happened in the lawyer's office between Yvonne and her parents—the decision she then made—still resonates deeply in her memories.

"All us kids—Leon, Karen, Minnie, Kathy, me, and Perry—were lined up on chairs outside, and I was called in last. Even Perry was called in before me. The lawyer was smiling across his big desk, Dad sat on one side and Mom on the other. That lawyer said nothing, so finally I asked him,

"'Who's going with Mom?'

"'So far,' he said, 'they're all going with her.'

"Well, I knew Leon would for sure and Karen figured, and Minnie, but—'Even Kathy and Perry?'

"'Yes.'

"'Who's staying with Dad?'

"'Nobody.'

"I thought Mom looked cocky, like she does when she wins—despite her obvious pain of this pulling apart. Dad sat bent forward on his elbows, then he threw back his shoulders and head, brushed his curls flat on his head like he always does with his right hand, and stared straight ahead, stiff as a Marine.

"Oh, I remembered the pictures of Mom, so beautiful when she was sixteen. Slender and stunning with her olive skin, black eyes, and long black hair—every Indian in Great Falls must have been nuts about her. I'm sure there was plenty of growing-up to do after nothing but priests and nuns and five prayers every day and seven on Sunday. She knew exactly what she wanted: she married a tall, blue-eyed, curly-blond American ex-Marine. And a short time later she took him back to Canada with her—to the Thunderchild Residential School as they had named it, though Chief Thunderchild had never allowed anyone to baptize him—the school she had survived and somehow gotten out of at age fourteen just before it burned down to its very foundations in a fire of unknown origin (but it still continued, of course—the Roman Catholic church can never permit a fire, no matter how big, to wipe out its program), and with her big White American husband standing beside her Cecilia told the priests and nuns she was taking every one of her younger brothers and sisters away: Richard, Evelyn, Rita, Roy: she was married, she was of age, she had a home in Montana, and she would be their guardian—her family needed no residential school, she would take care of them."

And Clarence in his Butte house shows me the pictures of the beautiful teenage Cecilia he met in a bar in Great Falls; who married him in Coeur d'Alene, Idaho, in late 1950. Earl was born in January 1951.

"Yeah," Clarence continues, "and besides that we had all her younger brothers and sisters in Butte, different ones at different times in the fifties, till they got bigger, before our girls were born. I helped raise those kids, all except Josephine, the oldest. I worked in the mines—hell that was work, those narrow shafts, and deep!—and brought in the money and she cooked and cared for them. Once when they hauled her little brother Roy off to a foster home she went after them and said, 'Where's my boy, where've you got my kid?' and she took him away from them, right out of their car. Even after they were grown up they'd come here when they got in trouble, or me and her'd haul them back across the line to Saskatchewan because their parents were living together on Red Pheasant again. We raised those kids with Earl and Leon in the fifties, and their kids were here often enough too. Ask them, there's dozens, they always knew there's a place here."

Yvonne tells me, "I told that lawyer, 'I want to stay with my dad.' "

I ask her, "Why did you do that?"

She answers quickly, "I love Dad. I felt sorry for him, all alone." And after a pause, she continues thoughtfully in her resolute, self-searching way. "He looked so crushed . . . but not just that. I thought if I was an only child, if he only had me, I'd get everything. Huh!" She laughs sardonically. "I should have known all I was going to hear from him was, 'I can't afford it.' "

The Caddy was gone—repossessed and hauled away—and Cecilia had a Ford pick-up truck, black and so old the floorboards of the box were wood with steel bracing. She packed everything she could into it, piled high, tied down under canvas. Clarence had the flat-bed logging truck, and he and Yvonne followed the pick-up. There was some delay about how many children the Americans would let Cecilia take with her—and then her truck wouldn't start. Clarence had to push it to the top of a hill to start it rolling down across the border into Canada.

In Butte, Yvonne had to face the little bigots of Webster-Garfield School alone. Though she had missed twelve of forty-five days of school in the previous quarter, her performance in every subject was simply checked as "S"—satisfactory—and at the end of May 1973 she was promoted into Grade Six. It was the last year she would receive a regular report card.

"In June, after school, Dad took me north to Taber, Alberta," Yvonne tells me. "Mom and our whole family was working there, hoeing sugar beets. Her oldest sister, Auntie Josephine, was there too, and her oldest daughter, Shirley Anne, who was shacked up with a White guy——"

Yvonne breaks off; she rises to her feet, picks up our coffee cups, and goes out quickly. When she comes back, her cap is pulled down low over her grim face; we drink barely warm coffee.

Finally I ask, "What's the matter?"

"Oh, nothing . . . ," she begins, but she's too honest to deny herself. "Shirley Anne." And I know: accused with Yvonne in the murder, she actually served only a year for aggravated assault. "I can't mention her," she murmurs. "I get upset."

Then she adds in a rush, "She'd lived with us quite often in Butte before. I remember Shirley Anne when I was little in the White House: she's ten years older than me. I would watch Shirley Anne, I didn't know anything about her then, or what she was doing, I was a little kid, and she'd spend all morning putting on make-up, taking it off, putting it on, and most of the afternoon too, and then she'd go out for the evening. That's all she did."

She sits there, pulled together and small in her chair. After a while I remind her, "You were talking about thinning beets in Taber. That June, after the separation."

"Yeah," she says. "I . . . we were in Alberta all summer, and I went with Mom to Red Pheasant when we were through. Dad didn't thin any beets. He dropped me off and drove back to Butte. He was alone until I got sent to him again, I think it was after getting in a fight in school in Saskatchewan that fall."

When did this happen? How?

I am small and I'm being taken—stolen away?—into Canada, Mom is taking me. Leon has escaped from Swan River Reformatory or maybe it's Miles City, and he has to get over the border into Canada too, and Dad can never buck Mom once she's made up her mind, but he warns her: nothing happens to Vonnie. And she agrees, Yes yes, Vonnie will get to Red Pheasant safe and sound.

Leon is sitting on the hood of the car with a flashlight, Mom is driving very slowly, carefully, down a dirt trail. She avoids, she follows the high running lights of semi-trailers, but we're barely moving, she crawls along, concentrating ahead so hard her big chest pushes against the wheel, she has to stay within sight of the top row of tiny lights but the huge truck churns so much dust or when it dips into a hollow she can mostly see nothing, the flashlight is caught like a broken pencil in the rolling dust of darkness. A huge black shape sits in front of us, Leon.

The car is stopped. Outside the open windows the grey line of land rises into a double-hump of immense, high hills, I cannot tell how far away. There are stars and the twitchy sounds of sweet summer grass singing. The car motor clicks, clicks when Mom switches it off. The dash lights cut sharp shadows on her face; she looks angular like Big Bear in the photograph taken in jail almost a hundred years ago where he seems to be staring into the sun forever. We are driving to my grandma's place in Canada. Grandpa John will be there and he'll say nothing to me, but Grandma Flora will, in Cree, which I do not understand but I know anyway.

The yellow car lights feel carefully along the endless gravel road going north. For days and nights I am going to sleep on the floor in that corner of Grandma's grey house behind her warm woodstove. She will do ceremonies on me to help me forget.

In the counselling room inside p4w Yvonne explains to me:

"Dad's a binge drinker: he'll sober up for months and then he'll drink for months. After they split up, for a long time he drank more than ever. He'd sit and cry in his drunkenness. For a while Perry was brought back to live with us and I watched him."

"Didn't you have to go to school?" I ask. "You were in . . . what . . . Grade Six?"

"Dad didn't work steady, he was on the small pensions he has now—I can't remember, not much. But I know Elvis Presley had a song out then, 'Daddy, Daddy, Please Don't Cry.' A man who was in the war with him would be there, drinking too, and he'd razz Dad:

"'That time, your Indian woman sure hung a licken on you!'

"'Yeah,' Dad would say, 'but my back was broke then.'

"'Sure sure, and the next thing you'll say you was dead drunk too!'

"'Hell, you gotta stop the pain somehow!'

"They'd drink and talk about the gruesome stuff they saw in the war, competing with each other. Dad said he saw a man blown in half, and the jungle grew so fast, the next day grass was growing through his guts and out of his asshole."

Twelve-year-old Yvonne cooked what she could: "Spaghetti, beans and wieners, beans from a can, pancakes that turned out to be five-pounders, a lot of peanut butter and bread. Dad went out on his drinking sprees. During one of my stays in Canada someone gave Dad two dogs, Prince and Princess, and he'd moan they were all he had, all that loved him—and I was sitting there. I stayed, and he drank till he passed out, pitying himself, and never offered me a touch of comfort. It was just as well I guess; a man's touch was never anything but dangerous."

I have brought copies of various papers with me from Butte, and together Yvonne and I try to puzzle some order into the records of her life between 1973 and 1978. There are almost no objective data to guide us. Even Clarence's cardboard box held only a few dated disciplinary notes:

West Junior High School: Yvonne suspended one week for smoking, [signed] George Foley, January 6 , 1975

West Junior High School: Yvonne involved in a fight within the classroom, [signed] R. Kuecks, 1–17–75

West Junior High School: Yvonne suspended for two days for skipping classes, [signed] Miss E. Nixon, Jan. 6, 1977

Clarence has no report cards beyond Grade Five, May 1973. Yvonne has memories of a school-yard fight in Cando, Saskatchewan (where she would have gone with her sisters by bus while they lived on Red Pheasant Reserve), and getting her mouth damaged and being sent back to Butte for the continuing operations paid for there by the U.S. Crippled Children's Fund; of a time in junior high in Bell School, Winnipeg (Cecilia had gone there to work), where she mostly played hookey in the girls' room; of a school in Leaf Rapids in far northern Manitoba where she "fell in love." It may be that in spring, 1974, after they left Leaf Rapids, both she and Kathy returned to stay with Clarence in Butte; she is certain she refused to return to Webster-Garfield alone and was sent to McKinley School, which she remembers as much quieter for her.

Clarence tries to explain to me the endless movements of children between wherever Cecilia was working in Canada and himself stationary in Butte:

"Vonnie lived with me for quite a while, and so did Kathy sometimes. Perry was with me a lot as a little guy, when Cecilia was working somewhere. But Karen and Minnie never came back here for long; they'd show up one day and then be gone before I knew it. All the kids back and forth. Once the four girls were here together. By then Cecilia couldn't do nothing much with them either, and I was sitting here, and them asking each other, 'You going back to Mom?' They couldn't agree. They'd go uptown to the bars, and next day they're off, all back up to Canada.

"Leon . . . he was back and forth as he liked when he wasn't in jail either here or there, often running from one country or the next 'cause he was in trouble. In Butte I'd know all about him from the papers: he'd live with a girl and was in the papers every week, drunk or smashing something, paying a fine or slopping out the jail to work it off. He's never worked except in jail, he can't work: he lives off the girl, Welfare, and thinks he's so smart and strong he's the ultimate of all creation—he actually talks like that. He must have six, seven kids at least, and I can't let him into my house any more: he'll just take what he wants and if I tried to stop him he'd break my back. When he shows up now I talk to him on the porch; if he wants to come in, I tell him I'll call the police. He laughs or swears, but he never gives me any trouble that way."

Yvonne tells me school had never helped her learn much of anything except how to disappear. And how to fight, although as she grew older the speech-therapy classes they gave her and the continued plastic surgery aided her a little in coming out of her silence. She had taught herself to read by breaking words into parts and pronouncing them in her head, following the model of speech therapy, and during Grade Six in McKinley School her teacher "didn't bug me"—which meant he ignored her if she caused him no trouble—and she would go to the library and read on the machines where the text would be illumined for a brief time, and you read it and then tried to answer the questions that followed. It became a game: she practised setting the light for shorter and shorter periods until she could answer correctly as fast as the reader could be set. She read half *The Godfather* and other books she found interesting. There had never been any books at home, except for a set of Bible-story books that her mother bought from a travelling salesman. The only time she spoke up in grade school, it was because she loved *Charlotte's Web*. One entire winter she never played hookey in the afternoon because the teacher was reading that book aloud to the class.

"I loved that story so much," she tells me. "The spider, the pig, everything—it was the only time I wanted to go to school, and once I was drawing a spiderweb on my desk, ink on wood, and the teacher saw me and was furious. She demanded I repeat what she had just read. I was so excited I stood up and talked! I quoted the book back to her, almost word for word from the beginning, and she was so stunned at my memory and talking aloud she just said, 'All right, all right, sit, sit,' and didn't punish me."

Grade Six mostly in McKinley, Grades Seven and Eight moving back and forth between Manitoba and West Butte Junior High, who knows how often; it seems she may have spent two years in Grade Eight until she refused to go to school any longer; she failed at least once. She was always outstanding in physical education (Clarence shows me a certificate of award for P.E. Volleyball she received on 25 May 1973), and good to very good in art and music, but her academic record in her first five grades was consistently "unsatisfactory" and "needing improvement."

"I flunked Grade Eight at West Butte Junior High," she tells me, "and I quit."

She failed in spring 1976; it seems she tried again in fall, but quit for good early in January 1977, shortly after she turned fifteen. Just stopped going. In the meantime she had lived on the road between her mother, who moved over three Prairie provinces looking for work wherever she could find it, and her stay-put father. When she was in Butte she tried to stay out of her father's way, not attract his attention. "He never talked to me anyway," she says. "We never talked about what our life, our family was about, why we lived like this and what we kids could actually do to change it. 'Go to school,' 'Get a job'—that was it, orders, arbitrary orders but never a conversation about choices, about what might be possible. He ate at home and went out to drink. He drank to get drunk.

"There was something about me as a beginning teenager that somehow warned me: hang on, don't call attention to yourself, you can't do anything anyway, just adapt, do what any available adult does; hang on.

"Everyone told me I was stupid anyway. I'd flunked Grade One, then I flunked Grade Eight—I must be like they said, stupid, and probably crazy too. No family around, eat whatever you can find or pick up in homes where I baby sat. There's usually something in Dad's fridge when he's away or asleep. Or you go into a bar. Butte bartenders never bother with your ID if you're tall and sit quiet and drink. You can always get a pizza there, pickled eggs, some bar food. That's where I learned to manage on three or four meals a week. And I always had a place to sleep. Either I'd babysit somewhere and sleep over, or I'd sneak into the house basement when Dad locked the door on me—he didn't like what he thought I was doing; I was alone with him and only fifteen, sixteen; he might have talked to me about it beyond an occasional yell, but he didn't—and after I couldn't trust him, I lived like a mole in his basement. There was only one way into it, a big thick door Dad never knew I had a key to. I was small and flexible, and I could withstand great pain. Even if I had to cut or bend myself to fit some place, I did. I've had to stay some place so long, my body formed into that small space and when I finally could leave I had to force myself out and let my body unfold itself in its own time.

"When I came into the basement I would look at the woodstove, to see if it was stoked for evening. If it was, I'd sleep stretched out on my pile of rags; if not, I'd hide in a hole like a small tunnel. When Dad wasn't home I'd dig the hole bigger at least to curl up in, and over time maybe stretch out. If I was willing to sleep balled up, it was in this hole tunnel. All the time he thought I was running the streets, I was mostly there.

"Just stay alive, hang on. Dad never knew where I was. Nor, it seemed sometimes, cared: he was too busy drinking, trying not to remember much, looking for some kind of happiness, you know, just getting past one day into another.

"But he was always a laugher too, always. Every one of us kids learned that from him. In the next minute telling a crazy story and all of us laughing so loud our ears hammered. And 'stop feeling sorry for yourself': he and Mom agreed on that, absolutely. But he never paid her even the one dollar a year he promised her for child support."

How could this happen?

A cop car brakes beside me and I run—they killed my brother, they can kill me—run to a house, banging on the door, and I scramble in as it opens. I try to hide under the dining-room table, its lovely lace cloth hangs down to the ground, but cops are at the door. They come in and drag me out, clamping their big hands over my screams. I'm in a padded cell in the uptown police station by the courthouse. Take off your clothes, they order; there are perhaps six or seven uniforms around me in a semicircle. I hunch together, crying. One uniform says, I don't want no part of this, and two of them leave. I'm curled naked in the corner of the padded cell, and they give me coffee. When I wake up groggy, I'm all wet, as if I've been hosed down to clean me; my hair seems glued to the floor. The matron covers me with an itchy blanket and she leads me out of the padded cell upstairs to another cell. It has beds, and a cop looks at me through the trap-flap in the steel door and I scream out the second-floor window at people on the street, Get my dad, Clarence Johnson, 410 South Jackson! A man is listening to me, but a needle is poked into my arm and, when I come to again, I wrap myself in the blanket and the cell door is unlocked and I run. Somebody yells, Hey, she's loose! but I'm outside, running down the street till the dope kicks in again; I'm falling on the sidewalk, people try to grab me; I'm running through a barrier into the bus depot; I curl together on the moving baggage belt so I'll disappear into the black hole with it. Then my father is there, picking me up; he carries me wrapped in the blanket into our house.

I am lying on the couch, and Dad is giving me shit for whoring around and who knows what else. So I show him what they did. His thick lips mumble curses steadily as he touches the belt marks whipped across my chest, around each thigh. I cry, cry; he rubs my head and his own head in rage and frustration as he checks me all over so gently and begins to cry with me. Then he shoves me back onto the couch, opens his pants, pushes himself down on me.

I can't breathe. My mouth is stretched open, my head twisted, my nose bent against the back of the couch so I don't have to see, though I have to hear him on top of me. The little cowboys woven into the couch covering are against my eyes, so close they're just blotches.

Dad is crying, sobbing out loud and begging forgiveness, he's sorry, so sorry, he got carried away, but I can get up and I run. Our neighbour finds me curled under his big tree. He takes me into his house, but when he says Police I slip away and back into our basement. I sleep and sleep. When I wake up I wait for Dad to leave, and then I climb up into the bathroom and lock the door. I'm covered by gentle water, as hot as I can stand, then Dad comes back before I'm out and I find him sitting with his gun. I think he's going to shoot himself. We struggle. The gun goes off and blasts a hole in the wall behind him.

———

When I call Clarence and, in the course of our conversation, ask him whether he ever fought physically with Yvonne, he admits he did. Once, when he found her with a "boy in the back room, I went in there and threw him out." But he denies, categorically, any sexual assault on her. "I spanked the kids some, sure, and I fought with Earl the one time, but there was no sexual assault. No way, nothing like that. I kissed them goodnight, I never penetrated any of them."

———

Yvonne: The police say when a girl turns sixteen Montana law requires that all her juvenile court and police records—sixteen and under?—be sealed for ever. But you can't seal memories for ever. To me they sometimes seem more like nightmares, but it is broad daylight. I am not asleep.

I know I tried to kill myself once with the gas stove and Dad found me after I was unconscious, but not far enough to force him to take me to the hospital. Twice he finds me passed out on his bed, holding his gun—I don't know how I got there. Leon is out of jail and back in Butte and shacked up with Liz Green, who's got one child so she can get welfare easily and live on her own. Finally I move in with Ellie Waite's family, but her mom kicks me out when Ellie and I go joy-riding in her car, and then one evening I meet her cousin Ed, who's just passing through. He's from California with some hillbillies in a blue car, and a biker and his wife travel with him. They're really decent, and one of them, Denny, says to me, You're a good kid, Indian. Where you're not welcome, I'm not welcome either. You want to light out west, California?

So we all pile into the blue car and go.

Denny and his wife drive, and another guy, Sammy, is such a fabulous talker he cons a man we meet in a parking lot out of his shorts, and then his false teeth too! They laugh like crazy on the road, but I'm quiet. The car leans into winding curves along valleys and between mountains. Ed won't take me over any state border, he tells me. "If you want to go, walk across by yourself."

So I walk across. I'm fifteen, I can take care of myself, and they wait in the car for me on the other side. The trailer in La Puente, California, where I'm left, is infested with cockroaches and for a while I babysit for a woman who's shacking up with her own brother and she gives me something to eat sometimes, but then the brother tries a heavy run on me and I move under the trailer for a while. Nobody knows I'm there.

One day Sammy and Ed find me under there and they say this is no good, they should never have brought me. They decide they'll take me back home to Butte after we go to Indianapolis, Indiana. I have no idea how far that is, but Ed and I have a bet going: he sings a line from a song and I sing the next, and I always win, until one day he sings an Elvis song I've never heard and he finally wins his bet. Denny and his wife are gone; there are three other people travelling with us and we live by Sammy's "artistry" as he calls it—hotels, fast-food places. We never steal or rip anyone off; sometimes Elaine, a girl travelling with us, turns a trick, but I don't, nor am I asked to. I see Death Valley, the Houston Astrodome, Knotts Berry Farm with the biggest roller-coaster in the world; we travel old Number 66 till it connects to the new Interstate outside St. Louis. I see the San Francisco bridge from a distance, the island of Alcatraz, and the Grand Canyon. I walk on the beach where they shot *Jaws*, though I don't touch the water; and we cross the wide Missouri, coming all the way from Montana, at St. Louis.

Ed's family lives in Indianapolis, Indiana, all hillbillies now in the big city. We're on our way back to Butte, the long way round, but we'll get there, and we're having a farewell party in a park and I've never drunk much, though all of them are winos, but now I drink and start to feel good. Elaine goes off with someone into the car, and a guy, Red, is talking to me. I want to have a boyfriend, I've never had one, and I like him. I try to talk to him, all giggly with wine, and Red pours wine down my legs. I'm wearing shorts and I go quiet, I let it happen.

Red and I are in the car when the guy who took Elaine there tries to get in too and I jump out the other side. It's Red's friend, but Red promises me the moon and the stars and I decide to stay with him, so Sammy and Ed leave without me, heading west I think. We never meet again. I live in one house, then another, and Red's friend tries to force himself on me again and Red says, okay, that's it, I'll get rid of him and when I do, I'll come back for you. He drops me off outside a bar and I never see him again either.

I hang around a few days, shoplift a few cans of ravioli and spaghetti and eat them cold. I sleep huddled in parked cars when I can find a door open, but finally I beg a dime outside a bar and call the cops on myself. In the big Missing Persons Bureau the walls are literally papered over with missing people; the summer of '77, it looks like a thousand pictures of bodies of all races and ages and sex reported missing or Jane and John Does they've found dead. Who am I? I give them my name, and Dad's, and our address in Butte, but they say they have no interstate police reports of me missing. They place me in a building with steel mesh for windows and three chains locked across the mesh on the steel door. I'm there seven days with over three hundred girls. I've never been near Black girls before — there was only one Black family in Butte — and one of the hundreds in here whose pale grey skin is scarred into ridges because her mother tried to disappear her by burning threatens to kill me. But then Dad sends money and they put me on a bus for Montana. It took so long because no authority could verify I was missing.

Dad says he always knew I was alive — I don't know how and he never explains — and here I was back in the tilted house on Jackson Street. I tell him I'll pay back the bus fare as soon as I have it and he just says, fine, fine. I move into the far side of the house, barricade the door to the one room I need, and go in and out through the back door on my side of the house; his side has the only bathroom, but I won't use it unless he's out. It's only fall; at night I can easily do whatever I need to outside in the dirt yard with its lilac bushes.

I know when this happened.

When I was back in Butte, the night I felt I must get Dad out of the White Spot Bar.

He's driven the logging truck he'll never get rid of uptown again. The night before, he came home and drove it right up on the sidewalk and almost crashed into our house. This time he's left the keys in the truck parked by the White Spot, so I stash them under the seat and go in after him. There's a girl in jeans— so tight, if she had a quarter in her back pocket you could tell if it was heads or tails—sitting on a stool with her booted feet up on the bar, crying to the song, "Don't It Make My Brown Eyes Blue." Dad heads for her, he buys her a beer. He can't kill himself or anyone else without keys, so I go out.

Frank Shurtliffe appears suddenly on the sidewalk. I know him, we talk. Someone comes out of the bar; he's dressed well and more or less stays on his feet.

Hey, you guys, y'know where there's any pot?

He holds a bottle, and a roll of money in his fist thick as a thick cigar. I say, Maybe I do and maybe I don't, and he swears he's no cop, shit, he's been drinking for days, does he look like a cop? I turn away, but he's clinking keys. Car keys.

A beautiful wide car, automatic. I've never driven more than a tractor baling hay. Frank doesn't say anything, so I say, Okay, let's see what we can find. Frank gets in the front too.

In the car, the owner—he's in the middle—tilts against me and tells me what to do. I can reach the pedals easy, my legs are as long as his, and I drive. The car floats like the Caddy. We drive to a guy we know, but he doesn't have anything, nothing; he's mad at me for asking, and who-knows-who sitting out in the car. The car owner tells me his name is Douglas Barber and he's much older than I thought, maybe fiftysomething, but he tells

us if there's no pot he wants a party; hell, winter is the best time
to drink and party, drive him to a party. Frank looks at me behind the wheel and says, Sure, why not? My experience of a
party is, I tag along, so the party just continues in the car.

It's cold, night, our unfound party stops where snow covers a
field and a barbed-wire fence and the forest on a mountain—is
this where every summer our family came to cut poles? There's
a snowdrift higher than the car, the hood of the car must be
shoved into it, the motor roars but the big car won't budge.
Forward . . . reverse . . . nothing. Snow is piled halfway up the
trunks of the tall lodgepole pines, ice drips glistening from the
spikes of the barbed fence. There is a wind, starting to howl like
a pack of hounds. A door is open, oh, I'm so cold, I feel like I'm
sitting in a meat locker, the steering wheel a ring of ice. I can
hear yells, maybe the sounds of hitting, but I don't look out.
Inside the car it is black; outside, the world turns grey, the grey-
ness of open sky and driving snow and the dark, spiked wall of
trees drifts everything into shadow. Even my hand in front of
my face is grey, shimmering; it's freezing as I move it to cover
my eyes. I can't see, or feel my own flesh touch my skin. The
wind groans, kicks up snow devils; ice wipes over my face; I'm
shuddering.

Frank gets into the car behind the wheel and slams the door.
Where's Doug? I ask. He gestures outside, somewhere. We wait
for Doug, but he doesn't come. We wait longer, I think I'll see
him any minute in the car lights, they're so bright over the drifts
of snow. Suddenly I know these trees, and this field; it was here
we once found an eagle hanging on the wire—but that was
summer and Earl isn't here. It was here Mom cried, and said I
couldn't play with Earl any more. He is in heaven and won't be
back. I recognize this beautiful silver place—it's so grey, and
cold, and horribly ugly. I want to go home. Please, to Mom.
Drive me to Mom.

Where's she?

At Grandma Flora's.

Frank's smoking. Finally he gives me a cigarette too.

Where's she at?

Maybe Taber. In Canada. Please . . . that's where we thin beets.

It's snowing fucken December.

Yeah, in winter Mom's in Winnipeg, yeah. That's right, drive me to winter.

———

Yvonne: Frank drove me to a motel in Boulder, Montana. After he fell asleep, I took the keys and drove back to Butte alone. I left the car with the keys inside parked in front of the cop shop and walked home. By then it was early morning.

———

Yvonne tells me the Barber story detail by steady detail. When the police came to the house a few days later to ask her why she'd been seen driving a car whose owner was missing, she lied at first. She said she just wound up with the car after the owner left a party. When the police came to the house a second time, she tried to run away, but was caught, and then she took her father and the police to the spot where she had last seen Douglas Barber, where Frank eventually got the car turned around. The police began their search in snowmobiles while Yvonne was returned home and ordered not to leave town. Barber was the son of a well-to-do Butte family; his body was found and ruled dead by reason of hypothermia; on 5 January 1978, charges were laid against Frank Shurtliffe and Yvonne.

And for once in her life Yvonne was fortunate: the presiding magistrate was District Judge Arnold Olsen, one of the few humane and incorruptibly honest officials Butte ever had. The initial charge laid against Frank was manslaughter, while Yvonne was charged with "driving a car without the owner's consent." At her trial in late February 1978, on her lawyer's advice, she pleaded guilty.

Yvonne writes in her journal on Independence Day, 4 July 1993: "Leon always called me zombie. Even at five foot ten and sixteen I carried myself this way, silent, head bent down, not wanting to be forced to talk because I spoke with such difficulty despite all the operations.

The roof of my mouth had been closed since Grade Four, but even that didn't help enough. A bartender later told me, 'You never smile, but you have a beautiful smile. Why don't you smile?' And I told him, 'What for? I've got no reason to smile.'

"But I do have," she continues in her journal. "The smile I have now was made possible by one good judge. Judge Olsen, you were one of the good things that happened in my life. You changed me, though you could not change the world in which I lived, and I thank you for trying anyhow. You have a special place in the good memories of my life."

Olsen ordered Yvonne to stand and speak to the charge. She stood, but spoke so quietly he could not hear what she was saying. So he asked Clarence to bring her closer to the bench; she came, but she could project so poorly when frightened that the judge still did not understand. He asked what was wrong, and Clarence explained the double cleft palate at birth, the many operations Yvonne had already undergone, and the problems that obviously remained.

Arnold Olsen, who was the Butte district judge for the last fifteen years of his life, invariably wore a white-striped blue bowtie with his black robe. He was born in Butte, served two terms as state attorney general before being elected four times to the House of Representatives in Washington. Like Clarence, he was of Norwegian ancestry and had served four years in the war of the Pacific. "He knew our family, all we'd gone through," Yvonne explains to me. "Leon had been in his court so often, he gave him break after break but it never helped much. He knew about our struggles concerning Earl's death. And here I stood in front of him: barely sixteen, a man had died. I couldn't run, facing him I couldn't speak, my breath was so uncontrolled and choked, if I'd made a sound it would have come out a scream. I could only do what I did so often: cry.

"He looked at me thoughtfully, then he leaned forward and told me a story. He said a teenage boy was always in trouble, always showing up in his court for sentence until finally he found out that the boy had impaired hearing. So he sentenced him to an operation, that he have his hearing repaired. It had been done, and that boy never showed up in court again.

"Judge Olsen told me, 'Yvonne, part of your sentence is that you, at State expense, receive the needed plastic surgery to your cleft palate, and dentistry for your teeth. I hereby order you to stay in Butte, to serve fifteen months' probation, and your probation officer will escort you to all your medical appointments. If you don't go, you'll answer to me. Do you understand?'

"I understood all right. He told me, 'I hope never to see you in this courtroom again.'

"And thank the Creator he never did," Yvonne says. And the excitement of what happened to her then, what shaped her truly lovely smile now, her fluent, often overwhelming flow of speech, springs from her like electricity.

"The most skilled dentist in Butte started work immediately on dentures to fill the teeth spaces in my mouth, and the State brought in a plastic-surgery specialist to Silver Bow Hospital on Continental Drive. He examined me and said he wanted to try something radical. I don't know where he came from, but he was the smartest, gentlest doctor I've ever met; all the nurses were in love with him he was so good. When I was on the operating table I suddenly came to. I was screaming for them not to give me a needle, it would kill me! They were holding me down and as they put another tube into my IV, I was gone. He told me after the operation they were having trouble with my heart, and if they had gone on as they were I might have died, but he'd caught it in time, I was on a heart monitor, just take it easy, everything's okay. And it was.

"I had a full bottom lip like my dad; the doctor cut a triangular wedge out of that lip and inverted it, sewed it into the cleft he opened again in my upper lip. To supply my new upper lip with enough blood so it could heal together properly and not reject the insertion, he sewed the big vein from the bottom lip into the upper he had made and then sewed both lips together so I could not stretch them and break the temporary vein connection apart. Once it was healed and blood circulation established in the upper lip, he told me, he would separate my lips.

"I was mute again, I could only moan sounds in my throat. But now there was hope."

For weeks, first in the hospital and then at home, Yvonne could take in food only through a straw which fit into the small hole left for that purpose on the right side of her sewn-shut mouth. We sat together in P4W and laughed about her stories of the great smell of food drifting along the corridors, of being given another patient's meal by accident and sliding threads of chicken through that tiny hole until an entire breast had vanished; and the consternation of the nurses and doctor, whose major concern seemed to be not her hunger but how to avoid infection. But Yvonne was a quick, healthy healer. She even smoked, which was absolutely forbidden, but she managed it with tiny pencil cigarettes she rolled from butts she collected in the hospital. The fire escape was good for that—no smell on the ward—but once the emergency exit locked behind her and she had to climb round to the senior citizens' ward and walk as if in erect, stately unawareness between the long rows of beds, clutching her hospital gown tightly behind her to cover her bottom. When she went home she cooked herself noodles, inserted and swallowed them one by one.

"One month, two, maybe three months, more operations under circles of blazing lights," Yvonne tells me. "Inner-jaw carving, whole rows of teeth anchored to the ones I already had. I used to snip and pull at my stitches as they healed out. When I went in, they froze me and took out the rest, cut the blood connection from the bottom to the top lip. I had always wondered what I would look like if I had been born like my sisters, who were all so pretty, my brothers so handsome—where was the beauty of my inheritance for me? And the radical surgery worked, the doctor knew how to do it all, exactly: the vein established itself and despite the obsessive things I did I got no deforming infections, and now some people tell me I'm pretty. Judge Olsen ordered the dentists and that incredible doctor at State expense to work on me all that time; no one but a multimillionaire or a rock star could have afforded it. The surgeon was so proud of me and his architecture, six hundred and seventy-six stitches!

"At last, I could speak."

———

There are questions I should have asked Clarence Johnson about why, in 1977 and 1978, Yvonne had such a difficult, ugly life while trying to live with him in Butte. It is clear that much of the time she lived in the dirt cellar under the house; she attempted several suicides; she ran away twice, the first time in the early summer of 1977, when she lived hand to mouth and wandered across twenty states, wherever her temporary friends would take her. Clarence did not even explain why he hadn't notified the police when Yvonne disappeared; if I were to be generous now, I'd say he had forgotten to tell me. Yvonne thinks that her mother did come to Butte while she was gone, worried about her, but as far as she knows her parents did nothing. Cecilia returned to Canada and they filed no "Missing Person" statement; perhaps they were afraid that, if they reported it, the Butte cops would make sure Yvonne stayed missing for good.

What Clarence did tell me—he has a good memory for money—was that Greyhound had a special on that summer. For seventy-five dollars you could travel one way anywhere in the United States; when he heard Yvonne was in Indianapolis, he sent her that ticket to come home.

Yvonne tells me she was back in Butte by late September 1977, and tried to overdose on pills again, but it didn't work. She turned sixteen on 4 October, so she was no longer legally required to attend school; a volunteer organization called Teen Challenge tried to help her: twice a week a neat woman with styled hair took her swimming at an indoor pool. Two hours a week, but there were 166 hours left to live. She was looking for possible work beyond random babysitting when Clarence told her that Grandpa "Fightin' Louie" Johnson was confined to a retirement home. He was 101 years old, and Yvonne felt sorry for him. At the same time, she realized he might help her to a different life.

Clarence shows me a picture of his bald, ancient father with a smiling woman of about twenty leaning against him, she with a cute baby on her knee. At the age of ninety-three, "Fightin' Louie" had declared he was the father of the baby, the young woman said that yes, he was, and so Blaine County gave her both child support and welfare. By 1977 Louie was still the independent individualist he had always been: whenever he could possibly get out of the senior citizens' home, he'd run away. Several times the Montana Patrol found him two miles out on the shoulder of the highway, bobbing doggedly along with his walker, heading for the town of Chinook. In late October 1977, public health services, not knowing what else to do, had him living in a hotel room. Yvonne volunteered to care for the old man.

"The nurse in Chinook," Yvonne explains to me, "found us an apartment and I went up and moved in. It was one large room with cooking facilities on one side, and on other side my bed was separated from his by two chests of drawers. We shared the bathroom with the woman next door, a former madam of the local whorehouse, Grandpa told me—no messing with her. And taking care of him was no big deal: all he wanted me to do was get him to the bar. As soon as the bar opened, every day.

"He had a buddy there as regular as he, and they played checkers. His old buddy was blind and Grandpa'd try to out-cheat him in checker cheats. They'd sit with a twenty-sixer of whisky on the table and play all day. They must have been alcohol-preserved, and cheating, more than checkers, was the going game between them, blind or not. I'd play pool by myself, and occasionally Grandpa would sneak a shot of whisky into my pop. One day a cowboy hat called Wilt showed up, he talked and laughed with the old men. Grandpa told him to marry me.

"I went to a movie with him, but I didn't like him much. He held my hand crooked the whole evening; it was painful and I didn't know how to tell him. Grandpa questioned me when I picked him up at the bar, said he'd fix me up to marry this guy, but I said nothing. In bed Grandpa drifted off into some nightmare—he drank steadily but never appeared drunk. He always had a big bottle in the apartment and the only way I could stop him drinking was to place it too high for him to reach—remembering a nightmare long past, either reality or dream: 'I didn't shoot that man. It was a fair fight, fair and square.'

"Grandpa Louie didn't like the handsome Native cowboy who started to play pool with me, but the two of us started visiting anyway. After a while I brought him home. Grandpa thought it was the hat he wanted me to marry, but when I told him it was my Native friend, he hit the roof! He called me bitch, whore, Indian squaw; he swiped his cane at me and I begged him, 'Grandpa, don't do this to me.' I got down on my knees: 'Please, please.' But he slammed me with the cane and I swore, 'That's enough!' I grabbed the neck of his whisky bottle off the table just as he called me something else horrible and swung that around at him. If I'd hit him I'd have split his skull. I intended to miss, I just wanted to scare him, but he wouldn't scare, and in the mêlée I backhanded him, knocked him sideways onto his bed. Fuck this, I thought, I'm outa here—run, my usual way of handling a problem—I tucked the blankets under tight so he couldn't fall out and hurt himself; he kept on yelling and spitting, and I left. I went to the Elks' bar and told them Louie wanted a twenty-sixer. They gave it to me, but I couldn't open it in the bar. I played a few games, walked out, cried, felt angry and useless, and ashamed. Then I went back.

"He was still yelling murder. I gave him some whisky, but he wouldn't calm down. He swore he wanted to move into a flophouse with his buddy where no bitch would tie him up. I called the nurse. I begged him again, but he kept cursing me, and when the nurse finally came towards morning to help patch things up, he just jerked his hand away from me. So the nurse called an ambulance to take him back to the home. And then, in front of the nurse and the two attendants carrying him out, he called me a fucken whore who'd sleep with any bastard that got his hands up between my legs. I couldn't stand any more, a whole night of being yelled at.

"'If I'm a whore,' I screamed, 'you're the one who taught me, you did it first!'

"'You little bitch, you wanted it.'

"'I was four years old! I wanted it? You were ninety!'

Yvonne shakes her head as she tells me this; her voice is barely audible as this memory rasps over her raw remembering. She has not yet described how Grandpa Johnson fits into the long abuse of her childhood, but I know she will, eventually.

"We were both howling by then, the men carrying him out the door into three feet of winter snow, belted to the stretcher and everyone in the apartment house watching and listening. I put the cowboy hat he always wore on his head. I bent down and told him I loved him, and I kissed his cheek, I felt so dreadful. He'd loved having me care for him, wash and shave him, give him enemas and bathe him all over, help him onto the toilet, feed him, take urine and stool samples, tuck him in at night, everything, and now when I kissed him he head-butted me! 'Fightin' Louie' Johnson all right. He liked me spunky, but on his terms."

Yvonne sighs, looks at me. "One stubborn Johnson against another stubborn one—a hopeless idea, I guess. Like most of my ideas. I've never had any luck. Seven months later he was dead."

A slight twitch plays at the corner of her mouth; I've noticed it before when she refuses to break despite memories too painful to speak of. "He died because he fell, crashed down the staircase in the old folks' home in his wheelchair. Dad figured the nurses couldn't stand him any more and gave him a nudge.

"Or maybe he cashed himself in. I think only he himself could finish off Fightin' Louie."

———

Yvonne: Back in Butte again, late fall of '77, and my life is worse, though Teen Challenge is still trying. I'm always hungry. If I smoke shit I can pretend I float away. A guy will offer me honey oil and disappear with me into one of the many empty houses of Butte. We can vanish into the shadows as Doris Day sings the hit song at that time—"*Che sera, sera*, Whatever will be will be, the future's not ours to see"—just learn not to block punches with your face. I'm sick to death and Dad is swearing at me for overdosing again and all the hospital bills. Ellie Waite is in the hospital bed beside me, isn't she living with Leon? No, but she'll soon be pregnant by him.

In mid-January the nice head of Teen Challenge visits me, rolling out paper to show me like a scroll. He's laughing, he's so proud. They finally got me accepted for a Job Corps program in Nevada, even though I'm barely sixteen. And I have to tell him I can't leave Butte because I'm court-ordered not to leave town; my trial's at the end of February. He can't believe it; he's walking away, shaking his head, and I stand watching until the falling snow fills his boot prints.

The older guys in the County Education Program [CEP] for adults, where the courts place me, are my drinking buddies. I'm the quick-reaction Fooseball Champion of the World there. We get ninety bucks every two weeks if we don't miss classes. So we're there every day, and one evening we go for a drink to a bar where cops show up in uniform but leave their revolvers in their holsters locked in the trunks of their cruisers, and the bartender takes a picture of customers for his collection. Elvis Presley is dead and Leon is separated from Liz Green, though sometimes I take care of the baby she has by Leon. I've just been paid by CEP, so I order bottles of whisky—I don't drink anything else yet, and I never get stoned or high for the sake of it; I do it to relax— and a few cases of beer for the others (I haven't learned to drink beer myself) and also a few pizzas to eat. The bartender locks up the bar and we drink by the light of the neon signs shining all over the walls. There's a girl in the basement doing tricks, but I'll never do that. My partner won't wake up and I can't leave him. I'm being rolled down the stairs, flashbulbs are going off, I'm locked in a place where they stack the booze. I scream enough till they get tired of that and open the door and peel me off the mesh, get me up out of there. I'm sitting on a bar stool, my head is so heavy I have to rest it on the level gleam of the bar; it's wet, so cool. A Spanish guy from CEP is there, and the red- head who I thought was my friend—for the first time in my life I black out.

When I come to, I don't know anything; it's never happened to me before and I'm really scared. But I do know, instantly, I've been raped. I don't know how often, or by whom, but it has cer- tainly happened. I know this took place because I drank too much, and I lost control, but I've never blacked out before, how . . . my head is still down on the bar, I'm sitting on the Spanish guy's lap and I'm being moved back and forth; he may be caus- ing it, the moving. I burn inside like white steel and I try to stand up as he stays on the stool and I can barely move, he's trying to pull his pants together. I go through the bartender's pockets for keys to open the door. He's passed out on the floor. There's a hairy cop I know as Mike stretched out on the bar with his official shirt and official belt buckle hanging wide open. He tells me without moving his head he was just holding me on the barstool, that I kept falling back and hitting my head on the jukebox.

I can't walk steadily, I can't get the deadbolt of the door open, and finally the redhead is up. We manage the door some- how and it's bright daylight out there; we can see to stagger home. We make it to the house, into my room, and we konk out.

I awake burning and I have to pee and I discover to my surprise that I'm naked.

And Dad screaming outside the door, Open up! Who're you sleeping with, you fucken whore, whoren around in the bed I give you in my own house! I brace myself to hold the door shut, but the redhead is still passed out and Dad comes through the door all over me. He's slamming me around like he's never done before; I'm bouncing off the walls, off the floor, he's clawed tight into my hair and hammers me with his fist, beating me stupid, drags me out of the room to his couch. He stops an instant and rips his hands back through his hair and starts again, Used fucken goods anyhow—you give it to him, you'll give it to me. I'm a man too.

He starts going through the motions, but stops. He'll get rid of the redhead first, but if I leave he'll kill me. He goes into the bedroom and I run out of the house.

—————

"After the attempted attack by my father," Yvonne tells me, "I was grown up. I moved in with Leon. He had taken over Liz's apartment; he beat her up once too often and she finally left with her little boy and new baby girl she had with him."

"You moved in with Leon, alone?"

"I was figuring things out, how to stay alive. I couldn't live with Dad; even if I barricaded my room, or slept in the dirt basement again—which I didn't really want to—I still had to use the bathroom, and the fridge to eat sometimes. And Leon was actually okay: he had ass around, so I seemed safe. Ellie lived with him now, she and her baby girl, and several other women were there too. He took them in turns or all of them in his room at once. I tried to find a boyfriend to keep me safe from him. He'd picked up an expensive stereo and tape player by giving the log peeler we used for logging as collateral, and he was mad when one speaker was broken after he threw it at Liz and took a chunk out of her leg.

"That was the only furniture. I slept on a mattress in my own room with an American flag for a blanket. We didn't pay rent and the electricity was cut, but he knew how to jump-wire it at the meter. We always had music. There was never anything to eat in the fridge and I went to parties and ate what I found, and drank. Only whisky then, only the smoothest Kentucky, Kessler's. Same as Grandpa Louie."

Yvonne started to learn day-by-day, take-whatever-whoever-comes life. The Community Education Program had focused her days, though the so-called life-education courses themselves, she tells me, taught her nothing except how to get involved with people twice her age, mostly the biggest dope addicts and dealers in Butte. She never got into heavy drugs—she had neither the interest nor the money—but she smoked to relax at parties when it was offered, and began trying beer as a chaser for whisky. She drank with Leon and his friends. She drank with almost anyone.

"I felt so low and shy, I could not talk to anyone except when drinking. You could not get me to talk sober, least of all to Whites, professionals like doctors, cops, priests."

She was learning a particular kind of survival from street experts.

"There was no family to show me," she continues. "I was alone, hiding, knocking around alone. When stoned, I could fool myself into relaxing. But always alert not to get caught. At Leon's at least I had an empty room to sleep in.

"Sometimes Leon would send his buddies to invite me to join them, but I wouldn't. Sex was something people did, I never got anything out of it and when men did it to me they felt so manly they usually wanted more. I was never in my life a hooker, but I think I know how they can work because I always felt uninvolved—huh! if every man who fucked me over had paid me, I'd be rich. I couldn't figure out why everyone thought sex so important. Mom always told me it was all men were after—they'll fuck anything—which never made sense to me, though it obviously did to some girls I knew. The best I could say for sex was I got through it without too much pain; if I had the choice and felt I had to please a man, I'd let him do it. And I could really fake it—men only notice themselves anyway—and I could be any man's dream, they went nuts for me. But I never made eye contact: just concentrate on something else, fake it, get it over with."

After a long pause she adds, staring across the counselling room at p4w, "I know I've sometimes been a fool. I know I've often hurt people.

I know I was involved in one monstrous act. And I've hurt myself, so much, so often. How can it end this way? It's got to be for some reason that all this happened. There are times in my life when I've thought: if this is reality I'd rather be insane. I guess you could describe me that way: insane by reason of reality."

She adds later, in her journals, concerning the coming summer of 1978: "My life continued horrible, though I did not try to kill myself, not then. My operations had been very successful but trying to live with Dad in the same house was impossible. Suicide was always there, starting in Grade Seven. I don't know what had set me off . . . being alive, I guess.

"I see now that most children, growing up, are taught options, choices, personal strategies. I never was, and even though I understood that choices must exist, they couldn't mean anything to a dirty 'breed' like me. There were just two possibilities: get by, or commit suicide.

"I can now understand Jung when he talks of suicide as a goal. It can become, as it seems, the one goal you can always try hard to reach if life becomes too bad. It's the final release, though by death."

And she shifts to an earlier suicide story: "Once, on a school trip to Yellowstone Park, that must have been about Grade Eight, fourteen, when Kathy was in Butte for a little while, they'd been calling me 'pud-lips, suck-your-brother's-cock lips,' and a big cop's son beat me up on the bus, and when we got to the geysers I kept on walking and tried to jump into one. Just end it, disappear in the hot, boiling earth. Every-body was yelling as I stood on the fencing around the pit, trying to think my final thought, crying, then Kathy got me down and led me back into the bus. I locked myself inside the bus toilet till we left. I wouldn't go back to Grade Eight, and the woman from Teen Challenge came and I toured a home and a reformatory for girls with her, but there was no place; I belonged nowhere.

"Mom roaming Western Canada looking for work with whatever kids could trek along with her, Dad rooted in his house in Butte on a five-year drinking binge—our family didn't have to stay together to prey on each other."

Another sardonic frown: "Our family wasn't much for weddings either," she says. "I don't remember being at one, but we had plenty of funerals to keep on bugging each other. Dad was so mad when

Grandpa Louie died, he was convinced 'those nurse bitches' had shoved him down the stairs—he was only 102, I guess he was supposed to live forever—but he took Leon and me with him in his logging truck to the funeral."

I have jotted down that essential date from the papers in Clarence's indispensable box: Louis Johnson, born 15 April 1876, buried 11 July 1978, Chinook, Montana.

"In a mortuary hall," Yvonne tells me. "Both Grandpa and Dad hated everything churchly. He said life must have come from a big bang volcanic eruption under the sea or something. It's six, seven hours to Chinook in that truck, and all the way Dad was drinking—we'd make a pit stop at every bar and gas station for beer. And he was mad at me. 'You're such a liar,' he'd yell at me. I'm right beside him on the seat with Leon driving but he yells, 'He lives all these years, born in the centennial year of the Republic and celebrating two hundred Big Ones and what does he get for it? His fucken granddaughter calls him a dirty old man. Jesus Christ, you're a natural-born liar!'

"He kept on, he really rolled into it. 'C'mon,' he's nudging me, crying and drinking from cans he doesn't even shove out of sight when a car passes, 'you're a natural, say something and it'll be a lie. Say something!'"

"So I say something. 'You're really good-looking,' I tell him.

"'Shit,' he says. 'Finally she tells the truth.'"

Yvonne continues, deadpan: "Leon started laughing. He pulled over, got out of the truck, and leaned against the hood. He was laughing to bust a gut, and I got out too. We were bouncing off each other.

"And Dad was cursing us. He goosed the motor and took off. Leon and I were left on the shoulder of that long Montana highway, nothing left but to hitchhike into Chinook. The funeral was next day and Mom and the other kids were already in a hotel. Dad got mad when they opened the coffin: 'Where's his cowboy hat? He won't be buried without his hat—and his boots? He's got to wear his boots!' They brought Grandpa's hat and he put it on him and that was better. So we buried him; a few of the old guys and the head nurse said something and that was it.

"And afterwards, as usual, there was arguing. Mom and Dad were together again, nothing to do but quarrel, this time about why it hadn't worked out with me taking care of him. They never asked me a word about it. In our family the grown-ups argued and we kids shut up, not a word out of you, especially me, who if I wasn't completely stupid was probably crazy. They got so well into their old fighting groove that Mom came to Butte for a few days. I went back to Leon's place. It was empty, no food, just two mattresses and the stereo on the bare floor."

I ask Yvonne, "Did you look at him in his coffin?"

She's remembering hard, very inward as she often is. "His face was always white, round, old, and bald, smiling. But they made him up so badly, like they do. I felt sorry I hit him, I felt so sorry I let him down."

"So, you went back to Butte," I say. "Your operations had been successful. You could speak."

"Just because I was capable of speaking doesn't mean I did. I had nothing to say, even if I wanted to talk. Hell! What people take for granted—nothing was 'granted' to this little bitch. I was always hiding. If I was sober I felt so low I couldn't even give simple directions to people when they asked me."

"And you were still in Butte. Did you go live with your dad?"

"Never again."

"You stayed with Leon?"

"Not long," she says, looking straight at me. "I ran. That's all I really knew how to do. That son of a rich Butte family was dead, Frank Shurtliffe now in jail charged for his death, I think, and the whole town gossiped about me being there."

"But you'd gone to court, you'd pleaded guilty to the only offence you were charged with."

She smiles grimly. "Sure, I had dealt with official law. But in Butte there's cop law too, and that one really counts. Inside a week of Grandpa's funeral a big cop saw me walking and stopped his cruiser to explain it to me, in case I didn't know for sure.

"'Johnson,' he says to me, 'you're a nobody, and you killed a somebody. If you're ever in jail, you might hang yourself.'"

"That's pretty clear."

"Two evenings later," she continues, "he has me in his cop-shop, not the one where they killed Earl but that makes no difference. I was walking with Minnie—she stayed on with Dad after the funeral—and I'd tried a beer, and this cop saw me throw the can over my shoulder on the sidewalk and he arrested me for littering. Handcuffs for a beer can. He slugged me so fast, so hard, I was sprawled out on the back seat of his cruiser before the can hit the ground. He orders me to sit down in a chair, and when I try he kicks the chair aside and I crash to the floor. 'See?' he says to his deskman. 'She's out of it, book her for drugs too.' "

She sits motionless, staring into space. Finally I say, "How did you get out of that?"

After a while she answers, and I can't tell whether she is speaking of now or then—perhaps both. "I was thinking of Earl."

"But . . . you got away?"

"That's a long story too." And suddenly she grins at me, her quick, luminous smile. "Canada."

6

Growing Up in a Beer Bottle

Answer: Back then I used to drink lots, so that wasn't much for me.

Question: That's twenty-four beer?

Answer: Yes.

Question: Okay, and on this trip . . . would you have been drinking in the same fashion, about twenty-four beer a night?

Answer: Not really, 'cause I slow down when I have a hangover.

– Sharon (Minnie) Johnson,
   North Battleford courtroom, 22 June 1995

I T WAS AFTER MIDNIGHT when Minnie and I got to the edge of Butte onto Interstate Fifteen. I was running from what I knew was a death threat by the Butte cops and Minnie said, "Fuck that, we're outa here." She'd just saved my life by proving to the cop-shop deskman that she was my older sister, she was eighteen and she'd be responsible for me, I was a silly kid and they should just let her take me home. The cop who'd hauled me in couldn't push the deskman too far in framing me on a littering charge, and to prove how really concerned and responsible she was, Minnie slapped me down right there in the shop. She put on a good show.

"You stupid brat"—she grabbed me—"don't you know any better?" And slapped me back and forth. She nearly knocked me out. I fell against her and whispered, "You don't have to do it so hard!"

Minnie stung me, but she convinced them; she got me out of there and I was more than glad to follow her. And out of Butte altogether.

We were not well prepared—I had less than $90 from my CEP cheque—but we knew Mom was back in Winnipeg again. She'd found a job there cutting rags after working at a sawmill in Edson, Alberta, till she came to Montana for Grandpa Louie's funeral, and Karen and Kathy were with her. I once started Grade Seven—maybe it was Grade Eight—in Winnipeg when Mom lived there before, so I thought if we headed through Havre and Chinook, going more east, we'd get to Manitoba quicker.

But Minnie said she wanted to go north through Sweetgrass, and I presumed it was to get into Canada as fast as possible. After what she'd done, I had to follow her. But a song by Burton Cummings was blaring on a car radio:

Runnin' with a gun
And it isn't any fun as a fugitive
God I wanna go home . . .

Home. I was "sixteen goin' on seventeen," as a real different song has it, and I'd been shipped back and forth across the border so often in six years, where was home? I guess it should be Butte, 410 South Jackson Street, but only Dad was left there—with little Perry for the time being—and trying to live the last year with Dad had been mostly worse than horrible. I couldn't imagine the last three or four places where Mom had lived, I hadn't seen them, and if my "home town" cops held me overnight I was as good as dead.

We caught a long night ride north through the Rocky Mountains to Helena, and so we made Great Falls by early morning: very good. The one suitcase we had was too heavy; we were already tired of lugging it. And I was thirsty, Minnie was dry, and she saw a Fast Gas on the Great Falls overpass and she groaned and pouted, "I bailed you out . . . you'd be hanging off a ceiling pipe by now, c'mon," till I gave her money. And then she came back with nothing but a twenty-four flat of beer and a bag of chips. For the road, she said. I said, How do you hitchhike with open beer? She told me, Very carefully, so we had the bright idea to toss all except a few select clothes into the ditch. We were teenagers, half wiped-out for sleep, and nothing and nobody but wide-open Montana all around us. The beer made the suitcase a bit heavier than the clothes, but Minnie said she'd soon fix that, and we were headed north again for the Canadian border.

We walked past the highway exit east to Havre, but I asked her again: Shouldn't we be going that way? No, Minnie wanted to see her boyfriend first; he lived outside Lethbridge, Alberta, and maybe he'd even drive us to Winnipeg himself, later.

"Anyways, you're slim and young and pretty," she said, relaxing. "These cowboys'll stop quick for you anywhere."

I sat on the suitcase and laughed at her; she was making herself comfortable in the ditch, wrapped in a blanket a guy gave us outside Helena, opening the next beer. We'd used this tactic earlier, and about sunrise a car had pulled over to pick me up, but when the driver saw I was Native and there was Minnie's broad shape—"The Human Tank," they called her in Butte—wrapped in a blanket rising from the ditch to come along too, he just sprayed me with shoulder gravel, his door slamming shut as he took off. We were mad, but we laughed about that, how he looked when he leaned over and pushed the door open, saw us, and just stepped on it, outa there.

I told Minnie,"It was you, a big mistake coming wrapped up in that blanket, you scared him!"

"Ugh, me Big Mistake." She laughed, pulling a Hollywood. She was about five foot two and maybe two hundred pounds, solid from logging in the mountains every summer. She began to powwow around in circles, "Me plenty big squaw, me happy Big Mistake!"

Overacting so badly I had to laugh too, and join her dancing. We played on the shoulder in the car lights coming down that straight flat stretch outside Helena, heading north for the next long line of hills. "Spinny Minnie" in our family—when we were little she was always Dad's favourite, his pet; in the White House, when he came home from the mine before he wrecked his back, we girls would jump all over him, but Minnie would grab his lunch box and run. She always hid it in the closet, and he would have to go look for it, pretending he couldn't find it, but when he found it he always had some goodies, candies or something, in there and he'd give them to her.

The heat burned up from the pavement outside Great Falls, and in full daylight Minnie found too many spiders in the shade of the overpass, so she wasn't laughing much, even while sipping cool beer. I was very thirsty. I didn't drink beer, so I said I'd go to a farmhouse I saw across a big field and get water. They were a nice old couple there; they gave me hot breakfast and a jug of water and biscuits for Minnie. Minnie always travelled easy; she'd drink and fall asleep when we got a ride, so I stood guard—"six-man" as it's called in prison. I had a ball and chain of Earl's, the only thing of his I had left, an eight-inch brass chain with a chrome-plated gearshift knob filled with lead, just right to hold in your hand or spin on the chain; the last link was shaped like a claw I could lock around my wrist and no one could get it off me. Minnie was talkative, lots of fun, but I wasn't. She'd either ride in the middle or alone with the driver up front, but I always rode shotgun or in the back and watched and said nothing. We finally got a lift north of Great Falls in a truck with a guy picking up garbage at the highway rest-stops.

Minnie nudged me, pointed silently. The guy's fingernails were painted and he was wearing red spike heels. Big brawny guy. I'd never seen anything like it. At the next rest area he got out, heels and all, and hauled out the garbage sacks and I said to Minnie, "Let's go." So we left him. The next pick-up Minnie rode up front and I sat low in the open back, leaving the Montana mountains behind in the cool, whistling air, the level prairies stretching east to the round pyramids of the Sweetgrass Hills. The guy dropped us off on the last rise, where we couldn't be seen by the border guards.

We walked past the U.S. Customs in Sweetgrass into Coutts, Alberta. Minnie did the talking; she told the Canadian guards we were going to Lethbridge just up the highway, and she had a Lethbridge address from when Mom once lived there. All I had for ID was my long-expired Grade Seven Butte school pass, which luckily didn't show how badly I'd done, and they opened our suitcase and relieved us of the unopened cans but left us the empties—nice of them. Then they said, Okay you're in, but a Customs guard escorted us to the bus depot. We hadn't counted on that and Minnie had to buy two tickets to Lethbridge with money I gave her, and we checked our suitcase in. The guard finally left and Minnie went back to the agent and got a full ticket refund. She said we'd changed our mind, and nobody was arguing with her when she glared at them. They even rerouted our suitcase, so our few possessions and all the empty beer cans were on their way to Winnipeg while we snuck out over the next hill on the highway, out of sight from Canada Customs, and stuck out our thumbs again. Spinny Minnie, stupid me.

I was worried. I had gotten away into Canada all right, but I was still under Montana probation, Judge Olsen's order not to leave Silver Bow County because Frank Shurtliffe was being held for trial in the death of Douglas Barber and they wanted me to testify.

"What's so hot about Lethbridge anyways?" I asked Minnie again as we walked out of Coutts.

"The Blood Reserve," she finally told me. "It's right next door."

More like fifty miles west as it turned out, but that made more sense than most of what we'd done so far. Mom's sister, our beautiful aunt Rita, was always bragging she had this great boyfriend Doug on the Blood Reserve, but now Auntie Rita had taken over Minnie's boyfriend state side, so the Blood Reserve made revenge sense all right.

Late in the day a small man in a huge black Chrysler stopped. I was wiped out, but he was so kind I could relax. I drifted off, so I asked him if I could stretch out on his leather back seat and he said sure, that's okay.

Runnin', runnin' as a fugitive. . .

The song rolling in my head and on his radio

God I wanna go, wanna go home. . .
Break it to them gently when you tell 'em
That I won't be comin' home again. . .

Lying safe in a decent man's car, travelling, I finally had space for a few tears about what was happening to me. The only other car I had ever relaxed in was Mom's big blue Caddy, sweeping down the road, all I could see was sky, feel it soaring through air, the whole family—as it seemed for that moment—happy. If Mom and Dad had stayed together, maybe she would still have had it. A hundred years ago Big Bear's son, Little Bear, escaped from the Canadian prairies to hide in the mountains of Montana; I was born and raised all over those mountains; now I was running back to hide north of the border. My mother, my sisters, me—running, looking over our shoulders, hiding—Big Bear's descendants, we had become nomads again; we were hunters hunting whatever we could find to stay ahead of hunger and homelessness. Still running from Whites.

Only Leon was fixed in one place – set in his own violence and almost always in some jail. Never imprisoned, of course, like Big Bear for standing up for his people. The winter before, he'd got out of jail in Duluth, Minnesota—I think Mom even moved down from Winnipeg to live close to him—and he came back to Butte, bringing a girl named Laurie. One night he had me watch while he pulled at her pubic hair; he asked me if I had any hair there yet, and I just left. A little later he got rid of her, and now he was back in jail for running lights through Butte while drunk and then smashing a cop-car hood and windshield with his bare fists. Leon never did anything in his life for anyone but himself; he was too mixed up, or maybe too stupid, to even help himself without damaging himself too.

The Elders say Indians today are masters of change: they have had to be or they'd be wiped out like the Beothuks. Be proud, we have survived! And yet here I was, a century after Big Bear, and I still cried for the freedom he fought for, and lost. Running from one country to the other.

I lay in the back seat of the big black Chrysler and cried for myself, for Big Bear, the suffering and pain of Indian people. Driving west of Lethbridge around the huge fields bending down to the Oldman River of the Blood Reserve, and towards the mountains again. That good man was so concerned about Minnie and me not staying on the road at night that he drove out of his way to take us to Stand Off, the town on the rez. It had only nine or ten houses and a water tower, not anything Minnie wanted, and he risked ripping out the bottom of his beautiful car, driving right to the door of the house on the hills overlooking town. You could see the long front wall of the Rocky Mountains from there, especially Chief Mountain on the border in Montana, the sacred mountain of the Blood/Blackfoot people.

The standing joke on that rez, the biggest in Canada, was that Blackfoot kill Crees; but Minnie and I survived—more or less. There was no one at the house when we pulled up, but in a minute two carloads of mostly young guys arrived and Minnie just got out and walked up to this huge man and started talking. I felt off-balance even being there, and I must have been a sight, a straight-out-of-Montana mixture of Native and cowboy and hippy, long black-brown hair with no bangs and parted to one side, worn blue jeans bell-bottomed enough to sit on my cowboy boots a size too big curled up at the toe, dark plaid man's shirt two sizes too big with its tail hanging out, tall, slim, flat, no make-up. But I was strong, well tuned from years of logging, silent and on guard. No one could tell my young age from the way I carried myself. I was always thinking one step ahead of others' actions so as not to be left behind, always serious, dark, and never started anything, then: I just followed in silence. If I went to the bathroom in a house, I'd feel the air out beforehand and be quick about it; in bars I watched the washroom door to see how many, or who, would be in there when I had to go; before I went I'd always tell Minnie. You have to know what you're walking into.

There was a long beer strike in Canada that summer; they could only get hard stuff or wine for parties. Everything was happening, night and day, and I drank steadily to keep up. I discovered again what a blackout was—it'd happened to me once before in Butte at the CEP party, and losing it like I did then and not knowing anything that happened terrified me—but I hadn't dared ask anyone about it for fear they'd say I was just crazy, truly nuts. We were at Stand Off for weeks; a young guy named Beno became my boyfriend and initiated my drinking with stories about Bloods who slit the throats of every Cree they meet—it's hereditary he said—sometimes even with skate-blades! Well, nobody was skating that hot summer. I stuck close to Minnie, and a couple of times we drove with them south to Montana and came back cross-country with a pick-up full of beer, but other than that it was all whisky and wine. Once Minnie went someplace and Doug wrapped his giant arms around me and tried to haul me into bed while Beno was outside, washing his bush of hair in a rain barrel. I yelled to him, but maybe he didn't want to hear. As Doug and I wrestled on the bed, we heard a car: it was Minnie, back unexpectedly, and he jumped up and ran out. So nothing happened except Minnie and I made a deal she would not leave me alone again.

I wandered around a few times and got lost, not knowing how to get back to Doug's house—they told me prairie don't come natural to Crees—so I stayed put in the little valley among the nine houses and water tower of Stand Off till Beno found me, laughing. He said they should put up a plaque: Yvonne Johnson, the only person in history ever to get lost in Stand Off!

Then suddenly Auntie Rita showed up, and before I could turn around Minnie had moved into my room with me. To "celebrate" the arrival, two carloads of us drove into Lethbridge. In the Bridge Hotel, Rita was all over Doug, Minnie over Beno, and I got disgusted—You guys are all frigging nuts—and I went out to sit in the car. Within a few minutes a stocky Native man came by, wearing a floppy-brimmed cowboy hat, and I asked him if he had a smoke. He said, no but he could get some at the liquor store, we could get them together. I knew Minnie and Rita wouldn't be out till the hotel closed, so I went with him. He got a twenty-sixer but forgot the smokes, and as we walked back we started to test it and he told stories, sort of flirting. He said he was a real cowboy riding horses on ranches for a living, and he told me of all the crazy fights he'd had and the tough bulls he rode in the rodeo. After a while I couldn't hear him too well. I just wanted to get back to the car because I never drank on the street—I hate the very idea of a "public drunk." Then he wanted a cigarette. I wanted one too, badly, so he tried getting some cigarettes off the people walking by.

All he got were looks of contempt. Even the passing smokers said they were on their last smokes. But then a guy at a bus stop shook out a pack and my friend went up to him; he told him No! and turned to the person beside him, "Useless drunk Indians, won't work enough to get themselves smokes."

And he lit one, blew the smoke into the cowboy's face. I could see where it was heading, so I walked away.

"C'mon!" I said to him. "We don't want nothing from this goof, forget it."

But he shook me off, "No way, that fucker insulted me," and he hauled out his pocket knife, opened a blade not two inches long, and I wanted to laugh but it wasn't funny: he went back and shoved it under the guy's throat. Whew, I kept walking fast and in a second he had the whole pack. This was too seriously stupid for me. But he ran after me, grabbed me, yelling at me to run, and his unexpected pull rocked me off my feet, I was somehow falling around and as fast as that happened a cop grabbed me. Maybe they saw the whole silly show; needless to say, I missed the ride back to the rez.

They charged me with being an accomplice in an "armed robbery with violence."

Cops are so slow—writing everything down, they never seem to understand anything. For a long time these Lethbridge police thought I was Minnie and eighteen. True, I was carrying her purse to keep my ball and chain safe, and for a while neither her ID which said she was five foot two and her picture which showed she had no neck on very broad shoulders, nor even the extra double-D bra they found in there could convince them I wasn't her. Who's this Sharon Johnson, they asked; my sister Minnie, I said. I'm Yvonne Johnson, *this* is my ID, I'm sixteen and my mom's in Winnipeg, but me and Minnie are heading there and if you don't let me go I'll miss my ride. You're not going anywhere now, they said, and what's your mother's name?

"Cecilia Johnson . . . or maybe she uses Bear again."

"What's her address in Winnipeg?"

"I don't know, exactly."

"So where's this big sister, Sharon-Minnie or whatever?"

I told them where I'd left her, but no cop will find Minnie once she knows they're looking for her. I did persuade them to let me keep my protection ball and chain. They took me from jail to the juvenile detention centre on the hill overlooking the Oldman River valley and the Lethbridge railroad bridge across it like a long black line pointing straight to hell. When they shoved me into that little room and the door locked behind me with nothing but a small high bed and dresser both bolted to the floor, not even a washbasin, I exploded: I had to get out! and the big window was right there. I jerked a dresser drawer out and ran it against the window to smash it and jump. But I bounced off, the drawer splintered into pieces: unbreakable glass.

The shock jolted me into some sense. I propped the broken drawer back in its place so it looked all right. It was the first time Canadian cops had talked to me, and here I was arrested. I didn't know how to behave, so I just became as small as possible, go unnoticed. After about a week Aunt Rita showed up and said she would help get me out. But one thing she wanted to know: had Minnie been sleeping with Doug? I said I'd never seen it, ask her. Well, Minnie said she did and Doug said they didn't, who should she believe? I wouldn't say, so Auntie Rita disappeared. She helped me with nothing, nor did Minnie.

The judge didn't take long when my case came up about a week later. The legal-aid lawyer did all my talking. They had contacted Mom and she was sending cash for a one-way bus ticket to Winnipeg. The judge ordered that when the cash arrived I was to be escorted to the station and *put on the bus*. If he ever caught me in Lethbridge again he'd throw the whole charge at me.

They placed me in a regular detention home filled with kids nobody wanted, lots of Natives of course. One was a little girl no older than six who had seen her parents die, a murder-suicide, kept there among all the older ones because no foster home would take her. We became friends; my nickname in there was Bigfoot, and she became my sidekick, Littlefoot. They held a summer carnival in Galt Gardens, and I rode with her on the Ferris wheel and we ate candyfloss.

Littlefoot told me her terrifying dreams, how spirits came into her room every night. I discovered the "spirits" were people going there, but they wouldn't let me sleep in her room; I was too old, they said, and stared at me as if I was a pervert when I asked. I noticed plenty, including how the male cook watched us sitting at the tables, eating—it was a very hot summer—at our bare arms and necks and legs. Once he grabbed me in the kitchen; we were wrestling and heading for rape when his girl-friend, a volunteer at the home, walked in and said, "This looks like fun," and I got away. What could I do, or say? I locked my-self in the music room and listened to Nazareth pound out "She's Just a Broken-Down Angel."

This "girlfriend" came in almost every day to play with the kids. I thought she looked like one of those worn-out madams from a black-and-white movie. She'd sit flat-assed on the floor with her legs spread open and have the boys shoot marbles be-tween them, and one day it got too much for me. I said to her, "How will these kids ever be normal if you have them shoot marbles up your snatch?"

"That's the point, darling," she told me. "They have to learn to deal with it, that's all. I never lose at marbles either."

Finally the money arrived and I was escorted out and put on the bus marked WINNIPEG. I arrived there twelve hours late— I got talking with a Native guy on the bus who had a cleft palate too (it's not as common in men as women), and I missed a con-nection in Medicine Hat—but Mom and Karen were there to meet me. They worked in a rag-cutting place and lived in North Winnipeg, east of Main, on Selkirk. Skid-row Indian turf.

Mom lived in Winnipeg so she could work, but the only place in Canada really important to her was her ancestral place, the small Red Pheasant Reserve in Saskatchewan, where our relations lived. They would never turn us away, always take us in to eat, sleep, get cleaned up, and rest and stay as long as you feel like it, there's always room. Even hide you among all the bush and valleys if you felt you needed that. There our heritage was dug into the very ground, and there we never felt poor or dis-placed or useless freaks.

Compared with Butte, Winnipeg was a huge city, with all the extremes of society from the very rich to the poorest possible, and right at the bottom was a thick layer of Indians. Off Main, in the seventies, you could live for weeks and not see a White except for an owner or a bartender or a cop. If you wanted to go Indian, Canada, and Winnipeg especially, was the place. I had no idea there were so many Indians in the world, whole bars full of nothing but Indians, especially the day the welfare cheques arrived. Karen was living with Gil, Kathy was living with Dan, both Natives, and Minnie was still somewhere in Alberta, and Perry with Dad in Butte. I stayed low, venturing out for no more than chips and gravy. The top song then was "Hot Summer in the City," and it fit, I guess. I knew how to be quiet, become a shadow, quite still, cross my arms and legs and stare at one spot, shut my body down, but I also learned how to deal with two situations where I was vulnerable. One was when I walked alone: I learned to put on what I thought of as "the Johnson strut," long, smooth strides, not running but gliding along really fast, I'd be gone before you knew it, a straight-ahead "don't fuck with me" walk.

The other situation was when I danced. I loved dancing, I'd become one with the music. In Canada women often danced with women, so it was simple to find a partner and I'd just disappear into that endless rhythm and movement. If no one jarred me I could dance all night. There were never any live bands or dance floors in the bars in Butte, but here there were many and they were one big reason I got addicted to skid-row Winnipeg.

We Johnson sisters dancing together would clean up a dance floor: everyone sitting around, watching us. They were used to old, slow waltz-style stuff, but we shook them up with *American Bandstand* style; I personally liked *Soul Train* music. Then, when I turned seventeen, 4 October 1978, Mom decided we'd all go drinking together at the Savoy Hotel. She asked me to do the robot dance; I could do it perfectly—I'd had enough practice all my life!—head and arms and hair dangling slack, moving like a mindless, completely controlled, robot. Mom loved seeing me do that dance, so I danced for my mother. I was wearing all white, and Calvin (or Aaron—he used both names for welfare or unemployment-insurance scams) was at our table. Mom had once lived with him; he'd left, but now he'd showed up again, a romance for Mom that my presence in her home didn't fit with very well. While I did the robot dance, Calvin started a bar fight.

Last call had been made as the lights flicked off and on and he wanted to impress Mom, so he yelled out his order with all the rest. I don't think he'd ever ordered in his life, he was a living mooch, he lived mostly at the Sally Ann, and the waiters thought him a joke and didn't listen. Calvin had a head like a rock, and when a short waiter passed with an empty tray, to attract his attention he head-butted him and laid him out. When the waiter got up off the floor, he banged Calvin with a butt of his own to the forehead. Calvin scrambled up, grabbed the waiter's hair with both hands, and smashed him dead centre. So the fight was on, Indians against the world, one entire side of the bar was breaking up. I tried to keep guys off Mom, but she was already fighting. Then the bartender cut the lights. In the dark there was screaming, tables and chairs crashing; when the lights came back on, the waiters and bouncers were yelling at everyone to leave, outa here, it's over! I was heading for the front door fast when the nasty short waiter shoved the firedoor open and threw me out across the alley against the brick wall. And there were the cops with nightsticks—they called them "Indian licorice sticks"—rushing us.

They slammed me over the trunk of a cop car with my arm twisted behind my back, and then more cars arrived fast as the Indians shot out of the door, and they clubbed them into a heap on the pavement—Winnipeg cops seemed to love caving in Indian heads, and I was just lucky being thrown out first— finally they threw me into the cruiser. Then Mom came out and I watched them beat my mother.

Her knees never buckled. She had two cops literally hanging on her arms, clubbing her with nightsticks. I tried to kick out the window to help her—my sad life with break-proof glass!—I was scared to death for her. They were breaking her arms back, pounding her head. She was clubbed on the forehead, and her face squashed down onto the trunk, but she twisted around and yelled, "Vonnie! Stay in the car!" when they got her cuffed, but the door was locked, I couldn't get out anyway, and a special car drove up just for her, and they stuffed a lot of people, most of them bleeding, into the back with me. They pulled us out inside the basement of the Remand Centre on Princess Street, I guess there were too many for the cop-shop cells, and there I saw them hauling Mom handcuffed into an elevator.

She shouted at me, "Just shut up, do as they say," before the doors slammed on her. They threw me out of the other elevator onto the main floor, the front entrance. There was nothing there but a few chairs and two memorial wreaths leaning against the wall, me in my white outfit covered with mud and blood, my graduation night into the happy, carefree world of skid row.

I was worried. One wreath had a purple sash with golden words: "Winnipeg City Police, the Finest Force," so I stole that as a token and searched around till I found the receptionist at the front desk. She didn't know where Mom was, or why I was there. She sent me up in the elevator and it stopped inside a huge steel cage with a cop glaring at me. I asked him about Mom, if she was all right; and maybe she had made a deal with them to leave me alone because he looked royally pissed off at me. My mother was cooling out in the drunk tank and if I didn't get the hell out I'd be in there with her. So I went home, walking down Main Street alone and embarrassed at my dirty clothing. One thing I knew: my drinking career was launched.

Next day Mom came home all black and blue. By evening the house was full, everyone talking about their war wounds, especially Calvin, who somehow moved in then, and all the White pigs they'd wiped out the night before. I figured with that many of the "Finest Force" lying on the streets, not a cruiser could have moved in Winnipeg all weekend.

An odd knock came at our door in the worst cold of the winter. I answered and saw a gigantic pile of coats, scarves, and jackets, heard a faint voice I recognized. I lifted the hood of a jacket—it was Minnie, her face so frozen she could not speak. I got her inside onto the couch, turned up the heat, and tried to help her undress: the scarf over her mouth was solid ice, the fringes snapped off when I unwrapped it. She screamed in pain as she started to thaw, but I ran a warm tub and helped her into it. I could hear her soft cries coming through the door. She had been drunk hitchhiking, got raped and left naked, but she got herself dressed again and walked almost thirty miles from Portage la Prairie. She told me the bare details once. She never spoke of it again.

Sometimes I can't believe what women have to survive.

When I was in Winnipeg a few years before, in Bell School—barely fourteen and not learning much, mostly playing hookey in the washroom—Mom lived with a man called Wes, and they, with Kathy and Perry and me, moved to Leaf Rapids, where Mom was hired to drive a pit truck in the new strip mine. Leaf Rapids, Manitoba: so far north and so new it wasn't on any map, so cold the snow was hard as the rock for seven months every year. They were bulldozing mines out of the spruce and muskeg and rock, and that's where I fell in love and lost what I thought I still had, but didn't.

My virginity. I had lived with certain parts of my consciousness shut down so completely, refusing to remember for so long, that I actually believed then in the deepest awareness of my mind that I had never been penetrated. I had not even masturbated. Mom always told me my crotch was a bad place; when you bathe never, ever, look between your legs or feel there, wash quick and leave it alone. You hide your body from everyone, including yourself. Especially men, and in particular the men in your own family. I knew I had grown hair there, that my body was changing, but for a hundred reasons I avoided it. In Leaf Rapids I fell in love with a Native boy named Nelson and we hiked to a trapper's cabin we knew. We were alone and I was so happy kissing him, I was completely, romantically in love, and this would be it. O, I was so in love with this marvellous boy, he could dance better than Elvis! And then I scared him witless when I started to scream, "My feet, my feet!"

I screamed so loud my own ears rang and I could not stop. It was my legs cramping back, my feet bent outwards rigid as rocks.

I tried to get up, to stand, and my feet and legs twisted tighter, harder. I fell down on the floor still screaming. He jumped up and ran out, but after a while he came back and tried to help me. I was groaning, rolling in pain, my legs and feet splayed out stiff as if they were bent iron, but when he touched them it was even worse. He tried his best to calm me, poor boy, but he and I never got to try again and find out about possibly good sex because he was long gone. I couldn't understand why his touching me like that twisted my body into an excruciating contortion. It just terrified me more about sex. My mom must be right: the fire of hell lived between my legs; just leave it alone and keep everybody away. At some point in spring we moved back to Winnipeg, on Selkirk west of Main, and from there I was shipped back to Butte again. For more operations on my lip, and Dad living alone, waiting for me.

Minnie was tough beyond belief. The same evening that she arrived in Winnipeg frozen, she asked me how much cash I had. One dollar. She said, good, that's entrance fee, get yourself fixed up, it's time for you to live and learn. She was older. I still thought she knew what she was doing, and off we went to the Manor Hotel. Beer cost ninety-nine cents a bottle; she ordered one, poured half into the glass for me, and swallowed twice from the bottle. Then she left me alone at the table—I didn't know it but I was being used as young meat set out to attract attention—and in a few minutes she was back with guys who kept us supplied till closing time. She drank and I covered her back, got her home safe. I learned to drink beer, and settled in with her showing me how to start every night. We came to be called the Gruesome Twosome, and for good reason.

In the next months we were eighty-sixed out of every bar on the skid; only the toughest, the Occidental Hotel on North Main, would have us, and that became my home bar, my daily place, my hell on earth. No one knew or asked our real names, or where we lived; she was "Four-foot-fuck-all" and I was "Long Streaks of Misery." It suited me, I was grim-faced, quiet, deadly when I had to be. I could fight alone like a man and never spoke unless spoken to, and then only a word or two. I never smiled, only a bit when I danced. Serious, don't cross me or I'll fight to the finish. Minnie never called me Vonnie; she'd yell across the crammed Occidental bar, "Hey, Streaks!" and everybody'd look over at me and laugh. That was the time in the seventies when the streaking craze of running naked through a crowd was slowly fading, but I was all dressed and never cracked a smile, I'd just go to her.

I learned how to handle myself. I never travelled in a pack like most street women who can't fight; they gang-pile their ene-mies. I thought them gutless. I could always count on Minnie to stand with me if she was around and sober enough, though basi-cally she had the attitude "So you couldn't handle it and you got fucked, well, you'll get fucked again, forget it," and I learned to take care of my own back.

Minnie tried to stand with me, but she really didn't care: she accepted abuse — it's the price you pay, forget it, c'mon, let's party — she never had the reaction, like I always did, to fight back until either you win or you're beaten down to the ground. By age nineteen, Minnie had already resigned herself to take whatever kind of violence she got battered with. However often it happened, she simply refused to think about it.

But if you refuse to take the shit the world dumps on you — if, like me, you fight back — it's actually safer being alone. My rules were: never drink or appear drunk on the street, never sell your ass, never hang out with horny old White guys, stand alone. Then you never have to confront anyone with "Where were you when I needed you?" That's how vendettas start, and some day you get jumped anyway by someone you thought was your friend for something you can't even recall from years back. Depend only on yourself was my rule, and if they crowd your space or gang-pile you and you're going down, take as many as possible with you, maybe they won't try it again. Both women and men tried to recruit me, but what was the point? Fight their problems too? On the street I decided I was born alone and that's the way I'd go out: alone.

Of all the fights I won or lost or got out of, I know I'm part of the hidden, sometimes forgotten-for-a-little-while-but-never-erased sorrow of the many people I knew who, like me then, lived on Winnipeg's Indian skid, one of the biggest aboriginal peoples' hell-holes on earth. I never worked the street as a hooker; on welfare days there were lots of Indians splurging, showing off their temporary money. I had casual work here and there, always temporary. I went to parties for the booze, but mostly I walked the streets by myself or spent time at "party houses" where people drank night and day, steadily.

I basically lived on the streets because Mom wanted me out of her house. I was seventeen; she told me it was time for me to get out and live with someone. But I didn't shack up; I'd go home to change, have a shower, sleep, heal from fights, whatever was necessary, but Mom really did not want me around. She always worked, and her hang-around Calvin hated me.

One summer day Calvin came in with a baseball bat and smashed it down in the centre of the table where Minnie and I sat quietly having a drink. He yelled he'd beat us both to pulp, useless bitches. Panfaced, I walked to the kitchen cupboard and took out two butcher knives. I laid one on the table in front of Minnie and sat down with the other in front of me and took another slow swallow of beer.

"If he hits me," I told Minnie in my calmest voice, "you split his guts. If he goes for you, I will."

That was me then at seventeen: no talk, never smile, walk alone, never look anyone in the eye to make them feel threatened. Never a word of personal talk to anyone, not Mom or Karen or Kathy or Minnie. I didn't know or think what was the matter with me — and something was seriously the matter — but if a direct threat was made, an action required, I knew exactly what to do: lay it out clear and simple as a bat in hand and two knives on the table.

Calvin couldn't face Minnie and me. He walked off, yelling, into the living room, came back without the bat, and grabbed one of our knives, started waving it around in the air, ranting even louder. Performance. He was all shithead actor and I lost it. I jumped him, knife and all, with a beer bottle. I beat him over the head till the bottle broke and so did he; he ran to his room, grabbed his clothes, and left. i looked out the window: he was sitting by the garbage bin without a shirt on, bloody all over, and drinking a twenty-sixer. Finally he was gone. After an hour the city police were at our door, looking for him. I said I didn't know, but gave them the bat.

"If you see him, tell him he forgot this. He tried to use it on my sister and me."

They took it, and left.

My shadow tactics and silence kept me out of the worst. Nevertheless, I could not avoid completely being preyed upon, violated.

For me, North Main, Winnipeg, is skinner city, full of pathetic, feeble, sexless men with their conscience destroyed. They wait till women are passed out, either from booze or drugs, and then they brutalize and rob them, and sometimes it's done by a crowd of men daring each other on. Native men do this a lot, especially to Native women—a dreadful shame on our people, but they prey on each other's suffering. To be taught how to suck, fuck, drink, and fight is a very hard, cruel way to live; to survive it you have to act adult before you know you're doing it. Becoming an adult in a beer bottle is small and limiting; you never have time to grow wiser, you never know better than to try and stay where things are familiar and you can somehow handle them because you've already had to. You notice other people of course, especially the rich and apparently happy ones driving by in cars, walking into neat houses, but you know that can never be you. That's already impossible.

By example I was shown how to drink and fight, but I was never taught what it meant to be a woman—except what I understood to be the shame of it. All Mom ever told me was, "Mark my words, you'll find out! You're asking for it and you'll get it." Despite all her experience of residential school, working and looking for work, drinking, marriage and giving birth, and suffering, she never explained much to me; she lived as she could until forced to plough straight ahead into whatever awaited her. She'd say, "Look at Jane; she gets drunk, she passes out and men take turns on her—so don't get drunk!" Easy to say.

Or she'd give me her brand of comfort, "You got hurt, the damage is done. It's not my fault. You made your bed, now lie in it; stop pitying yourself; don't cry over spilt milk; get on with it . . ."—all the useless clichés of a beaten life. So I never told her anything of what happened to me; nor did she ask.

She did come with me when the police caught up with me about the Douglas Barber case in Butte. One day around New Year's, 1979, four cops stood on the porch of our house in Winnipeg when I opened the door: two RCMP and two plain-clothes Montana State marshalls. I was alone at home, and they were so enormous they surrounded me like a wall sitting in the living room. I had broken probation in Butte, I was subpoenaed to be a witness at the Frank Shurtliffe trial. The initial charge of manslaughter in the death of Douglas Barbour had been changed to one of murder, and Yvonne was to be called as a witness for the Prosecution. So Mom took leave from her job and flew with me a whole day, through Minneapolis and Great Falls, to Helena. Dad, with Perry, drove up from Butte to meet us.

The prosecuting lawyers told me how to comb my hair and gave Mom money to buy me a dress. Mom said nothing. She took me out and bought the ugliest dress in Helena because she said anything nice was whorish. The trial was in Boulder, and there Frank sat with his lawyer, the first time I'd seen him since that nightmare night. Mom and Dad were in the gallery, side by side. I kept my head down, looked at nothing, and said what the lawyers told me: I knew nothing, it was hazy and long ago, I didn't remember. I felt really bad for Frank, but what could I do? He and Barber were grown men fighting each other in the snow up on the mountain, why had they hauled a young girl into it? His lawyer was terrifying to me; he used words I couldn't understand and I told him so. He finally threw his pen in the air and said, "She's either lying or just stupid—no further questions!" and the judge let me go. I was to be escorted back to Canada.

In the motel Dad slept on the floor, Mom and Perry on the mattress, and I on the boxspring. We were all packed up to leave when suddenly Dad was yelling at Mom that she'd stolen the top plate of his false teeth! We looked everywhere, unpacked the car, every bag—nothing—and he wondered if maybe he'd swallowed them. He began patting his stomach to see if he could feel them, and then he got a strange expression on his face and ran into the washroom: his teeth were hanging in the crotch of his underwear. So when we took off in opposite directions we were laughing.

I never personally knew what Frank was convicted of until 1993. Then, when Dad visited me in P4W, he told me the sentence was 77 years for some degree of manslaughter, but that he had now been granted parole and was out of prison. On our flight back to Canada, Mom said if Frank ended up in the same jail as Leon and something happened to him, it would be my fault. Otherwise she said nothing. When I tried to talk about it she told me to shut up, there was nothing to brag about. The last comment Mom made on the whole Barber– Shurtliffe mess was when we landed in Winnipeg. She told me:

"I've never been as ashamed of any of my children as I am of you."

All I had left was street people, and I really took to skid-row.

My first pregnancy came about by rape when I was seventeen, and a pretty Native woman set me up for it. At a house on Pacific Avenue, after she invited me to a party and drugged my beer so I passed out and remembered nothing, all night with six guys. Some were her relatives, she told me. I knew something vile had happened, but not what, and it worried me. A few days later I was in the Occidental again, having a drink with a new friend—young, beautiful, and a complete skid innocent—and this same woman came over from a table where she was sitting with those same Indian men and asked if she wanted to go to a party. I said maybe, and she said, "Not you, just her."

I said I wouldn't let her go alone, and the woman just laughed. "Those guys? You fucked them yourself, every one of them—remember the party in the green house on Pacific?"

The guys were braying at me from their table, and somehow I knew it was true, I just couldn't remember. She controlled them in her house and she'd watched them do it. I was enraged, I called her on it then and there, but the bouncer knew I'd clean her clock and pushed me out before I could do it. I put the young girl in a taxi and I swore revenge on each of them, as long as it would take. I beat up two of those fuckers, sitting and laughing at me, later that night when they left the bar, and then I waited till closing time and I got the pimp herself coming out. I have never beaten anyone that badly, but this was a different level of fight and rage: she had won my trust and set me up to be gang-raped, and then she bragged about it.

It seems to me now I beat her with all the pain and fear and misery for all those people who had violated me and whom I could never catch. Rage for ever bottled and screwed up tight inside me, acts blacked out, or unremembered, but nevertheless still, for ever, there.

We were off the sidewalk, fighting between parked cars, down on the pavement, and I heard someone shout, "A bus is coming!" I kept hammering her when I heard the swish of the bus, the light gleam on the shiny nuts of the big duels passing two inches from my face. Then someone kicked me in the face and I was out cold. I never saw that woman or those men again.

Only men can rape and hurt you the way they do but, worse still, sometimes women help them.

Rape and fight, I guess they go together like blood and miscarriage. I found out the rape had made me pregnant when I lost the foetus after another beating, this time from the brother of a man Mom wanted me to live with. Calvin didn't like anyone around, anyone to notice what he was doing while she was at work. When Perry came from Butte to live with us in Winnipeg, one of the first things he told me was he woke up to find Calvin peeking under his blankets; in no time Perry was gone, Mom gave him up to the Seven Oaks Home for troubled children. By age sixteen (1982), he was in Stony Mountain Prison for armed robbery; I don't think he knew his great-great-grandfather Big Bear was in a small cell there in 1885. And I was on the street more than ever. I never told anyone about my miscarriage.

And yet I tried, I tried. I got day-labour jobs. I was raped again and laid charges and the guy got three years and then walked on appeal for "lack of evidence"; I got arrested for public mischief, ordered to pay a $600 fine. Things were getting worse on the street for me. I got the drunken idea to steal a car and drive to Butte to live with Dad again, but I blacked out and had a severe accident. I was in jail a second time the day John Lennon was shot. I knew I was on the suicide road; I knew as certainly as every beer I swallowed that life on skid row is a slow, sure death. But even in that hopelessness I had a longing to live. I was barely nineteen, and I got away from the endless "parties" in the flophouse by committing myself to a dry-out centre; I tried the Pritchard House for further treatment and attended dry AA socials. I'd been basically sober and working at Swifts Meats when I met Fred at an AA social at the Native Friendship Centre.

Fred Ferguson was an Ojibwa, single, a hard-rock miner just come into town from Wawa, Ontario, and living on unemployment insurance. A big man, good-looking, he seemed solid and safe, so I asked him if I could move in with him and he said, "Sure." We went to bed that night and we were together.

And I was truly lost.

Mom liked Fred. "He's the best you'll get," she said, "a working man who sobers you up." So I tried. I got a job in a scrap yard and played the wife, gave Fred what—as I began to find out—his warped sexuality desired. I met him in winter; by summer 1981 he had a job as blast-hole driller with the Eldorado Company in Uranium City, Saskatchewan, and when they flew us up there I realized he had me completely under his control. Uranium City is on the north shore of Lake Athabasca, so far north you can see the Northwest Territories border: the only way in or out was by company plane, and then only if the Eldorado employee gives permission—which Fred never would. I wasn't there a week and I knew I needed to get out. Going there with him was a brutal mistake.

Because Fred now has money, he starts to go out a lot, drink, smoke dope, and becomes stingier than ever. I'm so lonely I become a born-again Christian, and I try to become the perfect submissive little wife. I'm terrified of getting thrown out, and there is no one, anywhere, for me to go to. He calls me slut, whore, drunken Indian. Every two bits of cash I get for groceries I have to justify with a store receipt; I can't stash a penny for an eventual getaway. He monitors my phone calls and tells me stories of how he tricked both his little niece and nephew into playing games with him by having them believe his cock was what he called "monkey." On Hallowe'en I go out to a tame costume party, and when I come back our apartment door is locked, a new deadbolt inside; he won't let me in. I sleep on the inside steps of the building, and in the morning he finally opens the door when I agree to his warped sexual demands.

I tried to fulfil my obligations as wife and house mate, I was fully committed to that, but I didn't count on abuse. Now I endured him, the way women have to. When I despaired I'd often bump against the thought "It's just you, Yvonne. Forget it. What can someone like you expect?" We had been together eleven months, but with all my born-again trying I was more than ever alone; I was sober, but Fred said my religion would not keep me sober long. I began to pray and pray for a child. One night as I fell asleep alone again I dared something. I said out loud, "Okay then, God, if you think I'll make a good mother, give me the gift of a child to love. So I too can find love." And I never prayed about it again.

What I knew about sex was: do as you're told or lie like a log; take it, perform. What I knew about having a baby was nothing. In December my breasts became sore and swollen, and when I stood in front of the mirror I laughed. Hey, I'm filling out at last! Fred and I went to the hospital for tests, and I asked the nurse, "Has the rabbit died already?"—I'd read something about that, somewhere long ago. She laughed and told me nobody did anything like that any more.

I had promised myself and Earl that, when I was his age, twenty, I too would be dead. But now I was barely twenty and I knew I was pregnant. After all I'd been through, a baby seemed impossible, but there really was another life growing inside me, and it wanted to live. I truly did not understand how I had survived so long on the skids. I drank and fought out of hopelessness and no one in my life had ever asked me for a date. I never met any love like I saw in movies, so gentle and happy and kissing, or had any idea how it could exist in the world I lived in—and yet I had a new life growing inside me. I could not understand, but I knew it was there and I loved it; as I knew it would love me.

But Fred became worse than ever. Growing bigger, grossly fat, he drank harder and his pounding sex disgusted me. It seemed he was smearing my unborn baby with filth, and sometimes I'd protect her by giving him the warped sex he wanted. I'd bury my face in a pillow and cry, and he was so twisted he thought I liked it.

I neither drank nor smoked dope once I knew I was pregnant, and my beautiful little Chantal was born on 9 September 1982, in the Winnipeg Women's Pavilion. We were there because, the winter before, Eldorado Mine with all of Uranium City had shut down, a disaster for thousands of people, but Fred would have lost his job anyway: too many days off drunk. And with his record they could not place him, as they did many miners, at any other mine in the world, so we were in Winnipeg unemployed when Chantal was born. But Mom was there at the birth, and after she came to see us. I hadn't seen her tears for a long time.

"All the pain she'll have to suffer," she whispered, "her face like that."

My first child, my own tiny *raz-ma-taz* baby. All of Mom's pain resurfaced while she counted fingers and toes, crying as if she actually understood, at least for a moment, what it was like to live as I had, hiding my face all my life—for there was the cleft in the tiny lip, my inheritance from her mother through her which I had now passed on to her granddaughter. Burden or gift? And Fred cried too. At first he could barely stand to look at her. But the head nurse at the hospital was wonderful. She said there was proper medical attention now, it would be fixed perfectly.

Mom was having her own difficulties. She had an excellent job at Bristol Aerospace, but she had had to recognize Calvin's real nature when he ran back to a male lover in Toronto. Fred was beating me as soon as I came home from the hospital—we moved in with his mother for a time, though once I fled to a house for battered women and tried to get Fred arrested—but in the end I went with him to Elliot Lake, Ontario, on the promise he got of a job in the gold mine there. Dead loss that too; he was nothing but a drunk wife-beater now. I found a job training for high-school janitor, but Fred bitched so much about babysitting I got worried for Chantal and finally I gave up and moved back to Winnipeg. He followed me, beat me up again, and then kidnapped her to try and make me come back to him—a real smart persuader, that one—and his family sided with him. The cops' behaviour was typical: waste time, refuse to accept my charges against him. Chantal was only eight months but already walking, and after two weeks Fred finally gave her back to me because he couldn't feed her properly, and besides, she was too much trouble to care for all day long. I was living with Mom and wanted out of Winnipeg desperately, and so did she. She had gone to visit her sisters in Alberta, and when she came back she said we should both go to Wetaskiwin, where her sister Rita and her husband, Albert Yellowbird, had started a construction company; they'd give us jobs. So just before Christmas 1983, Karen and her husband drove me and Chantal with all of Mom's stuff out of Winnipeg. I had to sell what bit of furniture I had left after two years of enduring Fred to pay the expenses.

Wetaskiwin is little more than five kilometres away from the northern border of the four Cree Nation reserves at Hobbema. This Wetaskiwin job turned out to be bullshit, of course. Albert had gotten a big oil payment from his band at Hobbema, but his construction company came to nothing. Nevertheless it was the best move for me: I was away from the big-city skid, and for four months I was completely independent, which had never happened to me before. Mom lived across town; I ran my own life in a decent apartment on welfare, taking care of Chantal.

It was wonderful. I played with her all day, every day; I never touched a drink; I never even went out, except to buy groceries down the street from Heritage Apartments. The Alberta winter wasn't much like Winnipeg's; chinooks came at the strangest times and the cold and snow melted away. Perry came to live with Mom, and sometimes he'd come over. He was so easygoing and handsome that women—usually older ones—fell for him quickly. His life was sleep, eat, screw, but no problem for me. He never tried to beat me or sass back.

Playing with Chantal was my life. We sat on the floor, and I dressed her up a dozen different ways every day, combinations of undershirts and dresses and frilly panties and socks and little button shirts and T-shirts and pants, and hats and fancy little coats too—there's so much to get at a Goodwill Store, every style you can imagine, and you can wash and trade them back in so easily. I never knew such a quiet, good world could be possible with a living child totally dependent on you alone. I never thought about drinking. Teaching Chantal how to eat and potty training and telling her stories, anything I remembered or could make up, and singing all the songs I liked, dancing, showing her the round spaces between her toes, how her hair tangled and all the patterns it could be combed or braided into, playing, everything you can do with a child is play if you love her, are gentle, and care enough.

Then, in late January 1984, I met Dwayne Wenger and we fell in love. Soon after, Leon got out of prison and appeared from Montana, and of course he moved in on me—you can't lock out family, at least this Johnson can't—he knew no one in Wetaskiwin. Within a few days he asked me if I would sleep with him. Amazing: he didn't just grab and force me, he actually asked.

I told him, "You've got two loves badly mixed up here, sister and lover."

"Other sisters do it," he said. "Why not you?"

I was shocked. I didn't dare ask who, I didn't know what to do except clutch Chantal—was he lying to get me, or telling the truth? Nevertheless he left me alone—but for how long? I couldn't risk it with him waking up and prowling around any time of the day or night, and so one day I left the apartment to him and moved in with Dwa. Only temporarily, I said. I told him why I feared Leon, but he said he didn't want to talk about it.

But when the apartment rent I had paid ran out, Leon moved into Dwa's garage. I cleaned up the mess he left in the apartment to get my deposit back and fled for help to Mom, who was then in Winnipeg. Frying pan to fire: I got raped by that slimy pig she was living with. In her own bed. I don't know how I came to be left alone with him or why I was so weak, but I was wearing Mom's big nightgown and I remember I had no strength to fight him. I tried to protect Chantal curled and sleeping against my stomach and he just put her on the floor and then sexually brutalized me. All I could do was cry as quietly as possible, take it not to wake my baby.

What's so special about my ugly body, men forcing themselves into every opening in it—why don't they just slash open my belly and wash their face in my guts as I die in one piece. At least I'd know it was final. But no, they ram themselves into me and defile my life for ever.

The guy jumped off when he heard Mom coming; he ran out the back door, having stolen what he could never beat out of me. Mom came in and pulled down my nightgown. I tried to reach her, but my body would not work. I could only try to hold on to her, crying, "It was him, kill him!" Finally I fell asleep and woke to Chantal screaming under the bed. The house was empty. I got her sleeping again and took a bath. I asked Mom for a hundred dollars to leave. Yes, go, you're better off in Wetaskiwin.

When I got back from Winnipeg, Dwa and I agreed to live together. He was a new man in my experience: he ran his own small painting business; he had a house with a mortgage; he seemed a responsible, gentle, steady workaholic with a kind of easy stillness about him. His house even had a lot with space for a garden. Best of all, he adored Chantal, and she him. It was time for me, as Dad would say, to bite the bullet of the working class. Bite the bullet and shit out the shells.

I didn't want to recognize it then, but Dwa was also an alcoholic.

7

Wetaskiwin: The Place Where Peace Is Made

Neurasthenia: a neurotic state marked by tension and malaise. *Neurosis*: a functional nervous disorder without demonstrable physical lesions. *Neurotic*: relating to being or being affected with a neurosis. . . .

I would say I suffer from forms of neurasthenia. I would say I am neurotic, but at different levels, usually triggered by neurosis itself. But more on a mental level because of past abuse . . . relapses into mental anguish and body memories channelled into mental confusion, which in effect cause physical reactions to the nervous system, where all physical, mental, spiritual [faculties] can't have up-front knowledge to recognize what in effect is happening. Where memories and emotions arise. Yet [my] mental and physical [faculties] couldn't co-exist then to recognize what was happening. But now I do. I see for the first time in my life, to understand. I am not crazy. I must ponder this idea more. . . . I was defeated before I recognized it. But now I can put a name to it, to attempt to explain it now. It is not incurable. I can cure myself, since I have a reason that caused it. So if I deal with the reason, then I can work to make the problem go away.

– Yvonne, *Journal 13*, 11 November 1994

WETASKIWIN, a small city of 10,000 people, fifty kilometres south of Edmonton. Growing in a land of milk and oil. Everywhere you drive in your pick-up — whether on the rolling land to the east dotted with poplar coppice and lakes, or to the west where the roads rise to hills and long ridges to the point where, on a clear day, you can discover the thin jagged line of the Rocky Mountains on the southwestern horizon 150 kilometres away — everywhere the round domes of dairy silos sprout, the waste gas flares burn, the iron donkeys sink and heave to suck up oil. Sometimes, from any rise in the road, you see three or four small churches at once — Baptist, Ukranian Orthodox or Catholic, Lutheran, Roman Catholic — with the unique crosses of their cemeteries spread out beside them. The straight section lines of cultivated land are scrawled over by creeks cutting down to the North Saskatchewan River — Pipestone, Conjuring, Strawberry — or blotted by blue lakes — Wizard, Ma-me-o, Dried Meat, Pigeon, Bittern. And everywhere the rich farmsteads spread beyond their shelter belts with cattle feedlots, ranks of pig and chicken barns, machinery sheds, and grain-storage bins. The soil here, created by ancient forests, by glacial retreat, advance, and then another retreat, is black and deep; able to grow any grain or hay under the long, brilliant, northern summer sun.

Dwayne Joseph Wenger, my workaholic common-law, the best man ever in my life. My grandma Flora once called him "the

White Indian," and Grandpa John liked him too, they became quiet friends. The first time I saw him, even before I said a word, I noticed a screw in his boot holding the sole in place and I knew he was like me, neither rich nor stuck-up but nevertheless with some decent pride in himself, so I looked away so as not to embarrass him.

Mom was back in Winnipeg, working for Bristol Aerospace, and I was living with Chantal alone in Wetaskiwin. Chantal, my little *raz-ma-taz* baby. When I was free to care for her properly by myself, away from her father's interference and brutality, she gave me more happiness than I could have imagined.

An ironic name for us Bear-Johnsons, *Wetaskiwin*, "the place of peace . . . the hills where peace was made." I found the meaning a few blocks from the apartments where I lived, a granite stone cairn with a marble slab explaining, one word in Cree, one in Blackfoot, and the rest in English:

Wetaskewin Spatinaw
erected July 1, 1927 in commemoration
of Treaty of Peace made in these Hills
Between the Blackfoot and the Cree Indians
1867

Perhaps our great-great-grandfather Big Bear helped negotiate that peace between his people and the Blackfoot: he never found any with the Canadian government. The buffalo haven't existed here for over a hundred years, but it seems that even in the twentieth century my family are still nomadic hunters, in cars now and hunting Indian jobs, searching out relatives or friends who will help them or, as a last resort, hunting White welfare. And still trying to avoid the White law that rules everywhere, avoid its jails with their doors open like traps, waiting to slam shut on us.

Mom's oldest sister Josephine lived in Wetaskiwin then, moving between her apartment in town and the Hobbema reserves south of town. The four Hobbema Cree Nations—whose total population is almost equal to that of Wetaskiwin itself—are the resource-wealthiest reserves in Canada; their oil royalties are so big that for a while, when a young person turned eighteen, they were given anywhere from eighteen to seventy thousand dollars in one lump. Often they headed straight for Auto Row in Wetaskiwin, where smooth car salesmen were waiting to sell them the biggest vehicle they could. At times they took up apartments in Wetaskiwin, and lived by moving back and forth between city and reserve; then the tensions between Natives and Whites often ran very high. The easy-going, partying life-style — some called it lawless living — of the Cree often bumped into the White members of the more than twenty churches and missions, many with strong fundamentalist Christian beliefs, who were the middle-class property and business owners of the city. After some years this lump payment was stopped: the social problems on the reserves became almost overwhelming, with accidental and suicide death rates among young people six times the national average.

Auntie Josephine had been moving back and forth between Wetaskiwin and the four reserves at Hobbema for a few years, and when I came into town I found a place in the Heritage Apartments, where one of Mom's brothers and his common-law lived on the first floor, and her youngest sister Aunt Rita lived with Albert Yellowbird on the third. Rita was still very pretty, but not what she was when she lived with us in Butte — she told Mom she thought some jealous woman was doing Indian medicine on her to make her ugly quicker — but I thought it was more likely age and hard living. Minnie arrived soon after me, and through her I met a White man named Dale; I went to bed with him once and he moved right in on me, sponging off me. I didn't know how to tell him to get lost.

I didn't know how to lock the door on anyone; family was always bothering me. Soon it was Perry, which was not too bad, but then my cousin Shirley Anne — Aunt Josephine's daughter; we hadn't met for a long time — who was between shack-ups and had insurance money to blow, passed her two teenage girls off on me while she went to party until the money was gone. That was typical for her. I got along well enough with her girls then, especially the youngest, who liked school at that time. I stayed home, until one cold late January night I thought, what the hell, I'm going out—maybe then I'll get enough guts to kick Dale out.

I took Chantal to a woman friend in the next apartment and called a cab. The cab driver who answered had given me a ride once before: it was Lyle Schmidt. He looked at me hard when I got into the front seat—I never did that in his cab again—and for all my street living I didn't recognize what the look meant, but I remembered later.

"You want to go for a drink somewhere? All alone?" And he laughed, as phoney a laugh as I've ever heard. "There's only two bars in this fucken town!" And he drove me to the farthest one. The Wayside Inn south on the highway, all of six minutes away. His radio was on loud, with Doc Hook singing "Penicillin Penny":

> They say she's loved so many that she gives 'em all numbers . . .
> She calls me one thousand and one.

———

I had a beer alone in the Wayside, relaxing, watching a video on the big bar screen. Then I noticed a man standing by my table. "Mind if I sit down?" he asked.

Dwayne Wenger. Long hair, stocky, a bit shorter than me, nice flared nose in a quiet face. His baggy jeans were his "up-town" clothes, but even they were speckled by the thousands of paint cans he must have opened—looking seventies hippy, like I remembered them—with muscular arms from all his painting, his shoulders squared back and eyes friendly, not cocky and condescending like most White guys on a pick-up. I thought, this one won't be hard to handle if he gets out of line.

So he sat down and offered to buy me a drink, but I said, "No thanks." I thought, I buy my own beer and owe him nothing. He sipped water at first—he said, "I want to sober up and not miss you!"—but after a bit he ordered beer too. I didn't know then that he couldn't stop himself drinking, that he sipped whisky steadily all day long while he worked. He wore work boots crazy with paint, and that screw held the rim of one sole together, and we talked. He liked nature, he'd gone to California after he finished high school to study to become a herbalist and he seemed so natural, genuinely happy-go-lucky and not at all snooty, like so many Whites in Wetaskiwin I despised, who hated the oil-rich Hobbema Cree, and sneered and treated them like dirt even while they exploited them for their businesses. Talking to me, Dwa seemed so straightforward and strangely innocent; not tricky or game-playing.

After a time I talked too. The P.A. was playing like crazy, and here was a stranger who didn't push me, he listened. And I told him about the mountains in Montana where I was born and grew up. Butte, Montana, the Richest Hill on Earth as they called it, a mile high and a mile deep, really the asshole of the world, the stomping ground of the one and only Evel Knievel, who did show-off motorcycle wheelies in every parade and whom I detested, and how our house sat on the rim of the giant open-pit mine before it swallowed our lot and the house vanished, and how our family cut poles in the high timber when my brother Earl was still alive and I was little, I ran like a whisper under the branches of the pines. I could be so quiet: once I came up on a cougar stretched on a rock just below me, very close. I could have reached out and touched its bright skin, the muscles flexing under it like water. The cougar was watching my family work, and I did too—my mom and Leon and sisters piling brush, my dad and Earl placing the posts one by one onto our flat-deck truck. I told Dwayne Wenger all those things no one ever listened to, and I never could speak to anyone anyway, I was silent, especially with White men, but somehow this stranger invited words, so easy, and I felt natural, open, letting them run out. He sipped beer and listened.

I even told him how hard it was to deal with my life, that I couldn't stand up to anyone, including Dale, whom I didn't even like but who wouldn't get out of my apartment, who thought we were shacked up. How I hated myself for not being able to get rid of him, teetering on a tightrope and this was my night out as protest. And then Dwayne got up and walked away, into the Men's, and alone suddenly I felt ridiculous talking and talking like that.

In fact, I knew I was lucky he left when he did. I had been hinting enough, maybe I'd been about to blurt out how often I thought of killing myself.

When Dwayne came out, he stopped by another table. He bent over one of the men there and laughed, and the man looked around at me, smiled and laughed too. But then he came back, and sat down beside me again. His painty boot. He looked at me till I looked up.

"I was telling my buddy over there," he said. "You're the woman I'm going to marry." And then, when I didn't say anything, I didn't know where to look, he said to my bent head, "Do you like to dance?"

They were playing "Jump" by Van Halen and we were dancing on the Wayside parquet dancing floor. How I love to dance. He wasn't shy; he liked to dance too, so light on his feet. Perry and Dale came into the bar and I told him, "The slim one's my little brother, the other the guy I was telling you about." After our dance we sat with them. Dwayne bought everyone a beer, then Dale ordered a complete tray and drank it all down, one after another, not even coming up for air. Dwayne sat across from me and we continued to talk. He understood what I thought of Dale and he passed me his phone number. Dwayne told me about the nice houses he painted, even the cells of the Wetaskiwin jail; he was inside everything with his brush and roller and drippy cans. But then Dale began to loll and sag and they were going to throw him out; it was really cold that night, so we hauled him out instead and headed for Heritage Apartments. We were in Dwayne's painting van, a big, boxy 1961 Chevy, pretty cold, and the three of us sat up front while Dwayne drove and Dale rolled around, stretched out among the paint cans in the back.

Even with a few beers I didn't know how to act around Dwayne Wenger. I was so attracted to him, the way he danced with me, I got a kick out of his paint polka-dots and the screw in his boot. And then we were driving under a streetlight and I saw his face clearly, a big man, sombre and serious, and I knew he was playing the game with me he'd started when he spoke to his friend at the other table, a love game, and I could sense he was absolutely serious about it when he said to me, though talking to Perry, "Can I kiss your sister?"

I wouldn't have known what to answer. I felt no strength in myself, I was shy, giggly like a young girl—embarrassed almost—but I didn't make a sound. I didn't feel like saying anything, not yet.

But Perry answered; he wasn't even eighteen yet, but serious as could be too. "What are you asking me?"

"I'm asking for a date with your sister."

And Perry spoke carefully, as if he was explaining something very important, very exactly; I couldn't believe he knew how to think or talk like that:

"I have to tell you something about my big sister. I can tell she likes you, and you should know this—Vonnie is a very romantic person."

We all burst out laughing; we were kidding around, avoiding something special. I wanted to have a date—when in my life had I ever had a *date?*—and it all suddenly seemed too heavy and there was the Heritage and I had to get Chantal and my key from the babysitter and I was running around, and Dwayne Wenger hadn't come up to the third floor with everyone else. I hadn't said anything to him, but I was thinking of nothing else—what do I say to him? what?—and knowing if he listened I wanted to talk all night. I was running around, so busy with my sleepy baby, and Perry was laughing with stupid Dale—who was awake enough to laugh now—they must have just ditched Dwayne in the hall and he was too shy—I looked out the window to see if I could catch him, but on the street under the light was a space of blank snow. He was gone.

I was holding Chantal and staring around, dazed. Perry said, "Dale'll sleep it off, I'm going," and he was gone too.

A baby asleep and a drunken mooch in the next room snoring off a trayful of beer. Sit alone in an apartment, some sixties songs on the stereo, snow crawling across the little balcony out-side: live for months, motionless, just deal with what comes minute by minute and don't move, don't think, avoid, avoid, and then one small, sudden, hurt and the pain that's always waiting inside by the year kicks over into impossible. I always was so scared Mom was right, I was truly crazy, and how can a crazy woman raise a beautiful child? I instantly liked Dwa so much, but he's gone and I'm still stuck with Dale—I thought, I'm a loser, I've left it too long.

In the bathroom cabinet were two large brown bottles of mul-ticoloured pills. Shirley Anne's girls must have lifted them from behind a drugstore counter. They looked as if there were enough. I slammed them all back, opened my throat and poured them down with a pitcher of water. The songs sounded far away, I was getting groggy . . . but I needed to see Chantal once more. I stood by her bed. I had survived my life without love . . . but I loved her. I was capable of love now, I knew it. I did not really want to die, because I did not want to let go of Chantal . . . but . . . . I wanted to let the pills make the choice of life or death, let the pills decide—or God, if there is one . . . like a child with contin-ual abuse, you lie and take it, knowing you will surely die, there's too much brutality to live, and yet if you do survive once more you accept that outcome too, that's the way life happens to hap-pen, what could you do about it, maybe next time.

But I wanted my baby near me, whatever the pills or God or both decided. I picked her up, I would lie down carefully on the couch with her, I was slipping away and I would never drop her, no, but she fell and I tried to pick her up—my hands wouldn't work, I couldn't balance, I fell to the floor beside her, crying, and Chantal was awake, she knew something was wrong, she tried to help me up. I cradled her head, whispered, "Mommy loves you, it's okay, Mommy. . . ."

But she started to scream. I lay with tears running over my face. I should have left her sleeping in her bed.

Dale stumbled out and saw me. He phoned Emergency; an ambulance came. I felt I was deep inside myself, like padded walls; perhaps I hung on by listening, and the ambulance attendant helped: he slung me over his shoulder and carried me out, swearing about stupid women, mothers, drunken Indians, why don't they just go off in the bush and die like they do in the movies, or a car crash, oh no, I have to carry her sorry ass all the way down from the third floor!

They wouldn't take Dale along. The nurse called him so stupid—he had put on his own jacket and brought Chantal out in her night clothes—and what was an Indian woman doing with a guy like that anyway, trying to pass her baby off as White? I could see the lights flashing as the ambulance rolled and cornered, and a silly song did too: "When they come to take you down, when they bring that wagon 'round . . . and drag your poor body down . . . please forget you know my name, my darling Sugaree . . ." whining around corners, the nurses in Emergency rolling me out of the cold on a gurney, sarcastic and joking:

Woman: "Another Indian trying to kill herself?"
Man: "Too drunk to do it right, she's just a mess."
Woman (laughing): "So what do we do with her?"
Man: "I guess our civic duty."

They all laughed, the man giving them more punchlines about Indians—their Emergency got so many damaged and dead people from the Hobbema reserves we'd become a joke—the women laughing at his cracks. An older nurse was working on me, she tried to get me to drink something black and foul and ordered a tube, when another nurse came and said that stupid guy was in the next room with the baby, raising hell.

And I heard Chantal cry. With that peculiar sound of baby desperation; she had never had to cry that way before. I was stretched out with a will to die, but her screams called for me. I whispered, "I want my baby, please . . ."

One nurse said, "She's coming in and out," and the other one working on me was more sarcastic than ever, ". . . her kid's screaming and she lying here, useless woman . . ."

Now I just wanted to get Chantal and leave, all their insults— doing their "civic duty" on me while their self-righteousness chopped me in pieces. And as always my defence was offence; my arm shot out and grabbed the nurse by the throat, and she hit me in the chest, trying to make me let go. I had just one hand on her; I was lying motionless in too much pain to move. They were keeping the shell of my life alive and insulting my spirit, and another nurse ran up swearing about dumb Indians, so I let go the first and punched her in the mouth. Then the male nurse jumped on my stomach, hit me in the jaw, and pinned my arms until the nurses got my arms and knees strapped down. Chantal was wailing so close, and I was finished, limp as meat. Completely strapped flat, I broke down and cried.

The head nurse was gentle. "You never know how much they can hear." She was wiping my face.

I wanted desperately to help my baby and they worked on me spewing words as if I was a plank—Do we really have to do this? You help these people and they choke you, punch you in the face—but finally the head nurse said if I calmed down they'd bring the baby, and then Dale brought Chantal to me. They unstrapped one arm so I could hold her. She stopped sobbing, she crawled onto me, hugging me, and I knew I had to live. I was whispering to her, "Mommy loves you. It's okay, it's okay sweetheart, Mommy loves you."

Touching her, I felt overwhelming shame and guilt. I told Dale to take her to my aunt at the Heritage, and I swallowed their tube then, right down into my stomach. I passed out when the pumping started and came to in a hospital bed with my whole body ringing the way it does from an overdose. Pills creep up on you, they take too long and you can get stopped and be dragged back with your body ringing your self into life again like a thousand tiny church bells. Better to use a gun quick—and for sure.

My mother came with Aunt Josephine—Mom had driven back from Winnipeg to pick up her stuff, so now she was here on time to report to the whole family about my suicide attempt. They came to the hospital to see me loaded with tubes. But the two barely spoke to me; they always talked Cree to each other so we kids wouldn't understand them, and since in our family kids don't talk to their elders unless spoken to—Mom says that's the Native way—it didn't much matter. However, all their lives my mother and her sister have played a kind of cruel game, a competition about who's tougher in punishing their kids. Josephine has two daughters and a son, and in front of Mom she always calls Shirley Anne and Darlene down unbelievably—never Carl of course; sons are always perfect, especially only sons. So now to prove how strict she was, Mom really got into me. In English, running up one side of me and down the other, irresponsible, stupid, thick numbskull, nuts, crazy, slicing me into slivers—why o why didn't I speak Cree? It has no vocabulary for abuse like this—while Aunt Josephine listened carefully, nodding, and I had to take it. You don't talk back to your mother.

She finally ran out of words—"I'm not taking care of your kid too. If she's damaged it's your own fault"—and she left.

Then Aunt Josephine asked me, "Where's the sixty dollars I left with you, that Dale drank up? I need it now."

I told her she'd get it when I could get outa here. So she left too, and I freaked out, the pain hit me so hard; they'd play their cruel games over me if I was dead in my coffin. I was ripping out tubes, staggering around for clothes, I was getting out, who cares if I die, my mother coming from Winnipeg just to yell and my aunt demanding sixty lousy bucks! I was screaming.

A nurse came running, one of the kind ones. She talked me down, calm, and convinced me I needed help, I must stay till I was strong. I needed someone to talk to, and she found a psychologist at Mental Health for me. When I got back to Heritage Apartments the first thing I did was tell Dale he had to pay back Aunt Josephine's money and leave. And he did both.

———

Drinking was as common as sleep in the world where I grew up, and it had nothing to do with "social" drinking. In our family you drank head-on steady to get drunk. And so I learned by watching, and drinking hard liquor off and on in Butte until I hit the blackout and that scared me—I hardly drank again till the four-week drunk at Stand Off. I started on beer in Winnipeg and drank steadily for almost two years. I stopped for most of the two and a half years with Fred; I abstained completely when I was pregnant and until Chantal was a year old. I limited myself to two beers the few times I went out in Wetaskiwin before I met Dwa.

So I did not recognize that I was an alcoholic. Though I didn't know what, or why, I did know something was wrong with me; sometimes I was so horribly *down*. Except when I was alone with Chantal.

———

After the hospital, the apartment building was free of family: Auntie Rita had married Albert Yellowbird and moved out; the others had left too; and I wouldn't answer the buzzer, so no one I knew could gain access to the building. One day the buzzer went and I wouldn't open the door but I listened on the intercom: it was two girls, one a schoolgirl cousin. I heard her say to her friend, "Just as well we don't visit. Her mother says she's crazy."

Chantal came and hugged my legs; I was crying but she looked up at me with her deep black eyes and I knew all was fine; who needs to care what name-callers say anyway. A short, stocky little girl sixteen months old and lovelier than ever, a chatterbox all day long and speaking only the language we had between us. She'd sing and prattle and I'd ask her, "Is that right, really?" and she'd nod laughing, it was such a funny game; she always caught the words, the tone when I said it, "Is that right, really?" and she'd nod so hard her whole body bounced yes, yes! I just hugged her, both of us rolling around on the rug.

If the weather was a bit warmer, we'd go out on our little balcony to play on a blanket in the fresh air. I told her the story of the girl locked in a tower by a wicked witch and one day her prince came, she let down her hair, and he climbed up to her, and they had lots of babies, little brothers and sisters, and so lived happily ever after. The balcony faced a street going north, distant lines of trees and roofs of houses all around, but there was never a boxy 1961 Chevy van down there splattered with paint.

Once, soon after the hospital, I had seen Dwayne come into the bank and I hid behind a large billboard—bright daylight and what would he think of me?—I had the telephone number he'd slipped me, but now I didn't dare call it. What could I say? Finally one evening I talked myself into using the excuse that I had left my purse in his truck, and a man's voice said, "Hello"—but it wasn't Dwayne. The guy said Dwayne was still working. I was so relieved I hung up before he could finish his short sentence. I tried again, but I couldn't leave my name and he never seemed to be in. Then one evening his voice answered. I could just blurt out, "Howdy, howdy . . . is Dwayne Wenger there?"

A pause. Then he said, "Are you my tall, beautiful Indian girl?"

"I am tall," I said, and was going to start on the purse, "and I met you——"

But he cut in, "Hey, I've been waving at you all over town; you always disappear."

I never walked around town. He'd mistaken another Native woman for me; he'd been trying to get her attention for weeks!

He asked, "What are you drinking?"

"Tea."

"Don't move," he said. "I'll be right over."

I was overjoyed and terrified at the same time and tried to fix myself up fast. He hadn't seen me since that night and now that dumb drinking song kept reminding me of our first meeting: "All women get prettier at closing time." But he came to the apartment wearing his old paint coveralls, and told me he had spray-painted his boots just for the occasion, a perfect black. They looked very smart, but I could still see the screw; he was a man with nothing to prove, he was himself, which was fine with me. Dwayne Joseph Wenger; my Dwa.

And a strange courtship we had of it. That first time he arrived sipping Southern Comfort, and drunk. Most of the evening he spent on the floor playing with Chantal; and I was surprised both at him for doing it and at her: she was so independent with everyone, playing her own games and never bothering any adults. But when he came in she pulled him down and crawled all over him, playing with him, unsteady as he was. It grew late; I finally got her settled in bed and came back into the kitchen. Dwayne was standing there, passed out on his feet, a puddle of urine spreading on the floor.

So, he was staying the night. I set him in a chair and ran a tub of hot water; when I came to get him he reached up and smudged my lipstick.

"I don't like . . . that stuff," he muttered.

There seemed no point at the time in discussing make-up. I helped him to the bathroom and told him to get his dirty clothes off and get in there. But he slumped down on the toilet and passed out again. So I undressed him and tried to hoist him into the tub; he was heavy and he came round and fumbled to hold onto me, I should get in too, get in with him.

I gave him a push and he fell into the tub; that brought him round and he slammed about, thinking he was drowning in six inches of water—"I can't swim!"—but I slapped a bar of soap in his hand.

"Use it," I told him.

I didn't want him sleeping where I couldn't see him, so after he was washed I put him in my bed and covered him with separate blankets. He was asleep instantly but woke me at dawn, shaking me awake.

"Where are my clothes?"

"You pissed yourself last night," I told him.

"I gotta go work."

He stood there naked—he had to go work!—the only guy I ever cleaned up who thought about work first thing in the morning after a drunk. I gave him some of my large clothes and he was gone. I fell asleep again, and I don't know, maybe I was smiling.

———

Leon got out of prison in Montana and I invited him north: after all, he was my brother and maybe in Canada he could somehow break his self-destructive cycle of prisons. He moved in with me and began working for Dwa; they got along well, but Dwa's roommate, Jerry, didn't like him. Jerry would get coked up and head-butt Leon, which always scared me: if Leon got mad he might kill him. But Leon was actually more interested in finding out how Jerry could break beer bottles on his head without knocking himself out, so they practised doing that. Then Dwa and Leon went to a bar and ended up getting stupid together: Leon drank beer pouring out of a hole in the sole of his workboot, and then Dwa curled up his thong and drank beer using it as a funnel. Soon the bouncers were trying to throw them out, and Dwa went easy—in six years I never knew him to fight anyone—but Leon was too macho. He fought them till he lay on the floor sticking his tongue out at the guy trying to choke him, sneering, egging him on to choke him harder.

So Dwa and Leon became working and drinking buddies, but I still had to protect myself. Drinking and pot were never enough for Leon, he demanded women; he put the blocks to me about sleeping with him, and I couldn't stand it. I told Dwa and he said he'd fire him. "No," I said, "he'll still be around but with no job. It'll be worse."

I liked the independence of Dwa and me seeing each other whenever we wanted to, each at our own place. The first time Dwa came up for lunch he asked if I wanted to go see some land he might buy, so we drove out. He told me he'd grown up in the north, at Swan Hills, hilly country all covered with bush, and his first girlfriend had been a Native girl from there. Like me he loved forests and trees, plants. We met some Cree men he knew and we finished the day drinking in Hobbema. It was different; at one point the women there beat up the men with beer bottles. We drove back to Wetaskiwin, tearing over the gravel roads on the rez, and his hand slid up to my crotch and I dug my nails into his arm and drew blood. That frightened me: to men blood is no joke. But he just laughed.

"Serves me right," he said.

When he visited and had supper, he would leave money in the fridge to help me, but I didn't want to feel I owed anyone anything. Once when he was helping me move out what was left of Mom's furniture, he asked to kiss me; he said, "You want to neck?" I wanted to snuggle but it wasn't at all romantic; I was sober, he drunk; I was shy and self-protective—he's a man, if I give in he gets what he wants and he's gone—so I told him I'd just gotten rid of an abusive partner and I wanted independence—what I really wanted was a date.

So we had a date, and one night in my apartment we went to bed together. He said I was wild, though I knew I was drunk and giving him what I knew men wanted; I was robotic, I had no feelings to remember. And he got up early again and was gone to work without a word. During the day he phoned: did I want to go on a picnic? Of course, so we drove into the country and my hat caught on fire and so did the painting tarps we were sitting on. A few days later he cooked me my favourite supper— spaghetti—at his house. After we put Chantal to bed, we sat on the couch. I was shy and he would undo my shirt and while he was busy with my jeans I'd button my shirt again. That went on for a while, I got excited and enjoyed it. It was wonderful.

After that, either he was at my place or I at his. But I had Chantal to care for and we had to work around Leon, who lived with me, and it was no good. Leon takes over any space he lives in. Independence disappeared for me, so I paid the rent a month for Leon and moved in with Dwa. All I asked was that we not lie to each other: he knew some of the problems I had with my family, okay, and he should have enough respect not to cheat on me. We agreed on everything; he didn't speak about my troubles with Leon or anyone else; he just acted as if me living with him would change things for me.

———

Life was better. When Chantal and I came back from that dreadful trip to Mom in Winnipeg and moved in permanently with Dwa, Leon was still working for him and, after the fight in the bar, sleeping in Dwa's garage. Life was basically good: living with Dwa became almost a business adventure. I answered his business phone, listed appointments and calls, cleaned the house, cooked, and sometimes went to help him on a job when he was really busy. When he came home wasted from work and drink, I'd massage his tired body with baby oil and he'd pass out or drift off into sleep. He loved Chantal and she adored him, she'd have all her stuffed toys waiting at the door for him to come in. She even started to call him "Daddy," and whenever Dwa's little boy, Taylor—from his previous marriage—came to stay with us, Chantal and I took care of him while Dwa kept on with his daily work; he'd underbid on every job to get it, and slave away, work, work; his daily life was to disappear into work.

Taylor was three when he first saw Chantal; he pointed at her and said, "Dad, she's a nigger."

"No," I told him, "she's Indian."

He was a lovely boy, and we all grew close together; Taylor loved his dad and so did I. Dwa was so good and decent, never doing to me what other men had done; kindness was a deep and unending part of his nature, totally harmless when drunk.

In many ways our living together was convenient for us both; I loved him beyond all I can say and we four grew to love each other. We never went out because he did not want to. I worked on the yard, cleaning up junk buried all over in the long grass, dug the garden area bigger, scraped the picket fence and garage for painting. Dwa drank steadily, a little all day long—he especially like painting inside houses that had a liquor stash to sample—but it didn't seem to affect either his work or how he reacted to people. But I could not do that. I never drank in public at all, and hardly ever at home at first. He'd come home, eat, and pass out asleep.

We never went out together; it was almost as if he did not want to be seen anywhere with me. I tried to get him to go camping, but if he did he'd be drunk and miserable the whole time. He cared for me and he played with the kids, but I was to stay in the house and care for them; that was all. I tried to put up with it, though I knew it wasn't good for me or him, always being alone together. But our mutual need kept us together somehow. I had a home, family, a gentle man who was excellent with kids, steady food and a van: go with it. I told myself again and again.

Nevertheless, there are so many arms and legs to my life, and Dwa wasn't a person to ask me about any of them. Even before my nightmares became impossible to hide from him, I knew I had to start telling him about my abuse. But he did not want to hear anything like that. We were together almost six years before our Wetaskiwin world collapsed and we knew each other very well, though in certain ways we didn't at all. I should have told him more.

And then babies happen, of course. I was wildly happy for my three babies, always amazed I could actually have them after all that had happened to my physical body, a new, unspoiled person growing inside me. After Chantal I wanted a dozen babies because I knew I had enough love and experience to care for all of them. But I also knew I should tell him there was something hounding me, something huge always dragging itself after me. I thought of myself as basically a friendly, welcoming person, but I was home all the time with the kids—I really had no friends in the area where we lived, Dwa never took me anywhere to associate with his business people, and the rare times when his parents visited he'd often call me down in front of them, as if to put me in my place, and I felt so low about myself I'd just hang on, shut up until they were gone and the two of us were together again, alone, and it was okay. For a time I accepted that he have me just to himself.

———

But sometimes our life together became too much. I was too intense with the next-door neighbours, too in-your-face. They'd tell me I was so protective about my kids that at times I was downright offensive.

That in turn reminded me of Mom always saying I was crazy, and I'd suddenly become very angry that anyone leaning over a fence could make me feel I was stupid. I'd face them right down: children, family, property, everything closely personal about me became intense, from cleaning the house to standing up for what I believed in. And later, when I started drinking heavily again, then the old skid pattern returned again: if anyone bothered me and I felt I had to protect myself, I was ready to fight till one of us dropped.

Nonetheless, those first years with Dwa were the best of my adult life. An alcoholic needs someone who will organize the practical business of living and put up with him without nagging when he messes his bed. I had such low self-esteem—my own past made me feel I was a drunk myself—that I was happy to work hard like Dwa and not expect much. I tried to keep him happy and that was such a change from his former wife, who had always wanted more and more of everything—a better house, car, furniture, times out, whatever you can think of— that Dwa loved me more than ever: just keep me to himself, as long he could stay happily drunk and work driven by bennies, what more could he ask from life? Other people just caused problems; keep them away.

Things began to change for us in the spring of 1985, when I found I was pregnant. He said he felt he was trapped into marriage right after high school when his girlfriend was pregnant with Taylor. He said to me, "Get an abortion," but I said, "No." Okay, Dwa agreed, but he was around less, working more, and still drinking too, and I was busy getting ready for the baby. I loved being pregnant. Dwa and Chantal would kid me. "Big Fat Momma!" James was born in December 1985, weighing ten pounds eight ounces, a thirteen-inch head and his body twenty-four inches long; the placenta also weighed ten pounds—"O-o-o-h a big baby!" the Hindu doctor said when his head appeared.

By May 1986, I was pregnant again. At that time Dwa had to answer long-delayed impaired-driving charges in court, to which were added possession of pot as well. He was sentenced to Grande Cache prison for six months.

Dwa and I never did talk about sex. I just pretended whatever we did was easy and natural, I was satisfied if I made him happy. He accepted sex straight on, no frills necessary, and he truly thought he was satisfying me because I'm a good faker, he never suspected anything short of all right and mostly wonderful was happening. And to an extent it was, because he never seemed to expect anything beyond routine—he would not let me touch my clitoris during love-making, that was all his—he did everything he thought made me happy, and once a woman starts faking it you can never stop because then you'll destroy his manly self. So, if he was satisfied that satisfied me too, and best of all he wasn't violent.

But I know I didn't experience the profound depth of sex I heard about, how it can roll you over and turn you inside out—how could I? I was taught sex was dirty, and it was tied to too many drunken assaults, to my buried child torture, to the nightmares that began to erupt into my sleep: I was being raped by something half-human, half-goat, and I was terrified, I couldn't stop it, totally helpless. That horror began to seep into my daylight awareness. I couldn't forget this beast thing whispering. I would cry while it whispered, "Just wait, you'll really like this" and as it started to rape me I could feel my body react—I'd wake up screaming beside Dwa. It was too, too horrible. I dreaded falling asleep after, and then would wake up to another day of restlessness that I knew I could only numb with booze, not wanting to eat, yet trying for everyone's sake to appear fine—Vonnie is fine, Mommy is just fine. I never had an orgasm, and yet the comfort of Dwa's arms was all I really needed or wanted.

Nevertheless, inside the comfort of our little house and bed, I found the nightmares were like a continual video being replayed over and over, the grotesque reality of my life winding on, without end.

And when I was without Dwa they were worse.

———

With Dwa in prison my life started to rock; the vultures of my family moved in. I could not keep them away, I could not lock the door of the house and not answer when I knew they were out there because they would peek in the windows to see me and gossip among themselves, or more likely they'd break in and there I would be—why hadn't I opened the door? What was the matter with me? Too high and mighty, eh, with my man in jail for impaired like everybody else? Even the aunt I liked best came around with a guy—she was "marking him in," as they say. She passed out drunk on my bed and left me, pregnant as I was, with this strange man in the house. I finally escorted him out the door with the help of an unloaded rifle.

My cousin Shirley Anne and her two teenage daughters were the worst. I was suffering terrible loneliness. Before Dwa got sent off, we went to a reunion in his home town of Swan Hills and he cheated on me with two girls from his past. Now Shirley Anne moved in on me. Her oldest daughter was shacked up, and when the youngest said she wanted to live with me to go to school, Shirley Anne was afraid she'd be cut from welfare. I said yes to her daughter because I wanted to help her, but Shirley Anne and my aunt threatened to report me to the cops as an unfit mother who shouldn't be getting any support, whose kids should be taken away. That was a standard tactic: control each other by reporting on each other to Social Services. Welfare revenge, I call it.

I was pregnant and desperate about Chantal and James. I couldn't take it, so I let Shirley Anne's daughter go. I locked up the house, put the two kids in the van, and headed south across the border to Dad in Butte.

Leon was back in prison, so I was safe from him, though he threatened me from there through Mom about Dwa having tried to sleep with his woman when she visited us in Canada. I knew that was a lie. Then Mom called me from Wetaskiwin and told me the news, all in one breath:

"Your house is broken into and everything's smashed and you got robbed, but I checked your mail and you got a cheque and I want the cash for the van you never finished paying me for, and I nailed your house door shut."

Dad came back with me to Wetaskiwin and we fixed up the damage. He stayed for a while. We visited Dwa, and I got him home on passes, and finally they released him to me on probation.

———

My father and Dwa did not get started well. "It's a hell of a thing," Dad said to me. "A man meets his son-in-law for the first time in jail."

Once before, when I couldn't take Dwa's alcoholism any more and I thought of leaving him, I phoned Dad to come help me move back to Montana. I was at my wit's end, and Dad was always fixed in one place there at the end of his telephone in his little seventy-year-old house shoved full of stuff, with Earl's old van still inside the rotten garage and our rusty logging truck with its cable and pulley on the tripod hoist parked behind the fence in the yard. He said he'd come to get me and my kids, but I'd owe him. At the time I thought he was talking about work, but he wasn't.

I didn't have to go then, but later he asked me, "What did you think I meant, work? What work do I need?"

I said I thought he meant clean up his place. It was like a porcupine's den, a dark hole where the dirt and droppings the old guy leaves behind trail into his sleeping area.

"Work, hell. I knew what you're doing, no matter where you live and how many common-law husbands and kids you have. I'm a man and men need it in bed, you knew that."

I was always his daughter whom he loved, but, no matter how I lived, it seemed that to him I was also a whore. How to understand that? Though I should have known: that was the way he himself lived. Sometimes when we visited him he'd be sitting in his dark house, blinds shut and TV on, with one of two Butte sisters who traded off on him in his bed. If he was on a binge, he'd sit with them in his lap in his mouldering chair, smiling, sucking a thin black cigar. But at the time I called him I had forced from my memory what he did to me at sixteen, when I was hurt and made the mistake of coming to him for comfort.

———

My White father and grandfather abused me, but my Cree grandfather, John Bear, never touched me. He was very quiet, a dark, lean man in denim work clothes and broad-brimmed hat, a silent sadness carved on his sharp face. As if he was never inside a building, always the open air, in the poplar bush and clearings, like Allan Sapp of Red Pheasant painted him. I saw that picture once in a magazine, a beautiful painting like a crystal; the winter air hangs in hoar frost over the trees and sky and horses and the long load of poplars he has cut to haul home to Grandma on his sled for firewood. Grandpa John sits deep in the snow beside a tiny fire, drinking tea from a small, black pail.

Grandpa John Bear was a quiet man. He spoke very little when he came to Butte, or when we visited them in Red Pheasant: he rarely spoke English at all. When I was alone with them on the reserve, he left me undisturbed with Grandma Flora; he never so much as looked directly at me that I can remember. He must have known how deeply troubled I was as a child—he understood when Leon was hurting his grandchild Darlene, Aunt Josephine's second daughter, and took her out of our house—but he left me to Grandma's care. I love his memory for that, and also because I know he loved Earl. Dad has a framed snapshot under glass on the wall above his TV: Grandpa John and Earl together, head and shoulders only, their faces leaning close together. Beautiful of them both.

When Grandpa and Grandma Bear came from Red Pheasant to Butte for Earl's funeral—Great-Grandma Baptiste, Kokhum, was 108 years old and couldn't come—I don't remember Grandpa John saying a word, even in Cree. He only cried when he thought no one was watching him.

My first memory of my grandparents was visiting them in Idaho before I went to school. Grandma had dried meat hanging from the eavestroughs all around the house where they lived. We kids were not around the grown-ups, they talked in Cree, but we worked with them in the potato fields and huge hayfields. I sat on a bale and found a Wizard of Oz comic book left there by the boss's children. We were so poor: my great-grandma was born when the Whites came west in Canada, my grandma was that first generation born on reserves, my mom was taken into residential school, and I was born into the in-

between Indian–White world where you do year-around labour-
ing jobs and the Indians leave their reserves for the slave labour
the different seasons need: hay, fencing, potatoes, vegetables in
Idaho, or sugar beets in southern Alberta.

Grandma said Indians had no concept of "poor" before the
Whites came; the Whites created poverty. When our grandparents stayed with us in Butte they would go to the dump and find
lots of good things people throw away; once we loaded Earl's
van to the roof with useful things, all the grown-ups got the best
places to sit and we kids squeezed in wherever we could and we
headed north for Red Pheasant. I was stretched on top of two
mattresses, sleeping, and all pit stops were regular as clockwork,
boys piss on one side, girls on the other. The food was Klik or
baloney sandwiches, drinks Kool-Aid or water in a plastic jug,
and you never said a word of complaint. If you cried, Mom'd
give you one warning, "When we get home, I'll really give you
something to cry about," because she was very sensitive about
how we behaved around her Cree parents. Indian children are
supposed to be quiet, well behaved, and say nothing to their
elders, but we kids often behaved White, and Grandma Flora
especially didn't like that. So Mom, to please her mother—as I
now long to please mine—wanted us to be quiet and perfect.

My grandma turned away from anything Whites considered
riches, but the religious jail my mother grew up in—residential
school—taught Mom to want things. She could not deny that,
while her mother wouldn't acknowledge that property even
existed and lived as best she knew how, coping physically and
living spiritually. Whatever spiritual gifts Grandma saw in me—
and she did—she knew they had to be brought out from under,
she had to undo all that my White life had forced onto me.

I saw Grandpa John's tears one other time, long after Earl's
funeral. The summer of 1985—centennial year of the Canadian
Indian and Métis rebellion—when Mom brought him and
Grandma to Wetaskiwin and I took Chantal and we drove
southeast over the prairie to Sounding Lake, Alberta. A large
shallow lake, the edge of its water had dried back so far from its
original stony banks that only a dot of blue was left glittering in

the distance, and the cattle grazing on the fenced flats were tiny blotches in an immense spread of green.

"Ni-pi-kap-hit-i-kwek" Grandpa named it in Cree when we drove over the rolling brush hills and saw it far away below us. Sounding Water. The aboriginal people of the prairie say that this is the place where the buffalo were born; here they came out of the depths of the water, and the underground sound of their birth rumbled through the earth as they emerged. They say it still does sometimes, though I did not hear it when we camped there. Grandma Flora made our campfire beside the Cree burial ground on what was once the edge of the lake.

In 1883 our ancestor Big Bear wanted to claim the land for his reserve at this sacred place.

I knew nothing then about Big Bear except that he was my great-great-grandfather, but I know now that, after the buffalo were all killed in Canada and starvation had forced him to sign Treaty Six, he and his people travelled here past Sounding Lake, coming north from the Cypress Hills as the Canadian government demanded, in June 1883. Maybe it came to Big Bear and his people then that, if they could live at this sacred place, the Great Spirit would give them the living gift of the buffalo back again; if they could settle here, the buffalo would be born again, they would be able to hunt them properly once more, and so live again. But the government imprisoned and killed Big Bear with sickness before he ever got his land negotiated; over a hundred years and we, Big Bear's direct descendants, still had no land. They say there are over six hundred of us now in Canada and more in the United States.

Where we camped that night, we were looking at what had once been a lake. A three-strand barbed-wire fence, a straight line across it and out of sight, white cattle grazing. Dried up. No sounding water, no buffalo.

A few steps from the burial ground stood a stone cairn erected by the government. The writing on it remembered a North-West Mounted Policeman who died while on duty, but it said nothing about the Cree graves, nor the Treaty Six payment that took place here in 1878, and the long debate between Big

Bear and the governor. It was on this spot he tried to negotiate better terms for the huge land all the Cree chiefs had given away by "touching the pen." Land fed you, Big Bear told that White moneyman; it was not like bits of government paper the wind could blow away, or water rot. But the governor would change nothing, and so Big Bear and his people left Sounding Lake and followed the buffalo south into Montana. Living there only four years while the lake here started drying up; no more buffalo were being born.

When the sun sank behind the hills along the far shore, I heard coyotes howl; Chantal shivered as I held her, listening. Their long, scattered calls answering each other from everywhere around us sounded so strange, such sad laughter. The sky was dark and clear, the stars like icicles, and Grandma Flora in the brush of the hills sang her ceremonies. Grandpa John sat looking into the wolf-willow fire.

The next morning, Mom said she was going to find out once and for all who had this land. It should belong to Big Bear's children, no one else. So she and Grandpa drove to the nearest town, Consort, and nobody there could, or would, tell them anything, so she drove on to Coronation, and they had land records but were even worse to them, so by the time they got back to us on the shore above the dry lake, Mom was so angry she could barely speak. The Royal Canadian Mounted Police was right behind her, two uniforms in a cruiser called by the rancher who said the land was his, the cattle were his, I guess everything as far as he wanted to see in all directions was his, and the uniforms told us so. This was leased Crown land, whatever that means to crowned Queen Elizabeth II, and if we weren't off it in twenty-four hours—Cree Indians and relatives of Big Bear or whatever we were, it didn't matter—they'd come back to remove us forcibly.

I watched this happen. My "little big man" James was growing inside me, and I held Chantal tight against my stomach as he moved there so we all together would see this, and remember.

Grandpa John stood without a word. Grandma Flora had started to pack up as soon as she saw the cars coming over the hills.

Mom shouted at the cops as they got into their car, "We don't need no twenty-four hours, we can leave in fifteen minutes! But when we get the land back, we won't give you one minute to clear out!"

They were turning their car around, gesturing for her to calm herself. But she kept on: "And you've got the gall to bury this bastard in our burial ground, build him a stone statue— when we get it back he's coming out. I'll grab his boney ankle and throw his bones over the hills!"

The thick rancher was glaring out of his pick-up. "Oh yeah?" he growled. "And I'm gonna dig up your goddam burial ground and crush every bone I find into bonemeal to feed my cattle!"

The cops waved him away, and he spun around and both drove off as Mom cursed them. Grandpa John was leaning against our truck, hunched against its rear-view mirror, crying.

The two vehicles crawled away up the trail over the hills between wolf-willow in a long drift of dust. And, suddenly, rain began to fall on us. The sky was clear blue, the sun was shining, and rain fell like light falling. I went to comfort Grandpa, and it was so quiet we all listened—Grandma, Grandpa, Mom, Chantal, me—and we felt the Great Spirit blessing of rain run down our faces, and listened to it drop on the sandy ground that had once been hidden by the sacred water of Sounding Lake.

"It'll be all right," I said to Grandpa John. "The spirits see us, and they're crying too."

8

Down into Disaster

A dream I dreamed just before Grandma Flora died:

Earl is lying flat in his coffin. Suddenly his eyes open and they are solid black, empty. He sits up in one smooth move and he looks at me. I am afraid, I have never seen him dead in my dreams before. He looks so evil, I run across grass to Grandma Flora sitting between two men in robes. She says nothing. Earl is coming and she points to stone steps. I walk up the steps, and Chantal is there, playing jacks. She is so happy; behind her is a confessional booth. I can see Earl's feet under the curtain, and a pool of urine is spreading from his feet towards Chantal. I grab her and run back to Grandma. She is nailed to the branches of a tree, her arms spread as if she is crucified.

– Yvonne Johnson, December 1997

ALWAYS IN MY LIFE there was Leon.

Mom and Dad's first child, Earl, had such a strong, healthy personality it seemed he would be everything to everyone; both the Bears and the Johnsons loved him. And when he was killed by Butte police, he became our martyr. Leon, the second son, could not shoulder such a burden, and all Dad knew was to try to beat what he thought was good character into him. But by 1971 Leon learned to protect himself from every family expectation by being for ever in trouble with the police, whose external rules he always knew exactly how to violate if he wanted to, get arrested, and be beyond any possible responsibility. Sometimes he behaved as if he had no brain whatever: he'd be barely out of jail and he'd steal a car and drive it home, leave it standing in front of the house, make no attempt to hide what he had done, and next day he'd be arrested and fight the police and be in jail again. Inside, he was a model inmate.

And I, the last of the girls. The family story now is that, beginning with having to be held upright to sleep and fed by eyedropper, I was always protected and spoiled. Since I could only cry, everyone tried to please me. That's the family story; and maybe there's some truth in it, but I do not remember it that way. I remember clearly the many times I felt family love as a child, yes, but if my mother now stands in a public courtroom and calls that love "spoiling Vonnie"—as she has done—then she is betraying even the love she gave me as a child into a testimony to protect Leon.

For I remember also, very clearly, being used by everyone for whatever purpose they pleased, and all the more easily because I could not explain what was being done to me.

Used most by Leon. Though he was my protector too, especially when I was little. In school he saved me from some brutality, and when I had to run from Dad I lived with him in Butte and that worked because at the time he had plenty of women to keep him happy. He protected me from others almost as if I were his property—but he never protected me from himself.

Living with Chantal in Wetaskiwin and starting to date Dwa, I somehow felt strong enough to suggest he should come to Canada. I had not really known him for over five years and I thought perhaps a change of country, a job, could break him out of his hopeless crime cycles. But prison had done to him what it does, and as soon as he arrived I knew he was more aggressively Leon than ever. He seemed to have no conscience, no concept of right or wrong or decency, leave alone kindness: he knew no women in Wetaskiwin, so he simply asked me to sleep with him. A sister was less to him than a whore because he wouldn't have to pay her. He told me all the years he was in prison he thought about me, and in his mind compared all his sisters. At the time he did leave me alone when I said no, but I moved in with Dwa; I could see disaster looming over me like his huge body.

And when the rent I'd paid on the apartment ran out, he followed me, made himself a space to sleep in the garage outside our back door, where Dwa stored his painting stuff. And then he wouldn't work any more; he claimed at one point Dwa ripped him off in pay and so he did nothing; he lived off us.

Leon had to have a light on in order to sleep. He'd spent most of his life in reformatories, with chain gangs, in prisons where lights burned all the time. I didn't dare leave him with the children and help Dwa paint. I didn't dare stay alone with him while Dwa worked, sometimes away for days or late hours, coming home when the kids were already sleeping and he was tired and happily alcoholic and would eat and get into bed with me and fall asleep so he could get up and drive off in his van and do it all over again.

Dwa did what he did best: escape into steady drinking and work, and I couldn't explain my fears. Fears both for myself and for my children, dreading that my nightmares would resurface in them, even if I loved and protected them more than anyone else on earth could. Leon put the blocks to me simply by walking in from the garage: huge, growing a beard, glowering, enough aggressive personality to burn down Wetaskiwin crammed into my small house. His way of staring. Though I didn't dare show it, I was terrified.

How could I get rid of him? I've never known.

Oddly, a few times he seemed as weak and helpless as I. He told me that whenever he was in prison he could think because that world was real to him; outside he couldn't really think, the world seemed too strange. And when Earl died he went completely crazy; he had shared a room with him and how could he sleep alone in it then? He'd wanted to fight and kill every cop for what they did. But the cops didn't kill Earl. No.

"Earl killed Earl," Leon told me. "He wimped out, left me holding the bag. I've got to live and deal with it alone."

Deal with what? He would never say, exactly. Only a bright light burning kept him going, he said, only when he was dead for sleep.

As he told me this he put his arm across my shoulders and held my hand in his—not really hard, holding it in an almost caring way. I was alone with Leon, and afraid, but he was confessing something too and I knew I shouldn't stop him. Then he turned my hand and saw the scar on my wrist. He asked me if I had slashed it, and I said yes. After I got raped in Winnipeg. He ran his finger along the scar gently, not pushing me, and told me how he once had to listen to a man in Deer Lodge Prison, Montana, kill himself by smashing his head to pieces against a stone wall.

"But dying's easy," he said. "It's living that's so fucken hard."

Leon tried to fix Dwa's cars, but otherwise he didn't do much; he rented sex movies and asked me to watch them with him. I'd never seen any before and they were dreadful. Once little Chantal got up on a suitcase and danced while I was singing and he said, "She'll grow up to be a peeler," and Chantal said, "No, I won't." I was so surprised, and afraid too, and to protect ourselves I tried the only plan I could think of: I gave Leon money to get his girlfriend, Lucinda, from Montana. She came with her little kids and that distracted him for a while, but one night he was enraged because she wanted to drink with us instead of going to the garage with him—he warned Dwa to stay out of it, he was Lucinda's man and he'd show her—and he dragged her to the garage. After she came back out, I called the cops, and they put her up in a hotel for the night. When money came from a painting job, I told Dwa that Leon had to move out. But Leon had a plan; he told us he'd go to Montana with the money, buy dope, return with a load, and become a dealer. So Dwa told him, "If you're going to the States, you should stay there. There's no more work for you here." And under his breath: "You're not selling out of my house."

Leon was mad, and of course phoned Mom. She was furious: so I now considered myself too high and mighty to help my brother, eh? And of course she decided to do something for him. Bristol Aerospace was shutting down in Winnipeg, so she cashed in her pension and RRSPs and invested the money in an upholstery shop in the old band hall on Red Pheasant in Saskatchewan. Leon arrived back from Montana with a new girlfriend, Laura—who'd left her two children for him—supposedly to run the business. But Mom did all the work that was ever done in that shop. He and Laura lived there, but neither worked, and in a year he had run it into the ground: the cutting tables and the sewing machines just sat. But for a while at least he was away from me and my small, helpless children.

One evening after Dwa was home I got away alone. I was in a bar, having a solitary drink, when I noticed a young guy with two girls, having a tough time of it. He was stiff and very mannered, looking like a total jerk with suit and bowtie, and the two girls were playing him for the fool with two guys at the next table: the other two had muscles playing theme songs all over their arms and chests. I watched; the girls knew exactly what they were doing and the guy knew it too; he stayed polite and bought the girls drinks, but he had no idea how to stop these muscle idiots moving in on him.

Then the song "Good Old Time Rock and Roll" started clanging out of the speakers and I had an inspiration. I'd drunk enough to have the nerve to go and ask him for a dance. He came onto the floor with me; he could dance okay, but he kept watching the girls at his table.

"Hey, relax," I told him, "let anything you feel come out of your feet and arms. Let it go, have fun."

Finally he cut loose, and he was an excellent dancer; we danced several times and he felt better each time. The two girls were watching him now; he was starting to lift off, to spin on his toes like Michael Jackson, and I came on to him a little: if you can dance like this, implement it in your life, don't hide it, you're really good. And he came on to me, dancing closer, smiling, and I said, Thanks but I've got a husband and nice family; save it for those girls—lose your bowtie, open a few shirt buttons. He did that, dancing like a scene out of *Flashdance*, and finally he strolled back to his table with his jacket hooked on one finger over his shoulder.

And those girls were crazy about him. I couldn't quite believe what happened, but those girls knew they had all the man they wanted; the muscleboys leaning over from the next table had fallen off their planet.

I could do that with strangers in a bar, but in my family? No, I could neither convince nor charm them into anything. To them I was still the smallest, the wordless brat of the family. Dwa with his quiet reserve and few words kept most of the family members away, but when he wasn't around—working all day or in jail for being impaired—they still harassed me.

Both Mom and Dad had taught us in Butte: it's us against the world. Even when they split up, she made it her life to care and stand beside us; and I in turn shared with her whatever I had—money, food, a place to sleep or stay, anything. But the authority within the family was always hers, authority which began with "Never talk back to your parents!" and was underscored by hitting. As we grew older she didn't necessarily have to hit us; Mom is an incredible speaker. Snake poison you can cut at and suck out, but she can slice your soul apart with words. Especially when she drinks: then she turns mean and may say things that remain forever scarred on your heart. Afterwards, when everyone sobers up, no one in the family will say a word about what she said; we all pretend it never happened. But it happened all right.

No one in the family has ever hit Mom except Dad; and Leon. She denies that Leon has, but Karen says she saw it. I've never even talked back to her. I just take what she does to me, aching all over with a twisted hopelessness grinding me up inside.

Once we had a serious disagreement in my house in Wetaskiwin, and she slapped me with both hands so long her hits finally did not land with full force. I was crying, my nose was running and her slaps began to slip off my wet face. She was so angry she was sweating, and finally she stopped hitting me long enough for me to get her a towel; she wiped her face and hands, and then continued slapping me hard until I was literally rummy. I was falling off my chair, crying, sucking air like I had hiccoughs, just taking it because I wanted her to realize what she was doing, to finally stop and hug me, give me some kind of mother's reaction. But I realized she would not stop until she was either exhausted or had slapped me unconscious.

And then Chantal came out of the children's bedroom. She had awakened and heard us, and I didn't want her to see her grandmother hitting me, so I broke away, "Chantal's coming," and dashed away my tears and led her to the bathroom to pee.

She asked me, "Why is Gramma hitting you, Mommy?" And my tears started again. "Why are you crying?"

I told her we'd talk in the morning, now go back to sleep. So I carried her back in my arms and tucked her under the covers, fumbling, my head ringing with the dreadful burn on my face. Even then I knew that if I could not learn to pity my mother for what she was, for what she lacked, for what her life had made her be, soon I would only be able to hate her.

Next morning Chantal asked me again and I told her, "Go ask Grandma." She did, and Mom came storming up the stairs at me.

"You let your kid talk to her gramma like that, saying I was beating you?"

I said. "She saw you do it."

Mom got her things and left. I sat and cried and cried; then in a few days Leon came back from Montana with his new girl-friend, Laura—Mom had arranged to meet them at my place and take them back to Red Pheasant with her—and Leon and Mom together was too much. When they were in the house I had a panic attack, I could barely breathe; it was like having both a heart attack and a mental breakdown. I couldn't control my thoughts. I locked myself in the bathroom, curled up and crying. Mom took it personally and called me down until Dwa—who was scared for me too and didn't know what to do either—came to the bathroom door, where she was yelling at me to come out. Kathy, who was with her, was shouting at me too, to stop being disrespectful of Mom, so childish.

Dwa said to them, "Please, just let Vonnie alone."

Mom was enraged. But in her order of things, in his house Dwa outranked her, so she could say nothing. She left, and never came back again when Dwa was in the house.

———

At first with Dwa I thought I had my drinking well under control, my priorities in order. If you're fixed in a house, after a while in a small city the people you meet come round, neighbours like Ernie Jensen dropping by, or Erna Brown who's having a rough time and you can help with a few decent meals and a couch to sleep on before she disappears. And she'll show up again, you're not moving anywhere, with a new boyfriend and maybe this one won't beat her up and you say "Hi, there's a cold beer in the fridge." But even if an occasional party developed, for me the children always came first; I bathed them, always watched out, and never drank much until they were safely asleep. My love for them, their love for me, kept me on the ground, no matter how hard my life became. When Dwa was sentenced to six months in prison, I went on welfare; I worked hard getting food and clothing, and I managed.

However, thoughts I couldn't control often made me hate myself more than ever. There were times when I could not haul myself out of despair, no matter how bright the day or how cheerful and happy the children. Who would care for them if I were gone? I felt only I could save them from suffering as I had—as I did—and yet I despaired of myself so much that once I actually thought of killing them and myself—but that was too horrible. Impossible. So I tried to find help: women's shelters, mental health, even church; nothing helped basically.

People praised me for how beautifully I took care of my three children, and Taylor too, Dwa's boy, when he visited, how we worked together in the garden I dug much larger. But neighbours' praise didn't help much. I could not understand it, but I had to be numb—especially after Susan was born and Chantal began school, when I really thought I had my priorities in place—I never drank alone and yet towards the end I was drinking a great deal.

I tried to keep Dwa out of trouble till he was finished parole. One day, when I was heavily pregnant with Susan and Dwa took Chantal with him to work, he got very drunk on the job and she came into the house crying and covered with paint. Somehow it had spilled over her in the van, and Dwa and Jerry followed her into the house, just laughing while she choked, she was sucking up paint. They had run laughing from her when she had turned to them for help. I yelled at Dwa as I tried to clean her up; it was in her eyes and even between her legs. I was completely enraged, and he started to call me down; he jumped up and told me to shut up.

And, pregnant as I was, he gave me a hard push. But I'd had enough of his calling me down, especially in front of Jerry, who had told me he thought I was always covering Dwa's ass, without me he'd be in jail permanently for impaired. I shoved Dwa over and he crashed on the table, but tilted back up with his fists high. So I went into my boxing stance too. I connected once and he fell back, then rushed me low and bull-dogged me in the middle, hard. But Jerry got him away from me, yelling at him that I was pregnant, and then they were fighting and I grabbed the kids and ran. A woman down the street let us into her house. When Dwa arrived she told him to beat it and he did. I ended up at Aunt Rita's, who nicely told me to go home, and when she took me there Dwa acted as if nothing had happened. He said, "I don't remember anything."

But my trust in Dwa crashed. I had trusted him with Chantal's very life and then he stood there, laughing, while she choked on paint. I felt betrayed; my past surfaced in my dreams and thoughts worse than ever. One drunk in a family is manageable, two is disaster. I begged him to move away, let's start fresh somewhere else all by ourselves and the kids—painting is an easily portable business—but he said he wouldn't leave the mortgage on his house. He did not want to hear anything of my past; just forget about it, he'd say.

My cousin Shirley Anne was often in and out of Westaskiwin, sometimes using her mother as a place to stay. But Auntie Josephine was usually on the Hobbema reserves, her in-town apartment locked up, and so my house was handy when Shirley Anne came. Her personal life was an ongoing mess and she became very jealous of me, my house and apparently stable family life. She started to create part of the problem I had with Dwa because she wanted him—and the seeming security he gave me, what she could see of it—for herself. If she complimented me to my face about how nice I was to my kids, that was the back side of knocking me and my mothering when she could get herself alone with him.

Shirley Anne was an old hand at family feuds about men. Though she herself was never as pretty as Aunt Rita, she was a few years younger, and for a while in Butte they competed in a vicious game of screwing as many of each other's men as they could and screwing each other up at the same time. Family gossip of course would follow, and yelling matches and fights; sometimes painful, hair-pulling brawls when they were badly drunk.

In fact, for a time my sister Minnie made that competition a threesome with her cousin and her aunt. She was the youngest by far, physically the strongest, and so aggressive she didn't give a damn. She'd go for the jugular: "Yeah, I did it," she'd tell them, "and this is why. You want to make something out of it? Then let's settle it right here and now." But Shirley Anne and Rita knew Minnie could whip both of them, so they stuck to vicious talk, telling Mom all the ugly stuff Minnie had supposedly done, but Minnie never cared about that. Talk shmalk—she dealt with life by shutting down her feelings: if she wore her shame for the world to see, as she did, then why should she justify her actions to anyone?

I could not, I dared not, shut down like Minnie—though she could have taught me how, and sometimes I longed for it—because I had children to protect as she did not.

After Dwa fought me when I was carrying Susan, he also cheated on me; so I went out and got deliberately drunk. Then I felt so bad, I went home and put a knife on the table between us.

"You filthied my child," I told him. "You slept with another woman and came home and slept with me. You shared my pure unborn baby with the whore you fucked. How dare you! And you just sit there, say nothing. Why don't you just grab that knife and kill us both, as you already have. I hate you."

And finally he said something. "Why do you hate me?"

"You made me love you. I never wanted to love anyone, look where it gets you."

And that was it; he wouldn't talk. There was no way I would have another child with him, so when my Suzie Q was a year old I got my tubes tied. He said nothing, always away working. Escape by working is more like it. Stay away and call it work.

At home I tried to keep the inevitable drinking bouts quiet enough so the kids wouldn't wake up. But when I went out to drink, which I did whenever I could after my last baby was born, all hell happened to me. The echoes of my life on Winnipeg's skid came back strongest then, and I realized that for some reason, despite my little family, I was still trying to be the solitary loner I had been there, to become a person without shame, guilt, or pain—not even to feel anger or hate. To just live for this moment. Be empty.

And I could not understand why I felt that way. When drunk I got into fights, and after a while I wouldn't even bother to wrestle anyone. I'd just go straight at them and take them down. Wetaskiwin, "a place where peace is made"—in that town I fought a lot and never lost a fight, was never gang-piled, never suffered a blackout. I had a camperized van, and if I got too wasted while out by myself, I'd lock myself in and sleep it off. It got so bad my van became known as a party house on wheels, and by the early summer of 1989 people had reason to fear me: "Take-no-shit Johnson."

Except my kids. They kept me alive: inside myself I was an empty space, all I kept intact was "Don't you dare touch my kids."

Dwa and I were killing each other slowly and we knew it. Something was building up, it was inevitable, and in fall 1988 he went north to Yellowknife on a job and just stayed there that winter till spring break-up. Moved in with a girlfriend he found. In Wetaskiwin I had the kids—he talked to them sometimes on the phone—and the house, did odd jobs, went on welfare, and it was dreadful. We couldn't live together, but we couldn't live without each other either.

Other than Dwa, the largest part of my gathering disaster was Leon. I knew what I had to fear from him when he came to visit, but I also felt that with him my children were in particular danger, though I did not quite know how. I remembered that when he was small and started to steal in Butte he began to wet his bed at night, and now he always slept with a light on: how was that dangerous? I could not fathom my fears, but I tried to turn them inside out, as it were expose them by doing the opposite to what

I feared. Once, when Chantal was about five—the summer after Susan was born, 1987—she came running into the kitchen, waving her arms, "Mommy, Mommy," she wanted so badly to tell me something.

But she had gone out to play before she finished cleaning her room, which she knew she must do every day, and I yelled at her.

She stopped, abruptly silent. I wanted to teach her something, I did not want to see her pain because discipline was in order; when I grew up a child had to be hit hard, immediately and quick to make it remember. I never treated my children that way, but as I yelled I watched her too and I saw the shine vanish from her face, her shoulders fall, her eyes so large with excitement grow small. She stood half-turned and silent, and my heart broke.

She was me, the little girl who never spoke. Head down, not daring to look up. What was happening inside her? I understood more about her than she needed to explain. I squatted down to her.

"Chantal, what's the matter?"

She looked at me and I could see tears gather in her eyes.

"You hurt my feelings."

I opened my arms and she came to me. I sat on the kitchen floor and rocked her in my lap and sang Christmas carols to her because I didn't know any lullabies, and we cried. After a while I pulled a chair close and lifted her up onto it and we had a long talk. I told her I often felt the same way when I was little, but no one would take me in their arms; this mom stuff was all new to me; but she had me, maybe she could teach me something. She should tell me every time I hurt her feelings and we would cuddle and talk about it. I never, ever wanted her to feel alone.

We talked, and then she said she wanted to clean up her room. So we did that, and when we were done we had a quiet time together, and after that we drank pop and ate ice cream. I felt so much better; she had helped me more than I helped her.

Little children are the purest gift of the Creator. The Elders say if you put your children first, you will do well.

In 1973 Aunt Rita's baby boy, Edward, was only fifteen months old and living with Mom and us four girls and Perry in an old house at Red Pheasant when Leon got out of Prince Albert Prison and came there. Within a week Leon was raping our cousin Darlene, Aunt Josephine's second daughter. She was fourteen, and staying with us too, rather than with her older sister Shirley Anne and her two kids in Biggar, because Karen was close to her in age and she could go to school with us in Cando. Minnie was barely thirteen, but she was the one who took care of little Edward. She often stayed home from school, fed him, would get up at night and carry him into the living room to change his diaper and rock him to sleep when he woke up beside her crying. The first word Edward ever said was "Minnie!"; he crawled around the whole house calling: "Minnie, Minnie." She was wonderful with children, she's loved them all her life.

Changing little Edward was when Minnie first saw Leon pull Darlene into his bedroom in the middle of the night. Kathy and I heard them too. He just went in and got her out of Karen's room, which was next to ours, but he was so huge by then—seventeen and experienced from any number of jails—we listened and finally covered our heads because who was there to tell, who would protect us from him if we did? Mom was away driving a gravel truck on highway construction near Battleford, so who could dare say a word?

Kathy's baby boy, Billy, had just been born when, in July 1988, all us Johnsons—without Dad, of course—got together for a family reunion on Red Pheasant after Uncle Frank's funeral. Mom and Kathy had persuaded me to come—I was afraid Leon would beat me for having Laura deported back to the United States while he was in prison—but Laura had returned to Canada and Mom volunteered to care for all the kids at Grandpa's house—"Go, go, have a good time"—within sight of the old band hall where Leon lived when he wasn't in custody. All of us Johnson kids were at the hall with our spouses, and Kathy had driven over from Manitoba, with her husband, Dan, even though their little Billy was only two months old. I cooked over an open fire and Grandpa John ate and drank with us, but the next day he wasn't there when we had a keg party. Soon drunken fights broke out, and grew until finally everyone was scraping someone, all the men, except Dan, who had passed out, and all the women. I put Billy in a chesterfield chair on top of the big cutting table, all that was left of the upholstery business, so he wouldn't get hurt or trampled. He lay there rolled up safe in his blankets, and Laura got into a fight with me, then Karen sided with Laura, and Kathy jumped me as well. I didn't bother with them, I concentrated on Laura.

But then big, glowering Leon came in. He came in bulging macho and glared around, feeling so good, filling the doorway, and he saw Laura was back. He considers himself the guard-dog of the family, and the boss: if Mom isn't there he decides what happens and sure as hell nobody fights unless he says, Go ahead.

When I saw him I got away from Laura and my sisters and ran to him to explain. I didn't know then that he'd kicked Laura out of his house, and that she'd just spent two weeks in Saskatoon with Karen, healing up and moaning about how horribly he abused her: I just knew he would certainly beat me to pulp for fighting with her. So I went to the door and got him away from the fighting in the hall. We went for a drive and I tried to explain to him why I had hit Laura. He slammed on the brakes. He has this way of going dark. He said, "You hit her?" I was in terror, and okay, he didn't beat me up then; what he did was worse.

My tears meant nothing. After he did everything he wanted, he laughed. "I always knew you liked it rough," he said. He felt great.

In such a situation, Dwa was no help. He always told me he was not a fighter, he didn't like enemies, and I had seen him take bad beatings without fighting back. I had often loved this non-aggressiveness in him, but now, at the hall, he did not notice what was happening to me. I knew that, among the Johnsons, I was strictly on my own. So, a few months later Leon got to me right in our house in Wetaskiwin, and Dwa wasn't there either, he was away cheating on me with some woman on the night of my birthday. It was Mom herself who drove Leon over, she was delivering furniture to Hobbema and she dropped Leon off with a twelve of beer and some cash—she didn't remember it was my birthday—and left.

I was desperately hoping Dwa would come home soon, but he didn't. The kids were sleepy and I tried to keep them awake while drinking with Leon, but they were so little, they were falling asleep on the couch and I had to carry them to bed in their room off the living room. I kept saying Dwa will be right home, and then, thank God, a woman named Dora showed up; I kept her happy with booze so she wouldn't leave. I should have remembered—for Leon, the more women the better.

After a while I broke away from them, got into the bathroom, and locked the door. Crying. But then I realized my children were in the house, and I went out quick and sat in the doorway between kitchen and living room. That was the only way to get from the bedroom where they still were to the children's room—past me.

Finally Dora came out of the bedroom. She was dressed again; she said something and left the house. Then I heard Leon get off the bed. He came straight into the kitchen and took me back into my bedroom.

I could not make Dwa understand; he simply would not let me tell him about what happened. I tried, but he thought it was all about him and his cheating, especially his cheating on my birthday. Men and their hopeless egos—okay, okay, I cheated, I'm really sorry but it happened—as if what actually happened to *me* didn't matter. The first time Leon violated me in the bush during the family reunion because he would have beaten me helpless and done it anyway. But the second time was even worse: he did it in my own house. Because I had no protection *in my own house*. That's what I wanted Dwa to see: I didn't care about his cheating as much as that *he was not there*. If he had just been present it would not have happened.

And once it happened a second time, with my kids sleeping in the next room, a pattern had been set as far as Leon was concerned: he'd use me as a regular thing whenever an opportunity arose or he could arrange it. I did try to stop him by telling him

I'd tell Mom. Leon said he'd already told her because she'd asked him about me, and so he was already one up on me. I understood then that no one, not even Mom, cared; I was just a daughter who willingly lets her brother fuck her.

Leon came to Wetaskiwin again, very soon, and Dwa was, of course, working and I didn't know what to do, so we drove out to Ma-me-o Beach with Minnie and her shack-up for the kids to swim. I was too terrified to do anything but the usual: drink. By evening he was ready to lock the kids out of the van and take me in there, but I couldn't endure that, I sent them back home with Minnie—Leon didn't care if she knew about us or not. I thought maybe he'd settle for oral sex, and after that I crawled back in the van, away from him while he drove back into town. All I remember is the loud gravel road, and vomiting. But then he parked and came at me again, six foot four and two hundred forty pounds, on top of me till I blacked out.

Even at Grandpa John's funeral in January 1989, he tried to get me—no respect for the dead, not him. He threw me into the bathtub and almost crippled me, but I managed to escape because there were too many people around. And then he got arrested and I was safe from him: he was locked away in prison.

But the problem was I could tell no one. I could not tell Dwa, not the complexity and tangle of what was happening to me. All he could see was, "Okay, I cheated—so you cheat and we're even." He could not understand that I forgave his minor transgressions, I just could not forgive my own.

When we were charged with murder and finally met again, flanked by cops and chained, in the lobby of the Wetaskiwin Courthouse, Dwa told me what he had told me before, "Vonnie, I thought I could just love your pain away."

———

Even as our world was grinding down into disaster, he taught me how to cry. Not just alone and in pain but for a certain kind of release. That last summer became one horrible blur of drinking, fighting, and sex that filled my wasted days and nights. I'd stumble home and Dwa wouldn't question me. "You make me love you," I'd yell at him, and he'd mutter, half-asleep, "Hey, isn't that good?" and all I could answer was "No. No. I'm not supposed to love anyone but my kids."

He was that special, he taught me it was okay to cry and he'd pull me tight and tell me, "'Let it go, let it go.'"

I was always worried I'd go completely insane, the big guys in white would come and tie me into their long-sleeved jacket and haul me down the highway to Ponoka. Once I started to scream; a deep gutteral scream; it tore out of me endlessly and it overwhelmed Dwa—he fell back looking so terrified I forced myself to stop. I didn't dare let go that deeply again. I just tried to shut down: let guys use me while thinking I used them more, a kind of sexless, feelingless, drunken fuck that seemed necessary to perform even when neither of us felt anything, having someone else involved in a strange hope that always failed to manifest itself; instead, just do it and get away fast.

But then everything changed because a relative by marriage raped me. Again in my house, again with Dwa gone—in my basement where I'd gone to get away, and fell asleep. I screamed the bastard out of the house, and I felt so vile and dirty I ran a shower—but I couldn't handle another secret. I drove to the town RCMP and reported I'd been raped. The police took me to the hospital, and the doctor who examined me was the same one who delivered my Suzie Q. I was so horribly ashamed, I could barely cry. I'd washed and that was bad for evidence, and I just could not tell him I'd been anally raped. I was hoping he'd find the bruise I felt inside my vagina, against my pelvis, but he only found traces of possible evidence in my underwear. Not enough, the police said, to get a conviction. The best they could do was take my statement, to place in my relative's file.

Brutalizing me in my home wasn't enough for this swine; a few days later he had to brag about it to Dwa in the Riggers Bar. Dwa came home furious.

"It wasn't sex," I cried, "it was rape! I was drunk and asleep and I woke up screaming. He had something stuck in my vagina and doing anal rape!"

Dwa yelled, "You never felt that? To wake up?"

"The pain woke me up!'

"Was his cock so small you didn't feel that to wake up?"

"I woke up! And yeah, his cock's small, if you want to know, it's that small."

"And you think I'm a wimp because I don't beat him up?"

"You don't have to, I can beat him up myself! But you're never here when I need you."

"And you think I'm a wimp."

"Okay! If you think you're a wimp, maybe you are. You just think about yourself, you're mad because some asshole tells you, 'I fucked your wife,' and you don't care how hurt I was, you just want to know his size. Well, fuck you! I'm never telling you anything again!"

We could not talk about the rape or any other problem I had. My nightmares became more grotesque, beyond anything either of us could deal with, especially in August when Dad sent me the newspaper about the crooked Butte cops; I remembered them all, every one. That last summer, whenever Dwa was home he'd go off and drink or toke with his buddies and just come back to the house to crash. I began to see anger building in him and I was afraid. I hid on him when he came into the house, knocking things around, but he found me. He seemed to be coming after me in a rage and I was so scared I jumped up and knocked him across the room.

"Bastard, you'd beat up your wife, but not the guy who spreads lies about her!"

He lay a minute, surprised; if I'd done that to Leon, no matter how drunk, my head would already have been smashed against the wall. But Dwa just slowly got up. "You think I'm an asshole, right?"

And he pulled his penis out of his pants. "It's all because of this, eh? A dirty prick."

And he began to slap his penis. "You want to hurt a man, hurt me. This is the way to hit me, see, like this, like this!"

He was punching himself out, pounding at himself, he really did want to help me so much—and he wanted to know nothing.

All I could do was hug him, stop him. We were hurting each other so badly: if he couldn't handle a rape, how could I tell him anything about Leon or my nightmares? I remained silent, and I held that against him. He would take me in his arms when the nightmares hit and flung me around the bed; he'd wake me by holding me until my shuddering stopped and I knew where I was and could say whatever to reassure him, "I'm okay now . . . I'm okay."

He couldn't handle anything I actually was, not really. Except the bit of me that was a mother and working as hard as he, and easy, simple sex in bed and drink a bit, steady, don't you overdo it like me, make sure there's always enough money around to keep us going. And I tried. I had tried as hard as I could at the beginning to be the perfect mother, lover, wife, housekeeper, and business partner.

But my past was too much for us both. And I knew the nightmares were not that, nor were they dreams. They were memories; there were more of them alive in my head when I was awake.

Now when my relatives arrived, Dwa turned completely quiet. Barely a word, and soon none of them came unless he wasn't home.

All except Shirley Anne, who wanted him for herself. He didn't even like her. "Why don't you kick her out?" he asked me. Some time before our arrest she tried to get him to sleep with her and he laughed her off. When I asked her about it, she denied it. But Dwa told me, she was sitting behind me, shaking her head at him with her finger on her mouth so bloody-red with the lipstick she always keeps fresh. Dwa didn't care about her signals. He told me right in front of her.

A few minutes before I had taken a colour picture of her trying to flirt with him. There he is, his grey duck-billed cap and long, flared nose as he looks out of his van window at her open mouth talking, talking, looking like such a wonderful person with her brown-red hair neatly curled, and sweating a little. Behind Dwa on the seat, in the shadow of the van, stand our blond James and baby Suzie Q; her hands up around her mouth and little bare belly curved over her shorts. They're watching Shirley Anne too. They were usually frightened of her and would run to me when she tried to pick them up. But they were fine at that moment, Dwa was between her and them.

Chantal was three when James was born in December 1985, and six months later Grandma Flora Bear died. Susan was born February 1987, and Grandpa John Bear died in January 1989. The deaths of my grandparents, especially Grandma's, were far more significant to me and my children than I then recognized. I was falling apart—for reasons deep beyond my own understanding.

9

Three Days in September 1989

Before my arrest, a lot of shit happened to me. If I had not been put in prison for this charge, I would most likely [have] been in [prison at] some point thereafter, if I never got helped. Or dead by suicide. My love for my kids kept me barely touching ground when I was just hanging onto existence and reality [. . .]. I felt evil, nasty, and dirty and lost [. . .]. I gave up trying to feel, except with my babies, I took to being so overly protective. Yet I still drank, I knew I was losing ground fast [. . .]. Never in my whole life [have] I been to such a low level, with no will, striving, dreams, or hope [. . .]. It truly was the most dead time in my life.

– Yvonne, *Journal* 13, 11 November 1994

F OR YVONNE, a house was a place to care for, to try to make beautiful for living. When, in August 1996, I park my car and again study the house where she once lived on the southeast corner of 43rd Avenue and 53A Street, Wetaskiwin, I see the trees, shrubs, the rows of raspberries she planted; but they are all untended, wildly overgrown in ragged grass gone to seed and volunteer saplings; pickets broken, missing in the fence; grey plaster on the walls fallen out in blotches; at one corner of the house a wooden barrel cut in half is filled with black rainwater. The Realty World FOR SALE sign appears to have been leaning there for several seasons.

It was different in 1989. Not even the sterility of police photographs can hide the particular care with which Yvonne decorated her house. When they were taken on Saturday, 16 September, the long, narrow-leafed plants she had hung in planters in her living room were still there, and pictures were neatly arranged on the wall; when the Wayside Inn replaced its dance floor, she had salvaged enough of the best parquet squares for her and Dwa to cover the living-room and children's bedroom floors with the very surface they had danced on the night they first met. Outside she planted shrubs along the sidewalk and expanded the vegetable garden around the garage, lined the walks with flowers.

"I felt I was rich," she tells me; "a home, a husband, healthy children. No matter how terrible my problems seemed to me, I tried to share that."

Her three children, aged seven, three, and two, played with everyone, and one day Dwa laughed as he counted fourteen little kids either running through the house or playing in the yard. One of the reasons they loved to play there was Yvonne's games: she was strict, she had them clean up the messes they left, but often she made games out of the cleaning by hiding dimes or nickels around the room they were to tidy, or in the vines or roots of vegetables they were to bring in. Any money they found working was theirs to keep. She maintained her house and yard, watched them carefully; she never left her door unlocked when she was gone, never left her children unsupervised. And it made her happy, it rested her, she tells me, to see children happily at play.

And what do you do when your wider family—all of whom certainly don't make you happy—arrive at your door? You open it.

On Tuesday, 12 September, early afternoon, her cousin Shirley Anne phoned. Yvonne was surprised: the last she'd heard of her, she was on the wagon and living near Toronto with her baby and nice Christian husband; now she was alone in Wetaskiwin and feeling really sick. The reason was obvious in Shirley Anne's slurred voice, and Yvonne wouldn't invite her over, but admitted she might have some "cure" in her house. In ten minutes there was Shirley Anne on the porch, alone, peering through the screened window in the door with nothing more than a shoulder purse; looking pitiful.

"O Yvonne," she sighed into her beer, sitting at the kitchen table, "you have such a wonderful place! I can just . . . relax."

By the look of her, Yvonne was certain Shirley Anne had been partying hard for a few days, but now, with an ear available and a beer in hand, she could spin out the version that she preferred: her heartless daughters had kicked her out when she got to Saskatoon, they were so cruel, right on the street, and she had to pawn her wedding ring to get money for a bus ticket to Wetaskiwin, and now her mother wasn't in town and she didn't know where she was, but at least she'd got little Sparky away from her cheating, two-timing husband and if she could just . . .

"What about Sparky?" Yvonne asked. "Where is she?"

"Oh, I left her at Darlene's, in Thunder Bay. She wanted to take her so . . ."

Oh sure, Yvonne was thinking. Your sister really wants to take care of that poor little kid.

Yvonne: Sparky is the same age as my baby Suzie Q. A year ago Shirley Anne came to Wetaskiwin too, but that time she had little Sparky with her. I was sitting on the living-room floor, breast-feeding my baby, and Sparky lay flat on the cork kitchen floor, whimpering.

"She's hungry," I said to Shirley Anne. "There's milk in the fridge; you can make her a bottle."

But Shirley Anne was sucking beer. "She ain't hungry," she said, "she just does that."

Baby ran everywhere, all day, but at eighteen months little Sparky could barely raise her large head. I knew her skull had been split once—family rumour insisted it was an accidental fall—but now she appeared healed and okay. She lay wherever she was placed, the fluffy hair on the back of her head worn off into a large bald circle; lying like a six-month-old. Suzie was in my arms, nursing, and I felt my heart stir; I wanted to give Sparky my other breast.

"She ain't hungry," Shirley Anne repeated. "She always cries for nothing; she just lays there, never even tries to help herself."

I went to the fridge holding Baby and made up a bottle with one hand. "Here. Feed her."

Shirley Anne stuck the bottle down and Sparky reached for it eagerly. But she had no strength to hold it: the bottle fell aside when Shirley Anne let go; the nipple pulled out of her mouth and she began to wail.

"See," Shirley Anne said, "too lazy to even hold it."

Baby was finished; I set her down to run off and picked up Sparky and the bottle. The little girl drank the entire bottle, her thin, almost muscle-less body gulping, it seemed, as if in desperation. I laid her down on the table when she finished the bottle; I cuddled her gently in my hands. Shirley Anne came to the fridge, looking for another beer.

"Don't touch her," she said. "She doesn't like to be touched."

I stood up, grabbed Shirley Anne in both hands, and shoved her against the fridge so hard the door slammed.

"Don't you ever—ever!"—I could barely control my voice—
"be mean to a child in this house. And right now you're out of
here, I'm driving you back to your mom's. Move!"

I shoved her towards the door, slopping beer and all; at that
moment I hated her. I picked up Sparky—Shirley Anne was
walking off the porch without her — and took her into the van
and called for the kids. A small flood of them came running
from the park across the corner of the street, always eager for a
ride. Shirley Anne climbed into the front seat, nursing her beer;
she made no gesture to hold Sparky. I belted the baby into the
child's seat bolted onto the floor.

I drove past a park where children were shouting, running,
tumbling each other, and I couldn't stand it. I stopped, unstrapped Sparky, and got out.

"C'mon," I said to my kids scrambling out, "there's swings.
Let's play."

I carried Sparky after them, running into the park; I propped
her in a small tire swing and pushed it a little. She smiled,
then she giggled, and soon she was laughing; such a large,
beautiful laugh I'd never heard from a child before. It was
marvellous.

Shirley Anne sat in the van. Once she started it, as if she
intended to take off, but I wouldn't react so she began to lean
on the horn, honking. Finally, she shut it down, got out, and
walked across the street to where we were playing. She stood
there, finishing her beer, then tossed the bottle among the noisy
kids. There was a small cry from somewhere but that was all: the
children were playing and Sparky was swinging gently, in small
circles.

———

On 12 September, a quiet Tuesday afternoon in small city Alberta, the
shrubs and poplar leaves along the straight streets are turning gold in
the sunlight. The preschool children were in the yard outside, water
splashing, glass clinking: they were cleaning what they'd collected in

their bottle drive around town. Their haul was spread all over the grass, and Yvonne's acquaintance Ernie Jensen—he worked only off and on, handyman stuff—came by, sniffing out a cure for what ailed him. Dwa had taken Chantal to Edmonton for a doctor's appointment, but soon the older neighbourhood children would come from school and then the work would go really fast.

Shirley Anne was still talking, but with Ernie Jensen there Yvonne knew she could leave for a bit, make a trip to the pawnshop to be helpful and get him a cure—and herself a starter. She could see various straps peeking out from under Shirley Anne's loose red-knit sweater; it looked as if she was wearing a large men's undershirt and what seemed to be a body girdle—silly woman, at thirty-nine or forty, and all those tons of beer, to still think she could cinch her belly in.

And play sexy games with people. Just looking at Shirley Anne reminded Yvonne of how the women in her family competed for each other's men, and it made her sick. They didn't do it even for the sex; it was just to gain bragging rights on each other. Yvonne could feel Shirley Anne's rambling talk "playing with her buttons"; it bothered her, it twisted her inside.

Shirley Anne said, with her usual edge, "You're thin and boney, but I'm sure you keep Dwa warm on those cold nights. How much are you, one twenty, five ten?"

"He's never complained," Yvonne answered back, and then couldn't resist. "Who knows what shape I'll be in—when I'm old."

"You're always lucky," Shirley Anne said snidely, "tall and slim, like your Dad, nothing like the Bear family." She took another long swallow. "I've got a cheque here"—she was digging in her purse. "If you help me cash it, I'll take the bus to Edmonton for a few days."

She handed the slip to Yvonne; only fifty dollars, but it wasn't made out to Shirley Anne—Yvonne had been stuck too often for countersigning NSF personal cheques, with the fee added.

"My bank won't touch this. But I'll lend you twenty, let's go."

But before they could get the kids together and leave—the bus depot was only four blocks away—Erna Brown was at the door; with her was a big, heavy-set guy in his mid-thirties. It took a moment for Yvonne to recognize him: Charles "Chuck" Skwarok.

Then she remembered Chuck was the man she had once given a lift home from the liquor store. Apparently he was now Erna's friend — good, she needed all the friendship she could get. Yvonne had met her a few weeks before through another woman, and when she persuaded her out of her desperate shyness, she heard a long, sad story. Erna needed to drink, she couldn't live without it, and had often been violated while passed out. She could barely walk; her leg was crippled from once trying to escape abuse by jumping out of a car going sixty miles an hour. Now the family she was staying with was ripping off her disability cheques; Yvonne offered her her house address to receive mail, and Erna slept a few nights on her living-room couch, safe, where no man could get at her. But soon she went away, and here she was, back, with maybe a decent man, not too badly drunk yet though it was already mid-afternoon. Maybe she'd have a bit of luck.

As Yvonne tells me four years later in the Kingston Prison for Women: "I had no idea the ultimate disaster of my sinking life had walked in."

She and I sit together in the windowless counselling room at P4W and often she remembers aloud, returns to the events of those three days in September 1989. But there is always a certain point she cannot pass — not necessarily the same each time — a point where she will say, "This is too hard. . . . I can't talk about this."

Sometimes when Yvonne says this she is huddled back in the upholstered chair, her arms hugging her knees tight against her body. And all I can respond is, "Okay . . . okay . . . say what you can."

Shirley Anne was "all over Chuck, bingo, just like that," batting her eyes, giggling, flaunting her "cock-teaser" tone right in front of Erna, who had limped in to ask if a cheque had arrived yet. She looked deeply depressed even before she knew none had. And Chuck said almost nothing; he simply ignored Shirley Anne's looniness.

Outside Ernie Jensen's young friend Brandy had come to help the kids load their bottles into a van; Brandy was the ex-boyfriend of one of Shirley Anne's daughters, and now her behaviour became even more drunkenly bizarre. She said that she'd once had an orgy with those two guys out there, what a pa-arty! When Brandy came in to say hello, she snuggled up to him and tugged at his belt buckle and the zipper on his pants, trying to persuade him—"C'mon, pull it out." But he avoided her, and Chuck simply looked more disgusted. He gestured to Erna and said he'd come back later when the men were around, and they all disappeared one after the other.

"There's still time for the bus," Yvonne remembered. She dug into her jeans and gave Shirley Anne a twenty-dollar bill with profound relief. "It won't have left yet."

She had the kids in the van and they were rolling for the bus depot when the motor started sputtering. Out of gas. Wetaskiwin Motors was right there, so she wheeled in, but she couldn't coast far enough; everyone jumped out and pushed, Yvonne steering through the open window and little James kneeling on the driver's seat and steering, too, for all he was worth. The attendant saw them and came to help, and together they got it to a pump.

"I guess we missed the bus," Shirley Anne said.

Yeah, Yvonne thought, my usual dumb luck.

She drove to the grocery store, bought food, and then stopped at the liquor store for a few twelves of beer and headed back. She cooked supper for the kids, who were running in and out as freely as they always did. A bit later Ernie Jensen was there again, and they sat in the living room, having beers. Immediately Shirley Anne began her usual games with him.

Yvonne had known Ernest Egon Jensen for less than a year, and considered him quiet and decent; later, on the trial transcript, she wrote in a note about him: "He is a good gentleman, and a good heart." He was a smallish man in his early thirties, separated from his wife and son, his parents dead, his younger brother in jail somewhere, and he himself had been badly burned in a car accident to the point of being visibly scarred and crippled. He'd been at the house a few times before to sit, talk, have a beer, and when Yvonne bought a second-hand stove, he hooked it up properly for her, despite his mutilated hands.

Ernie took Shirley Anne's games in good humour; Yvonne could see he might be interested in her.

"His life must have been lonely enough. He was no prize catch," Yvonne told me in P4W. "I had no idea of his personality besides how quiet and decent he was to me. A few times he complimented me on how well I treated my kids. He knew enough about that, he said, he'd been in plenty of foster homes."

Yvonne had never seen Ernie in a group of men, how manic he could become when surrounded by what he experienced as the heavy demands of masculinity. Nor did she know he had a long history of violence, or that he had been in prison several times for assault and being impaired.

———

Ernie Jensen: [from a "cell shot" taped by RCMP undercover constable Harvey Jones in the cell with Jensen and Dwayne Wenger in Wetaskiwin, Alberta, on Monday, 18 September 1989]:

I was seventeen years old and this guy was beating the fuck out of me so I fought back, and give it to him and I got my finger in his eye, that hurts, eh, so I thought, you cocksucker, I'll show you. I got my finger right in there and fucken got him to his knees.

Then I says, "I want you to say you're sorry."

"I'm sorry, Ernie! I'm sorry!"

"I want you to say 'I'm sorry, Mr. Jensen.'"

"I'm sorry, Mr. Jensen!"

Then these two cops smashed his head against the garage wall . . . [me] against the drunk-tank door, just fucken wham! and knocked me right out. Then they took me to court for that, they wouldn't give me a lawyer, there was only that court reporter, the Crown, the cops, the three cops testifying that I was trying to escape [from jail] and I fought. And the judge give me an extra year for that. [And later they bring me] back, and whoever's the boss he says, "I'm sorry," he apologizes. And I say, "Yeah, lot of good that does me, put me in fucken jail for a year, you cocksuckers."

[That first time] they said, "You either leave town or we're gonna put you in jail." I said, "Where the fuck am I gonna go, I live with my parents." I says, "No fucken clue where to go." So they put me in jail and she [my mother] died while I was in there, it just ripped her [. . .].

And then, what the fuck, I was on either the last week of my parole or just finished it, then I caught her [my old lady] in bed with this guy. Another three years.

———

A warm evening, 12 September. Dwa sat in his white shorts in the living-room sofa chair with a beer. Chantal's visit to the doctor had been okay, and all the kids were bathed and asleep on their mattresses in their room off the living room. Shirley Anne sat beside Ernie on the couch, talking, but now talking only to Dwa.

She had often seen him playing dolls with the little girls, sitting on the floor—no Native man they knew would do that—and so Shirley Anne tried to play small with the children too and hug them when he was around as if she truly loved them, to impress him with her tender motherliness. But all she managed was to scare them and annoy him. When he saw her there when he returned from Edmonton, he'd asked Yvonne in an undertone: "Why do you even open the door?"

He wouldn't, of course, say anything to Shirley Anne himself; he had no confrontational bone in his body, but this late in the evening he could avoid her clumsy, drunken attempts at sexy play now that the children were asleep.

"I'm bushed, I'm hitting the sack."

And Yvonne, exhausted and wiped on beer, followed his cue fast, her mind strung out by too much Shirley Anne drone all day. She said they could both stay for the night, she had lots of sheets, she'd just make a bed for Shirley Anne on the couch and one for Ernie on a foamy on the floor, no problem at all.

No sooner were she and Dwa in bed in their room beside the bathroom in the short hall off the kitchen than they heard whispering from the living room. They nudged each other, listened; soon the noises, the sliding sheets, the mutterings were obvious enough. Yvonne and Dwa laughed a little together and Dwa said, "Hey, maybe Ernie's getting some tonight," and Yvonne turned to him and he put his heavy arm around her and fell asleep. He always smelled the same: paint, beer, an irrefutable base of rye whisky; a bottle of Southern Comfort to sip steadily, just a bit, but steadily, keeping the world nicely balanced, mostly level. His wide body, muscles thick as trees.

Yvonne slept.

———

Wednesday, 13 September 1989. Yvonne lay in bed, listening. Dwa was out so late most evenings that morning had become his time with the children: Chantal getting ready for school, and then James too, were playing their game of finding animal shapes in the pancake batter Dwa ladled into the pan. But someone else was in the kitchen too, bustling around—Shirley Anne. Up early to impress Dwa. Or maybe she'd fallen asleep with Ernie on the floor and didn't want Dwa to find her. Who cared?

Shirley Anne was cleaning, which was the Native way of saying thank you for hospitality, though she'd never done it before. This was for Dwa's benefit, of course. And she was talking.

"Does Vonnie always just lie in bed and make you make the kids' breakfast?"

But Dwa said nothing. He could block anyone with silence; especially Shirley Anne. Dwa came into the bedroom, kissed Yvonne, and left. Then she got up.

In the kitchen she thanked Shirley Anne for cleaning. Dwa came back in, asked Yvonne to pick up a cheque owed him for painting, and then deliberately peered into the living room; past him Yvonne could see the burn suit Ernie wore lying crumpled on the floor. Ernie himself wasn't on the foamy, he was asleep on the couch.

Dwa grinned, going out again. "I wonder who wiped out Ernie."

Shirley Anne stood there, nonplussed, going red. She was stuttering something about Ernie being so drunk he must have taken his clothes off, but Dwa was gone and quickly Yvonne asked her, since she hadn't used the twenty dollars yesterday, maybe she wanted to catch the noon bus to Edmonton today. And in a minute Shirley Anne was gone.

James and Suzie trundled out into the yard to play, but before Yvonne could eat breakfast Ernie appeared, heading for the bathroom. He came out and found a beer in the fridge.

"So," Yvonne said, deadpan, "you got some last night, huh?"

Ernie's smile was relieved, and big, "If you're anything like your cousin, whoa!" And he elaborated in detail how she'd pulled him up for a second time. Yvonne was astonished at his frankness, and then realized it was pride: maybe he was no handsome man, but he'd had his fun.

He turned back into the living room—maybe get a bit more sleep—and amazingly, Yvonne found she actually had the house to herself. Five minutes to savour that, then Shirley Anne was at the door again, opening it. She carried her purse and two gallon jugs of Royal White Wine—the wino's special—and no bus ticket to anywhere.

The two small children were digging in the garden, grubbing out vegetables; when Chantal came home after school she would help them do the job properly. Shirley Anne sat drinking wine, denying she had slept with Ernie—no, she was a married woman, she'd never do that—and at the same time saying that all night she had dreamed Yvonne's beautiful house was a Taj Mahal and Ernie a sheik—she's got her "knights in shining armour" mixed up, Yvonne thought, but it's her game, let her run it—and then elaborating again on how she had not, she had never, ever, even tried to sleep with Dwa. Yvonne knew Shirley Anne would have been happier if she had accused her of sleeping with Dwa than Yvonne knowing, as she did, that he had turned her down.

Minute by inevitable minute, 13 September moved on.

Thursday, 14 September 1989. The last day Yvonne Johnson would be free of the iron of criminal law. For literally years, as she wrote to me, "I only ran it over in the silence of my mind."

By the time she dared to speak her memories of that day, could try to order the facts of action and thought and impression and image into words, the weight of it filled notebooks, tapes, videos, pages upon pages of comments on the trial and appeal records.

I have studied them, at length, and researched more—including, of course, the trial records—and to create a reasonable account of this day I can only draw out the absolutely necessary strands of details, sketch what seem to be the most crucial and inevitable scenes. What is clear to us both is that, until the very last minutes before midnight, nothing criminal at all need ever have happened.

The first and most fundamental of the inevitabilities of that day was Shirley Anne in Yvonne's house. Drinking, talking. She had claimed to have a computer course to register for in Edmonton, but she stayed, immovable.

The second inevitability was Chuck Skwarok. He arrived at Yvonne's house at two o'clock in his Hornet hatchback, alone. He said Erna had signed herself into the hospital; she had almost died from a grand-mal seizure while drinking.

Yvonne was deeply disturbed. What had happened? Why? But Chuck explained nothing, just "She's not doing too good," and stood there as if expecting her to do something. The kids were hauling vegetables into the house, running water over them in the sink, and Yvonne had to supervise things. So Shirley Anne hauled Chuck into the living room with a beer.

Outside, the gentleness of a September day, trees gold and shedding. Yvonne could see children jumping in the leaves in the park across the street; her littlest ones were there and her heart gave a jolt, and suddenly she ran, she had to for ever be on watch for them every minute, every second, like a deer or caribou mother. The television news had been full of warnings about a man hanging around schools, of children disappearing for a few hours and then showing up again in the same place, and some talked about a man who had picked them up, fondled them while he played with himself, though apparently not more than that yet — she ran, perhaps someone was behind the school bushes watching John, or her blonde Baby jump and land in the leaves, her chubby legs waving out of her training panties and the frill of the embroidered dress she wanted to wear today — no, no man seemed to be watching: five children playing under the spruce and poplars, their small bodies unmolested.

James was throwing leaves. . . . Baby was not there.

If only a stare would stay frozen in the air.

Baby! Ernie was in the garage, helping Yvonne out again, this time with the freezer, wiring laid bare, but it would soon — no, he hadn't seen Suzie. Yvonne was tearing through the garden, into the house, every wild glance, nothing! But there was her baby. Safe in the living room, with Shirley Anne. And Chuck.

The little girl stood rigid with her arms stiff, pushing herself away from Shirley Anne's attempts to pull her close—but her pretty dress was bunched up, her panties down around her ankles. Shirley Anne and Chuck were looking at her.

"Baby!" Yvonne said sharply. "Baby, what is it?"

Shirley Anne, startled, snatched the panties up over Baby's bottom. Yvonne could not even look at the adults; she just led the little girl into the kitchen. "What is it?" Trying to control her voice.

And to her astonishment, Baby pulled down her panties again and pointed to the raspberry birthmark high on her leg. Yvonne turned back into the living room.

"What's going on?" she demanded.

Shirley Anne said, "Nothing. I was just showing Chuck her birthmark."

Chuck shrugged; perhaps he was mildly embarrassed, but Yvonne couldn't really look at him. "Don't you ever do that again," she said to her cousin and turned quickly back to the kitchen and settled her child's clothes properly on her little body.

"No, no," she spoke carefully, trying to sound ordinary, "remember what we talked about: the only time you pull them down is to go pee-pee, only when you're with me, or alone. Never with other people—not even James—remember? If you want to show your birthmark"—she pushed one side of the panties up a bit higher—"see, then they can see, okay?"

The telephone rang; it was Erna at the hospital. Sounding pretty bad. Had her cheque come in? No. Could Yvonne bring her some cigarettes? Sure.

Baby had run out with a swarm of vegetable diggers, and Chuck was coming out of the living room. Looking angry.

"That was Erna," Yvonne said to him. And she felt a chill through her: had she seen him—she was looking so hard at Baby, but out of the corner of her eye—had she seen him leering at her baby's naked bottom?

"Erna admitted she's a drunk," Chuck muttered. "She's got no brains, and admits it. I can respect that about her. She's trying to help herself anyways."

Dwa had the van, so Chuck drove Yvonne to a house Dwa had painted to pick up a cheque for his work, over $400. The IGA knew her well, and she cashed the cheque there when she bought groceries for supper and cigarettes, then they went to the liquor store and she bought a bottle of Southern Comfort as a special for Dwa, and more beer. In Erna's room in the new red-brick hospital off Northmount Drive, she opened the whisky and poured some into a Tupperware container, but Erna shook her head, no, she could only have cigarettes. They talked a bit, then Chuck drove Yvonne back through downtown, between the old false-front and brick businesses and the line of peaked grain elevators along the railroad track, back to her little house among the trees on the corner of the dead-end across from the park and Parkdale School.

"I told you," Chuck said suddenly, "I don't like kids. And women are bitches, good for nothing but a fuck—but you're different. I respect you. You have a mind, you're not just a cunt."

Chuck bothered Yvonne. How could he not, saying such gross things? And from his tone and repetition really meaning them. Yet to her he was courteous, even opening the car door for her, which no one ever did.

When she had first seen him standing outside the liquor store with two bags of heavy bottles, and she had remembered the teaching: if you see someone in need, help them, for some day you too will need help.

So she offered him a ride then and he gladly accepted. He tried to climb into the bucket seat of her Dodge van, but her Baby was already sitting there, so he had to pick her up to sit down. And then he held her far away from him, as if she might contaminate him. She asked him what was the matter.

"I don't like kids," Chuck said.

"Why not?"

"I like them better if they're someone else's," he said. Which she found odd: her Baby was "someone else's." "Me and kids just clash."

He passed the little girl over to Yvonne, and she sat on her lap, helping her drive.

Yvonne dropped Chuck in front of a bungalow; she didn't even notice the address.

"That was my only meeting before with him," Yvonne wrote later.

But now, Erna had walked into her house with him, and the same night had to commit herself to the hospital.

It appears to me, now, that Chuck was much better acquainted with Yvonne's house than she realized. It was not until four months later, at the preliminary inquiry into Chuck Skwarok's death, that Yvonne heard that late the night before, 13 September—or the fourteenth, as perhaps it was already past midnight—Chuck and his cousin Lewis Bonham had driven around looking for a party, any party. Bonham testified that Chuck had been certain that there'd be one at Yvonne's, but when they got there the house was dark. Chuck stopped anyway, got out, and went up to try the porch door. It was open—Yvonne says that's impossible, they were at home, and at night she always locked the door—but Chuck didn't go in. Instead, Bonham testified, he came back down the porch steps, stopped, looked around, and then opened his pants and pissed against the spruce tree.

Yvonne knew nothing of this when Chuck took her home from visiting Erna at the hospital. She simply thanked him as she got out; he grunted, said again he'd come by later "when the men were home," and then his old hatchback grumbled away.

Shirley Anne was watching them, sitting on the porch steps. She looked angry. And coming up the walk with her shopping bags, Yvonne was suddenly, startlingly, aware of silence.

"Where are the kids?"

Shirley Anne took her own sweet time answering, and Yvonne strode up to her.

"Hey? Where?"

"I sent all them brats packing, and yours," she shrugged her shoulders, "are in the basement."

"What!"

"I locked them in there to protect them."

"Protect them from what?"

"From your 'friend' Chuck Skwarok! I thought he might sneak back here and kidnap one of them."

Yvonne exploded: "What are you talking about? I barely know him, he just drove me to see Erna."

"You oughta know him better. He could have kicked you out anyway, easy. What could you do, big bugger like that?"

"What do you know?" Yvonne was bent towards her, suddenly terrified.

Shirley Anne's lips twitched in that self-satisfied, catty expression she had when she was certain of her knowledge and of another's fear.

"He told me," Shirley Anne said.

"Told you what!"

"He told me this when all the kids were running around, back and forth," Shirley Anne declared, drawing it out. "He was looking at them kinda funny; he said they had nice buns, and then, just out of the blue, he told me, 'My wife charged me for molesting my little girl.' And he was looking at one of the kids kinda funny when he says this, and I says, 'Well, did you?' And he told me the whole thing."

Yvonne's breath caught in her throat, her mind racing . . . but it was too much, she couldn't believe Shirley Anne, her smug, fat face.

"Yeah, right." She picked up her groceries. "A strange guy who doesn't even know you is going to spill his guts to you about molesting his own kid—yeah, right."

"Yeah, really, he did!"

Yvonne just walked into the house.

Yvonne recognizes now, whenever she talks and writes to me about that day, that what she did after Shirley Anne's statement makes little logical sense. She tried to hide it from her cousin, but she was shocked beyond belief: the man she had been driving around with, who had sat in her house, watching her children, had actually once held—no. She couldn't face that, she wanted to avoid it, she had to feel better. So she got busy.

She brought the kids up out of the basement, where they'd been playing on the slide she'd built them for winter days. They promised not to leave the yard. She wanted desperately to feel better, so she got out the Tupperware container of whisky Erna wouldn't accept and sat at the kitchen table. The more she drank, the easier she felt and the less she cared about her cousin's yapping.

But Shirley Anne kept picking, picking at any possible fear, reminding her that Chuck had said he'd be over later, "when the men were home."

"So if he's after kids," Yvonne countered, logically enough, "why does he want the boys to be here?"

Once Baby ran in and showed Yvonne her raspberry, just the way Yvonne had told her too—that's right, good girl!—and Shirley Anne rolled right on:

"Just imagine," she said, "your little blonde Baby in diapers, her little finger curling around his finger as he leads her to the bedroom, she's so trusting, you've protected her so good, he's laying her on the bed, he slips her diapers down, and then he's squatting down, smiling, spreading her little legs, wide, his big fingers spreading her little lips open like——"

"O shut up," Yvonne interrupted harshly, not daring to reveal her deep reaction. She had to be big and tough; no stupid cousin would play with her mind. "Lay off that shit."

With every swallow of smooth Southern Comfort, the power of her foreboding dulled. Shirley Anne was playing her; the whole basis of a child molester's life is secrecy; if he really was one he'd never admit it. Chuck was big, White, handsome, no mousy beat-up Ernie—Shirley Anne was trying to use Baby to get him, and he just left her sitting while he drove off to see poor Erna. Yvonne hated herself for thinking this; she detested herself even as she detested Shirley Anne for sitting there, soused, making her think it.

Chantal appeared with carrots, Baby and James trudging behind. They wanted supper. Yvonne had bought meat and they had all that good garden stuff. And Ernie was still working on the freezer in the garage; he'd be hungry too. Cook, get up and cook.

When Ernie came in, Shirley Anne had someone else to tell. He got very disturbed too—that goof said that?—and Yvonne could see Shirley Anne loved it. She knew something dirty, she was the centre of attention.

"Yeah, and when he comes," Shirley Anne said, "I'll tell him right to his face in front of you guys, what he told me. I'm not lying."

———

Shirley Anne Salmon: [from the statement given by "Remanded Prisoner—Charged Murder" to RCMP at the Red Deer, Alberta, Remand Centre on 30 August 1990. The two-page text is signed by Salmon and witnessed by "J.R. Bradley, Cpl."]:

[Bradley]: Shirley, what you tell me, must be the truth and whatever you say, will not be used against you in any criminal, judicial proceedings. Do you understand this?

[Salmon]: Yes [. . .]. I was so devastated over the loss of my husband. I came to Edmonton to start over. I was really devastated. I stopped in Saskatoon to visit my daughter and grandchildren. My daughter got mad at me and kicked me out. I got to Edmonton and wanted to be with my mother. I couldn't tell Yvonne because she'd make fun of me. I was so alone. I decided to go straight to Wetaskiwin to see my mom. I got there Tuesday morning, got some money, and started looking for my mother and a place to stay. The only person I knew was Yvonne and I had avoided her because they were always drinking there. I went to Yvonne's, as it was a place for me to wait until maybe my mother came home.

This turned into a three-day drunk. On Thursday morning 14 September I wanted to leave. I went to the liquor store to get two and a half gallons of wine. Both Yvonne and I had hangovers. . . .

[from "Interview—Cpl. J.R. Bradley with Shirley Anne Salmon at the Red Deer Remand Centre 90 Aug 19, 1234 hrs." This witness statement has seventy-three pages, signed.]

Salmon: I didn't feel like sleeping outside like I did the night before [so I went to Yvonne's. . . .] And I admit I've always been scared of Yvonne. Not only that, she's always been kinda jealous of her husband and me, eh. Nothing happened. She's jealous of my mother. See my mother's sixty years old and she's always been like that, and uh . . .

Bradley: So when Yvonne says, jump . . .

Salmon: Uh-huh.

Bradley: You jump.

Salmon: Yeah. Sort of, sort of.

Bradley: Yeah.

Salmon: So did the boys [. . .]. Dwayne, you know, he was, he was always scared of Yvonne. . . .

Bradley: Well, why did it go as far as it did?

Salmon: She's [. . .].

Bradley: If Yvonne hadn't been there [. . .].

Salmon: Um-hum. It never would have happened [. . .]. I don't think they would have beaten him up as bad as they did [. . .]. I know it's hard to really believe this but, I don't believe the boys really, really have that killer instinct in them. Dwayne's always been a wimp. She always called him a wimp and she was, he was always listening to her [. . .]. It was more or less her that did all the planning. The boys didn't plan anything.

Bradley: Okay.

Salmon: Nobody planned anything except her.

Bradley: Let's talk about the planning [. . .]. Did Yvonne say, we'll phone him and suck him over to the house.

Salmon: Yeah.

Bradley: Okay, tell me about that conversation.

Salmon: Well, I, we're sitting there and she didn't specifically just talk to me and she was talking to everybody and, we'll phone him and, uh, tell him to come over [. . .]. That's all she really, uh, she really said, that I remember of and uh, that's when she uh, phoned him.

Yvonne [her memory of the phone calls on 14 September 1989; written and sent to me in June and December 1997]:

Shirley Anne used the words "plan" and "planning" a lot talking to Bradley, and they were repeated before the jury at my trial. But Bradley is doing the thinking for her, she follows his words, and she never says how or when, or *what* was planned. There was no plan. I did not phone Chuck to tell him to come over—he told me, when he dropped me off, that he was going to come back.

It was my home, it was my kids that were in danger if he came. Therefore it was my responsibility to question him about what Shirley Anne was professing to. The thought scared me, if he flipped out, because if Shirley Anne was lying about him, what would happen? I thought she and Ernie were no back-up if he flipped on me. So I had to know if he was coming or not. I phoned him, and I was told he was sleeping. I hung up. I was no further ahead, and Shirley Anne kept on. I got more and more edgy. Ernie and I questioned her truth; she got more and more excited, he told her, she's not lying. She knew I phoned once, so she said, "You phone him, get him over here, I'll ask him to his face, you'll see." All the time I feared him coming over before Dwa got home. If Shirley Anne was lying she'd take it to the hilt now, she was in too deep, I feared having to handle him alone. So I broke down and phoned again. This time he got on the phone, saying he would not be coming over as he was going fishing with his cousins instead. I was very relieved actually; he would not be coming. I hung up and told them not to worry, he was not coming.

I'm not really sure any more how the next [third] call happened, but it did. It had something to do with Shirley Anne wanting to talk. I dialed the number as she could not find his amongst all the other phone numbers on the calendar, I dialed and handed it to her. I stood there for a while, to hear her, talk about buns, cousins, males. Then she said, "Why don't you come over? Yvonne's passed out and her kids are running around half-naked." I then grabbed the phone, but she pulled away as I tried, raising her fingers to her puckered lips, and then came her sexy voice and talk of cousins, males, and nice buns again. I left to sit with Ernie in the living room, piss on all this crazy shit, piss on Chuck and Shirley Anne. At the time I thought he was still going fishing. Shirley Anne went on with her routine on the phone, halfway in the kitchen, performing around. After a lot of that, she hung up and told us he and his two cousins were coming together to my house. I really got scared then, as I felt I'd have no choice but to ask him if he was a molester, as Shirley Anne said, and now I felt I had to face triple danger, triple anger, if he, they, got mad at her lies—or worse if he really was [what she said]. I knew no matter what, I had to question him about Shirley Anne's accusations, plus I knew he did not respect women or children. So who could guess what would happen? I feared the unknown; I knew both Shirley Anne and Ernie were no protection, I envisioned a terrible clash anyhow, of some sort, and Dwa was still not home. So I got the gun [from the basement], knowing there were no bullets and it did not fire, hoping if it got bad I could just scare the three guys off instead of getting beat up. So it was placed under the coach [in the living room] for easy access if needed. I was panicked at just the thought of what was to come. Tensions got higher, and I was telling Shirley Anne it was her fault, all this shit is your doing. No telling what they do when they get here, and three relatives to boot, and I have to ask them, and she'd better not be bullshitting. She went on saying, "He told me, I'm not bullshitting, thanks a lot anyways."

I was mad at the position Shirley Anne got me stuck in, I was scared, drunk and frazzled. The kids were in their room, but not sleeping. Then Dwa walks in, in the thick of things. Asking, "What's going on?" I say, "Shit, ask Shirley Anne," Ernie saying, "Chuck's a kid diddler," Shirley Anne saying her shit, acting it out, and yeah, Shirley Anne had invited him and his cousins over now.

And things went nuts and crazy. I was dumbstruck, but somehow felt some peace, as Dwa could now handle it, as he could where I could not. But I was still shaken up emotionally at him coming with two male cousins. The phone rang in the middle of it. It was Chuck; he said, "I'll be right over." All I said was, "Yeah, okay." Dwa was here, he'd handle it.

We still all thought he was coming with his cousins.

———

Shirley Anne Salmon [from the second "Interview—Cpl. J.R. Bradley with Shirley Anne Salmon (B. 50-8-19), Red Deer Remand Centre, 90 Aug 30, 1256 hrs." There are twenty-one pages.]:

Salmon: So when someone mentioned that he was coming over
    I said to Yvonne, "This man said that his wife accused him

and charged him for molesting his little girl," and I showed them, I, I, I exaggerated, and I said, I said that ah that he had her—like he said he had her on his lap, and was going like this—when indeed he only said he only played with her buns while he had her on his lap.

[. . .] I did this to scare them, and to warn them. I didn't completely make it out of the clear blue sky. He did mention that his wife charged him, but he admitted that he didn't do anything, but I figured he must have done something because why would his wife charge him? By this time I, I, I had so much to drink and polished off the Southern Comfort and the thing is, you see, my mother raised us like this, but she always—she only meant good, one time me and my sister were talking and I said to my sister, "You ever notice Mom exaggerates," and then she said, "Well, she only means good." [. . .] I only meant to warn them [. . .]. I didn't mean any harm.

Bradley: When you say you exaggerated.

Salmon: Uh huh.

Bradley: You motioned with your hands like this, like he was screwing the little one? [. . .]

Salmon: And, ah, but I didn't say he was screwing but—

Bradley: But you left the impression?

Salmon: Yes, I just did this . . . at the time I didn't say he was screwing this little girl. You know he said he had her on his lap and I—

Bradley: You made the motion.

Salmon: Yeah, like he would be screwing her [. . .]. I didn't mean anything by—the thought of killing him or hurting him didn't enter my mind, I just thought the guys would just tell him . . . to get the fuck out . . . if you know what's good for you.

———

Yvonne hung up the phone and went back into the living room. She told the three others sitting there, drinking, that it was Chuck. He had told her he was on his way over.

And someone said, "Let's do him in."

Perhaps someone said it. At the trial, on 11 March 1991, Shirley Anne testified under oath as follows:

Q [question by Crown Prosecutor Hill]: [. . .] What happens then?

A [answer by Shirley Anne Salmon]: And then the boys are just nodding. They're not really saying anything. Just yeah, yeah, and they're just looking, and then she [Yvonne] says, "Let's do him in."

Q: Who did she say that to?

A: All of us. I don't think the boys took it seriously [. . .].

Q: What about you?

A: Well, I didn't think she took it seriously. I didn't think she was serious.

On the trial transcript Yvonne writes over this: "All a lie. If I fight I say, 'Let's dance.' Or, 'I'll run up one side of you and down the other.'" And she also writes on Shirley Anne's statement to Bradley, where this quote also appears, "What can this really mean, death, or beating, what?" She comments on these words in her notes on the factum prepared by her lawyers for her appeal to the Appeal Court of Alberta: "These words are not in my vocabulary. I'd say, 'Let's dance.'"

It is clear that what Yvonne remembers is: if Chuck Skwarok was coming over and they accused him of molestation, she thought he would become enraged and they would have to fight him. Or, if he actually was a molester—perhaps even the man who was being talked about as stalking children in town—then they might have to rough him up and throw him out to let him know he was not welcome in their house. She was fiercely protective of her children, yes, but, as she had kept telling Shirley Anne, she barely knew Chuck and—with the possible exception of what Shirley Anne herself had set up that afternoon with Baby—all she knew of him and her children was that he had conspicuously avoided them. She thought of having to fight him if cornered—threats and fights and beatings were standard behaviour in her world—but she never once had the faintest thought of killing him.

And furthermore, Yvonne points out, if Chuck's two big cousins were coming over with him—as they all expected—was she "planning" to kill all three of them? Clearly, Shirley Anne's testimony was ridiculous as well as contradictory.

Nevertheless, Shirley Anne's four words at the trial, which she insisted were Yvonne's, made it appear as if a plan was being made to "do" Chuck "in." Then she tried to soften it for the rest of them by adding that neither Dwa nor Ernie nor she thought Yvonne was actually serious.

In her second "interview" with Bradley, Shirley Anne shifted and elaborated further on her "non-serious" state of mind regarding a man she was trying to convince the others was really and truly a child molester. She frankly admits she herself talked to him on the phone, and that ". . . I asked him over, and [he] said he would [come and] bring a couple of cases and he was bringing these cute guys with nice buns, and at the time all I was thinking about was the cute guys and more booze and partying a little bit and that's what I was looking forward to. I wasn't even thinking—didn't have killing on my mind. I didn't take it seriously [. . .]. I meet the deceased at the door, no guys and just one case of beer, and to be honest I was a little disappointed, that's how I felt at the time."

Yvonne remembers that her feelings at that moment had nothing to do with "cute guys with nice buns" and "partying"; Yvonne remembers: "I did not know what to do. I sat like a stone. It was Shirley Anne let him in."

A complex sequence of cause-and-effect actions followed Chuck Skwarok's arrival. From police and witness statements, trial records, and Yvonne's recollections, I have tried to clarify a logical strand of facts.

Three people sit on the couch set along the living-room wall: Shirley Anne at the end farthest into the room, Ernie in the middle, and Dwa beside a small end table. Out of sight under the couch lies a nonfunctioning rifle. Yvonne sits in the sofa chair with her back to the doorway into the kitchen; the end table and Dwa are on her left, a wider coffee table and lamp on her right. Beyond that, on her right, is the door to the children's bedroom. It is closed.

All four are drinking; the three on the couch discuss, interrupt, argue what to do when the men arrive. They are coming, that's that.

———

Charles Skwarok arrives. He is alone, not with his cousins as Shirley Anne had said he'd be. He carries a carton half full of beer and a heavy plastic bag. He does not sit in the other sofa chair in the living room: he puts his stuff down and goes into the kitchen and returns with a stacking chair whose thin metal legs are curved round at the back. He sits down directly opposite the three people on the sofa, a metre and a half away; Yvonne is within arm's reach across the coffee table on his left, and the door of the children's bedroom is immediately behind him. He opens a beer and digs into his bag and pulls out some magazines. He says Shirley Anne asked for them, to "spice things up."

Yvonne refuses to so much as look at them; she is thinking: *Don't look at this dirt he drags into my house, be stiff, be cold and he'll leave, don't move, don't say a word.*

Shirley Anne leans forward to stare at the magazine spread out in Ernie's lap, and she reaches under the couch. She asks Ernie: "Are there any pictures of small kids in there?"

Ernie stares up at Chuck directly: "Do you like men, or little boys? Their tight buns?"

Voices are rising, Shirley Anne is asking questions now, too fast to wait for answers. Chuck tilts back on the rounded legs of his chair with his gut stretching his T-shirt above his pants, a bit puzzled at first but seemingly not at all concerned. Finally he says to the two men, "Sure . . . sure, some men have nice buns. I was gonna go fishing with a couple today, but they left, so. . . ."

He shrugs, relaxed, the biggest guy there with a slit of stomach exposed, and suddenly Dwa, on the couch in his summer-white shorts, hunches around and crosses his bare legs.

"Stop staring at my balls," he says to Chuck.

There is a shift of feeling in the room, like a sliver of winter wind. Ernie and Chuck are talking very loudly now, not listening to each other. Shirley Anne is scrabbling her arm under the couch and mouthing at Yvonne, "Ask him now, ask him now," so eager to prove herself right.

———

"No!" Yvonne exclaims, thumping her empty bottle on the coffee table and jerking to her feet. Chuck reaches his long arm down and pulls up a beer from his carton and offers it to her and she says "No!" again. The room is so crowded, she is standing directly against his legs and she won't look at him. "I don't want anything from you!" She is hemmed in; how can she get past him and the coffee table into the open space of the kitchen? "I get my own beer in my own house!"

But she is trapped by his body and the loathing of who he may be, and directly behind her Shirley Anne shouts, "Tell them what you told me, your wife hauled you into court, you were molesting your own girl, tell 'em, you fucken kiddy fucker!"

Chuck tilts upright on his chair, his body moving forward against Yvonne, suddenly huge, his face almost in her chest.

"Move, please!" she says, loudly but terrified. He is peering at her, his body thrusting forward onto her, yelling something at the others. She never has anyone to protect her—"Move!"—she lashes at him with both her fists.

He tips backwards on the rounded legs of his chair, crashes against the bedroom door. It bursts open, and he falls back flat.

———

Now Charles Skwarok is halfway inside her children's bedroom. Yvonne hears one of their voices, waking up, and breaks into total panic. She grabs across him for the door knob. "Get out of there, get out!" jerking, jerking, but his head and shoulders block the doorway. She bangs the thin door against him till he twists, curls himself around, and she can finally slam it shut. He kicks some space for his feet, uncoils himself upwards in front of her, his fist comes up and he smashes her; she explodes backwards, head over heels, across the coffee table, knocking the lamp onto the floor beyond and crashing down with it.

Yvonne is crouched on the floor between the coffee table and sofa chair; she knows by instinct what she must do. She must remain small, tiny; she cannot permit herself to be beaten senseless, her children are in the next room; she must remain conscious and extremely small, her bare feet flat on the floor, her thighs resting on the backs of her lower legs, her upper body and head bowed low, and her hands quietly cleaning the shards of the light bulb aside so she will not cut herself when she has to leap up.

There is shouting, shrieking above her, Chuck bellowing, "You fight like a man, you take it like a man!" and "I never did nothing, you cunts," and Shirley Anne, "You told me what you did, you kid fucker," and Ernie, "Fucken skinner," and Dwa sitting there completely quiet, in six years Yvonne has never heard him yell. *Stay small, fake it till you have to make it.*

Chuck swings from side to side, poised to handle them all, and stringing curses he turns, walks into the kitchen. In three, four strides he'll be across it and out the door.

But Shirley Anne will not be denied, she won't allow it to end. She leaps after Chuck, grabs his hair and yanks him to a stop. He tries to tear her loose, fights her kicks and shrieking; he is sliding on the cork floor in his stocking feet; she has him bent over as he slowly drags her towards the door, straining low, but she knows hair fighting—she has him good and tight and he slips, falls to his knees, she is kicking at him and he reaches up, he has fists big enough to drive her through the wall.

"You stupid cunt, let go!"

And Yvonne makes the mistake of her life: she wants nothing but Chuck out of the house, and she straightens up, she jumps in to separate them so he will go, be gone, vanished.

But when she tries to get between them, Chuck explodes into a frenzy; he forgets Shirley Anne yanking his hair and kicking him, and instead hammers Yvonne. Instinctively she hits him back. Chuck has his fist in her hair as she falls under him, he's bent under Shirley Anne, and they are sliding on the kitchen floor. Yvonne shouts at Shirley Anne and Chuck to stop, for Dwa to come and break this up, and finally she hears Dwa yell, "Let go of my wife!"

Dwa is there, yanking at them, and then Ernie too, but punching, all five in a tangle and skating into chairs, slamming table, kitchen counter, walls, corners. They are ripping and beating each other into the tight space where the closed outside door and basement door stand at right angles to each other. They are one big ball of fighting now, with Yvonne at the bottom.

In that tiny square they slam and rebound heads, body edges, feet against the fridge, the two doors, and suddenly the basement door bursts back off its breaking latch, opening like a gigantic maw, steep steps slanting down into blackness. And inexplicable to Yvonne, she is still at the bottom of the pile and can see nothing, as they struggle to untangle themselves from each other, even as they seem about to break apart, it is Chuck who is on the lip of the top step of the basement. Who topples over, and falls. Disappears into the ominous thuds of his falling.

———

Three men beating each other always make a lot of noise, but contained in a short, narrow basement it is even louder. Ernie has charged down after Chuck, yelling to Dwa, who has followed. But Yvonne wants no part of this, she wants it gone; maybe it will vanish if she pulls the basement door shut. So she does that.

Shirley Anne is shadow-boxing around the kitchen, punching air hard each time a heavy slam or grunt sounds through the floor. "Yeah! Hit the fucker."

But sometimes there is silence below, an ominous space of . . . nothing . . . and Yvonne is afraid. It seems more likely that Chuck is giving it to Dwa and Ernie; she has no faith in either as fighters. Out of such a sudden silence Chuck may suddenly jerk the basement door open, loom up into the kitchen.

Shirley Anne sees her and stops her silly boxing; she disappears into the living room and returns holding the rifle across her chest like a movie soldier.

"That's useless," Yvonne says. Shirley Anne looks at her without comprehension.

"It's a gun, eh?" As if, if she holds it, it must be power.

Chantal appears behind Shirley Anne, frightened. Yvonne goes quickly to her. "Don't come out now. Watch your brother and sister but don't ask questions now. Go, sweetheart."

And she goes, quickly obedient as always, back into the bedroom. There may be heavy thuds and shouts and crashes in the basement, but that small room with most of its floor covered by mattresses for sleep or play must hold only quiet breath. The block letters of the alphabets they pasted to the wall begin just above the middle mattress, Chantal's, and rise like a mountain to the brightness of the T lit by the streetlight shining through the frilly curtains, and turn the corner of the room on U to Z by the window. Straight across, the ABCs begin again, slant down until M disappears into the closet doors folded open. The three children asleep.

There is no sound from below, nothing. With a jolt Yvonne cannot remember since when there has been no sound, and she is deeply afraid. Silently—her feet are bare—she walks past Shirley Anne by the sink, listening too, open-mouthed, and leans towards the basement door. The door catch has been torn out. There is a slight creak, and slowly she pushes against the door. Inch by inch the steep steps appear beneath her, empty.

———

And then Chuck's sudden face is below her. Surging up out of nothing, hard, fast, raw, a face and wide shoulders enraged and already eye-level with her bare feet and in a second he will be nose to nose with her again, will tower over her, and she jerks the door back, he has beaten down Dwa and Ernie and now he will do whatever he pleases, but his big hand out of nowhere grabs the bottom of the door and she jerks harder, she cannot break his grip, she has no space in her terrified mind except, *no, no, not up into the house, knock him loose, knock him back down*. There is only their desperately silent struggle, both the boys must be out cold and there is no one left but she has to keep him away from the bedroom. She cannot break his grip on the door rim and his other arm is going high, reaching for the knob, and without a thought she slams the door back on him. *Stay out of my house!* And the edge of the door hits his face, blood wells as the skin of his forehead dents and bursts.

She has drawn blood. A fight to the blood is very bad.

———

Chuck's face may be bleeding but he is too strong for Yvonne. With one hand he keeps the door open and with the other he grabs her ankle and jerks. She slips off the floor onto the top step, loses her frantic balance and falls forward, headlong into the stairwell. Her desperate hands hook onto the small cupboard she built onto the wall opposite, above the stairs, and she catches herself there, hanging with her full body length stretched out above the bloody, enraged man. He roars to pull her loose, dragging down on her left arm, but she has the strength of terror. If he can throw her aside he will certainly climb up and do whatever he wants in the house. She contorts herself to anchor her right leg on the concrete ledge of the foundation and he clamps onto her hips with both hands and pulls down with all his strength, all his weight. Shirley Anne is kicking at him from the top stair; Yvonne is gasping for help, she knows her backbone will snap. And then at last both Dwa and Ernie are coming at Chuck from below. Cursing, they haul at him, stupidly they add their weight to his on her bending back!

She is breaking, she cannot hold. She manages to scrape one leg free, to get her foot against his chest and shove, hard. And he flies down the stairs against the men to crash into the washer and dryer; even as she falls after them.

———

Within seconds Shirley Anne is down there with them. All five are now in the tight concrete basement; scrambling to their feet on its concrete floor. From above the kitchen light gleams on Chuck's bloody head.

10

If I Gave You a Gun, Would You Shoot Me?

In this case you are exposed to people who are obviously very different from you and me. That's reality. It would be nice if all the Crown witnesses to a murder were bank managers and accountants, but the cold hard truth is that Chuck [Skwarok] and Yvonne Johnson and Ernie Jensen don't hang out with those people. They hang out with Shirley [Anne] Salmon and Lyle Schmidt, people who drink wine at 11 o'clock in the morning. The point of all that is not whether they are people who do things like that, it's whether you accept what they told you about what happened.

– Crown Prosecutor J. Barry Hill, Address to the
  Jury, Wetaskiwin, 18 March 1991

S TREETS LEAD AWAY from Yvonne's house in three directions. The south is a dead end blocked by Parkside School. The door clicks behind her, the autumn air innocent as the corner streetlight, not a sound or motion. Her Dodge van stands in the drive where it belongs; she can walk around it and open the door and get in and twist the key and back onto the street easily and she'll be facing away, every road leading away.

The engine roars as the cold pedal hits her bare foot. *Move, move.* The van swings back, left, and leaps forward. For an instant as she runs under the streetlight at the corner, her eyes draw left, she can't stop them, and Chuck's dark Hornet hatchback sits there beside the sidewalk under the trees of her lot. Her thoughts rip like the flash of the streetlight across the back of her mind.

> *Maybe nothing happened   maybe he was just out cold and limp when we wrapped him in the tarp   so limp when we shoved him in the hatchback and slammed   maybe he'll wake up and kick off the tarp and drive to the hospital   maybe he'll drive and get his two big cousins and come back and beat us all up   maybe nothing happened   maybe*

She thrusts a tape into the player, concentrating on play! And George Thorogood's Destroyers' guitars clang, then Thorogood wails, "I come in last night . . . wouldn't let me in, move it on over . . ." and she flicks that up to blare, her head rocking into beat. The van drives, turns by itself.

At the Wayside Inn there's a big bus with blocked-out windows in the parking lot, which means Ladies' Night, no women allowed except strippers. Music so loud you can't think. Yvonne just wants a case of beer from Off Sales and she'll be gone, away, and the bouncer says, Okay, ya gotta wait for intermission. She stands in the space between the two padded doors of the bar, slumps, and hits the pay-phone. The kids—someone will have to take care of the kids now. But Mom has no phone at Red Pheasant; this time of night there's only Dad in Butte.

The stripper music crashes to a stop as she's dialling and the bouncer sticks his head between the doors, Okay, quick. Yvonne ap-proaches the Off Sales desk. One case. Her hand comes out of her jean pocket not with the twenty Dwa just gave her but bills, bills—the cheque she cashed earlier—so she says, "Three, no four cases, four."

Someone comes up behind her, some huge lunk, talking loud like he owns the world. "Hey, Bud, you can't serve her, she's barefoot!"

But both she and the bartender ignore the bossy bugger; she hoists the four cases of beer to her chest and is out of there. *The kids.* She stacks the beer on the entrance floor beside her cold feet.

"Dad," she says fast, "Dad!" interrupting the long-distance collect operator saying her name and will you accept—into his muttered waking-up.

"Vonnie?"

The door from the bar swings ajar; someone, a man, peers out at her, stands there, trying to listen? And she twists sideways, the receiver jammed into her ear. She's in Butte, Montana, the little crammed house.

"Vonnie, I can't hardly hear you, I——"

"Dad, I'm in bad trouble. Can you get hold of Mom, to come get the kids. Something really bad——"

"Where are you? I can't hear, just noise . . ."

"I'm between the doors in a bar, I . . ."

"Where? You in Alberta? Vonnie?"

"Yes! Yes!" she shouts. On the phone she trusts him. He'll tell her what to do and she'll do it. "In Wetaskiwin, the house's okay but some-thing really bad—Dad, a guy keeps peeking out at me. I'll phone right back, some other place; I'll phone right back!"

She hangs up, and the man is there again; he must have been lis-tening. "Yvonne?"

It's the loudmouth at the Off Sales, and she's seen him before, plenty, always hanging around, she can't stand him. "What's wrong? Hey, you're soaking wet."

"Nothing!" She's got two cases under her left arm, grabs the third by the handle, and tries for the fourth but she can't hold it, it drops to the ground, so she leaves it and swings around to knock the outside door open but it jerks away and she almost falls against two RCMP officers coming in. They back up a step, staring at her.

The biggest one says, "Hello, how's it going . . . Yvonne."

He's grey-haired and smiling slightly. *The cruel cop game of smile and arrest, maybe they've already got the guys.* She can do nothing, just play the game as long as it plays.

"How do you guys know my name?"

He laughs, points, so friendly he'll be the worst. "Right there, on your jacket." And of course it is, her old Butte, Montana, sports jacket; her mom made it. The shorter cop is staring at Loudmouth.

He says, holding the dropped beer, "Yvonne here forgot one."

"I can't . . . ," Yvonne says, "carry it all. I'll get it, okay?"

"That's a lotta beer," says the shorter cop. "Big party?"

Yvonne's fear cuts deeper. She steels herself to be normal. "Yeah, home party, just two blocks to go," and slips past them. She cannot let them smell her breath; any second they'll yell, "Stop!" But she hears nothing. The hardest thing is to walk normally. She's across the lot— their cruiser is parked right in front of her van—she's got her door open, she climbs in with her cartons. The ominous cruiser with its bar of flashers is shoved up wide against her radiator. She stacks the beer beside the seat; she is bent down as low as possible. *Go, go.*

The passenger door opens—Loudmouth. Past him, under the hotel-door light, the two cops stand, still looking at her. She can't start and drive away because they'll see she has only one headlight, they'll be after her in a second, and then they'll smell her and haul her in for impaired too. The guy hoists up the beer carton and leans into the van.

"I brought your beer. Hey, something wrong? Your old man beat you up, who were you calling there? Look, there's blood on your pants . . . you get raped?"

"I got in a fight, I gotta go."

He laughs, one foot inside the van now. "You look fucken great," he says. "What does the other guy look like?"

She doesn't know his name but he's always hanging around town, always staring at women.

"If it's rape," his voice lifts, drawls the word like it feels good in his mouth, "tell it to them cops. They'll get the bastard."

This is worse than a nightmare. Her van is her safest place on earth; in it she is surrounded by all the familiar steel which can move her away, away from anything—and now she cannot move it an inch on the busted pavement of the Wayside Inn! This snoop is hooked over her passenger seat and those two cops are staring at her—

"I'm going." The motor starts with a touch. "Get out!"

But he doesn't get out; he's scrambling in and her mind flips over, "Okay," she tells him, "you brought the beer, you can have it. I'll drop you anywhere you want to go."

He's yapping, yapping, but she swings the van back from the cruiser and around before she switches on the single light and she's driving slowly, carefully towards the street. No flashing lights behind her. She cranks up George Thorogood,

The sky is crying, look at the tears
roll down the street . . .

Loudmouth leaning towards her, yapping because he senses something's the matter. Something bad.

She's looking for her smokes; he finds them and passes her one. And she sees the booth by the dark Shell station.

"I gotta make a call."

"Who you gonna call, eh?"

Yapping on, trying to find out. She corners in quick, leaves the Destroyers wailing even louder.

Shielding her voice around the plastic phone: "Dad, I think . . . maybe . . . somebody's dead. I'm in a phone booth, but the kids—"

"Vonnie listen, listen, you go back to the house, make sure the kids—"

"They're fine, they don't know, they—"

"Listen! Go back to the house, make sure they're okay, now!"

"Dad, what will I do?"

"Okay . . . okay then, then phone me back, right away, from the house and——"

"Okay . . ."

"And you gotta tell somebody. If somebody's hurt bad or—you better tell somebody. You've got to. You hear me, Vonnie?"

———

Yvonne sits in the driver's chair, bent over the wheel, arms clutched tight around her stomach, rocking back and forth. Gasping at odd intervals, as if she is exhausted, or crying. Her untouched cigarette is smoking itself away and Lyle—he's told her his name, that he's the cab driver who used to pick her up before she had a car—Lyle butts it into the crammed ashtray. She rocks back and forth, her body swaying on the chair's swivel but never leaning closer to him. He's keeping things rolling, prying at her.

"If your old man did this, leave him. You deserve better. You need a place to hide out?"

"Leave," she tells him dully. "It's my problem . . . I gotta see if the guy I fought is okay. Go see if he's gone."

"Okay then," Lyle says, "I'll help you, we'll go get your kids, I'll take care of you, no worry."

He's carrying on his own conversation. Suddenly her arms unlock from around herself and she reaches over for the key, starts the motor, and the van jerks forward.

"I was in a fight, and I think, maybe, someone got hurt, bad," she says. "I don't know but maybe. And you can do shit. Now anywhere you want to go, I'll drop you off."

She steers with one hand, trees, stop signs, houses, streetlights blazing and gone, everything is blurred and fluorescent; shadows bulge and shift but her solid van blasts through anything.

I tell this asshole he's out and runs to the cops   I go back say goodbye to the kids and kill myself   if they get me I say I did it alone nobody else just me   Dwa's a good dad   I can kill myself in jail

She's roaring straight down the avenue heading back to the house.

"I don't know how bad he's hurt—pretty bad—I think I killed someone."

But Lyle is rocking in his chair, cranked higher than flying on sheer adrenaline; his eyes gleam at her like she's a miracle. She swerves the van to the curb.

"Get out!"

"Yvonne, I'll help you! It's your old man's fault. You'd never hurt nobody, I know that. I'll . . ."

She can't get rid of him. She drives, rockers pounding; she's reeling and can barely aim herself between the rows of parked cars. Where is her house? She knows every street. Where? She stops. The middle of a street; she is blind in flashes; the world twisted into streaks, lights like bare branches leaning down, her head hits the steering wheel; she is so wrung out and she sees Lyle's face inches from her face, talking.

"Please," she pleads. "If you want to help, get the fuck out!"

Staring at her. Never look directly into a man's eyes, it's too dangerous; never, unless you know there's nothing left but to fight.

Go home   drive   let Dwa and Ernie scare him off

The van is moving again, it seems to be alongside a park—the park; there's her house on the corner and she has to look and instantly sees Chuck's car is gone. The van rolls, stops.

"We put him in the back of his car." She hears herself saying that aloud. "And now the car is gone!"

"What? Where?" Lyle is staring around, wildly.

The car is gone   maybe Ernie drove it away   or Chuck woke up and went for his cousins to beat us up   or Dwa burned it   or Ernie drove it into a swamp   or Dwa drove it to the hospital

"Where?" Lyle has grabbed her, is shaking her, and with one last jolt of what's left of her strength she steps on the gas. The van heaves forward under the streetlight across the intersection; she is aiming for her driveway in sheer panic, her children have to be in that dark house and Dwa has to be protecting them. Let him get rid of this asshole!

But he's screaming, "No! Go, go, go, go!" and lunges over, grabs the wheel, twists it back, knocking her aside as he slams his booted foot on her bare one on the gas, guns the van past the house and down the street. For an instant Yvonne freezes. *My house gone   my children my children.* The van shudders to a stop past the next corner with his foot on the brake and she shudders too, crumples, crying hopelessly.

"Get your ass outa there!" He drags her over himself into the passenger seat, shoves her against the door. She sinks, weeping. He's in the driver's seat.

———

Gravel. A line of weeds along a ditch and big rolls of baled hay, a barbed-wire fence, fields. Yvonne is crying and crying, curled tight.

Lyle drives her van as he pleases, drinking beer and talking, but she does not listen: she is trying to make a plan. What she must do now is get him to kill her; then he can go to the cops and be a hero because he's solved the murder and that'll save Dwa, and then the cops will get him for shooting her and stick him behind bars for ten years and that will protect all the little children in Wetaskiwin for ever, that's a good plan. A really good plan.

She says into whatever he is saying, "If I gave you a gun, would you shoot me?"

He stops, he must be staring at her. He's trying to get hold of her hand and she jerks away.

"I couldn't," he says with the stupid hang-dog look of a man trying to be convincing. "I'm your friend."

"You make it look like suicide, you've solved their case, and you're famous."

She is crying, a hand gropes inside her shirt and she shoves, she hears a voice, it may be her own, it may be the cropped grass in the fields they pass whispering, ". . . so tiny, she's showing her raspberry birthmark, Shirley Anne told me . . . o my Baby, my sweet little Baby."

The van does not move; a wall looms over her, the edge of long roof, and a man's face is against her face, she can feel it.

"I'll get you," his voice says—did he say that?

He's driving again; drinking beer. It is night, the sun will never rise. Talking whenever she actually hears him, he has another reason for going nowhere in particular. She has to pee. He says, "Go ahead," he's so confident, and she gets out. The wash of black night air, stars all over like fireworks when they explode—behind the van or he'll see her in the big sideview mirrors. She peers back around the corner as she pushes her jeans down and yes, he's out of the van; he's stretching around, trying to see her, but she has to squat, it comes in a rush and he looms over her, knocks her back and she's fighting even as she falls, her jeans are soaked, her bare buttocks ground into the gravel. *He'll never get me not this stinking vulture NO!*

He's sprawled out full length, holding her flat. She cannot heave him off, but her jeans are still up on her thighs, he'll never spread her legs wide enough like that. She can time it; if he lets go of her wrists she'll wrestle him and he'll have to grab her wrists again to flatten her. Her back is shredded on the gravel, but all he can do is weigh her down, panting; he can't get his own pants off either. She's okay, she can lie here for ever with her van flashers blinking red, her head bent back into the gravel ditch, and everything's safe.

But she feels herself sink: she is too wrung out, too much beer, too much everything. She's going to lose it.

"You're gonna pass out," he hisses in her ear. "I'll get it, one way or the other."

The worst is, she knows that, either way, he'll do it: while she's awake, or just wait till she's passed out.

He chuckles deep and soft, the old male flip from real brutal to pretend gentle. "C'mon, you know you want it. And I'll take care of you; listen, we go to your house and pick up your kids and we're outa here. Let some shit take the rap, who cares, we disappear. I know how to do it, we'll be safe, c'mon baby."

She feels herself sliding into a black hole. Not even the gravel digging into her back will help her.

He heaves her step by step along the ditch to the open van door. He throws her across the two front seats. She sags between them, and he hauls back on her legs till her buttocks are on the passenger chair. He shoves his pants down and climbs up on top of her.

In the Kingston Prison for Women, Yvonne sits coiled tight in the upholstered chair across from me. She huddles down even smaller, her long, black hair hides her face. But she will speak this, every word of it.

She says, "Within myself, I cursed all creation of the stars above, and anyone sitting there watching this happen."

———

This pig has abducted her in her own van, forced her away from her house, and driven her around for hours, telling her how for years he's watched her around town, offering stupid advice, come with me, you and your kids, I'll hide you, I'll take care of you, I'll drop the body in the river, shit, I can sink a body in a slough, just come with me. While she cried, sank into comatose despair, screamed, drank in hopelessness, but he kept on driving, talking, drinking, until he finally raped her. And now he's content. He's so sure of his control he lets her drive again: go ahead, let's see what's going on at your place; hey, maybe the party's still going on.

She's driving, and with the van she can kill him. And herself too, of course, and then everyone in her house will be safe. If Chuck's dead, then she's guilty and dead, and the children and Dwa will be safe. She speeds up; there's a low bridge abutment ahead; she aims and speeds up. He's screaming, grabbing at her, and she can't see so well; she doesn't hit it square in the spraying gravel, and the tough van glances off. Okay, there's always a roll in the ditch, and she goes over and down into the weeds; the van's rocking, slewing wildly but it's not fast enough to roll, he's fighting her for the wheel and the brake, and he gets it stopped. Cursing. But he's so confident he doesn't drag her out of the seat, he doesn't bother to drive again.

In the grey morning light she slams on the brakes in front of the cop shop on Main Street. "Go ahead," she mutters through her crying, "go, tell them, get out!"

"No, no," he says, chuckling. "We're going home, to your house."

When she gets inside the small porch of her house, the door is unlocked! She runs through the house to the children's bedroom—but they're all there. Curled under their twisted blankets. She feels them, each one, and they stir under her touch. All breathing, perfectly.

Ernie snores on the couch in the living room—where's Dwa? Sprawled under a sheet on their bed in the bedroom. Sleeping.

———

Lyle Schmidt [from a statement made to the RCMP, Wetaskiwin, Friday, 15 September 1989 at 7 a.m. Witnessed by Constable T.G. Witzke]:

Last night I was driving around Wetaskiwin until 11:30 with [a friend] until he dropped me off at the cab company. I rode around with the drivers until approximately 12:30. Then I rode around with [a woman] and my daughter, and they dropped me off at the Wayside [. . .]. at around 1:45 Yvonne came in. I have known her as Yvonne for about five years. Rick asked me what was I doing, I said girl hunting, he said what are you going to find in a place like this. I pointed out Yvonne and said there is a girl I know and went and talked to her. She was leaving with two cases of beer and I walked with her. I asked her where the party was at. I suggested I buy some beer, she said, I have two cases we can drive around. She wanted to go to her place but I said no, let's go park someplace and have a beer. We drove past John Deere where I started to drive. She said if I gave you a gun would you kill me. I said no you are a friend. I then asked her if she would kill me, she said, no because you are a friend. She said, have you killed a person, I have, we drove around and talked. She said she killed someone because that person had tried to molest her youngest daughter [aged two]. She said she had caught the guy with the girl's legs spread and he was playing with her. She said she had cut him, she didn't know he was dead until she tried to lift up his head. She said she also beat him up and she shoved the knife up his ass and asked him, this is what it feels like when you shove your prick up her bald headed cunt. She also said Shirley Anne Cooke [Salmon] was there, they took the guy downstairs and tied him to a post with phone cord. She asked me how to get rid of the body. I made some suggestions and we returned to her house. I noticed what might have been a blood spot on her jeans just above the left knee. We went into the house and there was Ernie Fraser (Jensen [police correction]) sleeping on the couch. She woke him but he had had it. I then grabbed him and woke him up. He said that they took the body out to the dump but everything is covered. The guy was still alive and choking on his own blood when they buried him [. . .].He also said he burnt the car [. . .]. The husband came out, he said forget it, it is done with, we got rid of him, and went back to bed.

I should add, when we first went in she took me downstairs and showed me the blood on the wall [. . .]. A knife was stuck in the post and she grabbed the knife and took it upstairs and washed it in the sink. I took it out and put it in my pocket. I asked her for the sheath, she told me where it was and I got it. I put the knife in the sheath and into my boot. Then I woke Ernie up. After talking I called the [cab] dispatcher, who called the police, and I left [. . .].

Q: Was there blood on the knife?

A: I did not see any blood on the knife before or after she washed it [. . .].

———

[From a "Taped Interview of Lyle Schmidt (DOB: 51 Feb. 03)" made by the RCMP at 1647 on Saturday, 16 September 1989. The interviewer is not named.]

[. . .]. she gave me a beer and I started drinking beer. I said, "How'd you kill him?" and she said, "I cut him," not getting into any details. It was like that for about two hours [. . .]. So I'm really being the actor, or whatever you guys call it, and really getting into it. Literally, like 'I'm mad at you, there's no body, there's no car, what kind of shit are you trying to pull?' [. . .] I'd say within 15–20 minutes, like, she relaxed to a point where she suddenly has my trust. Like we're going to, she's going to show me everything, and she's going to let me help. By the time we got intimate, I did not force myself on her [. . .].

Q: So you had sex with her.

A: Uh huh.

Q: In the van?

A: Yes I did. Then right after that the girl really opened up. She said everything's a mess. I need help [. . .]. it almost got to the point where she at that time the feeling was of total trust and she was going to show me everything and I was really going to try and help her [. . .].

Q: Alright, you're back at the house, you go in the house . . . go over it again quickly.

A: [. . .] She also mentioned that when all she wanted to do was tie him up and just let him sit there for about three days [. . .].

Q: You had it in your mind from the beginning that if there was substance to this . . . you would find out what you could?

A: If there was any substance to it right from the total beginning, like . . . to play along with the game and fill you guys in on it later. Like if I would have had to dispose of a body there's various ways I could have done it, with them along. But it was just a matter of letting you guys know the exact spot [. . .]. Like this was all going through my little mind, like I'm working on this the whole time.

Q: Okay, and I assume you did this entirely on your own [. . .].

A: I do the strangest things at the strangest times and it's kind of like I said before, OK Lyle, let's see what kind of shit you can get into tonight [. . .].

Q: You did not have a reward . . . in mind?

A: No [. . .].I want to do this, it sounds like fun, let's see how far it goes [. . .]. Like if it would have been just something passing me by, I would have just forgot it. But everything in my mind, like I'm planning ahead, like I'm asking the questions, I'm playing the role, telling her things about my life, like I know what I'm doing [. . .].

Q: Just one other thing [. . .]. How did you . . . end up having sex with Yvonne there? [. . .]. You suggested it?

A: We both suggested it, like that part we had been tossing it back and forth all night [. . .]. A couple of times I asked her if she wanted to and one time she said no. Now later she said yes . . .

Q: Was she a willing participant?

A: She took off her own clothes [. . .].

Yvonne knows they're coming, it's only a question of how soon. In her staggering exhaustion of drunkenness and confused hopelessness, she sits at her kitchen table alone. The dull light from the stove angles shadows; they seem almost tranquil, lie so steady and usual across the table-top. Dwa is sleeping, or passed out, Ernie is sprawled on the couch. Shirley Anne is long, long gone.

Someone has stepped into her porch. Footsteps. A pounding, sharp and hard.

"Who is it?"

"It's the police. RCMP."

She lets the silence stretch out, just a few seconds more. The banging comes harder: "Royal Canadian Mounted Police. Open the door!"

The door is locked. In the living room, Ernie jerks erect on the couch as if the cop's voice had raised him from the dead.

"What do you want?" Yvonne raises her voice as loud as she can.

"We've had a complaint here."

"What complaint?"

"That someone's been hurt. Now open up."

"There's no one here hurt."

"Who's in the house?

Yvonne looks up; Ernie has appeared at the table, but at that question he turns and darts for the living room, shoves the sliding patio doors open silently and drops out, gone. Like Shirley Anne, he can run too; it's not his house.

There are two cops outside; she can hear them talking to each other. It'll be just a matter of minutes now.

"Open the door!"

"If you have a warrant," Yvonne answers, "I will."

"Yes! Now open up!"

"Then slide it under the door, so I can read it!"

Another silence. Suddenly powerful kicks hammer at the door, and Yvonne jumps up and slides table knives in the door jamb so they can't pop the lock—they sure as hell have no warrant—and then the first cop's voice shouts to someone and a voice answers, seemingly from the living room.

"Ray, the patio door's open!"

Yvonne shouts, "Where's your warrant?" as she runs into the living room. The patio doors are three feet above the ground—the patio isn't built yet – and the cop already has his hat and arms, shoulders in; he's hoisting up his leg as Yvonne gets there, yelling, "You can't come in without a warrant!"

And she's jolted into a shivering rage. She grabs at his hand on the sliding door, gets her hip and leg against him while she pries at his fingers, they loosen, she gives a final shove and he falls back on his ass. He's up in a second; he grabs her ankle as she tries to shove the door shut, and she kicks him back again as she falls. Then the other cop is there, yelling, "Don't let the bitch close the fucken door!"

He trips over the first one, getting up, but manages to jam his hand up inside the door. Yvonne pulls the door back a bit and slams it on his fingers till he jerks them out, bellowing. Then she shoves in place the board that locks the door.

She looks out; one of the cops is sitting on the grass with his hat lying behind him; the other is jumping around, holding his hand and swearing. She closes the vertical blinds; suddenly she can barely stand. Wetaskiwin Mounties always think they can do anything they please.

She grabs the phone on the kitchen counter and dials the RCMP number. When she hears the official voice she simply shouts, "You bust into my house at six in the morning with my kids sleeping, who'd you think you are! You think I'm the bad guy here, don't you?"

"Madam . . . madam, who is this calling?"

"Yvonne Johnson, and your guys know it, you sent them here, and they're prowling around outside my house right now!"

"Please stay on the line, I'll transfer you, please stay on the line."

And Dwa is standing beside her. He's in his boxer shorts, his smooth muscles pouring sweat from his hangover and everything else that's hit him. They're in their house together with their three children. They can't run anywhere.

He looks so sad, so strong, so pale. He says, "Vonnie, don't make it any worse."

A man's voice, it can only be a cop, says, "Hello, Ms. Johnson? Hello?"

Yvonne hangs up the phone. Dwa heads back to bed; Yvonne tries to cover the kitchen window with a blanket. The sounds of the police rustling around the house stop. After a time there is a quiet tapping at the patio door. It's Ernie. Yvonne opens the door, and he hauls himself up into the house again.

———

Seven thirty-five in the morning on Friday, 15 September 1989, in Wetaskiwin, Alberta, population 10,103. In the bedroom off the kitchen in the small house partially renovated with new cedar siding at 4123 – 53A Street, Yvonne Johnson and Dwayne Wenger sleep restlessly, tangled in light bedclothes and occasionally each other's sweaty arms.

Across the dead-end street from the house, between Parkdale School and a white bench on the 54th Street side of Parkdale Park, a Hornet hatchback has at some point during the night been parked on the grass, half-hidden by bushes. But an hour ago a tow-truck from Mel's Towing arrived, hooked onto it, and hauled it away backwards. Now a police cruiser is parked nearby on 53A Street, in a spot from which the porch door of the house can best be observed without obstruction.

Three kilometres away Harvey Schneider, who operates the packer at the City Sanitary Landfill—everyone except city council calls it "the dump"—is driving his shiny '87 Dodge pick-up down the slope into the landfill excavation. He glances aside at the new mounds of garbage he has come to pack, and immediately sees what looks like a pale manikin sprawled out, legs and arms wide, lying face up. He stops, backs up, and drives to within five feet of it. But he does not get out; he simply stares through the window and sees a large White man, that's obvious enough—the only clothing he has on is a dirty T-shirt caught up high and tight on his protruding stomach.

11

You Have Nothing to Hope, and Nothing to Fear

In Wetaskiwin the only thing in the cell with me is a *Reader's Digest* I was given. I recall reading the whole thing, but only two things stay in my mind. One was reading the story of a little girl collecting envelopes to take to the priest's collection plate, a woman asked her what she was doing and the little girl replied, "I am taking God his mail." The other thing I remember is Dwa yelling to me, from his cell, that he loved me.

– Yvonne Johnson to Rudy Wiebe, January 1998

WHEN, in late October 1992, I first heard about Yvonne Johnson, she had already been in prison for over three years. After numerous letters and several phone calls between us, in April 1993 I contacted the Edmonton lawyer, A. Brian Beresh, who had defended her at her original trial for murder and also presented her appeal from that decision to the Alberta Court of Appeals. I talked to him at some length—the appeal decision was still pending—and he gave me a complete 884-page transcript of the original trial.

That gave me the judicial version of what had happened in the basement of Yvonne and Dwayne's Wetaskiwin home; the version in which, on page 800, Crown Prosecutor J. Barry Hill addressed the jury with, it seemed to me, truly overweening condescension: "Now, you remember that I said to you that we don't videotape murders. Indeed, the whole trial process is in many ways an attempt to recreate for you, as best we can, what happened."

But I wanted much more than Hill's re-creation of the events in the basement; I wanted to hear Yvonne's personal account of what went on. Especially, I wanted to hear, from her, what she knew she had done. And in her written comments on the trial, in her letters, in our conversations, she did explain things—but never in sequence; never as one connected story. For several years she could not find it within herself to do that.

In the meantime, she and I were working on this book together. Many of the facts were clear and accepted: one fundamental was that four people had had a hand in killing Chuck Skwarok and in trying to dispose of his body. Another fundamental: within six hours of Skwarok's death, the Royal Canadian Mounted Police, who serve the city of Wetaskiwin as its urban police force, were informed of that fact.

By early morning of 15 September 1989, about a dozen RCMP officers were investigating the crime.

In order to have a clearer understanding of these events, I compiled a timetable from the verbatim record of the preliminary inquiry held in Wetaskiwin in January 1990, and then collated and supplemented it with data from the official transcript of Yvonne's and Ernie Jensen's trial for murder conducted over a year later. Here are the results:

Sequence of Events, Friday, 15 September 1989

Before 5:00 a.m.: On-duty RCMP constable Thomas Witzke investi-
gates a small hatchback parked behind bushes inside Parkdale
Park, beside Parkdale School. He sees "nothing out of the ordinary" and radios for a tow.

5:35 a.m.: Ex–taxi driver Lyle Schmidt contacts Witzke and talks to
him in his cruiser; Schmidt gives him a knife as evidence of a
possible murder in Yvonne Johnson's house.

6:00 a.m.: Witzke informs his superior, Corporal David Aitkin.

6:15 a.m.: Witzke, with Constable Ladoucer, tries to enter Yvonne's
house; she won't let him in without a warrant.

6:30 a.m.: Aitkin contacts Corporal James Bradley of the RCMP
General Investigation Section (GIS), Red Deer, for assistance.

7:00 a.m.: Schmidt signs a two-page statement about a possible
homicide; Aitkin sends Constable Ambrose Wolfe to close the
dump and Constable William Fraser to keep Yvonne's resi-
dence under surveillance.

7:30 a.m.: Harvey Schneider sees a body in the dump; radios police.

7:40 a.m.: Wolfe arrives; sees the body from the dump entrance but
does not go down. He radios to headquarters in code to avoid
scanners—"a 10-4 type of thing"—which simply means "Confirm." Aitkin does not understand that Wolfe has found a body,
but knows the dump is closed off and guarded.

After 9 a.m.: Red Deer GIS officers headed by Corporal Bradley
arrive in Wetaskiwin and, with Aitkin, organize a search of the
dump for a possible body.

10:55 a.m.: Aitkin, Bradley, and others, including a police dog,
arrive at the dump. Under oath Aitkin declares this is the first

time he knew that Wolfe had had the body in sight for over three hours.

11:20 a.m.: On a warning from Fraser that Dwayne Wenger has come out of his house, Witzke and Constable Pittman drive there and arrest Dwayne outside Parkdale School, where he has gone, he says, to check on his small daughter.

11:38 a.m.: Constable Dennis Travanut, GIS, begins to interview Dwayne in the Wetaskiwin RCMP headquarters.

When the law-enforcement system seizes you as a criminal, the world changes. You may never recognize yourself again.

Yvonne knows she can only escape into sleep, to take herself away with alcohol. If she forces herself out of sleep, out of bed, the phone is ringing, ringing, all she does is interrupt her escape.

"Yvonne! What the hell's happening?"

It's the neighbourhood pawnshop owner, telling her her name is all over his RCMP scanner. She hangs up, tries to crawl back into her escape, and notices Dwa isn't in bed with her, but the phone rings again; it's Jerry, Dwa's friend, shouting in her ear, frantic.

"Vonnie! There's cops with guns all over, they're swarming around your house, get out, just get out!"

"Get out? Where?" she asks him and hangs up. She flops back onto the bed, pulls the covers high; blankets can be trusted to be close and warm and——There's a tremendous bang, the kitchen door is breaking open. She sees there's a guy in a tan jacket hunkered down against the corner of the bedroom door, arms extended and locked together, and she is looking at the small, steady circle of his pistol barrel.

"Police! Don't move!"

What took them so long? She feels as if she has been sleeping for months, floating on alcohol; some weeks ago she wouldn't let them break in without a warrant, she could just let him shoot her, there's a shotgun with an RCMP standing in the doorway trying to cover her too, okay, enough guns, they'll do it, but the uniform blunders against the first guy, knocks him aside into the bathroom doorway, and then she is almost laughing at these Keystone Kops—Where's the camera?—

and she pulls the blanket up while they curse each other, thumping around, but her feet go cold, and she kicks to cover them too; the blanket jerks and she curls down to pull it back tight again and the big bastard in uniform is rushing her.

The plain-clothes man yells and shoves the uniform back into the kitchen. Yvonne lies motionless, watching them. Right now she's still okay with her T-shirt and jeans on, she's quiet in bed. But then the squatting cop with his gun levelled, the tan plain-clothes man, waddles in on her low; he is saying something, maybe identifying himself again, maybe barking to keep her hands in sight; and a horde of men in uniform are crowding into the doorway, all pump-actions levelled. She hears herself moaning, she is trying to somehow stay herself, be her own believable person, but he's moving in, his gun won't stop boring in, and then he jerks her blanket away, throws it into the corner. She tries to crawl after it, the reality of her blanket, but he shouts:

"Don't move! Do you have a weapon in your bed?"

She has nothing. Arrest strips her of every possible thing, especially choice. After Chuck, Lyle sealed it: someone had to make her choices and now they are made. She recognizes that this man she has never seen before with his revolver and tan jacket will do it. He is reading, very distinctly, from a card taped inside his notebook:

"You need not say anything. You have nothing to hope from any promise or favour, and nothing to fear from any threat. Whether or not you say anything, anything you say may be used as evidence at your trial."

If you want to, speak, but you have the right to remain silent. Silent . . . it's hard on the brain, it destroys the spirit—just go back inside the hole you already know so well; be silent. Yes, I can be that.

"You are under arrest for murder. Do you understand?"

The policeman attempts to turn her over, she is so limp her arm falls back on the bed where it was when he picked it up. She sees but does not particularly feel herself handled by this man with his gun in her face, rolling her over on her stomach. She is gone, not floating out of herself but gone inside. Like a turtle.

His knee is between her shoulder blades; he reaches for the other arm but the first flops back. Finally he tells someone angrily to come snap on the cuffs.

"... legal right to have a lawyer present when you are questioned ..."

She has heard that before. But never in her bedroom, never in her own house where her children live.

Yvonne sees two plain-clothes men are trying to wake Ernie on the couch; two uniformed police climb in through the patio doors and shove aside the chairs, let's get the bugger hauled out, but Yvonne's Tan Jacket yells at them, "Don't mess up a crime scene!" and they hastily try to push the furniture back where it was. They're dragging Ernie's arms together for handcuffs, "No!" Tan Jacket orders again, "He's gotta be awake; you have to read him his rights!"

Yvonne asks, "Where are my kids?"

"Hey," Tan Jacket says, "someone better round up the kids before Social Services gets here. How many have you got?"

"Three."

"Find three kids," he orders.

A uniformed officer brings her knee-high leather boots, her classiest shoes, into the crowded kitchen, bends, sticks her feet into them, hauls them up her legs, and then pushes her jeans down over them. She is being shoved out, moves mechanically, gripped by someone holding her elbows back; she's bumping into the huge men standing all about her like trees.

"I want to talk to my kids!"

But they've got her out on the porch, pushing her, helpless with her hands cuffed and ankles shackled, and a photographer is flashing pictures. "No!" her Tan Jacket yells behind her. "You, get that camera, take out all the film!"

She can hear James behind her and she jerks her elbow loose, turning, and he says, "Okay, okay—let her."

James—her Little Big Man—stands on the top step, staring about, very frightened. She kneels in front of him, into him since she has no hands to touch him; he nuzzles closer and she places her forehead against his. She tells him she has to go away for a while, these men say she has done something bad, but she will be back as soon as she can. His lips quiver, his eyes fill, and there's her Suzie Q squeezing between cop legs.

"Hi, Baby. Mommy loves you. James, you go take care of your sister, both your sisters, watch out for them ..."

She wants to hug them; it is unbearable not to be able to hold them, and she jerks herself away so they won't see her cry. She tells Tan Jacket, "Take me, now!"

Then Chantal comes running from school, bouncing through the trees, and sees Yvonne being pushed towards the cruiser, weeping, falling to one knee, and the seven-year-old freezes. The police haul Yvonne to her feet beside the car, and then she sees Chantal. She forces herself to think, to speak clearly through the pain that is breaking her, "Chantal, tell them you want to go to Aunty Bev's. Get them to let you."

And Chantal understands; Bev is a friend who takes in foster children; the kids are always playing back and forth between their houses.

But then her private life is over. She's pushed into the back seat of the cruiser, Tan Jacket follows, and already there are only questions.

"Where'd you guys take him? He may still be alive, where?"

"I don't know where he is."

A grand, public departure with an RCMP in uniform driving a uniformed car and all the neighbours at attention. She'll never see the door, the house again. Or her wide Dodge van, standing there, waiting for her to get all the children together, to climb in and turn the key.

They are pulling her out at the jail when she says, "Get my mom . . . Red Pheasant Reserve . . . she'll come for my children."

"Where, your mother, where is she?"

"Saskatchewan. Cecilia Bear Knight. No phone."

"Her name is Ceas—Ceas—what? Bear?"

"Knight, Red Pheasant . . . Ce-cil-i-a."

They are in control.

———

Except for one thing: her silence. Questions, questions, let them pull out strands of hair, even offer them more—here, take it—so that they will finally let her sink into a chair and she can tilt forward, lay her head face down on another chair, go away. Long ago she knew this, as a tiny child she was taught this over and over: cry if you must, but don't speak a word. Not to anyone. But the questions persist; surrounded by uniformed chests she realizes her menstruation has begun. They don't know what to do; they all leave and a woman officer appears. She leads her to a bathroom, strips her naked, and gives her coveralls of paper. And a pad, when she asks for it.

Then it's back to the interview room. Tan Jacket appears, more questions. She tells him that last night a cab driver named Lyle raped her and she is hauled to the hospital, to the clinic and lab; she's shivering in the monkey suit, very nearly hidden in it, but not her head, and of course her hands are sentenced to exposure in handcuffs, her legs to shackles; she's on public view and led about with her hands over her crotch—no panties are permitted, only the coveralls. Pulled by men in and out of cars, past hospital and clinic workers, patients, past policemen, prisoners, janitors, lawyers, all of them men and all of them glancing sideways at her again and again, at her handcuffed hands bunching her sagging paper suit up high between her legs because she must hold the pad in place somehow.

Finally, late Friday evening, the endless dragging around is over and she is locked in a cell; she can lie down. She knows that Dwayne and Ernie have also been arrested; that Shirley Anne is nowhere to be found—but there will be time to think, more than enough time.

Sequence of Events Continued

Friday, 15 September:

11:45 a.m.: Constable Daniel Konowalchuk, GIS, and other officers break into Yvonne's house and arrest her in her bedroom. At the same time, Witzke arrests Ernie Jensen asleep on the living-room couch. They are driven, separately, to the Wetaskiwin RCMP station.

12:20 p.m.: A legal-aid defence lawyer, Ken Sockett, arrives for Yvonne; he asks the police to give her a breathalyser and blood test. Samples reveal alcohol content over double the legal limit.

12:33 p.m.: Unknown to Yvonne or Ernie, Dwayne agrees to make a statement.

After 1:00 p.m.: Yvonne states she was raped by Lyle Schmidt; she is taken to the hospital and then a clinic, but only blood tests are made, no examination for signs of rape.

3:00 p.m.: Constable Fraser takes sample of "red smear in the dirt" around the body at the dump.

4:26 p.m.: Ernie Jensen talks briefly to his lawyer.

4:49 p.m.: Body is removed from the dump; Aitkin accompanies it to the Medical Examiner in Edmonton.

4:39 p.m.: Dwayne agrees "to come clean." He is taken by Bradley and Travanut to the house to re-enact the crime on video and audio tape.

5:14 p.m.: Dwayne is back in headquarters; he signs a fourteen-page statement, but the police say the video machine did not record anything, and he agrees ("showed no hesitation") to return to the house and redo it (6:31 – 7:06 p.m).

7:46 p.m.–8:20 p.m.: Bradley tries to interview Ernie; he denies knowing anything about anything.

Saturday, 16 September:

Early afternoon: Lyle Schmidt is taken to Yvonne's house for a video and audio re-enactment of what he knows.

4:47 p.m. – 6:03 p.m.: Schmidt completes a sixteen-page statement.

The Boys and the Cell Shot

[Dialogue selected from the official record of "cell shot" made between 10 a.m. and 2 p.m. on Monday, 18 September 1989; other details are added from the sworn testimony given by Constable Harvey Jones at the preliminary inquiry, 1 February 1990.]

The parkland world of fall evergreen and glazing gold aspen shimmers over the Medicine Lodge Hills to the west, and the Bear Hills of the Hobbema reserves to the east, as Constable Harvey R. Jones of the RCMP General Investigation Services, Red Deer, drives north to Wetaskiwin. It is Monday, 18 September 1989. He listens to the country-music station that highlights area news, and its "Top of the Hour" report is about the three Wetaskiwin people who have been arrested in connection with the murder, last Friday, of an unemployed man of no fixed address; another suspect, a woman, is still at large.

The three will appear before a judge this morning to be formally charged in court.

With his long hair, beard, and rough clothes, Constable Jones looks like a biker; his official assignment is to be an actor who fishes for information. He will describe his job to Judge H.B. Casson at the preliminary inquiry as follows: "I had been advised [by Corporal Bradley] that I was going to be placed in the cells with one or possibly two suspects in relation to a homicide. I was given no details—I heard some basic details on a radio broadcast [. . .]. It's generally found, if a person goes in in an undercover capacity . . . the less they know the better."

Around ten o'clock, he gets himself shoved into the largest cell in the Wetaskiwin City Police Station. He is armed with all he needs: a tiny radio transmitter concealed under his shirt collar, low enough on his neck so his beard won't affect it.

Dwayne Wenger is seated on a bottom bunk; he glances up as the guard locks the door behind Jones.

"How ya doin'?" Jones says with just the right edge of careless cheeriness to get a momentum started.

"What?"

Depressed all right; and worried. "Say," Jones says, cheerier, "how ya doin'?"

Wenger does not respond; he looks ill, his body hunched together in baggy prison coveralls on the edge of the bare bunk. Finally he mutters: "Watcha charged with? Remanded?"

Jones: What's that?

Wenger: Remanded, or you got [to] do time?

"Well." Jones drops on the other bunk at right angles to Wenger's, slumping over close into better pick-up range, "They're breaching me on my parole. So they charged me for the dope dealin' so I'll do some dead time, I guess. Fuck-all a guy can do about it. What ya in for?"

Wenger: Second-degree murder.

Jones: Hoo, fuck. Was that that one that was on the news?

Wenger: It was on the news?

Jones: Yeah.

After a moment Wenger mutters something that ends in "fuckin' queer."

Jones: What's that?

Wenger: The guy was a child molester.

Jones: Oh, you're kidding. Who?

Wenger: I don't know his fuckin' name. We only just met this once.

Jones: Oh, you didn't know him at all?

Wenger: I didn't know the guy. I met him twice [. . .]. The guy was still alive when we put him in the car and then they took off.

Jones: Well, they shouldn't be able to get you then [. . .] if he wasn't dead when he left . . .

Wenger: Well, they gotta fuckin' prove it.

Jones: You have to prove it.

Wenger: (Inaudible.) Figure out how long he was dead and what time it happened.

Jones: Well, that's right. And how he was dead, or what killed him.

Wenger: Oh they already know that. Dead by strangulation, or getting hit over the head too much.

Jones: White guy or Indian?

Wenger: White guy.

"Fuck." Jones leans closer as if in camaraderie, but actually Wenger is talking so quietly he is concerned about "inaudibles" and worried that Bradley, listening, making back-up notes, will mess up this run by hauling him out to adjust the mike. "I probably know him if he's from here."

Wenger: I don't think [he is].

Jones: [. . .] Like was he fuckin' around with some kids here in town?

Wenger: He told, uh, he'd come around, he takes 'em, he goes like this to 'em [Police note: Wenger displays motion of someone parting vagina lips] (inaudible) cunt. Says he was goin' up on a charge for it. Now that's what I gotta find out. That way I have something reasonable, a reason for it.

Jones: For doing what you did, yeah? So what'd you do, did you ask him about it and then just punch his lights out, or?

Wenger: [. . .] This all happened so fast and then the one, there was four of us there . . . the fourth one, I don't know where the fuck she is [. . .].

Jones: [. . .] You're sure he was still alive? When he left you?

Wenger: I'm not sure.

Jones: Well, you had to carry him like out, or what? [Wenger nods]
    Oh, so what'd the guy do, did he get caught with him right in his
    car?

Wenger: He was found at the dump.

Jones: Fuck. You ever done time?

Wenger: For impaired.

Jones: Oh fuck that [Jones changes directions] maybe you can get
    this down to manslaughter or something. If they go first [de-
    gree], you're lookin' at twenty-five.

Wenger: [. . .] No, its second degree right now [. . .]. I had three kids
    there [. . .]. He's telling my buddy, there, Oh, I like your kids. All
    this was happening, I wasn't even there (inaudible).

Jones: The other guy was holding the rope on him, so, that should
    get you off, eh?

Wenger: Ah, the other guy said he'd take it all.

Jones: He said he would? What, he told the cops that?

Wenger: He told me that.

Jones looks at Wenger in amazement; he is sitting curled up on the
bed now, his knees against his chest and his arms wrapped around his
stocking feet as if he were frozen. After a while Jones says quietly, "So
you got an old lady?"

Wenger nods, though it may be he is simply rocking himself.

Jones: She's in, too?

Wenger: Yeah. We all did [. . .] We all did the beating, but, the one
    guy did most of the damage. With the stick.

Jones: What kind of a stick, like a bat, or what?

[There are several inaudibles here; Jones explains them at the preliminary inquiry: "I know Mr. Wenger told me that the victim was
choked with a telephone wire [. . .]. it's probably repeated two or three
times throughout our overall conversation."]

Jones: Fuck, what the, you shoulda taken him out and dumped
    him in a slough or something [. . .] the dump, that's the first
    place the pigs look.

Wenger: I told [Ernie] that, he said fuck, he fucked up [. . .]. It all
    happened so fast, I can't sleep since I got in cells [. . .]. If it
    wasn't for me too, he'd still be alive maybe.

Jones: Why?

Wenger: I was the only one strong enough to (inaudible) him
[. . .]. Couple of times he tried to run (inaudible).

Jones: Yeah. Hindsight's twenty-twenty, eh?

Wenger: Shoulda, coulda, woulda.

Jones: What's that?

Wenger: Shoulda, coulda, woulda. If.

Jones: [. . .] So your old lady's charged too. That's pretty tough. You
guys got kids? How many?

Wenger: Three [. . .]. Six, three, and two.

Jones: Holy fuck [. . .]. Well, if this other guy'll take the fall . . . you
should be okay. Your old lady, she probably won't get fuck-all.
You know, unless if she wasn't involved hardly at all [. . .].

The cell door opens. Constable Witzke pushes the other male
accused in and is closing the door, but Ernest Jensen turns quickly.

"Got any more cigarettes there, bud?"

Witzke gives him some. "One more?" Jensen asks, but Witzke just
gestures and closes, locks the door. As Jensen turns into the room,
Wenger is already off the bed and facing him.

"Ernie, you going to take the fall——"

"Who, me?" Jensen interrupts and wheels aside, walking the length
of the short room as if he had been pacing there for the past three
days. He twists the tap and drinks long as the water pours out. "[We
all] take the fall, whatever happens. Don't say nothing about nothing!
It's all gonna come out, probably. The way it sounds. Fuck, the
cocksucker."

His speech slips away into inaudibility. But Wenger persists: "You
told me you were gonna take the whole bit. 'Cause I got kids."

"I told them," Jensen responds, "he was still alive when we took
him to the car."

"You told them that?"

"Yeah." Jensen stops in front of Wenger; he is chewing an unlit
cigarette and they are almost the same height, though Wenger is stock-
ier. "They showed me that video [you did for them]."

Wenger sags. "Oh yeah?"

"Yeah. They told me everything you said."

Wenger slowly retreats to the bed, sits down on its edge. Finally he
murmurs, "I fucked up eh?"

Jensen bursts out with something about ". . . according to your lawyer!"

And Jones cuts in quickly, "Fuck, you never know, man, you might get it dropped down to manslaughter. . . . if a guy can grab five years or something, keep your shit together inside, you're out in three."

Jensen almost screams, "[If I] don't keep my shit together I won't fuckin' live one, never mind! [. . .] They charged me with second-degree murder."

Jones has to contribute some acting to calm Jensen a bit: "If I didn' have this fuckin' parole hangin' over my head, I could get bail [. . .]. You done time in Drum[heller]?"

Jensen mutters, "Yeah fuck. Ten years ago."

The cell door opens again.

"Wenger, your lawyer . . . your parents are here now."

A bit of hope flickers across Wenger's face; he goes out quickly. Constable Jones is relieved; the raw exposure of facts through argument is gone, but concentrating on two guys, trying to ensure audibility, is always so complicated.

"This fuckin' kid," Jones says confidentially, "he's pretty scared, man [. . .]. He says you did most of the damage."

Jensen drinks water again and is pacing, "He said fuck-all."

Jones: Why the fuck would he confess like that, the dumb — [Jones changes directions] Just a kid, eh, that's why?

Jensen: That's (inaudible) confessed, but [he's] pointing fingers in my direction. Okay. I don't know fuck-all. So like he just hung himself [. . .] the re-make of the whole fuckin' thing.

Jones: What, a video?

Jensen: Yeah.

Jones: You're kidding. You mean, he did everything?

Jensen: Yeah.

Jones: Well, if he did that, he's probably hung you too.

Jensen: Well, touch and go [. . .]. Either way I won't do six months.

Jones: Well, you might end up doing a lot more than six months if they get ya.

Jensen: I'm thinking serious suicidal.

Jones: Oh fuck, don't croak yourself man, don't be stupid.

Jensen: [I'm not] fuckin' dying for somebody else.

Jones almost laughs at the poor guy's unthinking contradiction, but he has to stay sympathetic. "Hey fuck, settle down [. . .]. From what the kid told me I don't think you guys are going to have much of a problem, anyhow."

Jensen: What do you mean?

Jones: Well, you're gonna do a bit of time. Well, the kid says, number one, the guy's a child molester [. . .]. and number two, everybody kinda got a few licks in on the guy and then didn't mean to fuckin' kill him [. . .]. It was a fight.

Jensen: If worse comes to worse, I think we should all be charged with manslaughter.

Jones: So big deal, you're looking at a fuckin' fin.

Jensen bends to the sink over the toilet, takes another drink from the tap, and is pacing again.

"Yeah"—he laughs, without humour. "Fuck my old lady, beat the fuckin' charge, that would be funny!"

"You got an old lady now?"

"Oh yeah. I got a boy [. . .]. She's sitting in court [as we're charged], she's looking at us, and she's crying [. . .]. fuckin' Heartbreak Hotel."

Jones: Boy, there's nothing worse than that. She bring the kid?

Jensen: No, no, he's only three [. . .]. See, he thinks that I should take the fall because he's got kids; well fuck, I don't got kids?

Jones: Well, he said you told him you would take the fall. . . . If you get in a fight and everybody's all wound up and you fuckin' threw a phone cord around the guy's neck and choked him out, it's how can they prove intent outa that? It was a drunken brawl [. . .].

Jensen insists: They got very little, very little on me.

"Is that right?" Jones looks at Jensen bent over the sink again, the long drink of a confused, desperate man—hit him. "Why," Jones asks, "why the fuck did you put it in the dump? Why not in a slough? There's a hundred sloughs around here."

Jensen mutters, "Juiced, man."

"Juiced! A guy like you though, fuck, you've been around the block, you know better [. . .]. Hey, the main thing is as long as you don't crack to them."

"Oh, yeah. I can beat it. What do you call that, uh, pathological."

"Liar? Is that what you are?"

"Yeah."

Jones proceeds very carefully: "You mean, you beat the polygraph?"

Jensen: Yeah, I could.

Jones: Is that right, well, that's what you should do then. That'd give you an out.

Jensen: [. . .] If it comes down to that, I can say, well, okay I transported [. . .]. Just depends what he's gonna do and what his old lady's gonna do [. . .]. See I can play dumb until we see what the preliminary [inquiry shows. . . .] I just hope they don't fuckin' bug us here.

And Constable Jones must lie, quickly, but he's there as a lie for the cause of justice.

"No," he says. "They can't any more. No way."

It's working. For Constable Harvey Jones a cell shot usually does somehow, and if the dual recording machines stand up, a lot of useful evidence will be collected for investigation. Three suspects complicate things badly, but it isn't his job to analyse the legality of this "surreptitious effort," as Crown Prosecutor Hill will call his work at the inquiry. It isn't for him to decide what's admissible, whom they should break, if anyone; which one of the three—possibly even four—to use against the others in court. He simply follows Bradley's orders.

And he's already formulating his testimony—he knows it will be required—before the judge at the preliminary inquiry, and also the trial; there will likely be both in this messy business. Testify how the accused Ernest Jensen was distraught throughout: unsettled, pacing, drinking water at least fifteen times in half an hour, up and down, by turns confident and depressed. "Mr. Jensen," he will say, "was just almost beside himself, he actually sat down on the bunk and stayed there for maybe two minutes [. . .]. He didn't look well, he looked like he was hung over to me, his hair was soiled. He was a very—I don't know—he looked in bad shape."

Jensen is thinking of something else. "That poor guy's old lady though, fuck."

"What?" Jones has more to fish. "She gonna go down?"

Jensen: She's one violent motherfucker.

"Oh, is that right?"

Ernie is silent, pacing. Jones doesn't even know Dwayne's old lady's name, but he knows she's involved, so he goes for a quick, hard lie, something drastic to fish Ernie out.

"Well," Jones says, "he told me, he says I woulda, we woulda never killed him, except she kept saying hit him, hit him, hit him. Is that right?"

But Ernie won't bite; he says nothing, so Jones shifts fast to another usual police angle, "What is she, an Indian?"

Jensen: What's that?

Jones: She Indian?

Jensen: Oh, yeah.

Jones: Oh.

Jensen: But that doesn't mean fuck all. I don't know what it is, she's just . . .

Ernie's voice trails away. Jones can only continue lamely, work away from exploiting a standard racial prejudice. And like most sudden prisoners, Ernie really cannot stop talking to someone; he will talk himself around to the vulnerability of his whole past life, the violence of his younger brother Al who is almost continually in prison, and the bad memories of his mother's death while he was in prison as a teenager.

But then Dwayne Wenger is shoved back into the cell; his lawyer has been trying to work on "some kinda bail" but "people charged with murder don't get out."

And so the two blunder around the crime again, it's all there is to their life, round and round, with Jones trying to elicit or confirm any useful detail.

Jensen: We can't talk till the preliminary. If they show that video—

Wenger: I'm sorry, man.

Jensen: Don't sweat it [. . .]. There's no reason to be sorry that this happened. We shoulda been more fuckin' aware that night [. . .].

Wenger: Shoulda, shoulda, shoulda.

Jensen: Shirley Anne. She was the fuckin' instigator that one for sure.

Wenger: Started it, and we fuckin' finished it [. . .]. She's the one that started the argument [. . .].

Jones: So then, she was just inciting the fuckin' guy? This bitch?

Wenger: Oh, she started. She told everybody what he said and that got us all worked up and then he phoned back and then, in a way we had it planned that we were gonna fuckin' do this guy in.

Jensen is bragging, "Gonna die." [At the inquiry Jones states he understood that Jensen meant "if he was a molester, they'd kill him."]

Jones: Don't fuckin' admit that to the cops, man. Neither of you guys, like fuck, you gotta get your story together, for sure.

Wenger: I told them he came over of his own will.

Jones: Yeah, that's good. Well, who phoned him, did you? Or your old lady.

Wenger: He phoned over, but Yvonne invited him.

Jones: Invited him. Fuck, don't ever tell them that [. . .]. And you got rid of the piece of wood, eh?

Jensen: Oh yeah, it's buried [. . .]. He wanted to play hard ball, but he got the hard ball. I don't feel too good now, though.

Abruptly, Jensen is called out, and Jones works hard to take advantage of his absence. And Wenger talks, talks without seeming hesitation.

Wenger: Ernie fuckin' kicked him in the balls six, seven, eight times when he was lying down there.

Jones: Oh, is that right? It was, and Ernie was hittin' him with that thing?

Wenger: He shoved that thing up his ass.

Jones: Ernie shoved it up his ass. What, you guys stripped him? Before you did him?

Wenger: Ernie and I took his clothes off and said how do you like this (inaudible) fuckin' diddling little kids. You'll get your own medicine, and he shoved it up.

Jones: [. . .] Ernie says your old lady gets pretty wound up, eh? [. . .]. Because the guy was a skinner? That's what pissed her off or?

Wenger: Yeah. . . . (inaudible) Ya gotta defend yourself [. . .].

Soon Ernie is back in the cell, and on and on the story circles, for another hour. They try to co-ordinate each other's booze-spaced memories of a terrible night. Was it accidental? As Ernie says it, "I still can't piece it all together, that's the fuckin' worst part."

But Dwayne is dead certain of one thing. "Shirley Anne started it all and she was fuckin' right there until the bitter end."

To keep up appearances, and to change tapes, Jones is called out of the cell as well. When he comes back he tells the two, "You guys are the talk of the town."

For a moment they are diverted by their dubious fame, but Dwayne still feels bad about his video re-enactment and abruptly he confronts Ernie, who drove the body to the dump in Skwarok's car.

Wenger: The car, you got lazy, didn't want to walk home [i.e., from the dump, so he simply drove it back and parked it behind bushes in the park across from the house].

Jensen: That's right.

Wenger: That was you, fucked up there.

In the face of this growing blackness, Jones tries to be helpful: "Shoulda torched the car. You should've drove it over into a lake."

"Shoulda, coulda, woulda."

"Yeah." Jensen grinds it out; bending to drink at the sink again.

But neither can endure such confrontations. They know at any instant the door can open again like a sentence and they'll be separated, and all their defensive, momentary togetherness will be gone. They must hold hard to whatever fleeting camaraderie they can find, and Ernie grabs for it with a laugh:

"We gotta watch ourselves from here on in," he says. "But what can you do? Have another beer and go out and fuckin' do it again."

Constable Jones laughs uproariously. "I like your attitude!"

Jensen: Talk of the town, my in-laws will never, ever, ever talk to me now, never mind the last time.

Wenger: I never talk to mine, anyway [. . .].

Jensen: I don't know whether to shit, laugh, cry or go blind.

Wenger: Who's gonna paint my house now? I got this guy's house all masked off and ready to spray and there she sits, fuck!

They're all laughing, hard, feeling not too bad for a moment.

Jensen: I guess a guy should try and cheer up. It ain't gonna get any fuckin' worse [. . .]. It was just a party that turned into a accident."

They are all silent. They know they are at the centre of their small city, Wetaskiwin, "The Place of the Hills of Peace," where they live, work, hang out, walk warm along the sidewalk in sunshine, wheel their vehicles around to any bar they please and someone they know will be there, will say, "C'mon over, have one on me"—but now all they can hear are the heavy sounds of captivity, feel the density of every wall and door with their tiny sliding windows.

Dwayne Wenger says, "The thing that bothers me, it's Yvonne. She's always left alone. That could screw anyone up." He gestures across the hall. "She's next door, there."

Dwayne goes to the door, peers through the crack left by its window. Suddenly he shouts, "Vonnie!"

"What?" Her voice is distant but clear, as if buried.

"How you doin'?"

"Reading."

"How are you?"

"Fine. I love you."

"I love you too."

Ernie is beside Dwayne, on tiptoe, trying to peer out. Dwayne mutters. "They got 'em right over there."

"She's in the way," Ernie says, "we can't see."

Dwayne says, "I'll show you how."

"Straight," Ernie says, "straight from that window—you can't see her?"

"Yeah, I know. I fuckin' know every square inch of this place, I painted it."

"Can't cry over spilt milk, but I sure wish that prick woulda never showed up that day."

Wenger yells at the door, "Come on and feed us!"

Four hours in a cell is exhausting work. In a minute Constable Jones will give Bradley the prearranged signal that will get him out of here, but even as he thinks this, he studies the two doomed men once more, carefully, with the trained eye and memory of a professional witness who knows he will be cross-examined by lawyers in a court of law. Poor buggers.

———

Yvonne is silent; not even with a lawyer present will she speak. She does not know what anyone else has said, she knows nothing of Dwayne's video re-enactment of the crime; all she decides is, sober as she is now, from her they will learn nothing. At her brief court appearance on Monday she is charged with second-degree murder and then taken back to the women's cells at the rear of the Wetaskiwin police station, behind the desk in the hall where a matron is always on duty.

But shortly after noon on Monday, she becomes aware of stirrings in the hall; whispers outside her locked door. When she peeks through the blind in the window to see, a large RCMP man blocks it and begins twirling what sounds like a noisy ratchet to cover what is being said. Abruptly the door opens and she is ordered out so that her cell can be cleaned. When she protests that she's just cleaned it herself with a mop and hot water, the officer says, gesturing "Johnson, out, now!" and of course she goes.

They put her first in a cell with two bunk beds, down the hall near the men's section. She listens, and suddenly she knows she is opposite Dwayne's cell. She hears him talking to someone, though she cannot understand what they're saying. There is coming and going, and soon Ernie is brought in too, mooching for cigarettes even from the cop. Two co-accused together in a cell with a third prisoner? Coming and going, talking? She feels very uneasy—Are they playing the usual police games on them? Since when does it take all afternoon to clean a cell that's already spotless?

Dwa calls to her once, and she tell him she loves him before the policeman shuts them up. It gives her a jolt of happiness.

After supper on Tuesday, 19 September, Yvonne is moved again. And she is astonished to find her cousin Shirley Anne is already in the cell where they place her. Sitting on one of the lower bunks, close beside another woman inmate. They look up when Yvonne is escorted in, surprised as if caught whispering together.

Later, Shirley Anne would make various statements that when she ran from the house after midnight on the morning of 15 September, for some time she hid in terror of "Yvonne sending the boys after me"; that she tried for refuge in the house of a minister she knew, but he had moved—"I seen Satan that night when that [other] man answered the door"—and she fled; that after huddling in an apartment landing all night, next morning she hitchhiked to Edmonton to stay with her "stepfather," John Wheels.

Yvonne knows John Wheels as a man Shirley Anne lives and drinks with when the occasion arises. But Yvonne doubts that Shirley Anne ever went to Edmonton, because no street person in the city remembers seeing her. Yvonne believes she may have hidden in Wetaskiwin, perhaps with her mother or Lyle Schmidt, who stated in court he knows her very well.

But on Tuesday, 19 September 1989, *The Wetaskiwin Times Advertiser* carried a large front-page headline, "Three Charged in Slaying," just below a picture of a police officer photographing the half-naked body of Leonard Charles Skwarok, thirty-six, of no fixed address, lying in the dump. The news item stated that Dwayne Wenger, twenty-eight, Yvonne Johnson, twenty-seven, and Ernie Jensen, thirty-two, had been charged with second-degree murder in provincial court on 18 September. The article continued on page A5 with a headline: "Police Seek Woman for Information," directly above a dramatic picture of Dwayne in front of a police car, surrounded by officers and giving the photographer the finger. The article concluded: "They [police] are also looking for Shirley Anne Cooke, 39, who also goes by the last names of Bear and Salmon, who they believe has information about the murder."

On the afternoon of Tuesday, 19 September, shortly before four o'clock, Constable Witzke was talking to Cecilia, who was at Yvonne's house taking care of the children, when the phone rang. It was Shirley Anne. She said she was at the pay-phone in the Wetaskiwin bus depot; she wanted Cecilia to meet her, so she could tell her side of the story. Cecilia told her to turn herself in and hung up; then she informed Witzke. In a few minutes he was at the depot; a bus was leaving, he stopped it and asked the driver if a person fitting Shirley Anne's description was on it.

Witzke testified at the inquiry: "The driver pointed to a person walking away from me who at that time turned and looked at me, and then walked towards me."

The person admitted she was Shirley Anne Salmon, and added, "I was going to turn myself in to the police in Edmonton"—even though she later claimed she had just come from Edmonton. Witzke did not question her about that; he simply arrested her for murder.

According to Witzke's testimony at the inquiry, Shirley Anne told him in the car, "I want to tell the truth." At the station he read her the standard police warning about her rights, but then, just moments before a legal-aid lawyer arrived, she said, "I didn't know he was dead until I heard it on the radio the next morning. It wasn't premeditated. We just got drunk."

Witzke then asked her nine questions, all of which she answered; he testified that he wrote them down in his notebook immediately after:

"You want to tell the truth?"

"Yes [. . .]. I'm not a murderer. I was coming down for court yesterday. I got ten dollars for the bus and came down to turn myself in."

"How well did you know Chuck?"

"I just met him once."

"Were you there when it happened?"

"Yes, I saw it all."

"Did he talk about molesting his kids?"

"He said he was charged once. You can check his record."

"He has two girls, a six-year-old and a baby?"

"I think it was the baby."

"Did he say what he did to her?"

"He said he did it to her."

"Did he say if he touched Yvonne's kids?"

"I think he said something. I was kind of loaded."

"Did Yvonne and Dwayne fight with Chuck?"

"Yvonne did nothing. It was the guys. They threw him down the stairs."

"Did you and Yvonne go downstairs?"

"Yeah, but we just watched."

They say the first statement is always closest to the facts—or could it be closest to lies?

———

To Yvonne, being placed in this new cell, and with these people, "didn't line up right." She had been held in the women's cells, at the back, and suddenly she is moved in with Shirley Anne and a young woman. Why? She feels something is going on, so she ignores the two women, she looks around. But Shirley Anne gets up quickly.

"O, Vonnie . . ."

Yvonne sees a pear-shaped blob of off-white plastic stuck high on one wall. She tugs a blanket off a bunk and tries to flick it at the blob, to knock it off. But the new woman grabs the blanket from her. "I'll do it!" She flicks feebly, but achieves nothing.

"It's just . . . a bump," she says, turning away.

Yvonne is looking steadily at her. "Who are you?"

"I'm Mary. I got bust for cocaine today—when were you arrested?"

Yvonne considers her shirt and jeans; dirt smeared all right, but not worn in, nothing ground into seams as there would be if she'd been sleeping in them for a few weeks; and perfect teeth, like a toothpaste ad—coco-nuts are teeth grinders.

"A few days ago."

"Oh, so soon after the . . ." and the woman stops.

"So soon after what?" Yvonne asks.

"After they found the guy, at the dump."

"Who told you that?"

"She did, she . . ." Mary gestures lamely.

Yvonne turns away, goes and sits down on the toilet. She looks at her cousin and tells her, very carefully, "Listen, in here you shouldn't talk to her, you shouldn't talk to me, you shouldn't talk to the cops, you don't even talk in your *sleep*, you only talk to your lawyer. Got it?"

Yvonne believed she had foiled an attempted "cell shot" on herself and her cousin; she did not then know that within less than an hour Shirley Anne and Corporal James Bradley, a twenty-year veteran of the RCMP special branch of General Investigation Services, would have a long conversation in a "co-operative, congenial" manner. As Bradley testified at the inquiry, Shirley Anne told him she wanted no tape recorder, but she saw him make copious notes and did not object.

Shirley Anne began by asking Bradley if the other three had told the truth. He replied that some had, some hadn't, and then by directed questions led her into an extended explication of her life. When she got to the evening of 14 September, she said there was no phone call, no gun; she and Yvonne had just watched the boys in the basement.

After an hour and a half of this, Bradley, who had recorded Dwayne's double re-enactment of the crime (he did not tell Shirley Anne that, of course), testified:

> She asked me if Dwayne had told the truth and I said yes that he had. I said, What I want to know is, Shirley Anne, did you kick him just once? Now you know, and I know that you did not stab him, or strangle him, or drive him away and dump him. She said, "Yes! Oh God yes, I want to tell you this. I did kick him once in the basement…in my bare feet, once." She said that before she left Toronto she was close to God. She went to church every Sunday even if her husband wouldn't go.
>
> She said Pastor Goodman could verify that as he worked with the Indians quite a bit. She said that to her Sunday was a big day because she could wear her best clothes. I said that I used to be in a seminary to be a pastor too and I asked her if Goodman's first name was Bob. She didn't know but thought that he went to school out west somewhere. She asked me where I went to school and I said Saskatchewan. She said that the church was Pentecostal. I said I studied for two years before joining the Mounties. I said, "I want to know how many times you kicked him.
>
> "Like, Shirley Anne, when drunk, once, twice, three times can seem like once when you sober up. Like if he has bruises all over him and someone tells me he's kicked once, like do I believe that?" She said, "What I meant by once was I kicked him only one time in the basement, not each time I went [down] there."

In the next hour Shirley Anne told a much longer, and rather different, story about the beating in the basement; a very detailed one, as it developed. Including much more of her own, and particularly Yvonne's, participation in it. Finally, Bradley testified:

> She said, Can I ask one question; and I said, Yes. She said, Do I stand a chance? And I replied that it would be unfair of me to tell her. I told her that she should ask her counsel about that because if I was to tell her one thing and it didn't happen, then I wouldn't look very good in your eyes. She said she understood.

So at 9:15 p.m. on 19 September 1989, Shirley Anne was taken away to her cell "to relax," as Corporal Bradley told her, while he began the long and largely satisfying process of writing out two and a half hours of testimony.

Shirley Anne was arraigned in court the next day and officially charged with first-degree murder. That meant life—twenty-five years in prison. Not at all the "chance" she had asked Bradley about. As Yvonne explained it later in a comment on the trial:

> She ran, then tried to find out what was being said to cover her ass; while trying to receive this information—so she could tell her own story—[she got arrested] and she lies, saying she's turning herself in. So not being able to [find anything out], she lied in her first statements too, which got her nailed for first, and she later found out we were [only] charged with second. Then she tried to get me to talk, but I wouldn't.

———

Yvonne refuses to speak; even when she receives hints to contact the RCMP, she does not respond; she makes not one single statement. There comes a time, in the empty days of waiting for the preliminary inquiry while inside the Edmonton Remand Centre, when she begins to draw a few sketches, pictures. In grade school she always loved the art and music courses, and this seems another way of speaking to herself perhaps. She listens to a Christian minister who visits the centre, and after a time she begins to read a Bible again, as she did while living with Fred Ferguson. In November 1989, she sketches a message to herself, incorporating words someone else offers her.

She draws a bird-shape emerging out of a surround of words:

Do not fret!
Aren't we told His eye is on the sparrow—
That small fluttery brownness?
Imagine—a sparrow—
Sold two for a farthing. Almost two for nothing.
"Yet not one shall fall to the ground without His notice."

The bird Yvonne draws to encircle these words looks nothing like a sparrow. It seems to be swirling up from a seething cosmos, its head feathers swept back from its fierce black-masked eye, its strong beak open like any eagle's. Ahead and over this bird floats the tiny split ovum of the universe, and the bird is driving itself straight at the long tail that trails down from that egg.

Another drawing, from December, has the superscription

In the same way, I tell you, the angels of God
Rejoice over one sinner who repents.

Two immensely feathered wings below this text hold aloft between them the body of an angel whose single foot emerging from folded robes seems to stand on air. The angel's slender hands are folded over its breast, and one eye is open, looking straight at the viewer. But the other eye, the left eye on the side of the heart, is closed tight, blind to the outward world. Obviously its sight, in keeping with the Cree understanding of life, is turned inwards, searching for a revelation of that mystery which a human being can find only within herself.

Shirley Anne, of course, is being held in Edmonton Remand as well; Yvonne has to see her every day because they are in the same tier of cells. Shirley Anne is afraid; she doesn't know what the boys have said but she wants them all to "get their stories straight," as she says, for the lightest possible sentence. And she keeps confronting Yvonne with "You're gonna talk, you're gonna deal." But Yvonne refuses to speak about the case to the cousin who, she feels, has once again taken advantage of her kindness and then viciously betrayed her.

"No, I'm not talking to cops," she tells her flatly. "I can't judge what happened, who's wrong, who's right. The law doesn't care what happened, they only want to nail someone, that's all. They won't understand anything. I'm not talking."

Finally, the day after Christmas, their yelling matches turn into a physical fight. Usually the rule holds that if two fight, two go "to the hole," as the solitary confinement cell is called. Yvonne is interviewed first and says, "Guilty." But Shirley Anne, as Yvonne remembers it now, "had a wild made-up story, lie and bullshit, and put it all on me.

They returned her to my old cell with my daily cleaning job. I was the only one placed for fourteen days in the hole."

She thinks, if Shirley Anne can do this to me in Remand, what will she manage to do in court? Should she talk with the police, as they kept sending her hints she should?

As she comments to me years later, "I guess now I could have made a deal, but would not." Why? She could not bring herself to do that. Why? She does not know. She remembers her sometimes overwhelming depression then, alternating between anger and despairing guilt; when she emerges after two weeks in solitary confinement, she writes a long poem, "Loneliness," which ends with these lines:

> You try to walk
> But you're fearful of falling deeper
> Into another empty space
> That's within yourself [. . .].
>
> I touch myself.
> Am I warm or cold?
> I no longer know.
> Loneliness is existence within an existence
> Where nothing exists.

———

The official preliminary inquiry concerning the death of Leonard Charles Skwarok was conducted by His Honour Judge H.B. Casson in the Provincial Court House, Wetaskiwin, on 29 January–1 February, and 4, 6 and 11 April 1990; there were 703 pages of testimony and legal discussion.

It was during these days that, for the first time, the four accused heard all the evidence, and witnesses, that the police had brought together about the case up to that point. Ernie had said in the cell shot, "Play dumb to see what the preliminary shows" — well, now each of them knew what they had to contend with.

On 22 May 1990, Judge Casson ruled that the evidence presented at the inquiry satisfied him that it would be open to a jury to conclude that all four accused participated in the process of killing Leonard Charles Skwarok. He declared, "Accordingly, I'm ordering that the accused Wenger, Jensen, Johnson, and Salmon are to stand trial on the charge of first-degree murder."

A first-degree murder charge against all of them—it shocked the four defendants. A conviction meant a life sentence in prison, twenty-five years without the possibility for parole.

Though Shirley Anne had been arrested on a first-degree-murder charge, this judicial ruling terrified her. She had always insisted Chuck was still alive when she fled. Consequently, her lawyer, Stirling Sanderman, arranged for her to act as an informant on Yvonne in the Edmonton Remand Centre. Shortly after the inquiry ruling, she began to press Yvonne about details concerning the offence; to insist that Yvonne would deal. She was so awkward in her questioning that it seemed to Yvonne she was eliciting information, and finally, as she wrote it later, she yelled back at Shirley Anne,

> "It was you and Ernie kicked his neck, I heard it crack, then he gurgled, and then it was you who choked him!" At that, Shirley Anne flipped out, ran to the toilet and ripped off the tape of the bug she wore under her shirt and tried to flush the bug down the john, smashing it on the toilet and trying to stomp it down. To return to the bars gunning me off, with a shiny wire bouncing in front of her to her hard breathing, yelling, "I want to see my lawyer now!" I laughed at her as she stood there, I told her her shiny wire is sticking out. She was yelling, the matron came, and then a RCMP, to let her out and he retrieved the broken tape recorder out of the toilet.

Within days after that Shirley Anne was removed to the Red Deer Remand Centre, 150 kilometres from Edmonton, and on 19 August 1990 Corporal Bradley flew in 2,000 kilometres from Whitehorse, where he had been transferred, to interview her again.

When he was cross-examined at Yvonne's trial about these particular August 1990 interviews, Bradley stated he was told by J. Barry Hill, the Crown Prosecutor, "in no uncertain terms that there were to be no inducements or deals at all offered to this lady . . . and none were." Nevertheless, the first point he made to Shirley Anne was that she and her legal-aid lawyer, Stirling Sanderman, had agreed she should talk to him, and that Mr. Hill had instructed him to tell her that what she was going to give was a *witness statement only*.

"In other words, what you say to me now deals with what you saw as a witness, it cannot be used in any proceedings against you, it cannot be used at your trial [in this case]."

Further, he had written up his notes of that first interview of 19 September 1989—he showed her the typescript, from which he had quoted extensively in the preliminary inquiry—but since she had never signed it, it was now considered a *verbal statement only* and would "not necessarily, no" as he said it, ever be used against her in any trial.

Reassured on these points, she did a two-hour tape-recording with him, which became a seventy-four-page statement; he returned to Red Deer from Whitehorse again on 30 August 1990 to corroborate the typescript, and witness her initialled changes and final signature to it. He reassured her, "My commanding officer told me I can travel any time on this investigation because the Crown has basically said that they want me and you to deal with each other."

Shirley Anne was satisfied. She repeated and elaborated further on what she had already said, and in all signed three different statements totalling ninety-six pages of testimony.

———

Yvonne did not know that Shirley Anne was dealing in Red Deer, but she was proving herself in her own unique way at the Remand Centre. On 2 April 1991, the centre's senior psychologist, Dr. Patrick Thauberger, would write of her:

> During the past 16 months I have provided counselling to Ms. Johnson [. . .]. She has been the leading player in facilitating the adjustment and coping of mentally low functioning female offenders [in her unit]. These individuals are very difficult to place and are vulnerable to pressures and intimidation of less compassionate offenders. Ms. Johnson has consistently taken each and every one of these lower functioning offenders under her guidance [. . .]. She

is, in my evaluation, one of the most capable and sincere offenders I have encountered in 14 years of Corrections.

And, at the same time, she herself was beginning to speak. Not to a police officer, but to herself. She writes a document headed: "YVONNE JOHNSON / SEP-6th 1990 / Edmonton Alberta Canada." It is typewritten and single-spaced, fourteen pages loaded with words from edge to edge. From the very first page it is clear that she intends to write her life story:

[. . .] My life story may not be believable by most, but I bet a lot of people can understand [. . .]. Since I've been here waiting for trial for first degree murder I've come to know a lot about myself, and for the better. [. . .] I don't know how long my book will become, but at least it will help me deal with things in my head. I hope anyways. You see, to me writing this book will release long hidden fears, dreams, hurts, love, pain. [. . .] I'm doing this also in hopes of dealing with things that I never did before. Somehow maybe figure out some answers. I don't even know how to write a book but I will give it my best shot.

She continues with memories of her childhood, family, and personal incidents—funny, painful, many ordinary, some frightful. There is no detailing of any particular violent or sexual abuse, but several times she notes "I was a very scared child," and on page 8 her reasons for writing surface again:

I was not a child long enough. Maybe my childhood was not what my mom thought it was. Poor Mom, what this book has in store for you and Dad. Please believe me, I'm not doing this to hurt anyone. But I feel things must be said. I've held things inside for so long, and I can't deal with it [. . .] obviously something is not right, if only, if, if, if, if I want the ifs to stop. I want the whys to be answered. [. . .] I have been quiet too long. [. . .] I feel dirty all the time.

This amazing document of stories circling through Yvonne's life is filled with sketches of her father, mother, her siblings, and the continuing traumas of her cleft palate throughout her childhood: many facts and events we will use to write this book. And though Earl's death is not mentioned, pain appears often, and her admissions of her adult "hiding in drugs, booze, that never did give me any satisfaction, just confusion," and several of the incidents with her father and Leon edge close to the abuse she will later detail to me. The last page concludes with:

> [When I was small] I feared my dad not because of him and the spanking he was giving me, but because of other experiences that had happened to me. [. . .] Writing this and finishing it will be that thing in life that so many fear to look at. [. . .] As I always knew, but did not.

———

Nevertheless, for five years, Yvonne does not tell me about her memories of what happened in the basement. She drops a hint here or there, or makes a comment on the trial or factum records—"That's a lie" . . . "it didn't happen that way"—but reveals nothing consecutive or coherent.

On 1 September 1995, she writes to me, in her last words of *Journal 16*:

> I just can't seem to write in length of detail of Lyle or the offence. I feel it's not safe to do so. Or at this point in time. I just cannot do it. I will try to write what I can of things, but it's the best I can do. I will not write of the hours before, during, or right after the offence. I just can't bring myself to that.

To write the whole story, I need to hear her memory of the basement, but I cannot push her. So, I wait.

———

The preordained order of the legal process of Canadian justice and guilt and punishment in the death of Chuck Skwarok ground inevitably on, and with great slowness.

In its wisdom — presumably on the basis of the evidence it had gathered and the deals it had made — the Crown decided to try Dwayne and Shirley Anne in separate trials, but to link Yvonne's and Ernie's in one. Consequently, there were three trials.

On a serious charge such as murder, the trial usually takes place before judge and jury. However, if the accused pleads guilty the trial is conducted by judge only because there is no need to *prove* the guilt, only evaluate a just sentence. Since both Dwayne and Shirley Anne entered "guilty" pleas on which they could be judged, they did not need to face a jury.

Dwayne Wenger's trial came first. On 15 September 1989, he had been the first of the four to be apprehended; Constable Witzke arrested him at the door of Parkside School, where, he said, he had gone to make sure Chantal was in class. In the cell shot he also said that he'd gone to look for Chuck's car where Ernie had left it behind bushes in the adjacent park, though it had, of course, been towed away hours before. On 14 January 1991, Justice Nina Foster accepted his plea of "Guilty" to second-degree murder. Dwayne had hoped for the more lenient sentence of manslaughter since he had, to quote the prosecutor, "shown a great deal of remorse and cooperated all that he could," that is, with statements and video re-enactments, but rather than an extended trial he settled for a sentence that implied his intent to commit murder. Perhaps one critical point against him was his confession that, when the fight raged in the kitchen, he was the person who had thrown Skwarok into the basement. Judge Foster sentenced him to life in prison, but with the possibility of parole after ten years.

Within a week Shirley Anne Salmon's trial followed, and she got "the chance" she had so apprehensively asked Corporal Bradley about when he first talked to her after her arrest; she got her chance in spades. Her lawyer, Stirling Sanderman, reached an agreement with Crown Prosecutor J. Barry Hill and at her trial, on 21 January 1991, she pleaded "Not Guilty" to the first-degree-murder charge, but "Guilty to Aggravated Assault." Sanderman stated that she felt remorse and guilt for what she'd done, that her judgment had been affected by drink and also by pressure from the others involved. In an unusual, even astonishing move, Crown Prosecutor Hill accepted the much lesser plea of "Guilty to Aggravated Assault." Justice T.W. Gallant agreed to it and summarily sentenced her to an extremely light possible jail term of one year in prison and five years' probation. Peculiar as it was, the Crown attorney offered Shirley Anne less time than she wanted. She had already been incarcerated for sixteen months; however, at Yvonne's trial she testified that she herself asked to remain in the Red Deer Remand Centre for some time longer. As she explained, "There was one point that I was going to go out on bail last September [1990] and I asked my lawyer—I said could you ask for more time. I said I want to stay. My soul still feels bad because I believe I sentenced this man to death. So he said well, you phone me back in a few days. They're asking for more time anyway. Since you don't mind staying there. It's not that I mind staying there, but I didn't want to be going out somewheres down the line and think I hadn't done enough time for the death of this man."

Yvonne later wrote in the margin of the trial record: "You should be in my place."

As Shirley Anne stated under cross examination by Brian Beresh, she would "still be in the joint [ie: the Remand Centre] till May 21, 1991." That is, she would serve a sentence of exactly twenty months.

———

At this point I had become more than uneasy about the legal process which I had been attempting to assemble and narrate in a logical order. I felt I needed to have more comprehension of what, in terms of Canadian legal practice, was going on here. So I contacted several lawyers I knew, both those who served as prosecutors and those who act as defence counsels. To summarize:

> *Question*: All four accused had legal-aid counsel because they had no money to pay for their defence; does this raise particular problems?
>
> *Answer*: Legal-aid lawyers are paid minimal professional fees. They do their professional best, of course—legal aid is often the way lawyers build their reputations—but it is very onerous work and there are always more cases than there are capable lawyers willing to handle them. They are invariably rushed; they cannot

spend extraordinary amounts of time on any one case, however complex. Besides that, there may be little or no money provided for extra investigative work, beyond what the police are already doing.

Question: What kind of a defence lawyer is Brian Beresh?

Answer: He has a reputation within the profession as being one of the best. He's defended some very difficult cases. For instance, in 1987, in another well-known Wetaskiwin trial, he defended William Nepoose, who was found guilty of second-degree murder. Though Beresh lost that case, in 1992 he presented new evidence that two of the women witnesses had confessed to giving false testimony and indeed to "outright lying." A new trial was ordered, and Nepoose was declared innocent.

[In August 1997, Brian Beresh was chosen the defence lawyer for Larry Fisher, the Saskatoon man now charged in the 1969 rape/murder of Gail Miller, for which David Milgaard was once convicted. Clearly, Beresh has a wide reputation.]

Question: Is there a kind of "good defence strategy" for abused women accused of crimes?

Answer: They don't really teach you in law school how to represent abused women, or a raped child. And cases can't come any worse than the one you're talking about.

Question: What is this business of "making a deal" with one of several persons accused of the same crime?

Answer: It's standard legal practice. If someone agrees to serve as witness against other accused, they may or may not stand trial on a reduced charge and with a reduced sentence.

Question: But will their sentence be lighter?

Answer: It may well be, if they agree to plead guilty to a lesser charge. But a judge still decides on the sentence, according to the evidence presented.

Question: The evidence as presented by the Crown Prosecutor?

Answer: Yes, it's his or her responsibility to present the relevant facts of a crime gathered by the police, and for the judge to decide on a reasonable, fair sentence.

Question: And who decides with which of the accused "the deal" is made?

Answer: The Crown Prosecutor. Based on the evidence the police gather.

Question: So, the Crown Prosecutor has, in effect, already decided, before any trials take place, who the guilty parties are?

Answer: Well . . . that's not the way it should be phrased.

Question: Okay. But the Prosecutor decides which of the accused he or she will make a deal with, and then subsequently could present the facts against that "dealer" in the "dealer's" trial in a rather less stringent fashion?

Answer: (from a Crown Prosecutor): You must understand, you can only prosecute according to the legally defined laws of evidence. You have to weight where the clearest, most credible evidence lies, in order to get a conviction for the crime—in this case, the killing of a man—that has obviously taken place.

Question: Okay, so does the Prosecutor then decide that the party "most guilty" is the one for which he can most readily gather the clearest, most believable and incriminating evidence?

Answer: I wouldn't say "most guilty."

Question: And would you, as Crown Prosecutor, perhaps back off a little on the evidence against the party you're "dealing" with?

Answer: Some might. After all, it is a "deal." In any case, ninety-nine percent of the time the judge asks no questions whatsoever about possible further evidence. That's not his job.

Question: But a crime has been committed, you need a conviction, so you're looking for the most "believable evidence"?

Answer: That's true, but——

Question: And in weighing that evidence, in order to get a conviction, you might, for example, leave out of consideration that one participant could easily run away from the scene of the crime and claim—since no time of death has been established anyway—that the man was still alive before she left, while the other accused had to remain at the scene because her children were there and had to be protected? In other words, in this case the mother, because of her duty to her small children, provided the prosecution with the most believable motive *and* evidence?

Answer: No. You'd weigh the mother thing—but of course, there's no legal exemption for mothers to kill.

Question: But perhaps one could expect some *understanding* for a mother who believed her children were being threatened?

Answer: Oh sure—but a jury is a jury, if they say "First" no judge can do a thing about it. Because we have an adversarial courtroom system: the defendant is innocent until the prosecution *proves* him guilty beyond a reasonable doubt, and the defence will try its professional best, within its means, to expose every extenuating nuance and contradiction in every testimony. As Prosecutor you count on that—for the dialogue of oppositions to expose the factual truth. The fundamental concept is, the conviction does not depend on what either the Prosecutor or the defence says at a contested trial; it depends on what the judge or jury understands as being the most credible. In an agreed guilty plea, it's different, because the Prosecutor selects the charges and decides what evidence to call in support.

Question: Okay, that's the basic concept. Is that why, if you're rich enough to hire enough detectives and expert witnesses, you have a very good chance of throwing "reasonable doubt" on the prosecution's case?

Answer: Unfortunately, that's sometimes true. That may be part of the reason why jails are filled mostly with poor people.

Question: If so, if a person—especially a poor person from a racial minority seen generally in the community as being socially upsetting—if such a person goes to trial, one shouldn't really expect justice. One can only expect what the judge or jury, who are invariably of the majority race, will find "believable"?

Answer: I wouldn't say "only expect." One always hopes that what is believable and what is just to all concerned are the same thing. [One hopes.]

The trial of Yvonne Johnson and Ernest Jensen began on 4 March 1991 in the Wetaskiwin Court of Queen's Bench before the Honourable Madame Justice Nina L. Foster—who had already tried Dwayne—and a selected jury. The charge against the two remained first-degree murder to which they pleaded "Not Guilty." The Crown's case against

Yvonne rested primarily on the testimony of Lyle Schmidt and Shirley Anne Salmon, though they were both, to state it in the acceptable legal language of the defence lawyers, witnesses whose credibility "was greatly at issue."

Instead of pleading "Not Guilty" to one of the severest charges in the Canadian criminal code, why did Yvonne and Ernie not plead "Guilty," as Dwayne and Shirley Anne had, to a lesser charge such as manslaughter or even second-degree murder? According to Brian Beresh, he and Ernie's defence lawyer, Glen Allen, had several discussions with Crown Prosecutor Hill and Judge Foster to accept a plea of "Guilty" to manslaughter. But Beresh remembers Hill as having "a punitive attitude" towards both the accused, and towards Yvonne in particular. He recalls: "The judge was on our side in this matter but Hill would not budge." And without his agreement no change of charge was possible.

Hill was also adamant that Yvonne and Ernie's trial must be by jury as well as judge. It seemed to Beresh that Hill felt that such a brutal crime—beating to death an almost complete stranger—should "be judged by the community." Beresh and Glen Allen had at first elected to go with a judge and jury because, like all defence lawyers, they were apprehensive about having a hard-nosed judge preside over the trial. But when they learned that Judge Foster was to preside, a magistrate well known for her fairness and understanding, they requested a re-election to a trial by judge only. But Hill "would not back off" and allow re-election.

The defence lawyers had good reason to be apprehensive about defending such a widely discussed murder before a Wetaskiwin district jury. One of the accused was Native, and racial and social difficulties with the Hobbema reserves were well known. Also, Native people rarely accept jury duty, especially when a Native person is one of the accused. Generally speaking, they do not wish to sit in judgement on one of their own people, nor do they like to be seen as cooperating with a legal system that is so often pitted against them. To add to this, the area, which includes the densely populated, farming- and oil-based communities of Leduc, Camrose, Thorsby, Ponaka, and many others, is seen as deeply conservative, and a Bible belt of Christian practice and morality.

At every turn, then, the letter of the law as enforced by the Prosecutor, seemed to leave Yvonne no choice.

———

Besides the trauma of the trial itself, Yvonne faced several difficulties. By March 1991 she had been in prison for eighteen months. She writes: "I saw Xmas activities through the window bars of Remand for two years. I watched the people moving on the streets in dress for Klondike days. I lived through a strike there." Her three children were living together in one foster family, and if the charge had been minor, she would have simply said, "Yes. Guilty," and hidden and endured until she was let out.

As a child she had been trained and beaten to play the shadow, to be a rubber doll or an emotionless statue and take everything done to her; or to cry and so perhaps avoid somehow whatever brutal thing was happening to her. As an adult she had sometimes tried to evade problems either by fighting physically, with rage the only acceptable emotion, or by running away, or by hiding behind a bottle and all "the false bullshit and dreams" she could convince herself into. In short, from her cell in the Remand Centre she had come to consider the first twenty-seven years of her life to have been one jagged sequence of "ducking, hiding, dodging, diving, lying, fighting, running."

But none of these strategies was possible now. She would be taken to Wetaskiwin in chains—walk or be carried, it made little difference to officials—and the rest of her life would be decided for her.

The question remained: why not leave the Edmonton Remand Centre dead? Perhaps it was born-again Christianity, the moments of consolation she found in being convinced she was "saved." "Christianity," she would write later, "fooled me so well in prison for a while. It saved me from facing a lot of my reality."

But there was something more: her looming past which she could not yet order in her mind, nor speak of in any sequence of words because she did not yet know how to turn towards it; and if she could have so turned, it would have been impossible for her yet to face. Nevertheless it was there, and a small articulation of it began in the image of a poem she wrote on 16 June 1990:

There's a hole left in my soul
Where I fear to go.
There, once, a child should have lived.

Instead anger and hatred moved in.
They smothered the child
with filth and guilt.

———

In April 1993, I first talked to Brian Beresh in Edmonton several times on the telephone; he was efficiently courteous and professional, he returned my calls, he invited me to meet him in his office and gave me various boxes he had, full of the court records. At that time, the case was still before the Alberta Court of Appeal and, as he said, the decision was taking very long. But he would be happy to talk to me about it; it was, he said, "one of the saddest cases I've ever had."

It stands in the court record that Beresh requested that Yvonne's trial be severed from Ernie's, but Judge Foster's first ruling in the trial was: "I am not convinced that there is a need for severance. I will deal with that problem when it arises." As Beresh explained to me, severance is very difficult to get in cases where two persons are accused of the same crime. The law generally holds they should be tried together. Beresh also applied for a change of venue, largely due to the "emotive" language used by the local press, and that request also was rejected. Beresh then decided that his trial strategy would be to call no witnesses whatever: his defence would consist of his cross-examination of Crown witnesses.

As Beresh indicated to me later, he had an "ethical obligation" not to call witnesses who he thought might prove to be "unreliable." There are two different rules of professional conduct that he may be hinting at here: one is the "ethical" rule that you cannot call a witness who you believe will not tell the truth; the other is a rule of good practice, which is not to call a witness if you don't know what he will say, or how he will stand up to cross-examination.

"I had lots of good reasons," Beresh insists, and so no one was called to the stand to testify on Yvonne's behalf, or to challenge or contradict any of the statements made about her and her actions. Nor could she testify herself. Like her ancestor Big Bear at his trial for treason-felony in 1885, she did not speak a word in her own defence.

When I asked Beresh why he had not put Yvonne on the stand, he gave me two reasons. The first was that the two co-accused "agreed that neither would testify."

It is conventional wisdom, in trials with co-accused, that there is nothing a Crown attorney likes better than to have the two defendants pointing a finger at each other. Good legal advice would involve advising your clients of the fact that they could sink each other — either because their memories vary, or because they may implicate each other by finger-pointing on the stand. Unless their stories are congruent or mutually supportive, they can have a negative effect on the jury. Given the confusion and violence in that basement room, Yvonne and Ernie might remember things quite differently. And from his erratic comments in the cell shot, there was no telling what Ernie might say on the stand.

The second reason Beresh gave me for not wanting Yvonne to testify was "Yvonne does not present well, [she] does not look too good."

Yvonne herself says that at the time of the trial, "I was just totally shut down." Even in June 1997, she wrote of her reactions at that time in the third person.

> After the first day of the trial her lawyer told Yvonne, Try to smile a little bit, you look so hard. Yvonne either tried to hide behind her hair or find one spot in which to stare. Just sit like a zombie. She told her lawyer she did not want to go back into court, it could just go on without her, as her face being there just gave them an Indian face to judge and sneer at, she could say or do nothing anyway.

It seems quite possible that a Wetaskiwin jury would have been unsympathetic to the kind of woman she presented herself as at the trial.

In the end, Beresh said, a court decision depends on what the jury accepts. And the jury in this case was "mostly White men, local people." In fact, they were all White, nine of them men.

The jury of twelve Wetaskiwin Judicial District citizens retired to deliberate at 11:53 a.m. on 19 March; they returned to the courtroom at

1:42 p.m. on 20 March. Despite all defence cross-examination to the contrary, and despite Brian Beresh's concluding address, in which he emphasized that there was no credible evidence of intent to kill on Yvonne's part, and no evidence linking her to the injuries that caused Skwarok's death, the jury found Lyle Schmidt and Shirley Anne Salmon most believable witnesses. They also ignored Beresh's assertion that Yvonne could be guilty of nothing worse than manslaughter. Yvonne remembers:

> They came back with the verdict on me first. Unanimous, Guilty as Charged, first-degree murder, life, twenty-five years without parole. As they did, Ernie hit the floor, but I remained standing. And for the first and only time I looked each of the jurors in the eye; wondering, did they really feel better human beings for this, or self-righteous as some of their looks would say. Then came Ernie's verdict; guilty of second-degree murder. After a short break, the judge asked if ten years before possible parole was good enough, or more?
>
> They returned, saying ten was good enough, life-ten.
>
> Then the judge sentenced us in one final swoop. Like a drop from the gallows.
>
> I thought I'd comfort Ernie, he must be feeling it all, as I did. I told him, It's okay, if you look around, others got it worse than you. His reply was, "I won't get laid for a long time."

Throughout the trial, one source of support for Yvonne had been Cecilia and other family members who sat in court every day. On 21 March 1991 *The Edmonton Journal* reported: "Two relatives of Yvonne Johnson ran from a Wetaskiwin courtroom in tears after a jury convicted her of first-degree murder [. . .]. Johnson wiped away tears but remained relatively composed after the verdict and sentence."

12

The Power of My Name: Why I Must Remember This

It's confusing, it takes a lot of thinking to put it into some sort of—realism, some sort of life structure, something that says I was other than this. That I had some other life prior to this [. . .]. And how I could have lived and had memories . . . without recalling this. It [did] come back in dreams. But they were such horrific dreams that I didn't think that they were possible. In my healing process, in dealing with things and the memories coming back, I realize that they weren't hideous dreams. That they were actual things that happened to me.

 – Yvonne at trial proceedings,
  North Battleford courtroom, 21 June 1995

S NOW FALLING, lying flat outside my window. It's not real snow, it's just bits of white falling, a white space, and then a stone wall beyond my barred window. No rocks, no trees, no stubble or grass like there should be sticking out of it. And there is never darkness inside these walls, only floodlights all the time, lights brighter than ever with snow blinding the sky. I haven't seen stars for months. I came in spring, the end of April sometime, to the Kingston Prison for Women, and there must have been summer too, and fall, and now my first Christmas in Ontario has come, 1991. And snow is falling.

I have lots of time to watch it drift down against the grey limestone-concrete walls that go up into black. There is something black over me, like a huge trapdoor—and I can't move it. It's not my sentence, I can feel that in the hard walls around me, but something black made blacker by the sharp line of endless lights.

No one is allowed into the prison yard at night. If I serve my full sentence in P4W, I will possibly not see a star in the sky until 2014.

I work every morning as a general service barrier cleaner: I swab down the floors, doors, and bars with cleaner, and for two hours in the afternoon I go to school, writing and math. My nights are long, but also short-lived, and the nightmares that woke Dwa beside me in Wetaskiwin are beginning to come again. My bed here is made of steel, with a thin mattress.

I'm glad I'm not on the range any more. The range cells are like cages, six feet by nine; you can hardly turn around and you face tall windows across a wide corridor and can't see anything coming unless you angle a hand mirror—if you've got one—through the bars of your door. In the newer wings (they had to add these because more women are being sentenced to longer terms in Canada), the cells open onto an inner corridor and each cell has its own outside window. Mine faces a wall, but a small pane in it opens and a little real air can come in. The ranges are noisier, nastier—yells and shouting really echo around stone and steel—but I'm here for life, so after four months of range they placed me in the Wing, where it's quiet, and private.

That's funny—how private I am, will be—hardly funny. I'm one for the record books: the only Native woman in Canada currently serving a twenty-five-year sentence for first-degree murder.

Two women near me are together, getting involved with each other. I can hear them tonight louder than usual. A place like this breeds a new kind of woman; they're driven to anything, maybe as a last-ditch try to hold onto humanness. An act of sex may be the only free relationship you can have in here, and I don't know, when will it be my turn? I don't want that. But it's a reality behind bars, so it's acceptable; it's more or less expected. The women here have to find a new way of thinking, to live; they fear to act human, but who knows what that means in here, and so some keep trying. The guards can hear and see them of course, but do nothing. If they listen, it's just to tell each other ugly stories, and laugh.

Older women lifers usually have photo albums: of the years—family, friends, places—before, and then the years inside. They literally age before you in the seconds it takes to riffle through the pages, a reality they never talk about. I have no mirror hanging in my cell, because prison time lies so heavy on the mind and spirit I can see my age in the face of everyone around me. Women age faster in prison than men. A woman's body is made differently, and it deals with doing time differently. If you imprison what women are, what they were created for, they age very fast. Especially their sensuality and tenderness, their warmth; the world slots women into a certain kind of sexuality, and prison forces that to the extreme; a woman walking out of prison is a shell of woman, mother, lover, whatever it is to be female.

Men in prison worry about getting laid when they get out; women worry if they'll ever be loved again. Or capable of giving it. Many men pump so much iron they look better—like Leon, and with his hair cut—when they come out than when they went in. They'll say, "When I get out I'm gonna fuck everything that moves." and with men that's permitted, they expect it of each other. They expect to go back to their woman, or find another one, who's cared for their kids, who'll care for them—but women can never expect that. If a woman has borne children, they'll have been adopted away into foster homes; if she screws around like men do she's just a whore, and worse than any because she's done heavy time. A woman on parole can't run wild like a man because her children will suffer. Men generally don't care about their kids, in fact a lot of men brag they don't even know how many kids they have, leave alone where they are. Who cares—some woman, somewhere, is taking care of them.

A woman in prison can never think of her children that way. Her soul is full of grief and guilt towards them—are they suffering abuse, like she suffered it?—to keep insanity at bay she has to shut down. She's isolated, no lover, no motherhood. She ages fast into something dry; hard; shrivelled.

The reality of sex in a prison is, I think, very different for women than for men. There are, of course, homosexual people in both kinds of prisons, but beyond them, for male inmates sex is often connected with power games, protection, lust, dominance. For women it is more often a matter of loneliness, a need for affection, of feeling worthless. Women are the caregivers in any family; intimacy and tenderness is how they understand themselves, and when they're cut off from everyone they know in the completely controlled space of a prison, they mostly feel like less than nothing.

A prison for women breeds confusion, there's so much nothing to hold on to, and when you have lockdown, as they often do to us for any reason, which they may explain or may not—and you never know for how long, nobody knows—you just sit in your cell, alone, perhaps twenty-four hours after twenty-four hours. That's when you feel the years your arms have already been and continue to be empty.

And yet, I can't remember when in prison—I've been in over two years straight—when I've had the heart and body release of a good, complete cry. Sometimes there's a small sound, my nose runs, but whatever comes out is anger; it builds up, so I hold myself down, and I wake up with my pillow wet. Tears shed but useless. The door slams on my cell—I call it my house, with a note on the bars which says "Don't shake my cage." The door slams on my mind. What can a person think for twenty-five years?

By law they must keep our bodies alive in here, but what will we be when we're released? The human need for kindness, grace—it's impossible in prison. How can you ask for pity? All you do is try to shut down. Solitary is nowhere but inside your own head; and finally you really end up in there: your head only. I told an older girl cousin once what my grandfather was doing to me in Butte when I was four years old, but I didn't remember exactly what all he did, only that Mom kicked old "Fightin' Louie" Johnson out of the house as soon as she found out how he made me play with him for candy. And I remember once when I was even younger than four, I think, when I was tied to someone in a "sixty-nine" position, my ankles tied to this other person's wrists and my wrists to the other person's ankles. I don't remember doing anything, but now I recognize it as arousal. I cannot help but think. It lives on inside my head.

I found one good thing in P4W one day last summer: I sang in the winds of a rain. I was working on the yard crew—I love digging in the ground and making things grow in neat rows—and it began pouring rain. The rain cleaned the dirt of this place off of me, I wanted to ride the wind, I sang and wanted to fly with the storm.

I want to die, but not in here. Here there is pettiness, only pain is normal, love is one woman sucking another. God be merciful and let me die in my sleep. But not here.

My big brother Earl died in jail. He was in our home town, but every member of his family was far away too—Leon in jail and the rest of us in Saskatchewan. Earl told me when I was a child that I did not have to let people touch me.

Why did I once think, when a man has an erection, he's in pain? That it's my duty to help him relieve it? Any male looks at you, he wants sex? As I grew older I tried to get something out of sex for myself, I tried to tell myself I'm sexy—hey, look at these lo-ong legs!—but I knew I never was. I try to look back, and I can't remember any sober sex. I was too busy having to perform and I knew I could never handle it without liquor. I became more confused, numb. And I found men never seem to care anyway, as long as their lust is relieved, all that bulging, prodding pain.

My lifetime of doing what others demanded of me—if I couldn't stay out of their way. Except with my kids; and if only Dwa and I could have been together a little longer; a little while without booze. But I was hurting in ways I could not remember, then Leon came after me. Now I'm here, and Dwa is serving his ten years in Collins Bay Institution down the road. He got himself transferred from Alberta to Ontario so at least one person in my family would be closer to me. So we could try to stay together.

I don't know if Dwa and I stand a chance. I'll have a visit with him in the Little House in the prison yard, two or three days every two months, if we set it up right, but so far he's said he doesn't want to marry me, not in prison. I was trying to tell him of my first attack, and I was so emotionally drained I mostly wasted our few days together, I slept from three in the afternoon till three in the morning. I wonder if I'll make it through this, if Dwa has any miracle to help me, if my life can include my kids or if I'll have to teach myself to let them go. See them once a year on visits, as long as they can come, and let them grow up in the foster home where they are now. I won't go back to the Parenting Skills class they give here; it's mostly designed for short-term inmates and just frustrates me to hell. The first thing they take from you here is your motherhood, and by the time you're brainwashed enough to suit them, you're not even a woman. You're washed out, empty clothes walking past.

I sleep too much. But it's never enough anyway to make time move.

———

The "sugar shack" is what I call the Little House in the prison yard. Dwa and I have had a few three-day visits there now. I'm finally beginning to feel loved again, and comfortable with him. He's the same man I've known over ten years, but different, strange. We talk about more things, each other's needs. Even sexual, and we never really talked of sex before, just did it. When you're locked in prison, he says, you learn to think of women not only in a sexual way. Given the way other guys behave in prison, I didn't expect him to say that; he looks at me now as the one who bore him children, the greatness of women who are mothers, lovers, caregivers, giftgivers, sisters, aunties, grandmothers. In prison, he says, men can see life through a woman or learn to hate them forever, turned and twisted inside. The body reacts on its own, out of its nature, and a person's sexuality gets very tested when you are forced to abstain.

How can anyone imagine the loneliness behind all the masturbation that goes on in prisons? I was raised between Roman Catholic and Cree, both very demanding, but the Catholic religion has no mercy. And me with all my abuse, there is nothing good about sex, not even something simple like masturbation — I found masturbation was a big, big thing for me. Because I know now that sex was being done to me all my life, and all my body knew was that any touching, of any kind, had to lead to sex. I was never innocent in body or mind; there were only secrets, pain, silence. And when Mom told me my crotch was a bad place, don't ever touch yourself! I knew that already.

I can't recall ever enjoying sex, and I never came. Eight years into marriage and it was still performing, I could never come — even when I finally found out what coming for a woman could be. In dealing with my abuse, what I am become, honesty with Dwa was the first step because he has lived with me into the process and so I told him about never coming while on a

Little House visit. And he was so hurt, he cried. Well, what did it have to do with him? But he thinks it does, I guess he thinks it's his manliness. So I have to deal with him while I deal with myself.

Love, not sex. I wished to give him sex because he wanted it, it joined us so well sometimes. But what I truly wanted was the closeness it gave us. All wrapped together in and around each other, together in the dark.

Today Mom blames Dad for everything that happened to us. "I should never have married him, never," she said after twenty years and having seven kids with him. And Dad justified whatever he did to me by blaming all the rest of us for leaving him. "Families have to stick together," he says. "Families work when it's us together against the world."

I pity them both. The other person is always the problem.

When I told Dad what I remember Grandpa Louie doing to me, he said there's a difference between abusing and just touching or fondling. Maybe the old guy was just comforting and loving me to make me feel better. "And now," he says, "all my dad gets for living 103 years is being called a dirty old man."

Everyone in my family denies and denies the abuse I—all of us—suffered. "It's all in your head," they say, "you remember nothing straight."

It's in my head all right. And in my body, carved like stone. But Dwa and I are talking now in the Little House, we are telling each other the truth. And sometimes we both cry. There's nothing else to do, but still it feels better, saying it aloud.

As Big Bear said, "Words are power."

And it seems to me that the opposite is true as well. If no one ever speaks the words that should be spoken, the silence destroys you.

———

Would the guilt stop if I was dead?

If I die serving a life sentence the government has to send me home to Red Pheasant in Saskatchewan to be buried in the graveyard there with my family. I want a pine box, no air-tight shit, I want to rot and go back as I can to Mother Earth with my hugging pillow in my arms. No dress. Just pyjamas, the long-shirt-and-pants kind, with nothing on my feet. I want to be laid as if I were sleeping, and I sleep on my side with my hugging pillow in my arms, my head on another pillow in a curled, foetal position. On the little hill south of the church with my Grandma and Grandpa Bear.

My guilt feels endless. I can't pin it down. And still I try to stay alive, to laugh when insanity would be a release, to not become what I see around me in P4W, women inmates who seem to exist for nothing but to eat or be eaten. And me with my conviction of guilt, both legal and personal, my shame.

———

Now after three years of being locked away this strange thing happens: I begin to recognize my body. I recognize it takes practice, you have to explore yourself to know your physical and spiritual self. The first time I attempted an orgasm I stopped myself and cried. There was the shame, the pity for myself, why does this come to me now? To feel my body after all the horrible stuff it's been forced to do, all I've done, now this? But it did help me fall asleep.

———

O God, O Creator, help me.

And the Creator has. In the sweat lodge which the Ojibwa elder Art Solomon and others helped our Native Sisterhood to build in an angle of walls here in P4W, it was revealed to me what I have been given. Things beyond pain and suffering and grief. I have found the darkness and the light in that small circle, and I have blessed it, as it has blessed me, as my body poured sweat. I could not have remembered what I do about my life if the Creator had not come to me in the circle of the sweat lodge.

I will say it the way it happened:

We Native women in P4W are a Sisterhood, we are family, and sometimes we kid around before we enter the sweat lodge with our Elders. It was Vern Harper that time, and somebody says, "Let's go burn with Vern!" and we all laugh a little, it's so solemn, but wonderful too, and full of anticipation. When the lodge helper lays all the covers tight and darkness surrounds us, the heat and steam rising, the sizzle of water on stones, of groans, of screams barely kept in, a pain like birthing that rocks, gasps — I cannot scream, it is not respectful, but the pain and heat are unfathomable: my robe is blue and white. I am burning up and I slap myself because I was told wherever I burn I'm sick and need healing, slapping it acknowledges my pain, slap it to let it go, give it to the Creator. And for an instant the pain is gone, but then it returns even more intense. I was warned: you've made yourself sick, so it's up to you to heal yourself, do it, and in our circle all eyes are watching me invisible in the darkness but they watch, I know, and hear, the sound within my silence is a rumbling growl, it grows larger and larger until my body can't hold it, it bursts into growl, roar after roar, a huge animal towering over me, roaring out of me.

The second round is hotter, and then the third round hotter still, the water hissing on stones soaked through with fire. The Elder at the head of the circle sings his sacred songs, makes his prayers as if talking with someone we cannot see. Then he addresses me. He is saying sacred words to me as he says them to himself.

"I think you know why you are receiving this name," he says in English. "Your name is Medicine Bear Woman. And your colours are the Cree medicine colours, red and green."

Everything is quiet in the sweating darkness of the lodge. The Elder says, "It's your responsibility to learn how to say it in Cree."

My body is curled and wet, this heat and darkness may have been called by his words to deliver me into my coming life. And then I hear the Cree words again. Not from him; it is the voice of my grandma Flora Bear who speaks my spirit name to me. As I remember she did so often when I was a child:

Muskeke Muskwa Iskwew.

Without knowing that name again I could never try to help myself, or help my family. My spirit name, given me by the Spirit World People, now I have a place. Where I can stand to speak.

Medicine Bear Woman.

———

I must explain how my life was kick-started. Speak it out, word for word. I know my spirit name, and that I am the great-great-granddaughter of Big Bear. The Elders tell me that Bear sits in the north of the circle. Bear is the Healer: if you ask and believe, it will happen.

In the summer of 1992, I found *My Father's House* in the library and I started reading it. It's a book written by Sylvia Fraser [about sexual abuse within a family], and it just made me sadder. And one day one of the guards spoke to me — actually I never speak to them, just "Hi!" and smile and disappear as fast as I can so they won't ask me anything — but this one is a Native guard. She spoke to me first.

"Is something the matter?" she asked. "You walk around all day like a zombie."

It was the name Leon always used on me. And suddenly I just blurted it out, "I'm having these terrible — not nightmares . . . sort of pictures . . . things about when I was little, that have always been there, somewhere, but more and more, I don't know, I can't stop them."

Tears came into her eyes. "Are they about being abused?"

"Yes . . . yes. But if they do such things to a baby, I wasn't crippled, I don't know how I'd remember from so young?"

She looked at me for a minute, and then she nodded.

"You know," she said, her face deep and sad, "I was raped and molested when I was a baby. My siblings, when they were older, they confirmed it. It happens, yes."

Bear is the Healer: the Elders say if you ask and believe, it will happen. so I am asking. Please. Have mercy.

And every day I remember. I see as clearly as if I were staring at a picture I hold in my hand, hour after hour. The longer I look, the more I see in it.

This should not have to be spoken in public, or in a court of law. At best it should be talked through in my family only. If only that was possible.

I always knew I was abused, but I tried to forget to what extreme it had happened. At the time of my arrest in 1989, I knew of my brother's recent attacks on me. His attacks rekindled lost or pushed-aside or covered memories: the best way to explain it is when you sit and watch water in a glass pot come to a boil. It doesn't happen in one big rush and the whole pot is boiling. It's slow and steady, just one bubble at a time rising up from the bottom, then a few more, and more, and before you know it the water's pouring out all over the stove. My life is like that pot. I don't know *why* water boils, or *how* the stove works, but I do know I was simmering as a child and started to boil as I got older until, with Leon and all that happened in Wetaskiwin, I came to a full raped boil. And then, the worst of it, I was arrested when I was twenty-seven, and the cops and the law just covered me, locked me down tight with a lid.

So I sat in Remand, the holding cages—and I kept boiling. I tried to wipe it up, yet it kept coming up; I was shackled and cuffed and unable to turn off the stove. I was sentenced, I was taken two thousand miles to the Prison for Women. I am boiling away, burning up, and I am smothered by the rules of the law while everyone sits on their job and watches me burn; till one day—perhaps they're hoping for it—I'll be boiled out and cooked out of existence.

Then, in October 1992, while I was at my appeal in Edmonton, my sister Karen told me on the phone that Leon had raped her. When my sister Minnie told Mom about Leon's attack on Karen, Leon beat and beat Minnie, ripping her clothes off, all she had on when Karen finally got him to stop was her bra. And

I said to Karen, as she wept for us all, that I will not let this violence in our family continue any more without a fight. I will speak out loud. I will write these words down.

[From a *witness statement* Yvonne wrote on 2 November 1992, in Edmonton. Her signature on the thirty-page handwritten statement is witnessed by Detective Linda Billings, Child Abuse Unit, Edmonton Police Service.]

My first attack happened when I was between two to three years old. We lived in a pink house, next door to a two-storey house and down from the railroad tracks. My eldest brother got on a bus and went one way and the other kids went to a school that sat on the hill [. . .]. I slept in a bunk bed in a room off the kitchen. From where I slept I could see the kitchen table, and my plant that sat on the window. The boys slept in the living room.

The attack on me was by a grown man, by my brother Leon [eight and a half years old at that time], and later on by three other boys, one was tall with red hair. And one boy was our neighbour, and would be in later years as well.

What started my rape was our babysitter [the grown man] caught Leon messing around with me behind the fridge in the kitchen. The man told him, in other words, Leon was not doing it right. I was placed on the kitchen table and the bottom half of my body stripped. He was pointing things out to Leon, saying things like this is this, and this is this, And this is where you put your prick [. . .].

I cry and try to crawl off the table. The man would yell at me and slap my ass. At first. And put me on my back. He hurt me I think by putting his finger up my cunt. I'd cry and try to get away as I was crawling off the table, then he started to poke my ass as well. He yelled at Leon for letting me get away.

One time I put my arms around Leon, to try and carry me away, and the man would throw me back on the table. He bent my legs up past my head as I lay on my back. I could not breathe [. . .].

I was on the table, and Leon watching as this man tried to shut me up, he'd give me a sucker. First he gave me one and started to poke at me again, I'd cry out so he got some more suckers and shoved all of them in my mouth at once. I was suffocating and crying as this man kept poking at me. I'd pull the suckers out and cry and try to get away.

If anyone tried to come in the kitchen, like other kids, he'd get Leon to give them a sucker and chase them away. The guy beat me to shut me up, he banged my head on the table. Then when someone came he'd put his cock in my mouth and almost kill me. But also, he'd bend my feet, to where I swear he broke them, to spread my legs and poke at me. I think he went to put lard or oil on his hands, and then Leon would bend my feet.

I got away from Leon's hold and the man shook me, beat me, called Leon down, put me back on the table and bent my feet more. He took Leon's hands, and helped him bend my feet the right way. I could not move. He told him to hold me, and if I moved, to bend my feet some more [. . .].

At one point Leon lost his balance, he was off his own feet and his whole body was pressing down on my feet. At this point I could not move any more, or even cry out. I think I was close to death from all of it and them constantly choking me. I could feel everything, but feel nothing.

This is where I can't recall all things in such an order. [. . .] The last thing I recall was reaching out to Leon. I think I passed out.

The next thing I recall is Leon and the boys going outside, if not to keep the other kids out, they were running around and looking and blocking the windows. [. . .] I think I kept passing out, but pain would wake me up. And choking, I wanted air.

I don't recall much else. They then took me to the bedroom, and Leon, the man and three boys came in. Leon was happy to show off to his friends, I was something to him. The man told them to fuck me, they just stood there. Even Leon was quiet now. I think the boys felt sorry for me. The man went as far as to pull the boys' pants down for them [. . .]. But the boys jumped out of the window.

Then the man grabbed Leon. He started to beat him and threw him on me and told him to fuck me. Leon acted as if he was. The guy told him to put it in me, and tried to put Leon's cock into me. All the time Leon started to cry, and this guy told me to hug him, that's Leon, but I could not, I was too weak.

Finally Leon got mad, or the man got mad. He was now fighting Leon, he attacked him and I don't know if he succeeded in raping Leon, but Leon was crying and they fought some more by the door and against the other wall, yelling. Leon had blood from his waist down, I don't know if it was from me or from the attack done on him, or both.

The man put a diaper on me to soak up my blood. I don't know if I slept all day and into the night or into the next night. I could not move or talk, how could I talk, no one understood me anyhow [. . .].

The reason why I recall being two or three when the first attack happened was, when I recalled it, I phoned my oldest sister Karen to ask who that man was that lived with us in the Pink House. She asked why, and how come out of the blue, I recall something from so long ago? I told her he raped me. Then she said, at that time she was six and Leon eight, she said Earl beat this guy up and kicked him out, as he was Earl's friend, he was about seventeen or eighteen at the most. Earl was in junior high, and he found out this guy would line all four of us girls in the yard on the swings, take our pants down and bend us over the swings and beat us bare-assed.

He also tried to screw us, and I think at this time he had already raped me. Earl caught him trying the other girls and beat him for this [. . .].

I have a hard time writing officially, as you would wish. For the first time, I get a sense someone hears me, or wants to [. . .].

When I was first attacked, I could not speak to be understood, I did not know what happened to me, just pain and scared emotions and thoughts of pain recalled, I could not understand the yelling and beating I received, as it was not a spanking or regular punishment. I did not know I had a vagina or rectum, how was I to know what a penis or sex was? I knew nothing, let alone what they were doing to me. I reached for my brother [Leon] while I was in pain, and he could not, or was unable to, help me. Or worse, refused to. Or even worse, wanted to but did not know how. And could not. I often wonder, now, if the effect of it caused him to be as he is. Though this does not excuse him [. . .].

At that age I had nothing to compare, that act is all I had. You learn something because people tell you the story around it— well, this was not my case. I had no story. I registered what happened to me as pain, hate, bitterness, yelling, crying, mass confusion with no explanation [. . .].

I stayed in the room where they took me [. . .]. This man would change me, and rinse it out in the toilet. Leon was six man [i.e., the person on watch] for all this. I tried a few times to go where my family was watching TV, but the man would grab me and put me back to bed. One time [. . .] Mom took me aside, asked what was wrong and where did it hurt. She could not understand me, it made me cry more, I tried to show her how they hurt my feet by acting it out. And Kathy could not interpret, she was as little as I and I could not get her to understand what I could not understand [. . .].

My guess is I could not recall what happened to me because I did not know what is was at the time. And repeated abuse, with mental abuse revolving around fear of pain, caused me not to really remember. I do know I was safe when Leon started to go to jail, and reform schools, and finally prison.

———

I wonder now, how could a family, especially a mother, not notice such torture of a small child? Maybe, for whatever reason, no one wanted to.

I'd scream and scream, and tell Mom the shadows had come for me, I saw them move there! I pointed to the small area by the door: when I screamed the darkness curled behind clothes hanging on the coat rack and when Mom came into the room it slid out the door behind her. Mom turned on the light, moved the clothes around piled on the floor by the door and hanging on hangers, and I tried to say, "He ran out." But she did not understand. She told me it was just lights moving outside, to stop crying, go to sleep. The nights blurred together. I was awakened again, and again, by the person returning in the night shadows, blending into all the darkness of the house. One night I saw a man bent over, doing something on the kitchen table! I went hysterical with screams, Mom come running. She said it was only one of the boys making a sandwich before going to sleep, shush, shush up, she had enough of me waking everybody in the middle of the night. You go to sleep, now!

I hated to go to bed, to have to try to sleep. Shadows visited our girls' room, shadows that breathed, that made sounds, shadows I could feel touch me. I hated closets, clothes hanging on walls; breathing shadows came out of them.

In prison most women understand my story; it's so much their own. But when visitors come here to perform a play for us, the actors are so caring and filled with excitement, they carry such personality and energy of life that everyone is seduced to smile and laugh at abuse they themselves wear in their bodies being performed on stage in front of them. At one point in a play they put on for us the devil tells the pimp to beat the hooker and rape her: the audience in the prison auditorium went crazy with laughter, yelling at the actor, "Go for it, go, go!" First I felt anger, then tears; and when the Good Spirit stepped in to help the woman, I wept for her, her violation, her helplessness. But I also cried for the women here, laughing till they cried at her pain. After everything they themselves have to live with.

There is such evil concentrated in this place. How can anyone, ever, become better if she's walled up in here? What do plays and colour TV matter if you're in hell?

My thoughts tell me the warden knows there is a possibility I will take my life, and she's having me closely watched. But if people really want to die, they find a way. An Indian man in Edmonton Remand did it by shoving toilet paper down his windpipe; a girl there hanged herself from her sink, just sat there forcing herself to bend over till she was dead. One prisoner asked the judge for psychiatric help but the judge said no and the prisoner slashed his own throat right there in the courtroom. In P4W we lost eight women in eighteen months by hanging; one died a year and half after she did it, she was on life support all that time. Slashing is very common, so easy, I was almost tempted to do it the other day. I'd thought my husband being near me would help, but sometimes I don't know. I seem destined to die alone. No one here to trust or believe.

My mother insists nothing like this ever happened to me as a baby. I was abused, yes — but by the White side of my family. The two Johnsons: first my grandfather Louis and later my father, Clarence. That's where all my horrible memories come from. The ones that are true, she says.

Mom is Cree, yes, and I love her for that. It is the core of the person I am now and when I'm in the sweat lodge, which stands in the tight corner where the prison walls meet, the Mother Earth and the Creator come there, they are there to cleanse me. But I want her to face the fact that her oldest living son, whom she loves and gives everything to, every penny she has, even if he smashes her houses to pieces with an axe, that the "Squeaky" she loves is sick; to face the fact that she considered her four daughters, Karen, Minnie, Kathy, Vonnie, nothing but bad problems, that she treated us not like the babies we were but as if she thought we could be naturally born whores.

I remember when I was no more than five her warning to us, over and over:

"Girls, be on guard! Don't hug your dad, never your brothers, your male cousins, or uncles, or grandpas. If you do you're asking for it, it's your own fault. Never hold hands with any male, stay away from all boys, protect yourself by crowding together, by hiding in corners, never pump yourself high on the swing because a male might see your panties; leap frog is too sexy, sitting with your legs uncrossed is just asking for it."

Asking for what? Mom never explained. Once she caught Kathy and me, we were five and four then, playing house naked.

She beat us till the belt broke and she was hitting Kathy with the buckle. Didn't she realize someone had taught us to play that way?

When Grandpa Louie would babysit Kathy and me, we played house. And it was always nap or bedtime; it was always time to take off all our clothes, time to lie down on the blanket and put our heads on our little pillows and sleep with our legs spread out wide. Or he would let us play in the dirt or mud as much as we wanted, and then he'd say suddenly, "Okay, time for a bath," and bathe us, a long time, laughing and playing with us in the water. Mom is always yelling, punishing us, Dad is never around, but to Grandpa Louie we're special, he lets us play, he hugs us warm and gives us candy. He loves us.

Though sometimes he did strange things, especially when he and I were alone. Sometimes I was frightened of him because he was so ugly and hairy down there, but he had a hand-kerchief with a hole in it and he would stick his cock through the hole to hide his scariness and then I'd have to take off my panties and he would show me how to sit on the floor, or lie down flat with my skirt high and legs spread exactly the way he'd tell me. Then he'd put my panties over his face or on his head, or peek through the legs, and he looked so funny we'd both laugh, him playing with them. He'd give me candies while he held the panties and the handkerchief in place, till finally he'd stop and place his shaking foot between my legs and pull at himself while I lay there on my back with candy melting in my mouth.

Even so, sometimes I would become very frightened, or suddenly scared, and I would get up to run out.

But I know the lock on the door was too high for me to reach, I could never get out. And he would laugh and soothe me in his lap with his big hands, and give me more candy.

Strange but true, my abusers have often been my protectors. Grandpa could sometimes talk Mom out of hitting or punishing me. I know he was protecting me for himself, the way Leon did when he fought the boys in the school yard or on the street in Butte so they'd stay away from me. And so, in a strange way, I loved them both, then: what else did I have? I thought they gave me more attention and care and love than either of my parents.

Now no one of my family can get at me; but there is also no escape for me from the silence of prison. Is it that that's forced these memories out? Where is it all coming from?

I must continue to exist. To find out why I remember.

———

On 19 December 1992, Detective Linda Billings in Edmonton sent Yvonne's witness statement against Leon to the RCMP in North Battleford "for follow-up." During the same time, Karen in Winnipeg filed a charge of sexual assault against Leon as well. So did their sister Minnie, then in North Battleford, but before the police could include her accusations in a formal charge, Yvonne wrote me, "Minnie pulled hers back, scared I guess." She would not sign it. In Thunder Bay their cousin, Shirley Anne Salmon's half-sister Darlene Jacques (*née* Bear), also filed formal charges about a series of rapes Leon committed on her when she was fourteen.

Eight months later, on 30 August 1993, two RCMP officers "attended" — as they put it — Yvonne in Kingston to investigate further the matter of the "Leon Ray Johnson Sexual Assault." In a three-hour interview Yvonne repeated, with more detail, what she had written originally, both about the first attack on her "by Leon and other parties" when she was a baby in Montana, and Leon's rape of her cousin Darlene at Red Pheasant "around the years '74 or '75 in the house where my mom lives now," and also Leon's various sexual attacks on Yvonne while she was living in Wetaskiwin in the eighties. The five-page signed statement, witnessed by constables Pender and Viens, concludes ". . .to the best of my knowledge . . . these are the only attacks I recall on myself [by Leon] in Canada."

The Canadian legal system now took its ordered course, with Crown Prosecutor James Taylor in North Battleford building Yvonne's and Karen's and Darlene's cases against Leon for all the acts he had perpetrated in Saskatchewan. Yvonne felt his violence within the family had to be forced into the open, and if the family refused to discuss it, then it would have to be exposed in a public court of law, but she felt no satisfaction about what was happening. She was torn by her feelings about her brother, whom she loved, and still loves. Whom she hated and cannot help but hate. She wrote to me:

> *Brian Beresh, when I talked to him about this at my appeal, told me a court of law was no place to heal. He says if this case ever goes to court, Leon's lawyer will eat me alive. And I know, my whole family will blame me for taking a stand. But I have started it and I will say what has to be said, and if it isn't worth the paper it's written on, then so be it. At the least, it has been spoken.*
>
> *And I've given it all over to the Creator. That's what the Elder told me when we went into the sweat lodge: "Let Leon go. Give him over to the Creator."*

13

If I Don't Beat You Up, You'll Sleep With Me?

I told one cop I wish I was a split personality, I'd send one of them to court in my place.

— Yvonne, letter from North Battleford cells,
20–25 June 1995

O N SUNDAY, 17 October 1993, I drive from Edmonton to Saskatchewan to meet for the first time members of Yvonne's family. Karen's courage to face her brother has held: Leon will go on trial in North Battleford the next day. I have talked on the phone to her at her home in Winnipeg, and she has agreed that I attend.

Seven months later, on 11 May 1994, I'll be driving the same high-way to the preliminary inquiry into Yvonne's charges against Leon for similar offences: several counts of sexual assault and incest, plus assault causing bodily harm. And Yvonne's cousin Darlene (Bear) Jacques will be in court then too, charging Leon with a series of rapes committed twenty years before.

Leon has been arrested on Karen's charges and is being held for trial in prison at Prince Albert, Saskatchewan. The year 1993 is the first time a member of his family has taken him to court for sexual assault, as the former "rape" is now called in the Canadian Criminal Code. And it is Yvonne, his youngest sister, who has begun all this.

Four hundred and seven kilometres of cruise-control highway for me to think. The long rolling land of the North Saskatchewan River plain is superbly different, fall and spring, but I know the two court-rooms in North Battleford will look and smell exactly the same. On my first trip, just east of Edmonton scattered buffalo graze along the highway in Elk Island National Park, they bulk black as moving mounds among the bare poplars or willow brush; as obliviously concentrated within themselves here in the bush and swamps and meadows of the Beaver Hills as they must have been for Big Bear and his hunters 120 years ago. But now they are enclosed in a steel-mesh

fence. Brilliant fall weather, and a few yellow combines still gob-
bling up the endless swaths of grain that diagram the fields on either
side.

I hear the spaceship *Columbia* is about to launch itself into space; I
am told that in less than a minute after lift-off it will be travelling 3,300
miles per hour over the Atlantic Ocean and into the void of the solar
system.

From Kingston, Yvonne has sent me pictures of her family—individuals and groups of Johnsons at various times and places. They all
seem to be tall, broad, impressively handsome people, or, Vonnie
laughs, an unbeatable—that's a good one!—combination of Cree warrior and Norse Viking. But what does a woman look like who must,
finally, accuse her brother of violent incest? What does the brother
look like? What do they say? If the machinery of law pushes them into
the same room, where do they look?

On a long field sloping south towards the Cree reserves across the
Battle River and Cutknife Hill, I see a coyote loping through the grain
stubble. Coyote, apparently ignoring me but travelling steadily in the
direction I am going. If I saw two of them, I would turn around and
drive back home, fast, but with only one I think I should have a
fifty–fifty chance that the trick Coyote plays on me will be a lucky one.
The blunt steeple of the Delmas Roman Catholic Church appears
over distant bends of the highway—will that counterbalance Coyote
or, more likely, egg him on to something more tricksterish?

Beside the church, behind a straggly caragana hedge, I see the low,
crumpled concrete foundation of a large building: the Thunderchild
Residential School stood here, so powerful it sucked every Indian child
from the reserves assigned by the government to the Roman Catholic
Church (the "Anglican reserve" children had to go to Anglican
schools) behind its iron fence. I have seen pictures of it; it burned
down—cause unknown and never discovered—in 1948 and prairie
wind still plays over the empty space. Cecilia Bear remembers that
school only too well. At the inquiry in May she will tell the court, "I
was born in a tent in Red Pheasant and my parents split up—I was
raised in Delmas Convent. I left there when I was thirteen [1945–46].
Went to my folks in Alberta, they were together again, my father
worked there."

I try to imagine Cecilia—whose picture as a grandmother I have seen—Cecilia a child running in this school yard that is now shorn, unmarked grass. More likely she'd be working in the garden, or in the kitchen, less likely standing at a window and looking south to her home, mother and father miles away. The boys were let out of school to go home for spring and fall work sometimes, but the girls stayed there year-round; how often did their parents come to see them? Were they permitted to? The worst years of the Depression and the war: those parents found some comfort in the thought that, whatever else it did, at least the Church wouldn't let their children starve to death.

I first see Cecilia Bear Knight (the last name comes from a brief marriage that didn't work out), age sixty-one, in the small lobby between Courtroom A and B in the North Battleford Courthouse.

By 9:15 a.m. the area is tight with people. It is Monday, and the relatives and friends of all those arrested over the weekend are trying to get into the larger courtroom for the first session. We crowd in and wait as, with great deliberation, the unflappable judge and policemen and occasional lawyer sort out names and birthdates and addresses (if any), and misdemeanours relating to cars, drunkenness, fights, drugs. The arrested are arraigned in a glass cubicle in lots of ten or twelve at a time, and efficiency is aided by the large number of accused men (there are no women) who seem to have irregular but continuing appointments at the court, whose vital statistics of all kinds are on permanent record. Every accused pleads guilty.

Courtroom A is all business and order. Outside its double doors is talk and worry, laughter, tears of spectators passing in and out. To judge from this crowd, at least seventy per cent of Saskatchewan is Cree. To judge from the men the police bring in from the city cells—men with mostly battered faces and wearing worn clothes, but with their long hair slicked back as if they've all been hosed down—it's closer to ninety percent. As Yvonne says, aboriginal crime is very big business in Canada and, according to statistics, it's worst of all in Saskatchewan.

This isn't a good place to meet anyone; especially not me her Bear family. For she's warned me: "They all know I'm writing a book with you. You're the enemy, so be careful."

Leon's trial is scheduled for Courtroom B at 9:30. I look in, it's small and empty; a place to get away from the crowd, but I want to see all the prisoners arrive. Perhaps I can recognize Leon. But Yvonne has given me no clear picture of him, and there are too many large men with black hair being paraded by, too fast.

It's easier to identify Cecilia when she comes up the stairs with a group of younger women. She is short, broad, black hair parted and pulled back from her round, classic handsome Cree woman's face: a visible descendant of Chief Big Bear, solid and formidable as a rock. She glances past me, I'm just another person standing around; I hear her talk to her small circle but cannot decipher what she is saying. She and her companions seem nervous, but familiar with all the courthouse facilities.

After 10:30 the crowd is considerably thinned; Cecilia and a slim woman barely bigger than a child—that must be Laura, Leon's wife—sit in the tiny visitors' alcove off the lobby between the courtrooms. I still haven't introduced myself when three men come down the corridor: a younger and an older RCMP officer, both almost as burly as the handcuffed man they lead between them: this is Leon. Tall, pale skin, good-looking with swept-back, wavy black hair, clean shaven, in a new white-striped shirt, new Lee jeans, and white socks and Brooks shoes. Yvonne has told me it's tradition: Cecilia always buys Leon new clothes for every court appearance. Despite his shackles he advances with easy confidence, nods to the women waiting for him, a slight grin twitching his lips; Laura gets up and follows close behind. Leon is very big, and even handsomer in profile, despite a double chin. He wears no belt, and his jeans are a bit loose—he may have lost his paunch in jail—to shift them up he must use both cuffed hands.

The trial cannot begin with Karen Sinclair's testimony: Crown Prosecutor James Taylor spoke to her yesterday, after she arrived from Winnipeg, and there was no sign then that she was under the influence of alcohol, but this morning she was tested at 100 milligrams. Several hours will help, and the judge decides to begin with the testimony of witness Phyllis Stevenson.

While the court takes a short break to locate Ms. Stevenson, Laura returns to the lobby and reports to Cecilia, who has remained outside. The younger police officer talks to Cecilia as well, and after a moment she looks up at me, steadily. So I go to her in the crowd.

"Hello, are you Mrs. Cecilia Knight?"

"Yes."

"I'm very glad to meet you. I'm Rudy Wiebe, I'm a friend of your daughter Vonnie. I've visited her in Kingston."

She has already deduced who I am. And it is obvious that mentioning Yvonne's familiar family name and my friendly visits to P4W doesn't help; she suspects I know she has never gone to visit Yvonne in prison, though under the Correctional Services Canada visitation program she has been offered an airline ticket every year.

She confronts me quickly: "You the guy that's helping her write a book?"

"We've talked about that, yes."

Everyone, including the RCMP constables, is watching us, listening. Her heavy eyebrows clench over her intense black eyes.

"You write anything about our family"—she gestures at the closed courtroom door—"you'll answer to me."

Later this afternoon, after I have met Karen and listened to her testify, I will tell Cecilia: "Yvonne's life story is her own. No one, not even you, can forbid her to tell it the way she remembers and knows it to be."

But now, at her direct challenge, I can't find a single word—what did I expect? But in front of all these witnesses?—and she turns, walks back into the visitors' cubicle.

———

"The Provincial Court of Saskatchewan at North Battleford; October 18, 1993: In the matter of Her Majesty the Queen versus Leon Ray Johnson, who stands charged that between the 1st day of May, 1992, and the 1st day July, 1992, at Red Pheasant Indian Reserve in Saskatchewan, he did commit a sexual assault on Karen Sue Sinclair. That she is his sister is admitted."

———

Witness Phyllis Stevenson
    [from her court testimony and cross-examination]:

Karen Sinclair is married to my brother. We started getting close because we confided in each other, my husband was abusing me and my brother tries to control Karen by scaring her — she gets scared easily. Last year we were living in Winnipeg, I was separated from my husband then, and Karen wanted me to meet her relatives in Saskatchewan. [Phyllis tells the familiar story about an all-night party at Leon's house with lots of twelve-packs available. At one point] I went upstairs to the washroom, when I came back Leon pushed me and I was scared. He sort of shoved me aside, on my arm, he didn't say anything but I was scared, I went outside and sat in the bushes behind the house. It was somewhere after midnight and I was wondering how I'd get home. Then Laura, Leon's wife called me, so I went back in the house [. . .]. Laura said Leon and Karen were in the basement and I was going to go down there but she said I shouldn't go, eh, I shouldn't bother. So I went out [. . .] and sat in the car. I locked all the doors and fell asleep. Then Karen came out, she was in a really big hurry [. . .]. We drove to North Battleford. Her eyes were all red, and she picked up some Visine for her eyes and we stopped at McDonalds, [her daughter] wanted to eat, and when she was out of earshot Karen started to cry. She wouldn't tell me immediately what was wrong, but finally she just said that Leon was on top of her and she pushed him off and she didn't elaborate. She started to get hysterical, so I just comforted her. I held her in my arms and she cried on my shoulder.

    Crown Prosecutor James Taylor: Did Karen want to report it to the police or not?

    Answer: She did, and I told her not to because — because her mother had recently had a heart attack and I didn't think it would — I told her they should discuss it amongst themselves in the family before they went — before she went ahead and did this, like.

Karen enters the courtroom at 2:30 and walks, without looking to either side, directly into the witness box. When she looks up, she sees me sitting at the elbow of the policeman guarding Leon, and she smiles at me—a first from a Johnson other than Yvonne. Her dark brown hair is tied back from her pale, rather drawn face; a small, trim woman in black jeans and shirt. And handsome like all her siblings I have seen: physically, the Creator has truly been kind to this family.

Karen tells another familiar story, of years of enduring violent physical attacks by Leon, and of sexual advances—which, unlike Yvonne, she says she could rebuff. And then, the night of the party,

> we were drinking, smoking, talking. To be honest with you, I got loaded [. . .]. I drank till I blacked out, the last thing I remember is sleeping downstairs, next thing was being woke up on the living room couch, upstairs. Leon on top of me. He had ahold of my hips and was bringing my hips to him and his body was on top of me. He was very very heavy, I could hardly breathe.
>
> Crown Prosecutor Taylor: And what was Leon doing?
>
> Answer: He was having intercourse with me.
>
> Crown Prosecutor: What did you do?
>
> Answer: My exact words were, "Get the fuck off me," and I was pushing, with both hands against his chest. He got off of me, pulled up his pants, sat down on the couch that was next to the couch I was on. And I looked for my pants and pantie, I was holding my shirt like this and my bra was still on but I couldn't find the rest [. . .].
>
> Counsel for the Defence Mignealt: You don't know whether you were the aggressor in having him have intercourse with you?
>
> Answer: I know myself, no, I was not. I never said anything, I didn't want anybody to find out and then my husband went and got drunk and blabbed it all over the place. It was something I just wanted to keep to myself and not nobody know, but everybody knows now.
>
> Counsel for the Defence: I understand the Winnipeg police came to you because of a statement your sister Yvonne made against Leon. Did you see the statement?

Answer: I saw it. There was a very thick one sitting on the police table. I did not read it. The officer asked me if I wanted to charge Leon and without hesitation I told him, "Yes."

Counsel for the Defence: You say you didn't read Yvonne's statement, but were you aware of its contents?

Answer: Yes. I didn't have to read it, because Yvonne told me.

Crown Prosecutor: Karen, as you were growing up, living with all your brothers and sisters, during those times did you have any suspicions about anything happening between Leon and Yvonne of a sexual nature?

Answer: Yes.

Crown Prosecutor: Did you ever see anything?

Answer: No, not actually seen it. [But] I was pretty sure, yeah, the suspicions were very strong, yes, yes.

Cecilia never enters the courtroom. During a brief recess in the afternoon I see her alone in the visitors' alcove and quickly, gathering my nerve, I go to the door and ask her if I can come in, sit down. Her greeting is non-committal, she's obviously thinking of something else, so I sit down.

Over noon I have had lunch with Jim Taylor. He is a stocky, oddly gentle man for what I still think of as the necessarily aggressive profession of Crown Prosecutor; he's been doing it for many years, and not much that happens in or out of a courtroom surprises him. He told me that it was Cecilia and Minnie who had been drinking with Karen in her hotel room till four in the morning; it was he who put her in a cell for four hours to make sure she would be sober enough by the afternoon to testify.

But now, Cecilia is explaining to me how persecuted Leon is. She is full of defences for him: it all happened when he was a kid, everyone does stupid things when they're young, the police have got it in for him, they just want to throw away the key on him for life. She says nothing about Karen, or why she would lay such a personally painful charge against her own brother, though it seems to me she must know every detail of it—it happened only sixteen months ago. Rather, she tells me without prompting that she was in Winnipeg babysitting as usual at the time the alleged offence took place; that when she was young her brothers tried to do things to her too but they sure as hell never got anywhere.

Young? I think: at the time of the rape, Karen was thirty-three, Leon thirty-six.

Yvonne has explained a great deal to me of how her family works, its enormous capacity for evasion, and listening to Cecilia I see her account corroborated. Behind Cecilia's defiant words to me I recognize her attempts to save her beloved Leon from the charges of sexual abuse that two of his sisters and a cousin have, after as long as twenty years, finally dared lay against him. Getting Karen drunk before her court-room appearance did not prevent Leon's case from going ahead, but I know Cecilia is trying stronger tactics on Yvonne. She told Yvonne a few months earlier that if she dropped her charges against Leon and he got out of jail, Leon would run for a seat on the Red Pheasant Band Council and when he got elected he'd get the band to support Yvonne with money and lawyers in her appeals of her life sentence. The band, she said, would help get her out of prison.

This seemed to me no believable plan of action. It sounded more like blackmail: if you lay off Leon, I'll help you with your appeals. But help how? Keep Leon out of prison and he'll be elected to band council? That sounds ludicrous to anyone who knows anything about reserve politics. Yvonne refused to play along with Cecilia's suggestions, and on 6 April 1993 she went so far as to send a three-page personal letter to the Red Pheasant Council giving them a detailed history of Leon's unretributed violence against his family members. She concluded: "My silence kept him safe in the past, but I will not be silenced ever again."

Do I tell Cecilia I know any of this, in the few moments we see each other in the tiny waiting room of the North Battleford Courthouse? No. She is polite to me, speaking loudly about generalities I already know, but I sense she could as easily explode as she is, for the moment, civil. I ask her the most neutral question I can think of: how is she related to Big Bear? But she will explain nothing; by siding with Yvonne I have become, as Yvonne has told me, "the family enemy."

I ask her about Yvonne. Cecilia's very worried about Vonnie, from prison she is saying such things, writing such crazy letters—she does not mention the band letter directly—so many crazy things, some of it is hate mail. She tells me Vonnie's White grandfather abused her, yes, and her White father too, but nothing else that girl says now ever happened, it's just not true, and maybe all the drinking she's done all her life, and drugs, and now that life sentence in jail, maybe she is crazy. Gone just plain crazy.

I could ask Cecilia: if her daughter Yvonne is "crazy," why has she never once visited her in prison? Gone to talk face to face, offer her some comfort and help? Why this destructive, emotional blackmail for Leon's sake?

I could ask, and maybe I should. But I simply don't have the nerve, sitting there, her implacable face so close. Perhaps I'm too intimidated by all I know of this afflicted family where both social and personal violence perpetuate themselves like cancers, from one generation to the next until, in despair, they can only accuse each other of brutality and lies in a public court where any Canadian who cares to can come and listen and know of it.

And at least part of the reason for my silence is Big Bear. I am as White as the Treaty Six negotiators whom he confronted in 1876, and today, in these North Battleford courtrooms, I have seen the prophecy in Big Bear's declaration to those government men:

"When I see you there is one thing that I dread: to feel the rope around my neck."

A prophecy being fulfilled in Canadian courtrooms day after day, in dreadful ways not even he could have foreseen 120 years ago.

What I do tell Cecilia is that I've talked to Yvonne for days at a time, I have read thousands of pages of her letters and personal journals, and she not only reads but she also writes out analyses of large, difficult books of fiction, history, and psychology. I have worked with highly intelligent people at universities all my life and to me she appears to be not at all "crazy." Her memories are bizarre, yes, and sometimes horrible and grotesque, but they are invariably consistent. She impresses me as a very intelligent woman who is daring for the first time to think through and understand what her life has truly been, and what has been done to her.

I see the expression on Cecilia's face and I stop talking; we look at each other for a moment silently. I think: she has long ago chosen which child she will support absolutely—it seems she cannot support them all—and now she is as immovable as a mountain, a strength commensurate with everything I have grasped in almost four decades of thinking and researching and writing about Big Bear.

She is little more than a year older than I. We both know the sometimes overwhelming, inexpressible pain that can happen in families, pain from which our memories will never find an escape. But to simply deny it? Face to face in the small room, I am weak in the knowledge of all she has already endured, and must continue to endure.

And I feel relieved—even as I feel shame at my relief—when she gets up abruptly, walks past me, disappears into the crowded lobby.

———

Accused Leon Johnson
[condensed from his court testimony and cross-examination]:

I'm the leader there, the man of the house, I've got to watch my house and my kids so I slacked off on the drinking. Karen kept pushing the beer and the pot. So this time when Phyllis went upstairs, you know, it's one of the deals, you always watch where everybody's at in the house, especially on Reservations. I was listening downstairs for Phyllis, where she was at, and when she come out of the bathroom she went into our children's room, so I went upstairs to see what was going on. She was all the way into the bedroom so I got Phyllis and took her out of the room and I say, "You can't go in there." And I went downstairs and told Karen I'd threw Phyllis out of the house and why, because she wouldn't, you know, leave the kids' room alone. So Karen just partied on, she says, "Drink brother, here, drink brother," bringing me beers. I've seen my sister drink to excess before, but not like that night [. . .].

Counsel for the Defence Migneault: Okay. Now, was there any act of intercourse that evening?

Answer: No, none at all.

Crown Prosecutor Taylor: You say Karen's the one who's standing naked in the basement. Is it your view that this is all Karen's fault?"

Answer: Exactly.

Crown Prosecutor: How much of the past twenty years, since you were sixteen, have you spent in jail?

Answer: About eight to ten years flat time inside, locked up.

———

All day I sat in court, watching, taking notes. I tried at first to be inconspicuous, but that was impossible in small Courtroom B, where the single row of chairs for spectators is not more than a metre behind the two desks where the accused and his defence lawyer sit on the left, and the Crown Prosecutor on the right, facing the judge. I had to sit beside the RCMP officer who brought Leon in, shackled, and stationed himself directly behind him throughout the trial. Sitting at his red-serge elbow I was, presumably, physically safe.

His Honour Judge D.M. Arnot looked at me immediately, "Are you with the press, sir?" I shook my head. "No, very good." and since then he has ignored me.

So has everyone else; I've become conveniently invisible. I've watched Leon listen as the lawyers ponderously dug up details of his brutality against his sister and relatives, watched his thick handcuffed hands with large knobbly knuckles probably broken in innumerable fights, watched him staring around in defiance, sometimes even cockiness, or on occasion with head bent and profiled face expressionless, only his foot and thumbs twitching slightly. And I wondered: is there such a thing as a courtroom ego? To have one's most trivial actions examined so minutely, almost iconically, within one of the few ritualized procedures left in our society—the courtroom trial? Does Leon ever think: I bust one cop-car window, I fuck one drunken bitch, and I get all these big shots just a-hopping—hey! Look at me! I'm big news. I keep them in fancy cars and slick women.

And Karen recovering from a binge, for three hours in the witness chair, her rigid, painful emotion as the cross-examination questions intensify, right to the legal-aid defence lawyer's grotesque demand that she state the size of her bra. She is at the most painful moment of memory, she has just told him she became conscious of being crushed under the huge body of her brother, she finds herself naked except for T-shirt and bra—and K.M. Mignealt demands to know both inch and cup size. And then he makes her repeat it. As Yvonne will note when she reads the trial transcript: "A typical stupid male who has a position in the legal system to defile the victim."

But Karen gives the data again, flat and clear. It is Crown Prosecutor Taylor who finds the breaking emotion in her: when she admits it was her abusive husband's drunken, public blabbing about her assault that hurt her most deeply. And then, surprisingly, in what until then has been a kind of mechanical excavation of harrowing personal experience, it is the policeman beside me who gives her the only gesture of courtroom kindness: he gets up and offers her a tissue to wipe her tears. And she accepts it.

I had understood that the defence lawyer was hesitating about having Leon take the stand, but there he is, talking willingly. In fact, after the first few questions he just rolls on without question, of his own accord. It seems to me he savours the sound of his own story, as only he can tell it, though his answers to the Prosecutor's cross-examination quickly drop to monosyllables. But he sticks to his position, and he has no idea why his sister would accuse him of such an act.

All of which elicits from Jim Taylor the comment: "I didn't know Leon Johnson was such an exemplary guy, or I wouldn't have prosecuted him."

And Cecilia Knight. She has sat all day in the tiny visitors' alcove across from Courtroom B, never entered to hear a single word either of her children had to say; waiting for it all to be finally over. She asks from the doorway, just before the judge adjourns the court, "Can I come in now, without hearing something bad?"

The judge states he will pronounce his verdict two days from now. And Cecilia turns, leaves immediately. Leon's eyes follow her; from the angle where I sit I can't tell whether he has ever looked at Karen, but I don't think she glanced at him even once. I go out, outside into the breathable air of the sunny fall parking lot.

After a few minutes I see the judge emerge, get into a blue Mercedes 450, and drive away. Then Cecilia and Laura appear at the public doors, talking to Karen, who gets into the back seat of a worn, white station wagon with them. Cecilia drives it out of the lot, down a North Battleford street, between tall trees now stripped of their leaves. She stops opposite a bungalow; Laura goes in, comes out with a small swarm of children carrying duffle bags. They crowd into the seat beside Karen, spill back over into the baggage space. Slowly the station wagon pulls away, turns left at the first corner, then left again. Cecilia driving out of the city, towards the river bridges, south towards Red Pheasant Reserve.

———

[From the judgement of His Honour Judge D.M. Arnott on 21 October 1993]

> The issue in the case distils to a question of credibility. Karen gave her evidence in a straightforward manner, in my opinion. She was at times emotional [. . .] recalling the incident was very painful. She was precise, concise, coherent, and consistent, and credible in her testimony. Some of her evidence was [. . .] not entirely flattering to herself [. . .]. in the face of thorough and rigorous cross-examination . . . she remained steadfast in her position.
>
> I have placed considerable weight on the evidence of Phyllis Stevenson [. . . . She] was straightforward on the crucial elements [. . .]. Her comforting of the alleged victim, her descriptions of the emotion of the victim were something I place considerable weight on.
>
> The accused's evidence, I'm sorry to say, I found to be evasive, self-serving, conveniently forgetful and, on a number of important points, simply not credible [. . .]. The accused's evidence lacked candour . . . he rambled on without direct answers [. . . his] evidence did not have the clear ring of truth.
>
> In analyzing the evidence, I asked myself, "Why would this victim lie?" [. . .] This is not something that the witness, in my opinion, would fabricate [. . .] something she would merely hallucinate, misread, or misinterpret [. . .]. This matter distils to this point: I believe Karen Sinclair, and I disbelieve Leon Ray Johnson [. . .]. I find the accused guilty as charged [. . .].

I agree [with the defence counsel] that this must be a very difficult thing for Mrs. [Cecilia] Knight to deal with, and certainly it was a difficult thing for Karen Sinclair [. . .]. In balancing off of these competing interests, then, it seems to me that the appropriate sentence is one of three years and three months in a Federal Penitentiary.

———

While Leon was serving that sentence for sexual assault and incest in the Prince Albert, Saskatchewan, Federal Prison—he was granted no early parole—he was formally charged with eight other counts of rape, intercourse with a female person under the age of fourteen, sexual and physical assault, and incest offences against his cousin Darlene Jacques and his sister Yvonne. The offences had been committed at Red Pheasant Reserve and the town of Battleford between 1972 and 1989.

And while Yvonne anxiously waited in Kingston to be called to North Battleford to testify at a preliminary inquiry which would convince a judge that enough evidence against Leon had been gathered to go ahead with a trial, the Prison for Women erupted into violence. As Judge Louise Arbour later described it, in her official review of what happened: "On the evening of April 22, 1994, a brief but violent physical confrontation took place between six inmates [. . .] and a number of correctional staff. The six were immediately placed in the Segregation Unit [. . .]." However, the violence continued, to the point where "on the evening of April 26, 1994, the Warden of the Prison for Women called in a male Institutional Emergency Response Team to conduct a cell extraction and strip search of eight women in segregation [. . .]. At the end of the lengthy procedure . . . the eight inmates were left in empty cells in the Segregation Unit wearing paper gowns, and restraints and leg irons."

Fortunately, Yvonne was not personally involved in these events; but the six inmates who began the crisis were all Native women, members of the Sisterhood, and that, together with the general chaos in prison, affected her immensely. Nevertheless, her preliminary inquiry was set to begin on 11 May, and so, on 10 May, she was taken out of P4W and flown to North Battleford to confront Leon with her charges. She had not seen him since he knocked her down into the bathtub in 1989.

Yvonne's formal charges against her brother were two instances of sexual assault in Saskatchewan in 1988, and the concomitant charges of incest. The first involved the fight at the family reunion, and the second a visit with Minnie to Leon's house, both at Red Pheasant. In Yvonne's testimony of over a hundred pages, the Crown Prosecutor identified a key issue:

[From the inquiry 12 May 1994]

Crown Prosecutor Taylor: Yvonne, as you were growing up [. . .] what was the relationship between you and Leon as far as any control you felt he had over you.

Yvonne Johnson: [. . .] He was my teacher and I never had no control over anything [. . .]. He'd have me beat my sister down. And, if I tried to back away, crying or whatever, he'd say, 'Feel it, don't you feel it.' And he'd convince me to get angry inside [. . .].

Q: Okay. The times you told the court about, between you and Leon, the family reunion and the time at Leon's house [. . .].

A: He had control. If you are a survivor [. . .] of any form of abuse [. . .] it affects your thought process and everything is out of whack [. . .]. When someone tells you to do something, especially if it's been consistent over a lifetime, you just do it. You don't think about it. It's better off calling it soul murder [. . .]. I've tried to talk to Leon before any of this [i.e., this inquiry], when I had memories. I didn't remember what happened when I was two and a half [. . .] till I stayed sober for a while and I was sitting in Kingston Prison that the memories came back. I wrote and asked him and I says, 'Leon, I don't blame you for what happened [. . .] 'cause you were only eight, but tell me what happened so that I can try to get my life back.' And, all they did was pass my letters around, amongst family, saying I wrote hate mail and it never went no further.

It shouldn't be in a Court of Law. He's not going to get no help in a prison, but—then you got to think of the dangers. All it takes is one time and you're messed up forever. I don't want people to hate him for what he did, but I have to have my say. I'm tired, really tired. I guess it's pretty bad when your only escape in life is thinking, 'Oh, I can always count on killing myself. I want to die, and I don't want to go on like this.' What do I do?

Yvonne said this while facing Leon a few feet away. He was the accused, she the accuser, but the legal consequences of their individual actions had brought them both there in shackles; if they so much as stirred hand or foot, their chains clattered. When she entered the courtroom, she had looked directly at him. She had named herself to the Court as "Medicine Bear Woman," and had testified for over an hour holding an eagle feather in her left hand, which verified before the Creator that she was telling the truth.

And she had said to Leon directly, from the witness box: "One thing I do want to say, Leon, is I do love you. I don't love what you did, or what you've become, but I love you."

And finally, "I have to have my say."

And he gave her a kind of answer. The court tape recorder recorded it exactly:

Accused Johnson: It's not my fault.

A moment of "very high drama," as Jim Taylor described it to me; and also, as he understood it, a concession that part or all of what Yvonne had described had actually happened.

———

Darlene Jacques lived in Thunder Bay, Ontario, and the inquiry into her charges were heard in North Battleford later that year.

Darlene Jacques (*née* Bear)
[from her inquiry testimony, 14 November 1994]:

I moved around so much when I was a kid, it's hard to recall all the places. My mother, Josephine Bear, and my brother left and I was sent to live with my older half-sister Shirley Anne Cooke, now Salmon, in Biggar with her two daughters. I was really lonely and then the opportunity arose to live with my Aunt Cecilia on Red Pheasant, in the fall of 1973 when I turned fourteen.

There were Aunt Cecilia's children there, Karen, Minnie, Kathy, Yvonne, Perry, and Leon when he wasn't in jail. A baby too, little Edward, my Aunt Rita's son, still in diapers. The house was actually Grandpa John's old house, and I ended up moving to my grandparents in the spring. My Grandpa felt at that time that I was being mistreated, even though he didn't know everything that transpired. I never told him, I didn't think anyone would believe me.

The first time it occurred was in around September, October. There were no adults present. We were left in Leon's care, he was babysitting us. And I was sleeping in one of the bedrooms with Karen. And he—he had been drinking. He came into the bedroom, and he dragged me out of the bedroom. And he sat me down in the living room. He gave me a Bible to read, I don't remember what I read from it. Afterwards, like this lasted maybe ten, fifteen minutes, afterwards he dragged me into the bedroom. He locked the door with a knife and he raped me. I was absolutely terrified. To me he looked huge.

This happened twice more. Once I believe I was hiding, I'm not sure hiding outside or inside, and the same scenario played itself out. He found me, sat me on a chair, got me to read from the Bible, took me into the bedroom and raped me again. The third time happened right here in Old Town [Battleford]. I was walking by myself, out on the street when I heard Leon call from an upstairs window. And he called me upstairs. And I did go. Leon had been drinking. He grabbed me again and dragged me into the bedroom. He raped me.

There was no adult around that I could trust, or tell. But one thing that I made very clear in my mind, is that once I got off Red Pheasant Reserve, I would never return.

Crown Prosecutor: Did this have any effect on your school grades?

Answer: I believe it did. I failed, I spent two years in grade seven.

Crown Prosecutor: What did the Bible have to do with this?

Answer: I have no idea.

Counsel for the Defence: Did anyone ever ask you about any possible attacks?

Answer: Yes. Karen did after the last incident on the reserve, just before I moved to my grandfather's house. And I told her.

———

Leon's subsequent trial on the charges laid by Yvonne and Darlene took place in the Court of Queen's Bench in North Battleford began on 20 June 1995, before Mr. Justice I.D. McLellan and a jury.

Cecilia testified first. Though she was called as a Crown witness, and though she could not remember any exact dates, including the crucial date of the family reunion, one thing she remembered most certainly was that Darlene had lived with her and her family at Red Pheasant in 1971, not later. That was the year Earl died, and Leon, of course, was then a minor—only fifteen—and so legally he should not now be charged in adult court for raping Darlene, who would then have just turned thirteen. The Cando School records showed that Darlene attended there in 1972 and 1973, but that did not shake Cecilia's insistence, and since she had always been away working, she knew nothing about this story anyway. Besides, they had never had a Bible in the house until the children, including Leon, were all baptized at once, on the reserve several years later.

As for Yvonne, Cecilia was adamant that as soon as she heard that Louis Johnson, Clarence's father, was abusing the children, "I told my husband about it and he beat me up for it [. . .]. I never left my children at all [. . .] I refused to go to work till my husband kicked his dad out of the house. [And later, after we were separated] Leon called me from Butte. I was working in Winnipeg. Leon told me come get Yvonne, my dad is trying to bother her [. . .]. I quit my job and went and picked up Yvonne. As far as I know, she never lived with her dad again."

There were many things Cecilia could not remember on the stand—"Not right this minute"—and not a single thing concerning Leon and Yvonne's relationship as children—"Like I say, I had so many children to watch I didn't particularly watch one person as the years went by"—but now that she had had a stroke, had severe high blood pressure, and was a diabetic, Leon, of all her children, had especially shown his concern for her. "He comes to see me every day when he's home."

Leon's legal-aid lawyer, D.J. O'Hanlon, shrewdly pointed out *in camera* to the judge: "Effectively I do not want Cecilia Knight's credibility reduced in any fashion. I think she was a benefit to our cause. She was [. . .] a credible witness."

But not for Yvonne, as it turned out.

———

Karen had been brought in from Winnipeg to testify, but on the morning of the first day of trial she was again badly drunk. So the Crown Prosecutor had her put in the cells again, overnight this time, and she testified on 22 June.

She was curt to the point of being monosyllabic: as for what she remembered of 1973, there were two "incidents" of Darlene going into Leon's room, and neither time did Darlene want to go there. Karen admitted that before the second "incident" she told Leon where Darlene was hiding in the attic—under cross-examination she could not explain why she had told him—and also that at the time she had told her mother that she "suspected something was going on with Leon and Darlene, but [Mom] did not really believe me that it was anything."

The Crown Prosecutor asked Karen nothing regarding Yvonne, but Leon's defence lawyer did. Karen testified that at the family reunion during which Leon allegedly took Yvonne away and forced sex upon her: "I myself stayed away from Vonnie [in the hall] because Vonnie just seemed to want to attack everybody." Did she recall whether Leon remained in the hall the entire time? "Oh, I don't—it's really hard to say. Leon and I we pretty much, we did a lot visiting between ourselves [. . .] I did not want to fight, he did not want to fight."

Yvonne does not comment to me on Karen's evasions regarding herself and Leon; but she does tell me she believes Karen knew everything that happened to Darlene in 1973 because the two girls were very close friends then. Leon was the reality they all—Karen, Darlene, Minnie, Kathy, Vonnie, Perry—lived with in that house on the reserve, where everyone could hear whatever happened: the question was never one of being able to escape him. If he was around, it was simply a matter of what he would do, and to whom. Karen must have helped Darlene logicalize it in the only way the helpless girls could: don't fight or he'll beat you up and take you anyway; and convince herself: better a cousin than a sister. When Leon first comes into their bedroom, Karen pretends to sleep while nudging Darlene to go; when Darlene hides the second time, Karen tells him where she is because he threatens to beat her up. At some point Karen must protect herself; she locks herself in as best she can; Leon is huge and unstoppable—except by their mother, who is mostly away—eighteen and out of jail for the moment; he'll have anyone he wants when he's home, and Darlene is the newest.

Karen might have testified to all this and, Yvonne thinks, on her behalf too, but the family has closed down on Karen since her charges put Leon into prison. Karen will later tell Yvonne that she is afraid that, when he gets out, he will come after her and her children. In his own defence in June 1995, Leon admitted he had had sex with Darlene when she was barely a teenager, but said that she had co-operated completely. He went into considerable detail: she was a virgin and he had condoms, but the first condom he used broke. "I went into the kitchen and got some lard to use so the condom wouldn't break 'cause I didn't know how to use the condom because I didn't leave—the thing hanging off at the end. We had sex like that off and on different evenings [. . .] I was there only a couple of weeks."

As for Yvonne and the family reunion? "It started out it was the men who were fighting and I would go there and make sure nobody got beat up really bad. If they started getting carried away, then I would break up the argument. I spent my time talking to Karen and going on refereeing fights."

As far as Leon was concerned, nothing whatever happened between himself and Yvonne at the family reunion. He had no comment on the words Yvonne testified he had spoken to her: "If I don't beat you up, you'll sleep with me?" And after, as she lay curled up, crying: "I always knew you liked it rough." Nor had he done anything on the trip she and Minnie made to Red Pheasant, as listed in the indictment. A few beer cans were thrown, but otherwise nothing happened. To specific questions from both Defence and Crown, he answered categorically that neither in 1988–89, nor at any time in his youth, had he ever had, or had he ever tried to have, sexual relations with his sister Yvonne.

And as for Yvonne laying charges, Leon told the Crown Prosecutor James Taylor: "My opinion is that she's in prison and she's doing a long time in prison and using this to gain some kind of release."

Taylor: And to do this she's willing to go to the extent of making up a lie about you?

Johnson: Yes.

———

Minnie appeared as a defence witness for Leon. She testified that, while changing little Edward's diapers, she had seen Darlene go into Leon's room several times; she had no idea what Darlene was doing in there. She herself and Leon "never got along, I always got him in trouble and I always pick on him. He was always my dad's pet." At first she admitted they often had physical fights, but she quickly changed her mind and said, "No—they were really kind of like playing around." He never beat her up, no, nor terrorized her; they never engaged in physical fights. She concluded, "It was just more like—teasing one another."

During the family reunion she stated she drank a twenty-four of beer by herself. She said the only person she saw Yvonne leave the hall with was her husband, Dwa, and then they never came back. During the trip to Red Pheasant, when they visited Leon for a day, there was never any time that Yvonne and Leon were alone together.

Kathy refused to come to North Battleford to testify about anything. That was that for family testimony.

———

None of them had to face Yvonne in the courtroom while they testified as they did Leon. Except for her hours on the stand, Yvonne was alone in the holding cell in the North Battleford jail for seven days.

Yvonne: Once I was a young girl in love with a name, and with a voice I heard — twice — on the phone. Just across the river from here, in the old town of Battleford, Saskatchewan.

Now I'm in the North Battleford jail, waiting to hear what the court verdict will be on Leon for what he did to Darlene and me in Saskatchewan; to confront him with what he did to me in Alberta and Montana, I'd have to charge him in court there.

Leon has now served half his sentence for sexually assaulting Karen, but when the police brought him from Prince Albert for trial on my charges, Karen was there to greet him, with Mom and Minnie too, bringing new clothes and shoes so he'd look good in court. And then Leon didn't like the clothes: he wanted the yellow shirt Mom had brought for Perry, who's in jail just now too on a drunk and assault charge. When the cops hauled Perry out, he said the shirt was too fucking small to fit Leon anyway. And so it was. Despite Leon's crying over the phone to Mom that he had wasted away to a hundred pounds in the pen, he looks trim and muscular the way prison always makes him; he gets fat and sloppy when he's out.

I heard my brothers' voices, somewhere down jail halls, and Mom's and Karen's too, but the five days I've been here not one of my family has visited me, not a note, not a message, though Mom hasn't seen me for almost three years and my sisters for over five. Mom sat in court all the time I testified, but she did not look at me. Leon's the rapist, I'm the one who got raped, but I'm also in P4W for murder twenty-five and I guess my family believes I'm gone for life anyway, so try to get Leon off — basically, what does it matter now if he did rape her?

I saw all of them in court, of course; Karen hugged me fast before the cops could get between us. And whispered some words I couldn't understand. She got very drunk — something bad is happening to her and it's not just her violent husband—and the court threw her in a cell (not one near me) so she would dry out to testify, and so the evening of Wednesday, 21 June, there were four of us Johnsons—Leon, me, Perry, Karen—all in this small jail at the same time. During the court break I asked Minnie to try and persuade the cops to let her come see me. She just snorted.

"Yeah! If they don't throw me in too!"

I could only hope the one other Johnson, Kathy, is safe and far away in Manitoba.

Minnie hasn't come yet. But I waited, brushed my teeth, combed out my hair, washed my combination stainless-steel toilet and sink; I smudged the cell with sweetgrass. They allow me pen and paper, and cigarettes, nothing else. I'm in their small juvenile female cage, with four chocolate-coloured bunks, green cement floor, faded yellow cement walls and ceiling. And the names of my people surround me.

Their names are everywhere, scratched, cut deep into the bunks, the yellow walls. Relatives I recognize from storytelling, or a chance meeting, family friends whom I may have met once on Red Pheasant. If I worked at it, my name here would be recognized as a Johnson of the John Bear family: Squeaky's— strange nickname for a man that big—little sister, or "that murdering Johnson girl." I've never lived much on the rez, so I'm not well known there. And for years, when my family told a story about a person, I wouldn't know them, but I always thought that some day I would get to know my relations. But sitting here I realize I never will know all my relations. This is a loss I suffer in prison, a loss which can't be healed.

On the bunk above me is carved a "LEON J + . . ." but the rest is gouged out. Maybe a little girl my brother got, and then she wanted somehow to make herself vanish, so she mutilated her name.

Sad . . . to search prison walls for news of one's own people; to become like an archaeologist trying to read the stones of tombs about the lives of your own ancient dead. And lying on the thin plastic mattress in my bunk in North Battleford jail, I see on the wall one name I truly knew: "JOHN SWIFTWOLF."

It's enough to bring a smile to this lifer's mind and spirit. And tears. I fell in love with that name—I wasn't even a teenager, not quite—one winter when we were frozen out at the rez and Mom brought us in to live at the apartment house in Battleford we called "Sesame Street," a huge building where only Natives lived, crammed in every bedroom, just across the street from the bars so no one had far to walk when they were open, or far to stumble when they closed.

We stayed with relations in this building, and a cousin and I became friends. She was older than I, her body beautifully developed, and she had a crush on John Swiftwolf's older brother. Sometimes she babysat in one of the apartments with a telephone, overlooking the river hills, and she'd invite me to come too and we'd talk about going sliding with boys we liked. We made a plan: she said she'd call John's brother on the phone, and I'd go with her as a double date. I dreamed: my first boyfriend, my first date; sliding in the snow down the Battle River hills. John Swiftwolf.

So when I see the name SWIFTWOLF scratched on this jail wall, it lays a sour bitterness over a sweet memory that until now has kept itself somehow hidden—and therefore whole—in my mind. I didn't know how sweet it was until I remembered it. And in that instant, of course, it turns bitter.

John's older brother had a car, and I'd watch at the window when he was coming to pick up my friend. But when I saw the car, I'd tell her quickly, then run and hide. I didn't want anyone to see me. I felt ugly and thought that if he actually saw me he wouldn't even want to talk to me on the phone.

But we did talk on the phone, twice, and I finally agreed that next day we'd meet to go sliding down the river hills. I was so happy, so scared, I was almost thirteen and I had such a crush on him, his beautiful name, meeting him!

"Sesame Street" was a huge former hotel three storeys high with all its standard-sized bedrooms rented out as "apartments" to Natives. It was crammed full of men, women, kids, and everyone seemed to be drinking, fighting, screwing around from one apartment and along the halls into another. "Parties" went on non-stop. And the cops could show up at any time: no one called them, they showed up when they wanted action. When the patrol car rolled up, kids playing outside would disappear into the halls yelling, "Simakunis!"—"police" in Cree, like runners in the old days warning a camp—and everyone would vanish, the whole place lock itself down, nothing but dead silence. Like an old western before the shoot-out.

Because the police weren't just dangerous for adults. We kids were taught to stay away from them too. Every kid understood that, if the RCMP appeared, you could knock on any door and you'd get taken in; parents didn't worry, we all knew each other or were related, you were being taken care of in some apartment and you'd come out after the cops left.

The day of my first date I was in the hall when I saw a woman fall. She bounced down the stairs on her head and I ran to her; there were bubbles foaming from her nose and mouth. Mom came and the fallen women seemed to be breathing all right, so Mom said there was nothing to do, I should just stay and check her now and then lying on the floor. I stayed in the hall, and suddenly kids burst into the building yelling, "Simakunis!" The cops were looking for two men, escapees or parole breakers, and what better place to look than Sesame Street. I didn't know what to do. I was just scared.

The woman lying there with foam coming out of her mouth was young and almost as beautiful as my mom, except Mom never had to wear make-up. The woman wore her hair up in the high, combed-back ratted style of the time, and after that fall she was always called "Bubbles" because the rubby she drank—they called it "taster's choice"!—made her foam.

That day I was so frightened of the cops in Sesame Street I couldn't do anything but try to hide, run. One of the men they were hunting was tall and skinny, and he was dodging around, with a woman leading him from one apartment to the next, slipping out one window and into the next while kids running in the hall pretended to give the cops signals, "He's in here, in here!" The other guy was huge, arms like trees and drunk to boot, but he had a naked shank and he wanted to get away from his friends trying to hide him, swearing he'd scalp the pigs, just give him a chance! I was at the stairwell, ready to dodge up or down, but the woman guiding the skinny guy told me to yell, "He's going down the stairs!", so I did that, me at one end of the hall yelling and the cops at the other. Then I dodged down around a corner and a cop came out of an apartment and turned away and the woman ducked into the apartment he'd just left; he almost saw her, but I yelled and distracted him. Ahead of me a man leaped out of one apartment and dived across the hall into another like a soldier hitting a foxhole, and I pointed the cop to the next apartment—I had no idea who lived there—and ran back up to the third floor to see if Bubbles was okay.

But the big man with the knife was at the end of that hall swearing he could take on any pig, C'mon! C'mon! and a cop at the corner pulled out his gun to get him. Then a bunch of people jumped on the man, actually covering him from the cop, took his knife away and hauled him into an apartment. The policeman was yelling "Clear out, Clear out!" when three more cops arrived and then a real fight took place, in the apartment and out into the hall. The four cops beat the man, but he gave as good as he got till they pistol-whipped him. That was too much for the Natives; they all jumped in too. I got slammed into a toilet and told to stay there, and I heard the fight going on and on, but I was safe behind the door.

I looked out the toilet window, and I laughed. The skinny guy had jumped out from a second-floor window into the snowbank. He was flapping around trying to get out of the chest-deep snow when the Swiftwolf car drove up. John's brother coming for his date with my cousin. The skinny guy ran for the moving car, dived, rolled over the hood, and grabbed the door and jumped in. The car wheeled doughnuts around the slick snow and roared away.

About the same time the four cops were dragging the big guy out of the building, unconscious; a woman screaming and crying at their heels.

Mom had had enough of Sesame Street. When it was warmer she took us back to the Rez. And I never went snow sliding with John Swiftwolf. I never met him.

John Swiftwolf, if you ever feel unloved, know that there is someone who has kept an innocent love for you over twenty years. If you want to, maybe after the year 2014 we could still go sliding on the Battle River hills.

———

It was RCMP constable Nicholas Smyth who informed Yvonne of the jury's decision. Smyth had been the investigator gathering Crown evidence for Karen's charge against Leon; he also investigated Darlene and Yvonne's charges. He had even spent a week in Butte, Montana, trying to gather school, police, and FBI records on Yvonne's childhood there. Despite Yvonne's long negative experience with policemen, she found Smyth "a nice guy."

She tells me she did meet one other humane policeman: RCMP Staff Sergeant Cliff Burnett, who came with his wife to Kingston in May 1995, to escort her to North Battleford for the preliminary inquiry. "He treated me like a human being—a unique experience on a sexual-assault complaint anyway, as most women will testify, and even more surprising since I was a federal inmate on security escort. He never shackled me, just told me straight up if I wanted to jump out of vehicle going a hundred kliks, the choice was mine."

In fact, Cliff Burnett later wrote a letter to Kingston regarding that escort; he praised Yvonne as a "model prisoner" who "followed instruction to the letter and accepted our direction without question and a great amount of humour [. . .]. I found Yvonne a very intelligent and respectful person [. . .]. We had many preconceived ideas of this inmate before actually meeting her and were somewhat taken aback when she quickly deflated our images with her wit, humour and conversation. She is truly a book that awaits to be written."

However, by the time of the trial in June 1995, Burnett had been transferred to Regina, and a different kind of RCMP officer in North Battleford jail went out of his way to let Yvonne know what he thought of her. He was considerate enough to ask her whether she wanted something to read, but when she replied, "Yes, please," he gave her only the section of the newspaper that carried a long article about a backwoods Ontario family fighting the courts to leave them alone in their apparently consenting-adult, incestuous relationships.

"I got the cop's point, all right," Yvonne wrote to me. "He as much as told me, 'Indians are always fucking each other anyway, why bother the courts with it? Clog up our jails, endless arrests and paperwork, who cares if Indians bugger each other up. And these Johnsons, four out of six here in jail at one time and the worst one, this convicted murderer, yelling rape on her brother.'

"Women accused of violent offences are always viewed as worse than men. In Canada judges have stated this openly on the bench, so why shouldn't the cops?"

Another policeman told her the evidence Smyth had gathered in Butte would at best make an RCMP scrapbook. "That's the abuse in my life: scrap; cop entertainment."

Constable Nicholas Smyth did not behave that way to her, and he said he wanted to help her, but there was never enough time, even with seven days in the North Battleford cells, for Yvonne to discuss with him what he had found in Montana. He did tell her two things: he had found not a single living person—including her father—who would confirm her accusations of porn-ring abuse in Butte; and police officials had told him categorically that no policeman had ever been found guilty of a criminal offence in Butte.

I myself had seen the evidence in the long reports of police crime in the 11 August 1989, edition of *The Montana Standard*. It would seem Smyth had talked to police and investigated "official" records only, and perhaps it was not surprising that he found no evidence there.

When Smyth informed Yvonne of the jury's decision on Friday, 23 June 1995, he came with a woman officer into her cell and told her as kindly as he could that the jury had brought in their verdict after less than six hours' deliberation: three charges by Darlene, five by her, and Leon had walked free on all eight of them. He said that's the way the law is, the jury has to believe beyond a reasonable doubt, and they said not guilty.

Where did that leave her? She was crying, she had counted on honest police to gather honest evidence, but it was all the same: always a power confrontation and absolute, overwhelming force, and the abuser walking free again. And Smyth could only tell her that after his investigation in Butte, and what he'd heard about her brother in court—though she had said and written some pretty wild things—he still believed that what she said could have happened. But Leon had denied everything, and no witnesses had stood up to confirm what Yvonne testified had happened to her in Saskatchewan.

"No one from my family?" she asked.

"You better talk to your family, about what they said in court."

Yvonne phoned Karen later from P4W, but Karen told her little except that the police had "yanked them around," they would not allow them to visit her; security, Karen said. Yeah, Yvonne comments to me, "if they really wanted to come, they'd find a connection, Mom was in good with my escorting officers. I'm not stupid, I've been in the system seven years now." She knew that the RCMP had searched for Cecilia in town and personally told her to visit Yvonne. After Karen's case against Leon, both the prosecution and the defence had evaluated Cecilia as a "good woman" caught in a bad situation, having a court search through her children's violence against each other. She personally told Leon's defence lawyer after Karen's trial,

"I support both my kids, but you get caught in the middle, and you really don't know what's going on all the time. All my life my kids never told me things, that I'm starting to learn about now."

And the defence lawyer added at Leon's sentencing, "To some extent, I think if there's a victim, it's her. Because she's a . . . she's a good woman.

Yvonne says that she believes in her heart that her mother *is* a good woman. But she also thinks that at some point Cecilia made her decision: she would back her son, even if it meant going against her daughters. She refused to be drawn into Karen's trial, but in Yvonne's she chose to take the stand; once there, there was a lot she could not remember, or that she had never seen. But as Yvonne pointed out, "If Mom says she can't remember, or saw nothing, then how can she say nothing happened?"

For Yvonne, the situation ultimately turned again on her mother's life of deny, deny. By continuing to say, "It never happened, Vonnie, nothing was going on, if you say it did you're crazy," her mother—despite her good intentions—simply perpetuated the silence that allows abuse in the family to go on, and on.

Yvonne found the holding cell worse after the verdict, four yellow cement walls. She was there for two more days—"I smoke like mad, a smoke was all I knew I had [...]. my stay in the cells was spent crying"—before they flew her back to Kingston. Alone except for an Elizabeth Fry Society woman: "She came and stayed with me, she gave me real support. She let me ramble and pace and smoke, she was short and dark, from Asia I think, and I taught her old Johnny Cash songs to give her a flavour of jail. She told me she saw me as a very strong, spiritual person."

And one fifteen-minute visit from her mother.

Cecilia came for a security visit under supervision in the visiting room: Yvonne writes me she must have deliberately asked for that, in order to keep it short and controlled. There were police officers—at times as many as six—listening all the time, and Yvonne recognized in her mother that cockiness she gets when she has won something. Yvonne had taken Leon to court to confront and expose him for what he had done, but also to reach the family, to achieve some understanding and—best of all—change. But her mother had seen it as a challenge, and now that the jury had declared Leon "not guilty" it seemed to Yvonne her mother was in effect telling her, "You gave it your best shot, and you lost. You tried, but not even a jury of Whites believes you, three members of the family have gone up against him now and it's over, he's clean, now let the past lie." So the court had vindicated her for backing Leon all along: *she* had won.

Would her mother have come to see her even for fifteen minutes if the verdict had gone the other way? She wouldn't come earlier when Yvonne needed support, so why was she bothering now? Yvonne writes with some bitterness, "I feel she [visited me] for the sake of show. The whole thing was exciting to her." To show the cops here's this poor, afflicted mother with her violent, crazy kids, and she still tries, she still cares for them all, even the worst. It's not her fault, she's the one to feel sorry for.

The police banged on the door, "Two minutes!"

Cecilia said to Yvonne, "I love you."

Eight months later Yvonne writes me, still with the pain remembered from that moment:

"I told her I feared for all of them from Leon. That's when I saw fright, and what seemed almost a breaking of some sort in her, yet her comeback was quick. She said, 'I'm tougher than that, he can't get this old bag down.'

"Her big boy would walk free again, despite all she knows he's done. In her happiness, her words, 'Now don't cry, forget it,' hit me very hard.

"But I was obedient. I told her as I hugged her, 'And I too love you, I really do, Mom.' I looked in her eyes and I saw a little give, they seemed to fog a bit and she grabbed me for a hug.

"'Yvonne,' she said, 'I'll help you get out. But be careful what you write, we still have to live here, you know.'

"Then she parted my company, walking out of my life as always."

When Cecilia left, she cracked a joke Yvonne couldn't hear; the RCMP officers gathered in the corridor laughed, and then the door closed.

14

Spirit Keepers

Reason sets the boundaries [of life] far too narrowly for us [. . .]. Day after day we live far beyond the bounds of our consciousness; without our knowledge, the life of the unconscious is also going on within us. The more critical reason dominates, the more impoverished life becomes; but the more of the unconscious [. . .] we are capable of making conscious, the more of life we integrate.

– Carl Jung, *Memories, Dreams, Reflections*

In August 1995, Yvonne writes to me from Kingston:

Something low and dark came to visit me in the North
Battleford cells, and I feared it when I should not have, as to fear
is to give it a way in. I smudged and cleansed the area, praying
to send it back where it came from. I've had nothing but bad
luck [in P4W] since court, which, I believe, was caused by what-
ever came, to kill me or take my spirit. It could not, so it follows
me to raise hell in my life instead here. I know now not to
acknowledge it in spirit, I will let it die out by not giving it any
energy from my sorrows and worries. Then it must go away, as it
has no control. I must believe in the protection that's over me.

Yvonne had managed life in the Prison for Women for four years, living as quietly and as withdrawn as possible—doing her daily work, her
classes, her crafts, studying and writing, being active in the Native Sisterhood, and working with me on her book, which she told me "all her
family feared." Now, just days before the old "dysfunctional labyrinth
of claustrophobic and inadequate spaces"—as Judge Louise Arbour
called P4W—was to be permanently closed, this "something low and
dark" came there to raise chaos in Yvonne's personal life. And it used
the normal, ongoing inmate and guard interaction—"endless game-
playing bullshit" as Yvonne calls it, the worst elements of which she
had managed to avoid for four years—to do so.

Yvonne: I'm scheduled to be taken to Collins Bay in fifteen minutes for my regular visit with Dwa. I have to be ready, have to get cleaned up. I have to get back unnoticed to my cell, quick, get myself cleaned up!

I walk out of the crowded bathroom into the open area of the Activity Building. Twenty inmate women stare at me, some deadpan, others crying, all speechless. And I do a fast scan to see if anyone else is coming for me, no, and I see my jacket on the floor where I placed it. I scoop it up—but my fingers barely move, my hands are swelling up so fast now I can't get them through the sleeves: I have to unzip the jacket sleeves to the elbow with my teeth before I can get it on. My hair is in braids but sticks up where fistfuls of it were yanked out and I try to pat it down, and I can't with my hands and I have no brush on me, I get out the door and head for my cell, my jacket covers the blood on my shirt and I have to get to my cell, quick, alone.

I hear a knock on the security glass: a woman on the upper range lifts her arm high in the Native salute, "Well done!"

She's been in P4W longer than anyone. I nod to her, I'm walking on automatic in the right direction, walk normal, if the guards grab me it will most likely happen before I reach my cell. I know every wall and corner and staircase and iron bar in every P4W building, but now all I see is Jane's back, going away along the top range towards her cell.

It all started because of Jane, a Native sister.

Just get back to your cell, your own small hole in the long range. Walk normal.

Everything grows bright and sharp. As I walk I begin to shake. I smell something odd—it's on my own breath, like ether—and I can't feel my heart pounding, though I know it must be. I try to touch myself and I feel nothing. Because my hands are destroyed?

It was the young White girl who got us to stop fighting. She hissed, "Six! Six!" meaning the guards were coming, and she gave me a shove because she's new and doesn't know any better.

I get into my cell. Its familiar—false of course—feel of protection. I'm alone for a minute, and do a fast body check: if someone comes at me now, I'll really have to take it to my limit, head, feet, teeth, whatever, because my hands are gone. Like they're frozen, so I hold my brush between them and brush my hair down against my stinging scalp as best I can. The pressure in my hands builds, they're stretching tight from the inside out, my hands seem like they'll burst.

I have to look in a mirror, assess the damage. If the guards notice there'll be endless questions that have to be answered and I don't want to think that fast now — but there's not a scratch. I don't recognize myself. It's the face of a stranger.

And I almost cry out in fear: according to the Elders, if your spirit leaves your body, you will not be able to recognize yourself.

My body is the house of my spirit. If my body does something my spirit does not agree with, it may leave my body. My body will be empty.

Or shift-change . . . into what? The Elders say when you shift-change you have called something from within yourself to the surface; it has taken you over to deal with whatever is necessary. Has my spirit been ripped from me? Has it hidden itself because it could not endure what I was doing?

By the rules of P4W, what I did was fair enough. But brutal. I can only bend my head and hate what I've just done. I lost it in there. Twenty inmates in the Activity Building watching, and I lost it completely. For the first time in prison. In six years.

My downfall was trying to help Jane, an abused woman who's being abused some more in here. While I'm trying to get ready to go to North Battleford and face Leon in court, she comes day after day, crying, "I'm so scared, Yvonne. He's after me all the time, what can I do?"

Yes, what? He's Joe, a staff member who positions himself to watch us undress when we change to go to the sweat lodge. And takes pictures too, everybody knows it, using the P4W camera. Then here's this short, stocky Ojibway woman who's been beaten up all her life, crying to me, "Yvonne, you stick to yourself, you're strong enough to go it alone here, you got the strength to haul your brother into court! What can I do?"

So, what can I do? She's my sister in the 'Hood. Even the guards are so worried about her, one evening they ask me to stay with her in her cell all night. I do. And I know I have to make a stand.

I file a formal complaint against Joe, and shit starts to fly. In my complaint about his activities I make the mistake of dropping an inmate's name as well, a White woman involved with Joe for a long time, who hates our Sisterhood so much—when she first came in I was chair of the 'Hood—that she tried to organize a "White" group to give them as much clout, she said, as the Native and Black Sisterhoods had. She never got anywhere with that, but she keeps pushing us and now she says she's going to take me to court for libel. I tell her, "Fine, then I'll be able to tell the whole world, and you'll give me the legal means to do it."

But then suddenly, in February 1995, P4W hits the national TV news with a leaked film-clip of the 22 April 1994 riot where six Native inmates are strip-searched naked by an all-male Institutional Emergency Response Team (IERT) and thrown into isolation shackled, crouching naked for days in bare steel-and-concrete boxes. The IERT guys took the video of themselves doing it, and it's very rough. Correctional Services Canada (CSC) circles their wagons; they go nuts about inmate complaints, especially Natives. In April 1995 the government appoints a Commission of Inquiry into Certain Events at the Prison for Women, and Judge Louise Arbour comes right into P4W to see us. She's sharp, tough; she goes around looking at everything and talks to inmates with no CSC people around, they can't bullshit her. The warden of P4W was kicked into retirement, and CSC was spinning from all the publicity.

After seven tons of paper, I know my little complaint about one White guy screwing a Native inmate is impossible; there's no way after this investigation I'll ever come out ahead on this with CSC, and to get it out of the way I retract. I withdraw my statement as a lie.

Though every inmate knows what I reported was the truth. And Correctional Services Canada knows it too.

When I withdrew my complaint, it was open season on me as far as the White woman was concerned, the one I'd named. I had been moved from my house on the wing to a cell on the A Range when I tried to organize an abused women's group, and after I returned from the disaster in North Battleford in late June, I was just messed up, barely surviving. I felt so vulnerable I packed a shank when I left my cell; I held it between my teeth when I took a shower. Though I tried to cover up, never show weakness, I started to shiver when I walked down the long corridors. But when the deal went down at the end of August I didn't pack, because I was scared I'd use it—which would have been worse.

I was trying to stay low, I was trying to walk my spiritual path. I did not even know if I could fight sober—I never had. But if you feel forced to make a stand, you do.

I was completely exhausted by the Leon trial, my mind strung out with what happened there. The endless guard and inmate gossip about me got so bad, yet no one would directly confront me, that I couldn't go on, I had to get the bullshit cleared up, so one day in August, just before I was due to go to Collins Bay to visit Dwa, I went to the Activity Building, to the area where the Blacks sit.

"Look," I said, "does anyone have a problem with me? If so, let's go to the laundry room and talk it over."

No, they said, no way. And they're friendly, like they usually are to me. "Hey Yvonne, don't let no White bitches play with you."

So I went to the next room, and the women there said "No" too. So I went to the kitchen area and asked. Same thing, no problem.

But one of the Blacks was running her mouth up and down the ranges, saying I was challenging everyone. And as I was in my cell, talking to a new arrival, a voice yelled out down the range: "Unit meeting, in the Activity Building!"

That means all the inmates on one range are to hold a meeting without direct guard supervision. I go, but I'm careful; I don't pack a shank. We stand or sit in a circle and the inmate Unit Rep does all the talking: she says everybody's getting too tense, who gives a fuck about some staff asshole anyways. Then she comes to the point:

"Yvonne, stop getting in everyone's face. We all know what you did, you told us yourself."

She was talking about my dropping an inmate's name when making a complaint on a staff member, and she pushed her face up to mine, so close I could look right down her throat. She was talking, though I don't know what she said. I was watching her mouth move, her throat open.

Then she stopped. About twenty women sitting around or standing there, quiet. We're supposed to have privacy for unit meetings. The guards can't see us, but they've got two-way speakers and can hear it all, and sometimes they come around the corner and tell us whatever they please. But this time they didn't move out of their bubble.

I said to the face up against mine, "Okay, I did that. Now do you have a personal problem with me?"

She walked across the room to her friends, hesitated, then turned from beside her friends and said, yes. Yes, she has a problem.

"You got my old lady involved too," she said. "And I've got a big problem with that."

Her old lady was sitting right there, and I could see she's surprised to hear this. She works in the gym area, but I never mentioned her in my complaint, and all she had to say now was she knew nothing. But she didn't explain.

"Okay," I said. "I apologize if you got involved."

I stood by myself in a corner of the room and the Unit Rep yelled, she thinks loud is authoritative, "Anybody else got anything to say to Yvonne?"

Another woman spoke up. I'd challenged her girlfriend the day before because she sided with staff on an issue, and she backed down at my challenge. But then, to save face, she lied to her woman; she told her she'd backed down only because I threatened to shank and gang-pile her.

". . . if you get outa line again, Yvonne," the old lady of the woman who backed down at my challenge was still yapping, "I'll smash your face, I'll knock. . . ."

I was so sick and tired of all this, finally I just said, "You want a piece of me?"

She'd talked herself up, everybody had heard her. "Yeah," she said. "Fucken right I do."

"Okay, I'm here. Let's dance."

I took off my jacket, the one with zippers at the wrists. She came at me running, and I went into my boxing stance the way Leon taught me, legs braced, knees slightly bent. She came on swinging wildly, but when I fight I shut off my pain. I hit her with three rights and a left jab and she hit the floor.

"Get up again," I told her, "and I'll knock you down again."

She got up, and I came in with a right to the bottom of her jaw, followed by a left cross, and she went down again. She lurched to her feet, and the same thing happened, but she'd called me out and as long as I was up she was the one who had to call it quits. She was lying on the floor—and I never kick—so I dropped into a squat beside her and told her, "Say enough. Say it's over."

But she started to get up, and halfway there she grabbed my leg and I tried to push her down—I don't pull hair—and I had to hop on one leg with my hands on her shoulders so she couldn't flip me when she got up, both of us trying to keep our balance. I hate wrestling—box and get it over with.

Her old lady tried to break in on us, but the Rep yelled, "One on one, now fuck off!"

She was down and tried to bite my leg. I hate that worse than anything except hair-pulling, and as I hit her I bent too low and she got me by the hair too. So I grabbed hers and she groaned and curled up. But I leaned back, pulled her head up to meet my punches, and hit her face full force at the same time.

I said, "Say it's over!"

But she wouldn't. She heaved up and had me by the upper legs and was running me like a linebacker into the sightline of the guard bubble. The Rep yelled, "Not there, not there!" but she kept pushing me right back against the glass wall where the guards can see, so I used the glass as leverage to shove her away.

We both landed right in the laps of the women watching. They struggled to get out from under us, and I wrestled out from under her too. I couldn't feel anything in my hands any more; she bounced me on one leg across the room and grabbed my hair above the rubber band that holds my braid and it broke. She used all her weight to pull me over by one braid, I was bent across her but not down, I realized we were inside the bathroom door jamb and she had me up against the wall.

I yelled, "This's the last time you're touching my hair!" and I got a fistful of hers and banged her head against the steel door. I heard it crack, I could feel from her weight she was going down, but I was so enraged—my hair!—and then a shout: "Six! Six!"

Her old lady, and a young girl were in the doorway, both screaming.

Then: "Yvonne, Yvonne . . . enough already!"

———

I was in my cell. Shaking so badly I had to sit down on the bed.

———

Jane and the other sister showed up at my cell door. They came in, they started to brag me up. But I told them, don't get into that, I'm no way proud of what happened.

"Just stupid games. We went at each other to give you guys excitement off our pain."

Then a Jamaican inmate showed up. She said she had covered my back in there and I thanked her; though I knew it was partly because she hated Whites so much. But she didn't stop there: to my surprise she turned on Jane, whose abuse by Joe was the reason I had made the complaint in the first place.

"How come you left your sister all alone down there?" she said, her usually loud voice even louder. "She coulda been killed!"

Jane looked ashamed. "I really thought someone'd get killed, I didn't want to get pulled into it."

"So you just left her, to take it——"

"It's okay, it's okay," I interrupted. "Thanks again, for the cover, but I've got to go, visit my old man."

"No!"

"Yeah, so please."

"God, you just taken care of business and you carry on, clean up, go visit—you got jam, girl, and then some!"

I found I could stand again. And there was my name being called over the intercom; time to leave for the visit. The guards said nothing about my hands when they cuffed and shackled me for movement to Collins Bay; they seemed to see nothing and they never asked a thing. Dwa saw how strange my face looked.

"You musta really cut loose on somebody," he said. "Or did you go through a wall with your bare hands?"

"Real thick wall," I said. "I never got through."

He saw how much I hated what I'd done. I laid my head in his lap and we were quiet together through the whole visit. Then our time was up, and I was returned to my cell on the A Range in the Prison for Women. Sore, sad, stupid.

———

Some stories need to be told, then told again.

A prison like P4W is not a livable reality. You are bombarded with control and instruction and restriction and useless information, endless courses—but what is the point of it all if you're in for life and never get a chance to live freely what you're supposed to have learned? Inside you can't live it, and so you never actually know it.

So, prison is no place to recover. From anything, either the grief of memory, or loss, or abuse, or the diseases of addiction. But if you're a Native and you can get the help to seek and find and claim your spiritual name, a lot can be changed. You can discover your destiny. Your life can bridge back to the origins of your family and people, you can seek out your colours, your clan, your spirit keepers. You may find the self you never knew you were.

As Jung explains it, you can "emerge into your own myth."

I had laid Jung's book *Memories, Dreams, Reflections* down open, to keep my page. And I saw on the back cover that he died five months after my conception: 6 June 1961: four months later I was born. Something to think about. He writes:

> It seemed to me that one's duty was to explore daily the will of God (the Creator). I could only conclude that apparently no one knew about this secret [. . .]. I knew from experience that grace was accorded only to one who fulfilled the will of God (the Creator) [. . .]. It was then that it dawned on me: I must take responsibility, it is up to me how my fate turns out [. . .].
>
> From the very beginning I had a sense of destiny, as though my life was assigned to me by fate and had to be fulfilled. This gave me an inner security, and, though I could never prove it to myself, it proved itself to me. I did not have this certainty it HAD ME [Yvonne's capitals] [. . .]. I was outside time, I belonged to the centuries; and He who gave answer was He who had always been.

Jung was so right, to my own understanding, when he spoke of "bloody struggles" and "ultimate testing." I had those for sure. And at the end of his life, in the chapter "Visions," he is right again:

> It was only after the illness that I understood how important it is to affirm one's own destiny. In this way we forge an ego that does not break down when incomprehensible things happen; an ego that endures the truth, and that is capable of coping with the world and with fate. Then, to experience defeat is also to experience victory.

An ego that endures the truth. My great-great-grandfather Big Bear was deeply connected to Bear. He was a carrier of the bundle of the Bear Spirit, and his body died during a blizzard on the Little Pine Reserve in Saskatchewan, 17 January 1888, and—as they say—was buried on the banks of the Battle River where it flows on to Hudson Bay and into the world water of the oceans. Before I was born, before I emerged as flesh from my mother, my spirit's name was Medicine Bear Woman.

Receiving my name gave me a way to adapt the problems of my past to the possibilities of my future, however restricted and controlled it would be. My existence would fulfil what the Creator intended for me.

I must tell the story again.

One day in 1992, after I had been door and firekeeper for the sweat lodge inside P4W for over a year, I offered tobacco to the Elder who was visiting us then, Vern Harper, and asked him ("Be careful what you ask for!") if I could receive my spirit name. He was always joking, and this was so serious I joked too:

"I don't want, you know, a name like 'Speckled Frog Sitting on a Stump,' something like that!"

He laughed with me. But he said nothing, so I continued to keep the sweat-lodge area clean, to close the entrance of the lodge when he and the Sisters of the Hood went inside. I kept the fire burning to heat the stones, and I waited. He visited regularly but said nothing. I was struggling, trying to prepare myself for the appeal of my sentence in October.

Then one day when I was again carrying and placing the stones in the lodge pit, he said to me, "You're coming in today."

In the fourth round, after he had sung and prayed, Vern told me my name. And also my colours, which I had not asked for.

I knew the name was true. My grandma Flora had called me that; I could hear her voice saying it. My place was behind her wood stove, warm and quiet, and she talked in the shifting light of a wick burning in animal fat:

Muskeke Muskwa Iskwewos. Say it.

And now I knew certainly that I was a spirit in the physical world, I knew I had a destiny. Maybe now a lot of what I always thought was insane in my life, what drove me crazy trying to understand, maybe I could deal with it. As Carl Jung writes,

"We cannot think of the physical life of civilized man except in terms of problems. It is the growth of consciousness that we must thank for the existence of problems: they are the dubious gift of civilization."

When I got back from my visit with Dwa at Collins Bay, I was called to Medical, and they asked to see my hands. The nurse said staff had reported damage to my hands; they feared they might be broken. What had happened to them? They know I never report anything, I don't gossip or personally complain, but they could see my hands and I'd thought of something.

"I was late for lock-up," I said, "running too fast for the stairs, so I reached up and hit the steel pole on the handrails with my knuckles, the back of my hand."

She didn't look at me, just studied my hand. Then she said, "Both hands? It looks like there could be broken bones in there. I'll send you for x-rays."

They did not tell me what they found. I was given Tylenol Threes with codeine, a very big drug for anyone in P4W. I couldn't hold the little medicine cup they were in, so I dumped them over into my palm. They helped, immediately. And I walked away with my sleeves pulled down over my hands, but everyone knew I was on the Med line and the gossip went around, "How did she get Threes?"

The woman I fought couldn't get out of bed. I heard that some inmates were giving her their Meds for her pain and that she was deaf in one ear from a broken eardrum. I went to my cell and prayed; not for myself, but for what was going on, and all I now had to do.

For two years I'd been working in Crafts on a special shield. I finished it now with an eagle on it, the messenger of the Creator. Then I went to her cell on the range and asked if I could talk with her. Her girlfriend was with her; it was the first time since the fight that I had seen either of them. There was a strange smell in the cell: she was lying flat on her bed.

She tried to sit up. I could see it was hard, and she hid her face from me. I bent my face to the floor to give her as much privacy as I could in that cramped space.

"I brought you a gift," I said. "A sort of peace offering."

I presented the shield to her, and for a moment she said nothing. I couldn't look at her.

"If you accept it," I said, "then it's over. If not . . . well, I'll know where we stand. But I'm offering it to you, to let you know I'm really sorry. If you take it, then it's finished."

She said, "I'll be proud to take it. Thank you."

Both her eyes were black; her whole face one battered bruise. And I started to cry, knowing I'd done that to her. And I told her how sorry I was. I said, "Let's never play these stupid games for them again."

And she promised me that. I gave her all the Threes I had, and she told me about her visit to the doctor about her face. She told him she tripped and fell down the stairs, and we laughed aloud, our stories so close. But they also asked her whether she'd been in a fight with me. Why? I asked. Well, your hands and my face, and they keep a suspect file on everything, they're always piling up files, every inmate carries sixteen tons of paper at least.

I said, "Let them suspect all they want."

"Well," she said, "you're sort of yellow around the cheeks too."

"That's nothing to what else you did—every muscle is sore, every bone aches."

"Let's see your hands," she said. I showed her. "Pretty bad, eh?"

"Yeah," I said. "You've got guts, there's no giving up. You're a real Cool Hand Luke!"

So we laughed; and she and I agreed we would not shank each other. I went outside to my work in the yard. The Black inmate was there digging out dandelions; they sail in and grow, the stone walls of P4W don't stop dandelions.

"I told those stupid women long ago," she said, "leave Yvonne alone, I told 'em, quiet water runs deep. You became the Bear, you swatted her down with a huge paw."

But I just wanted to be low-profile again. To be left alone.

And I was. Whatever they wrote down on my secret file, my official security rating remained medium. The Healing Lodge for Federally Sentenced Women at Maple Creek, Saskatchewan, was about to open; it would accept only minimum-security inmates, but in September 1995 I was transferred out of P4W with the prayer I would never see it again. I was brought back to the prairies, and for a few months I was held at the Regional Psychiatric Centre, Saskatoon, Saskatchewan, less than two hours from Red Pheasant by car. My family has been known to drive farther than that for an evening beer, but no one came to visit me.

The year 1995 was my roughest in prison, even worse than 1993, when I lost my appeal. Maybe Sergeant Burnett's good letter about me—no one asked him to write it—after he escorted me to North Battleford had something to do with my luck turning. Nothing official was ever said to me about the fight, and in fact, after I was transferred to the Regional Psychiatric Centre in Saskatoon in September, my security rating was dropped from medium to minimum. Then on 11 December 1995, I arrived at the Healing Lodge built in the hills south of Maple Creek on the land of the Nekaneet Cree Nation.

Okimaw Ohci. Still a prison, but with no wall or fence. Just tall poplar trees and air, the sacred ground of the Thunder-Breeding Hills sloping down to the long horizon on the prairie. Thank the Creator.

15

What You Did, and Where You Did It

Today makes it two years I've been in prison. Today I remember the pain and suffering not only of myself, but all who were involved. [. . .] When I saw that man's family in court, I cried within myself for them. As I saw the anger they had. [. . .] I can't help but want to give the dead man's family love, love they will need so much. But they will never accept me as long as hate outweighs their pain. I pray they not hate us, because if they do, their little ones suffer. I know the man suffered, and was hurt in a most cruel and bad way. All dignity was taken away in his death. I don't know if what Shirley Anne said about him was true, and now a lot of people perceive him as a child molester. I don't know. And truly, who am I to judge? None of it was intended to happen. I did not even hate the man, I pitied him. I don't know why it happened. I can hate no one, and if I do, it doesn't last. I do know, if what happened had not happened, I would have tried to help him again. [. . .] I always need time to let the anger pass, then if he had come and we were alone, I know I would have talked to him.

– Yvonne, *Journal 1*, 15 September 1991

T HE HEALING LODGE in the Cypress Hills of southwestern Saskatchewan came into existence because of the Task Force on Federally Sentenced Women. In its report in April 1990, it recommended that the single Kingston Prison for Women — P4W — be replaced by five regional women's facilities across Canada, and that a "Healing Lodge be established in a prairie location where Aboriginal federally sentenced women may serve all or part of their sentences." Early in 1991, a Healing Lodge Planning Circle began to make plans and receive submissions, and in February 1994, the Nekaneet Band voted to grant a site for the lodge on its small reserve south of Maple Creek. The Maple Creek/Nekaneet submission was accepted because it "demonstrated a strong tradition of Aboriginal and non-Aboriginal cooperation, an offering of sacred land . . . and a strong sense of responsibility." Construction started in August 1994, and in December 1995 Yvonne Rose Johnson became the fifth federally sentenced woman to be accepted there.

It was in Okimaw Ohci that Yvonne could finally gather the courage to recall in sequence the crime for which she was sentenced, and the strength to speak it out.

After a ceremonial sweat led by her adopted father, Elder Gordon Oaks of Nekaneet, and further consultation with Elder Pauline Shirt of Toronto, Yvonne chooses a "good, wise" course of action. On 26 December 1996, in the Elder's apartment at the Okimaw Ohci Healing Lodge, she speaks for hours into an audio recorder.

She will make five tapes in all and, as she states at the outset, they are there for use by the lawyers who will help her in her case, for me, and also for Judge Lynn Ratushny, head of the Self-Defence-Review (SDR) appointed by the Government of Canada. The purpose of the SDR is to make a "review of cases of women convicted of homicide which occurred in the context of an abusive relationship."

On 29 December, Yvonne personally gives me a copy of the tapes when I visit her in the presence of Pauline Shirt. I began listening to them on 2 January 1997. I have heard and read about parts of these events before, but this is the first time I hear her speak, in a connected sequence, what she remembers of what happened in the basement of her house in Wetaskiwin, Alberta, on 14 September 1989. In the following excerpts, taken verbatim from the tapes, the events of that dreadful evening are seen through Yvonne's eyes.

> I have taken Pauline Shirt as my Elder, and she is present with me at the Okimaw Ohci Healing Lodge while I tell this, for spiritual support, guidance, counselling, and for friendship. Today is December 26, 1996. I do this in a ceremonial way, and it is covered under the medicine, and I believe the spirits are here to help me. My sole purpose in doing this is to give it to the Creator, to give it to the spirits in the hope to get some sort of understanding, to put some sort of closure to all of it. To make a bad situation better if possible [. . .]. It's time for me to be as a medicine bear woman and to deal with these things [. . .]. Please try to hear me with your spirit [. . .]. Then use your mind to do what you think is best [. . .].
>
> I have never denied that I was involved. I was angry at the possibility that this man ["Chuck" Skwarok] could be a child molester, sitting in my home, I was angry because I couldn't talk to him about it, I was angry at myself that I had to try to convince myself to get angry or mad enough to even start to talk about it [. . .]. And I couldn't walk away, I couldn't run away. It was my home. It was my children, I just didn't know what else to do [. . .].
>
> The next thing I knew all four of us were down there in the basement. And everybody was fighting and I was just standing there.

Ernie would like bulldog him, and run him up against the wall, and then Shirley Anne [. . .] would come up there and punch him right where his head was cut, she just made it bleed, punching him there.

A lot of wrestling around and blood was getting all over the place, he was bleeding pretty bad from his head. And I didn't know how bad he was cut.

They were fighting and wrestling all over the place, it was mainly Ernie and Shirley Anne, you know that Shirley Anne, where I come from you're taught to fight one on one, you fight until one guy says "I give up." Everybody fights in Montana, but you weren't allowed to pull hair after the fourth grade and if you want to fight you call that person out and meet them after school, it's equivalent to having a gun showdown in the street. Nobody is allowed to jump in.

I didn't like the way Shirley Anne would sneak in there. She was evil, she knew where she was hitting, every time. I didn't figure she had that in her. And I didn't like it.

Or Ernie, that he could fight that hard.

Here it was my home, my children I wanted to protect, and now I actually didn't want them fighting him any more—and yet I had to try and save face that I wasn't condoning his actions by telling them to leave him alone. So in my own warped way, and I know it's not right, I didn't say anything in the first place. I know it's a twisted way of thinking to somehow defuse the situation at the time.

When Chuck was getting the best of Ernie, then Shirley Anne'd jump in there, and it just bothered me. She did all this to get us started and now she was doing this. I just didn't like any of this.

So I would try to break it up, and told him, "Don't fight me," I told him, "All I want is get you cleaned up and outa here." And Shirley Anne was standing there like a vulture, "Go," I says, "go get some water. We'll wash him up."

She was mumbling around that she had to be sent away, but that was one of her chances to get out of the situation if she had wanted to—as she said later in court she wanted to so badly. She went upstairs and she came back, all she had was this tiny tin pot of water, what good was that supposed to do? I put a rag in there and it soaked all the water up.

Washing Chuck, all I did was smear his blood around. I told Shirley Anne she was useless, so I went upstairs and brought a big pot of water back down. I had him cleaned off pretty good, and then he started bleeding again.

And I felt sorry for him, I felt really sorry. I would try to hold the rags on his face where it was bleeding so it would stop, and then he looked at me.

And there was something about his eyes, it all becomes weird, something happened inside me then and I'd look away from him, and then I would convince myself to have pity again and I'd try to help him and I would look in his eyes, and I would see that again.

And I could smell his sweat mixed with the water. I don't know, just the smell and his eyes, I don't know what the hell happened, I just stood back and looked at him and all of a sudden the pity I felt was gone, and I felt anger, this real bad anger. I said something to him, something about his eyes.

"You breathe like a pig," I said, "you smell like a pig," and I couldn't understand and I says, "I can't clean you up, you're bigger than this!" I remember taking that whole pot of water and I spilled it on him.

And when I did that, I flipped again—I thought, I did that? why'd I do that?—it seemed really cruel on my part to have done that and I let out a scream and I just spun around and I took off across the basement.

And when I did that, then Ernie started fighting him again, and Shirley Anne too.

They accused him of being an abuser, fighting and yelling, and I don't know what it is, but I felt sorry for him again. I came in between them and I broke them up, they were pounding him and throwing accusations and at that moment I wanted to protect him and I don't know why but I turned around and looked at him.

And I told him, "Do you really know how it feels, to be raped as a child? Do you?"

He didn't answer me, and when he didn't answer me I hit him, and I told him, "Tell me, if you know, what it feels like for someone to rape you as a child!"

He said nothing and I screamed, and spun away from him and shot off across the basement again.

And the other two were all over him. Ernie yelled, "I'll show him what it's like, I'll show him how it feels." I was standing there.

Ernie was going to sexually abuse him. I was just standing there, I . . . I don't know what really happened. Somehow Shirley Anne got his pants off, he was standing, his head was facing the dugout in the basement and Ernie was by the slide we had built for the kids, Chuck was bent over. He was saying,

"No—no—no. . . ."

And Ernie was working himself into a frenzy and trying to undo the string of the jogging pants he was wearing. And I was just standing there, I didn't know what was happening, and Ernie yelled, "Take off his pants, take off his pants!"

And Shirley Anne reached over and pulled down Chuck's pants. Ernie was going towards him. And then I came between him and Ernie again when Ernie was pulling down his pants, and in my own way I tried to stop him.

I told Ernie, "You don't want to filthy yourself, you don't want to do that."

And somehow Shirley Anne was standing there and she had a table [stool] leg and she was saying, "Here, use this, use this," and Ernie grabbed it, and somehow Dwayne wound up with it.

And I remember looking at Dwayne and looking in his eyes and I took it away from Dwayne and I told him, "I'll do it!"

Because I knew Ernie would've done it, and I knew Shirley Anne would've done it, so I faked it.

I came in between them guys, and either Ernie or Dwayne was holding Chuck by his head in a headlock, I don't remember, and Dwayne was saying something, "You can't use that."

Because the leg had a plastic tip at the floor end and a screw in the other; so I knew you couldn't use this, but I was not intending on penetrating him.

And in the process of acting like I did, made me feel horrible. To be honest I did not penetrate him, I could never have did that or he would have bled. I just acted like I did, or otherwise Ernie would've raped him. I acted like I did, I took the leg and I threw the leg across the basement, "There!"

Everybody thought that I did, but I didn't. And I says, "Let him go, let him go now."

And I don't know what happened again, someone started asking him if he was the guy going around picking up all the kids on the street. And then he started crying. Ernie said, "I knew it, I knew it!" and Wham! they were all over him again, Ernie and Shirley Anne fighting him again.

And I never told anybody, because I could never explain my own stupid actions. It made sense to me, then, to act like I raped him, but I didn't. Otherwise Ernie would've did it, I did that to stop Ernie. But for some reason every time I did something to stop it, it wasn't final, it didn't, it made matters worse. It's just crazy.

Then Ernie ran him headlong into the sewer stack. And he started bleeding more, I don't know if it was from his head or any place else.

But now he had no pants on, only a T-shirt. And I didn't want to look at him [Yvonne is now audibly crying] 'cause when I look at him I hated him when I looked at his nakedness. I hated to see his nakedness. They were beating him again, and again in my own strange way, I can't understand, but I kind of hated him now when I saw his nakedness, I kind of hated him.

When they were fighting him I went upstairs and I got a knife.

I came back downstairs and said, "We'll just tie him up," you know, that seemed like another way to stop it.

When I wasn't looking at him he wasn't naked, but when I did look he was naked.

And I hated his penis. [Crying] And I hated his body. And I hated men.

And I didn't know what the hell I was feeling and I didn't want them to beat him.

I didn't want Shirley Anne to have control, I didn't like any of it—but I was there.

So I went over and I cut this big thick cable cord that we had for our TV [...]. "Let me tie you up," I says, "and they'll stop fighting you."

So he willingly laid on the floor and I cut the telephone cord, it was the really thin thin white see-through plastic that comes from a real old phone.

And I was over him, he was lying on his belly and I told him to put his hands behind his back. I attempted to tie him up but it wouldn't work, I was so drunk I couldn't keep my balance, I went back. I started falling backwards.

And I put my hand back to stop myself, and when I did that my hand touched his naked rear end.

And something happened to me. All of a sudden I was really mad at him again. I started saying that he's a child molester, no good—and I put the cord around his neck and I pulled back on it real hard and it broke within seconds.

And when it broke, I moved away and they were back on him, fighting him again. Dwayne was there but I don't remember him, the rare time, in the beginning, he'd only fight when Chuck was getting the better of Ernie and Shirley Anne. Later on he was just there.

Shirley Anne and Ernie were doing all the beating. I felt bad because I knew it was my fault, if I could have done something—so I suggested to them, "Let's tie him up, let's just tie him up."

So Chuck sat down by the [floor-beam support] pole which Ernie had thrown him against, he put his arms around the pole and there was an attempt to tie him with the cable cord. But it was too big, too thick, it was old, old cable cord, so you try to tie it in a knot and you would let go and it would come undone.

Somehow while this was going on we got back on the conversation of him being the guy going around molesting all these children in the area. He wouldn't say anything, he'd just start to cry. So I went to him.

"If that's you, you should get help."

And he said something about he would stop drinking, he'd sign himself in some place, he'd get help.

And it was really strange, all the time through that basement I was like a Dr. Jekyll and Mr. Hyde. When he said that I says, "You know you hurt people, you hurt children." And it was like I was shifted into another person, but I knew I didn't, I didn't have multi-personalities.

"Well, why don't you confess," I told him. "Why don't you tell us? What you did? Where did you do it?"

He just started crying then, and I started getting mad because I knew, I knew it was him. And I did something mean again — to help him be honest I took his wrist and ran the knife over his wrist and I told him, "You either make your confession now or I'll slash your wrist."

That's when he admitted that he was the guy that was abducting the children.

I let out a scream and I jumped away from him. I threw the knife on the floor.

And all I remember next is my old man picked up the knife, and he says, "Never, never leave that lying there!"

When Chuck admitted it was him, all hell broke loose and Ernie started fighting him again. So I turned around and I said, "Just knock him out!"

Because I thought if he was just out cold they would not fight him, while he's knocked out. I told Dwa, he was going up on charges for knocking out these two police officers, Dwa was an ex-boxer, "Dwa, just knock him out," I said, "it's the only way to do it." So Dwa tried to knock him out, but Chuck wouldn't even pretend he was knocked out. He just fell over, and got back up again, he was sitting there. And Ernie lost it and said, "I'll knock him out!" He came up with the side of his foot, hit him on the side of the head. Chuck went over, they were wrestling around.

I said, "I'll knock him out," and I took the cable cord and wrapped it around his neck and he went like this a couple of times to take it off [. . .]. When I pulled, I slipped. I was pretty drunk and soaked and wet from the water that was all over the place and when I fell over and got mad, I couldn't pull, I was sliding across the wet floor and I did something cruel.

I put one foot behind his head and one foot on his shoulder. And I pulled real hard for two or three seconds, and then I let go.

Chuck started gagging, and kind of coughing. I just got up and went [away] again, I just got out of the situation.

Ernie says, "I'll knock him out." Chuck was on his belly and his head was tilted sideways, but it was tilted back. Dwayne was standing on top of his back, and Ernie came and kicked him in the back of the head.

And I heard this crack. I don't know what it was. And Ernie kept kicking him on the back of his head, on the neck. Then Shirley Anne came and did the same thing, and I got mad at Shirley Anne and I grabbed her and threw her. And I heard a gargling sound. And Ernie got mad again, and took the TV cord that was around his neck and he just pulled it straight up, till he lifted him up off the floor by the cord that was around his neck.

He didn't seem to be fighting or anything. Ernie started pulling him around with it. Shirley Anne was siding with him, there was never no plan, for minute to minute or even second to second. I think Ernie was jealous because Shirley Anne was talking on the phone sexually to Chuck and since he had slept with her the night before, he would make himself look like a man for her [. . .].

So. Ernie was jerking him around with this cord by the neck, Dwa was still standing on him. And then Shirley Anne grabbed the cord and we were still trying to knock him out. And I said, "If you're going to, just, if he tries to get up then you can hold on like this."

But what she was doing, she would choke him and stop choking him, she was supposed to be doing this to the time of his breathing.

And Ernie was going crazier on him, and this is where I did something real stupid 'cause Ernie had another table [stool] leg and he was going to use this table leg on him and I wound up spreading his legs and Ernie shoved it all the way up his rectum.

And when he did that Dwa said, "Chuck pissed himself."

Dwa said, "He's dead."

I said, "No, he's not."

And Dwa said, "Yes he is, he pissed himself."

"No, he's not," I said, "just watch his breathing."

Dwa was standing on top of him and I looked over and Shirley Anne had that cord, and she just had it tight, she was pulling on it, she had it [so] tight around his neck that she was holding it back with her weight, her body was on a tilt.

And I told her, "Let go," but she wouldn't listen. I was trying to see if he was okay.

"Shirley Anne, let go!" Three or four times I yelled at her, and she wouldn't. Finally I got up and I just pushed her and she flew across the room, and I took the cord off him.

Dwa was still standing on him and I pushed Dwa, I said, "Get off!" And I was standing there looking at him.

Everything was quiet, there was no noise, no commotion, no nothing. We all just stood there and were looking at each other. I was trying to watch him breathe, and I couldn't see it, his chest going up and down.

Dwa said, "He's dead."

But I kept saying, "No, he's not. No, he's not."

Everybody wound up going upstairs, and we started kind of panicking. Ernie started walking back and forth really fast, and I looked across at Shirley Anne. She was sitting by the sink: she was covered with blood. There was none on me, Ernie was covered in blood, and Dwa was sitting there very quiet in a kitchen chair and he had no blood on him either.

Shirley Anne sat by the sink on some empty beer cases and it was really weird what she was doing. She had on a red pullover T-shirt and she pulled up the sleeves and her arms were just covered with blood. Just covered. It seemed like it didn't even faze her, she had her arms out and she'd twist them from one side to the other, she'd slink her hands, she'd kind of slap her hands together one on the other like that [slapping] and look at them. She was smiling. The longer I watched her, the more—she sat there, nothing was bothering her. I was being torn into a hundred million different pieces and she was sitting there calm, cool, collected, just looking at the blood on her arms and hands.

Dwa was sitting across from me at the table and he was still very quiet. I couldn't look at Shirley Anne, and I turned and looked at him, and I said, "He's not dead."

Dwa goes, "Yeah, he is." And after a minute, "Is that what everybody wanted?"

"No." I said. "No, he's not." Then I looked at Ernie: "Ernie, is he dead?"

Ernie was pacing back and forth, really jittery. And he goes: "Yeah, he's dead."

"No, he's not." And I looked at Shirley Anne: "Shirley Anne, is he dead?"

She says, "Yeah, he's dead."

And I said to her, "No. He's not."

I couldn't look at her any more, so I got up and I figured he was just playing like he was passed out, finally. I went down a couple of cellar steps to where the first step was missing and I squatted down there looking at him.

I was waiting for him to move. And I kept thinking, Don't do this, stop playing this game, and I'll catch you, you have to breathe sometime.

I sat there, and I was watching him. Waiting.

———

In Wetaskiwin, Alberta, sometime around midnight between 14 and 15 September 1989, four people fight one man in a small basement. Within eleven hours, that man's body is examined and verified as dead by police. At the trial in the Wetaskiwin Courthouse on 7 March 1991, Dr. Graeme Dowling, the Prosecution's expert in the field of forensic pathology, responsible for overseeing the investigation of sudden, unexpected deaths, testifies: "It was my opinion at the conclusion of my examination that this individual had died as a result of the combined effects of ligature strangulation and blunt injuries, but that the more important of these two causes was ligature strangulation." For the ligature (a "long, thin flexible object" like a rope or cord) strangulation to be fatal, he said it would have to be applied steadily for at least three to five minutes.

A factor that did not fit with Dr. Dowling's conclusion that a ligature had been the primary cause of death was the broken hyoid bone. This "tiny bone [. . .] which supports the voice box" is located "high up in the neck [. . .] and is well protected" so that only a sharp blow would break it. Or possibly "some manual pressure by hands on the neck."

Besides numerous contusions to head and body, one other forensic fact was that "the anus was bruised," an injury "consistent with the insertion of some blunt instrument [. . .] not to a great depth, probably not more than one, one and a half inches." This injury would not cause death; nor had it been made by a sharp instrument, like a knife.

Dwayne Wenger and Shirley Anne Salmon had been legally sentenced in January 1991 for their responsibility in the Charles Skwarok homicide: Dwayne pleading guilty to second-degree murder and Shirley Anne pleading guilty to aggravated assault. On 19 March 1991, Madame Justice Nina Foster carefully instructed the jury that the guilt or innocence of each of the remaining accused, Yvonne Johnson and Ernest Jensen, must be considered separately. She reviewed the crucial definitions of legal terms:

> *Manslaughter*: causing the death of a person, though unintention-
> ally and unplanned, while committing an unlawful act;
> *Second-degree murder*: when a death is
> a) caused by an unlawful act,
> b) the accused had the specific intent to do it;
> *First-degree murder*: when a death is
> a) caused by an unlawful act,
> b) planned and deliberate,
> and/or
> c) caused while committing or attempting to commit the
> offences of forcible confinement *or* sexual assault.

A jury gives no reason for its verdict; in fact it is always instructed by the presiding judge to keep everything about its deliberations secret: "If you disclose [your deliberations and your votes], such disclosure constitutes a criminal offence." The jury's only duty is to come to a unanimous decision on the basis of the evidence it believes to be true "beyond a reasonable doubt."

There was strong physical evidence against Ernie Jensen in the case—shoeprints, blood on his T-shirt, hair samples, paint chips. But there was no physical evidence whatsoever against Yvonne. The Crown's case against her depended solely on their "star" eye-witnesses, Shirley Anne Salmon and Lyle Schmidt. Shirley Anne had been in the basement during the beating, Lyle had been with Yvonne immediately after; the credibility of their verbal testimony would determine Yvonne's sentence.

———

From the trial record it would appear that Shirley Anne laid the basis in the jury's mind for Yvonne's first-degree-murder conviction; Yvonne insists that, in testifying as she did, her cousin lied over and over again.

The first of what Yvonne considers Shirley Anne's most damaging lies on the stand was that, when the four of them were drinking in the living room late in the evening and Chuck phoned and said he was coming over, Yvonne hung up and said, "Let's do him in." Then Shirley Anne immediately tried to temper the statement's meaning by insisting that "no one took the words seriously."

Yvonne has explained to me that she does not speak that way; such an expression is not in her vocabulary. She would say, "Let's do him," meaning to beat him.

Speaking about this critical matter in the cell-shot record, Dwayne told undercover agent Constable Harvey Jones that Shirley Anne "started it . . . and got us all worked up and then he [Chuck] phoned . . . and then, in a way we had it planned that we were gonna fuckin' do this guy in."

Ernie Jensen added, "Gonna die."

"In a way we had it planned" could be seen as Dwayne's careless surmise, with a general "we" that could mean anyone or all; the question is, which one of them actually said the key words, "Let's do him in"? Yvonne has always insisted to me that Ernie said them; and his statement recorded in the cell shot, "Gonna die," would seem to corroborate her.

Now, whether Shirley Anne took the words seriously or not, her testimony asserted that they had been said by Yvonne. And so the jury could begin to believe that Yvonne was developing a plan for murder.

Yvonne says Shirley Anne's second lie on the stand was that, during the calls made earlier in the evening, Yvonne invited Chuck to come to her house — implying that by supper time Yvonne already had "a plan" to "do him in." Yvonne insists she was then not capable of planning anything; she denies that she talked to Chuck at all on the phone before supper, and Ernie Jensen corroborates her denial. On 5 March 1994, Ernie wrote to Yvonne from Edmonton Prison, where he is serving his ten-year sentence.

> You did not talk to [Chuck] on the phone. You dialed the number and gave the phone to Shirley and told her, You talk to him, you are the single one, you talk.

Yvonne says she and Ernie heard Shirley Anne try for half an hour to "sex-talk" Chuck into coming over, and then he said he was going fishing with his cousins and hung up; however, about five hours later, he called and said he was coming over. Alarmed and worried, Yvonne simply said, "Okay," and in a few moments Chuck appeared alone with beer and a bag of sex magazines "to party."

The jury, if they found Shirley Anne convincing, could now begin considering a sentence of first-degree murder because the unlawful act was "planned and deliberate."

That "confinement" had taken place—another reason for a first-degree verdict—was stated by J. Barry Hill in his summation to the jury, but not spoken to by Brian Beresh in his jury address; apparently he thought it was evident that, if Skwarok was confined, there was no evidence to indicate that Yvonne had anything to do with it.

However, there was a final reason for a first-degree verdict. Sexual assault. And Shirley Anne testified that it was Yvonne who sodomized Chuck Skwarok: "Yvonne says to me, she ordered, and she says, 'Take his pants off, Shirley Anne,' and I was scared. So without even thinking, I don't know why I did it. I closed my eyes for a minute, and I took his pants off, and I looked and he was naked from the waist down."

[Yvonne writes on the trial record, an arrow pointing to these words, "I got first for this."]

And without any further directed question from Crown Prosecutor Scott Newark—the only time Hill did not present his witnesses— Shirley Anne immediately continued with her version of events:

"So Yvonne picked up a wooden stool leg, and she was hovering over the deceased. I couldn't see. She was blocking my view, and

I couldn't see exactly what she was doing, but I could see from the motion she was making with her arm what she was doing, and she says to the deceased, 'This is how little kids feel.'"

Q: What did she do with the table leg?

A: She took it, and I assumed she shoved it up his rectum.

Yvonne's defence lawyer, Brian Beresh, interrupted immediately with "Well, let's not *assume* anything."

One "wooden stool leg" was filed in court as evidence and labelled "Exhibit number 8"; later, "two small furniture legs" were added as "Exhibit number 31," but no fingerprints to incriminate Yvonne were gathered from any of them; nor did the prosecutor distinguish between them as which might have been used. However, if Shirley Anne were to be believed, then death could have occurred while "committing a sexual assault" with the wooden legs.

Both Dwayne's and Ernie's evidence support Yvonne's contention that she did not assault Chuck with the leg. In the cell shot, Dwayne said it was he and Ernie who took off Chuck's clothes and then "Ernie shoved that thing up his ass." And Ernie writes Yvonne in his March 1994 letter: "One important thing to remember is that Shirley said that it was you that stuck that thing in Chuck's ass when it was me." It is for these and other reasons, Ernie concludes his letter, "I am going to do my best to get a perjury charge laid against her as soon as possible . . . if we just point out that Shirley lied we should get a new trial."

Shirley Anne did not testify about—nor was she questioned about—what Yvonne insists are the facts:

1) that others, not Yvonne, did the minutes-long strangling;
2) that Ernie and Shirley Anne fought with and finally kicked Chuck long and hard enough when he was down that, according to Yvonne, there was a loud "snap" which possibly indicated the bone in his neck had been broken;
3) that Shirley Anne was completely bloody from the beating she helped give Chuck.

Instead, Shirley Anne testified that she mostly watched, that it was "the boys" who did the beating and it was Yvonne, "she says to all of us, 'Knock him out' and the boys are just bewildered and looking nervously, not knowing what to do [. . .] so she picked up a telephone cord [. . .] She took it and wrapped it around the deceased's neck, and she pulled it."

Shirley Anne tempered her testimony immediately and in this she is, for once, in agreement with Yvonne's account; she continued:

"Like I had timed myself already. She pulled it for about ten seconds. Fifteen seconds would have been too long, ten seconds."

Q: What about the other two, Ernie and Dwayne? What were they doing while she's doing this?

A: They're just standing there, and then she lets go, and he's just laying there, and we all thought he was dead, and so the boys feel his pulse, and they said there was none.

Q: Who was it felt his pulse?

A: Both of the boys . . . and then I felt his pulse, and it was there.

This is clearly contradictory testimony: Yvonne chokes Chuck, but only for ten seconds, which is not nearly long enough to cause death. Nevertheless, the boys find no pulse—so is he dead as a direct result of Yvonne's choking? No, Shirley Anne says she found a pulse. The question arises: can this witness be believed at all?

Under Brian Beresh's relentless cross-examination, Shirley Anne admitted that she had, at her first questioning, lied to the police when she told them "she had seen nothing of the beating." She lied, she said, "intentionally [. . .] to a police officer," but only, she insisted, because by lying she thought she could protect her cousin Yvonne, whom she loved. Consideration for herself had had, apparently, nothing to do with her lies. And she was now "so sorry I didn't tell the truth" then, but "in the last eighteen months, I have learned to tell the truth."

"Well," Beresh countered, "learned perhaps for a particular reason? Tell me, a judge heard the evidence at a Preliminary Inquiry and ruled it was sufficient to commit you to stand trial for first-degree murder?"

A: Yes.

Q: Wou met with your lawyer and, I take it, part of the discussion was that you might be a Crown witness?

A: Yes.

Q: You suggested that?

A: Yes.

Q: Right? So of course part of the arrangement would be that you
   would have to give a statement to the police?

A: Well actually I didn't suggest that. It was suggested to me.

Q: By who?

A: By my lawyer [. . .] But I was at that point—I was still trying to
   protect Yvonne.

Q: In a 70-page statement?

"Yes," Shirley Anne replied. "And I knew I was wrong."

She does not explain what she knows she was wrong about, but continues that whatever "arrangements" had been made after she had
given those statements, they were deals made by her lawyer. "Stirling
[Sanderman] didn't notify me all the time about the deals he made."

Q: The deal was that you would be cut free from the charge, that
   you would get a slap on the wrists, is that right?

A: In September, when he said that, I asked him if I could have
   more time [. . .]. I wanted to be punished for the crime that was
   committed. I felt, I should have been punished.

Q: Well, with respect, you were trying to get out of it, and—

"You see," Shirley Anne interrupted, "I'm not in control of the authority, and what kind of deals lawyers make. I just go along with them.

Q: I'm suggesting, madam, that on the contrary [. . .] you know very
   well what's going on.

A: Yes, I know that there's deals that go on.

Q: Well, what did your lawyer—

And Shirley Anne interrupted him again: "But I'll be honest with
you. I'm going to acknowledge something. If it wasn't for the power of
God, I wouldn't be here. I wouldn't be standing here, and I will never
be ashamed of him, because someday everybody is going to realize that
there really is a living God."

Brian Beresh made no attempt to hide his sarcasm. "Well, let's get
back to this courtroom for a minute."

Shirley Anne had been made to confess that she lied to the police
during much of the investigation into the case. In his cross-examination, Beresh had emphasized as strongly as he could that Shirley Anne,
the confessed liar, was now lying again because of the "sweetheart
deal of the century" the Crown had given her. The Crown had already
kept its part of the bargain in January: a ludicrously light sentence of

twelve months in prison and five years' probation for aggravated assault. And now Shirley Anne was upholding her part of the deal by lying, though he offered the jury no direct counter-evidence to prove exactly how.

Yvonne says now, sadly, "Shirley Anne was well coached. That cop Bradley flew from Whitehorse twice to interview her. And Brian just worked her over on all her contradictions."

It would seem that the two Wetaskiwin Crown prosecutors, J. Barry Hill and Scott Newark, knew their local jurors—four were farmers and the other eight were residents of two large neighbouring towns—very well. Shirley Anne's ringing declaration of her personal conversion, of her faith in "a living God" without whose power, she said—rather oddly—"I wouldn't be standing here," and her repeated regret for what happened because of her admitted "exaggeration" and her repeated desire to be "punished enough," these professions obviously carried the day. And so, despite the fact that her own original first-degree-murder charge had been reduced to a sentence of more or less time already served—evidence of a pretty good deal indeed—the jury now found Shirley Anne's testimony not only believable "beyond a reasonable doubt," but very likely, from their later conviction of Yvonne, believable in absolutely every detail. Believable in the most incriminating manner.

And it would appear that local hang-about Lyle Schmidt helped to solidify their opinion. The one physical fact he had to contribute to the case—the knife—had already been ruled irrelevant to the death by the forensic expert; in any case, it revealed neither blood nor fingerprints. Therefore, all of Lyle's evidence, like Shirley Anne's, depended on his word. The core of his testimony was that:

1) after they left the Wayside Inn, Yvonne made a phone call and then she told him she had killed somebody;
2) the death had been caused by a knife;
3) for the next four hours or so they "were just driving around, drinking beer, and the subject came out she wanted some help to get rid of the body, the murder weapon." When they finally went into her house, he woke Ernie on the couch, who told them "that he had taken the person out to the garbage dump, at

the time he was still alive and choking on his blood, and he had finished the person off with the power [gesturing with his fist]." Then, Lyle testified Ernie told him, "They buried him beside a group of trees that was out there, and burnt the car."

But almost all the physical facts that Lyle cited—concerning the knife, the burial, the burned car—had already been proven false in court by police and expert witness testimony. And Brian Beresh called no witnesses to further undermine Lyle's version of events. What he did do was to make a thorough cross-examination to try to undermine Lyle's credibility. Lyle admitted that for much of his life he had had a problem with drinking, and that his sister, whom he awakened at his mother's house with a telephone call before five o'clock the morning of the murder, told him he was "pissed," drunk. In response to that, Beresh asked:

Q: Your sister, I take it, has known you for a number of years?
A: My sister and me have hated each other for approximately twenty years.

Beresh also made Lyle admit that he had been committed to Alberta Hospital, Ponoka, by his mother when he was sixteen (i.e., over twenty years before) and while there been "diagnosed as having poor control of aggressive and hostile impulses"; he further presented a recent affidavit filed by Lyle's former wife for her divorce from him: particularly apropos was his violence against her to the point where she twice attempted suicide and was hospitalized both for having been physically beaten and for psychiatric care.

Then Beresh took up the detail, made in Lyle's first statement to the police, that he was at the Wayside Inn "girl hunting."

Q: I take it that means precisely that, that you're hunting [. . .] That when you first talked to [Yvonne], sex was on your mind.
A: Sex is always on my mind. I mean, I'm single.
Q: You were then?
A: Okay, [my wife's] gone, and what am I supposed to do, become a monk?
Q: Well, I suggest—
A: That—that I can't do. Like sex is always on my mind. If I'm gonna get it, I'm gonna get it.

Q: I suggest that the way you got it that night was not with Miss Johnson's consent.

A: You're suggesting I raped her?

Q: You gather what you can from that, sir.

A: Well, if it's not with her consent, that must mean I raped her.

For several hours, Yvonne says, she was forced to listen to the man who had first harassed, then taunted, and finally raped her—"an intimacy" was all he would admit to on the stand: Lyle Schmidt given a stage at last, complete with media reporters and a packed courtroom audience, pouring out details and smart responses that reflected so well on himself, on his brilliant deductive powers, details of that horrible night and what she in her blacking out, alcoholic despair had supposedly said. Most of it was distortion, Yvonne says, lies slanted to slam her, until finally he came to the matter of the knife.

Though the forensic expert, Dr. Dowling, had stated a knife could only have been used to make "a superficial bruise" on the right wrist, nevertheless Crown Prosecutor Hill questioned Lyle about the knife in language that must have shocked the middle-class jury with the violence of an assault:

Hill: And you indicated there was conversation about a knife. What was said about that, please?

Schmidt: Okay, she mentioned how she shoved a knife up his ass, how she had cut his wrists with it and cut him up good.

Q: Was there any conversation about why any of this happened? [. . .].

A: The reason why he—they were doing this to him was apparently he tried to molest her youngest daughter.

Q: In the course of using the knife, was anything said to you about the use of the knife, any conversation?

A: Just the fact that it was shoved up his ass and cutting his wrists and cutting him with it.

Q: And was anything said to you about anything she may have said when that was done, when the knife was shoved up the ass?

A: What she told me was that as she was doing that, she was asking the guy how that felt, having it up his ass, you know; and like the idea was that's what it would feel like to, in the words, shove his prick in a little girl's cunt.

It was then that Yvonne spoke in court; once, very loudly.

The Accused, Johnson: How do you know how that feels? I didn't say that.

It stands on the court record that these eleven short words were "taken down in shorthand and transcribed from [her] notes to the best of [her] skill and ability" by Jackie Moore, Official Court Reporter. I wanted to hear from Yvonne what she meant by them.

To begin with, she told me, the record does not indicate the long pause between the first seven words and the final four.

"But what did you mean when you blurted that out, interrupted the court?" I asked. "How did it happen?"

"Lyle was up there for himself," she tells me. "He had a platform and Hill was feeding him, whatever he felt like saying he said, and I wanted him to stop, all the terrible stuff, and I have to sit and listen, nobody's concerned about the truth, just this court game going on day after day and I can't move, I can't speak, and I'm getting my heart tore out. I just looked at Lyle and the words came out. I was shocked at myself. I just thought out loud.

"And there was dead silence when I said it. Not a sound."

I ask, "Lyle testified you said it while you were 'doing that' with the knife. Did you?"

"No, I never did anything like that with the knife, I only cut the cord with it and once touched his wrist. The medical expert said Chuck wasn't hurt with a knife. And when I pretended I was doing it, with the leg, I never said a word. I had asked him earlier, right at the beginning in the basement, 'Do you really know how it feels to be raped as a child?' I wanted him to confess then, but not later."

"So, I still don't understand," I tell her, "what you meant in court: 'How do you know how that feels?'"

"I was talking to Lyle, 'How do *you* know, what it feels like.'"

"In the sense that, 'You know how it feels, and you describe it accurately because you've abused kids yourself'?"

"No, more like 'What could you possibly know about what it feels like for a little girl?' I was looking at Lyle, he was grandstanding, making it up, talking 'ass' and 'little girl' and 'cunt' and it was all too much because I know what it's like, and he's up there with Hill, playing their games with my life, and I wanted him to stop! And he did. Dead silence.

"And when I spoke, Hill jumped and looked at me, and the judge and the whole jury were staring. All of a sudden I didn't want to be seen, it was too awful. So I stuck my head down, to hide, but I had to face them so I said out loud, 'I didn't say that'—to the court, in the sense, 'I never said what Lyle says I did.'

"And then I broke down, hiding behind my hair. Brian looked at me, and interrupted Hill who was gonna go on as if nothing had happened, 'Excuse me, My Lady,' he says to the judge, and something about have a little patience. And he come over and asked me, 'Do you want to take a break?' I shook my head, but he turned to the judge and there was a short adjournment.

Beyond the contradictions already noted between cell-shot and "star witness" testimony, at one point in the cell shot Dwayne flatly contradicted what Lyle and Shirley Anne said about Yvonne's action in the possible sexual assault:

> Wenger: Ernie and I took his clothes off and said, how do you like this? (Inaudible) fuckin' diddling little kids. You'll get your own medicine, and he [i.e., Ernie] shoved it up.

The jury did not hear this contradiction because on 8 March 1991, following a request from Glen Allen, the cell-shot evidence was ruled inadmissible by Judge Foster. She stated that, after Ernie Jensen was arrested, "Corporal Bradley was unhappy with the results of the interview [with him], and he arranged for Constable Jones to do an undercover operation [. . .]. No court order was obtained [. . .]. Jones persistently [. . .] and actively attempted to elicit information from the accused [. . .]. This undercover operation obviously and admittedly fails [as] acceptable police conduct [. . .]. This, in my view, is a most unsatisfactory way to interview a person facing a charge of first-degree murder [. . .]. The admission of these tapes as evidence would bring the administration of justice into disrepute. I therefore order their exclusion pursuant to Section 24(2) of the Charter."

Therefore, though Beresh worked hard to prove that Lyle's testimony was badly compromised by its factual errors and by his possible rape of the accused, the jury was not presented with direct alternative statements to some of Lyle's most damaging testimony. Nor, apparently, was the jury at all influenced by defence counsel's main argument that there was no evidence presented to prove Yvonne had, or could have, formed an intent to commit murder, though by calling no witnesses he had the right to address it last. Late in the afternoon of 18 March, he ended by exhorting them, "The test of 'beyond a reasonable doubt' [is] simply saying, Are you sure. Are you sure [. . .]. And I ask that you conclude Miss Johnson's involvement in this case is nothing beyond that of culpability for manslaughter. And that, quite frankly, is the verdict I request you bring back. Thank you."

But, despite anything Brian Beresh said, after Shirley Anne Salmon's and Lyle Schmidt's contradictory testimonies, the jury in its collective wisdom "was sure" about Yvonne. It would seem every member was completely convinced by Crown Prosecutor Hill's outline of Chuck's death, which he based solely on Shirley Anne's testimony:

– Yvonne said, "Let's do him in — that's planning murder;

– Yvonne kicked him, and he fell back into the basement — that's confinement;

– Yvonne attacked him with the stool leg — that's sexual assault;

– Yvonne choked him with a cord (for only ten seconds, Shirley Anne insisted, but Hill skipped over the small detail that his forensic expert had declared *it would take three to five minutes of uninterrupted choking to cause death*, and apparently the jury skipped with him) — that's murder.

But perhaps, even more than his summary of the case, it was the particular rhetoric of Hill's address that overwhelmed the jury with his argument against Yvonne. She remembers the repetition of his words: "*these* people . . . are very different from you and me," and then repeating "these two . . . these two" while his long arm and pointing finger stabbed across the courtroom from the jury benches to the prisoner's box: the sound, the tone of "*these* people," remain branded into her memory.

In any case, a decision was reached in short order. At 1:42 p.m., on 20 March 1991, the nine men and three women from the judicial district of Wetaskiwin, chosen from the Sheriff's list of some three hundred, returned to the courtroom, and the foreman, a farmer from nearby Leduc, stated their verdict.

Court Clerk: Your verdict as . . . the court hath recorded it is for Yvonne Johnson guilty as charged [first-degree murder]. For Ernest Jensen guilty of second-degree. Do you all agree?

Peter Kopp: Yes.

Janet Sprague: Yes.

Trevor Rosland: Yes.

Finn Oleson: Yes.

Ralph Berquist: Yes.

Lorne Jobs: Yes.

James Schnepf: Yes.

Allen Walkey: Yes.

Brenda Stadler: Yes.

Ray Kuchnerick: Yes.

Dale Sherwood: Yes.

Bonnie Schwartz: Yes.

It was 16 September 1993, and Yvonne and I were circling through her life, as we had so often done. She had begun to tell me the on-going story of her lives and deaths in courtrooms because the month before the Alberta Court of Appeal had finally ruled on her appeal of her sentence of first-degree murder.

She gave me a copy of the thirty-four-page ruling. In it, Appeal Court Madame Justice Mary M. Hetherington wrote that several of Brian Beresh's arguments were "without merit." Then she analysed the entire case to refute his major argument that the sentence of "first-degree murder was unreasonable," and she did so by depending solely on the evidence provided by Shirley Anne Salmon and Lyle Schmidt. She did not, at any point, raise a question about the credibility of that evidence nor the contradictions it contained. And finally, after discussing various relevant details of criminal law, including whether the trial judge had properly instructed the jury regarding Yvonne's level of intoxication, she ruled that "no substantial wrong or miscarriage of justice has occurred in this case. . . . [Therefore] I would dismiss Johnson's appeal."

And the two other justices—Joseph Stratton and Ellen Picard—signed her ruling, "I concur."

The three Appeal Court justices accepted the evidence of Dr. Dowling, the forensic expert, that the main cause of death was strangulation. They also accepted Shirley Anne's testimony that Yvonne had pulled on the ligature cord for ten seconds. However, they completely disregarded his evidence that "for death to result from ligature strangulation, pressure would have to be applied for three to five minutes." In other words, Judge Hetherington accepted that Yvonne participated in using the ligature on Chuck, but ignored the evidence that ten seconds could not possibly have killed him. As Clayton Ruby, one of Canada's most respected criminal lawyers, said of this Appeal Court judment, "I think this is a shocking ruling, and an outrageous miscarriage of justice." He said that in accepting one part of the evidence as significant but seemingly ignoring the other, it ignored crucial evidence and the weaknesses of the Crown's case.

Nevertheless, in such a situation, only an appeal to the Supreme Court of Canada remained. And since Yvonne's appeal had been turned down unanimously, the chances—her new lawyer, Felicity Hunter, advised her—of being accepted to be heard in Ottawa could be no better than five per cent.

While preparing a possible appeal to the Supreme Court, Hunter spoke to me several times. She was very disturbed, both by the Alberta Appeal Court ruling and the original trial. She felt that "clearly there should have been severance," and that cell-shot evidence would have assisted Yvonne's case. She was also convinced that Shirley Anne had perjured herself, and that sentencing Yvonne to "first" was a "gross travesty of justice." It "smells rank," she told me, and corroborates the reputation the Wetaskiwin Judicial District, from which Yvonne's all-White, largely male jury were drawn, has in Alberta legal circles: for certain crimes "the chance of getting a fair trial there is almost nil."

Now, Yvonne and I were deep inside the looming stone Prison for Women, not a window anywhere, only walls, the plate iron door, the neon light buzzing faintly as she talked. The bright curtain of the long black-brown hair which she has not cut since her grandfather John Bear died—she promised him she would never again cut it—muffled her voice, veiled her face into a narrow line of nose, nostril, lips, a touch of chin.

"Mom came to my Appeal in Edmonton last October, when I first wrote you," she said. "Courts are never any good, but Mom came, she hadn't seen me since I was first sentenced. Pauline Shirt, the Elder, came too from Toronto. She brought a pipe into the courtroom and the officers didn't want her bringing anything in like that, holding it up to give me courage. But they let her stay, and when I said, 'That's my mother,' they let Mom come up to the side of the box where I was shackled.

"And I looked at her, and she looked a hundred years older than I remembered. And I look at her. 'Mom!' I say, 'I'm doing good, I go do the sweats, I smoke pipe, I do the ceremonies, and I sing on the drums, and you know what? I don't sound half bad!'

"And she started crying. I leaned over and held her, and I cried too, and I took my hair—I had one side of my hair braided, tied in a wide cloth to signify my mind, body, and spirit, that it was together—and I left one side of my hair unbraided, hanging down, because it covered my heart, to signify sorrow and pity—but not pity in the sense of 'pity,' but just humbleness, the most humble way to be. And my hair that was hanging down, I took that hair nearest my heart and I wiped my mother's tears with it. And I told her, 'Mom, don't cry.' "

After a moment Yvonne continues, though her voice is breaking:

"And all Mom could say to me was, 'I don't want to see you in here.' Nothing else, she never told me, 'O, by the way we aren't doing so good outside either; your brother just raped one of your sisters and nearly beat another to death. No, nothing—just 'I don't want to see you in here.'

"I held her, and she's a sma-a-a-all woman, she's a big woman but she's sma-all, and she seemed to just need me, so I was strong for her. And I wouldn't cry any more, I wouldn't let her see me hurting."

Her voice grows stronger as she remembers: "That's why I didn't cry in Wetaskiwin when they sentenced me for Chuck's death. Mom was sitting there in court, every day she'd been there, beside her sister whose daughter Shirley Anne saved her own neck by lying on me, and with her lies finished me. I stood there waiting for the sentence and I wanted to scream, I wanted to run, I wanted to die. But if I broke—I thought of my father. 'No matter what,' he always said, 'you hold your head up, and your shoulders back.' So I put my arms behind me like a Marine would when they tell him to relax, and then I looked at the judge. And you could tell she didn't like that jury decision, she didn't want to pronounce it. I saw how her face changed when they said it, and I gave her a nod and I stood back further like, 'Okay, I'm ready. Do it.'

"And a tear snuck out of my eye, it wasn't for me, it was just to relax the tenseness of it. And I knew everybody was watching me so I wiped it away so they wouldn't see it when more would come. And then the judge . . . she slammed me with twenty-five years."

After a pause: "My first instinct was to put my head down and hang my hair in front of my face—but I didn't. They led me out, I couldn't look on either side of where I was walking. I just wanted to melt, to hide, but I found comfort in them throwing me into a little cell because I was out of the torture. They had finally decided.

"And I could have stayed in that little cell." Her voice is thinned out almost to transparency. "I could've stayed in that cell, I could've set my mind to stay there for the next twenty-five years because I would have shut everything out, just let me dry up. But no. . . ."

16

Since the Time When the Earth Was First Born

The old man said, to have been born imperfect was a sign of specialness [. . .]. The old man explained carefully that in the old days, if a child came with a hare-shorn lip, it wasn't a terrible thing or a hurtful thing; it meant the child's soul was still in touch with the Spirit World.

– Yvonne Johnson, *Journal 9*, Spring 1994

"WE ARE THE ABUSED," Yvonne writes to me. "Which does not mean we are stupid. It means in our pain we are always thinking, and always alone."

She is rereading Carl Jung's *Memories, Dreams, Reflections,* and discusses with me the "natural mind" he describes: "the mind that springs from natural sources, and not from opinions taken from books; it . . . brings with it the peculiar wisdom of nature."

Sentenced at age twenty-eight to a lifetime in prison, she has to understand what her mind may demand of her:

"My mind is alive, and there is pain. A small word, '*pain*' — confusion, the unknown, aloneness — if pain could talk, could it identify any limits to what it is? If pain could say what it is, would it ask, 'What do you think I look like? How do you think I smell, or feel?'"

She cannot answer that question directly; her writing, as she admits, is often "all over the place [. . .] as I jump back and forth through time and space [. . .]. [Because] I'm writing as if I'm reliving it as I am, and it tears me apart to do this."

But reading Carl Jung has widened the language within which she can understand herself. "Jung has the White words," she writes, "but to me he thinks like an Indian [. . .]. He writes this which is me. I wish I could speak to him."

He is certainly speaking to her in prison. On 19 December 1994 she concludes fifteen pages of her daily journal grappling with his *Memories*:

"He writes back then [1961, the year she was born] what is me right now. I become aware of affinity, I could establish ties with something, some one. As most of my life has been to let myself be carried along by currents without a notion of where it took me, or even consequence. My dear Jung as you are to me now. I now will sleep with this to ponder, though I feel I know it already. His new chapter begins, 'The Work', on page 200 and the clock tells me it is 1:19 a.m. Time to try to lay it to rest."

————

Yvonne: This is what I believe, Sunday, 17 October 1993:

> The Spirit truly goes on, it lives and never dies. I am certain my ancestor Big Bear and the Bear Spirit and the Creator guide me, strengthen me, protect me, now as they have in my past.

Mom took me to Grandma when I was little to help me forget. Grandma did help me, and when she did it she also saw something in my spirit my mother couldn't see: what my mother thought was crazy, her mother saw in me as a gift. Grandma told Mom, "Vonnie has forgotten, but I want her to stay with me and I'll give her teachings."

A child doesn't know how to protect itself, either its body or its spirit. Grandma Flora saved my spirit from being damaged beyond restoration by helping me forget, but now the Creator is again letting me remember. My question is, why?

I hear a woman crying. They just called lock-up, she's crying to herself, my lullaby tonight are tarps on the scaffolding outside my window behind the stone walls blowing and snapping in the wind. As the snow falls and the wind blows, this woman's tears are of a broken mother, a lost aunt, a sister, her anguish within these walls matching the howls of the storm. I heard say that the aboriginal nations of Turtle Island will not fall completely until the women's hearts lie upon the ground. Where are your women, your girl children? What has happened to your life-givers?

Grandma was a good medicine woman; she intended good in making me forget. But I never really did; it was in my spirit, a spirit only the Creator can take. The Creator saw fit to take it away through my grandmother, now he's given it back. But I'm in prison for life, what can I possibly do with these memories?

I remember, and I pray as the storm kicks up. The woman is crying. Through the barred window I hold tobacco outside in my left hand, sweetgrass in my right. I pray for the woman to be safe, I pray for what she knows happened. I pray to the four winds to carry my prayers, I call her name into the wind to comfort her. I hold the tobacco in my open hand, offering it to the Thunder People, the Creator and his helpers. A universal prayer that reaches the world in every direction, over and around and up and down and under all Creation.

It thundered that night of my prayer. It almost threw down the scaffolding around the prison, ripped off the tarps. I prayed as I watched invisible hands take the tobacco on the winds, passing spirits of creation, the thunder beings. I watched the smoke of the sweetgrass swirl and disappear on the winds in respect of all things. I slept with the storm as my protection.

I awoke the next day. I heard, at the instant I awoke, a bird, unseen, fly away from outside my window with heavy wings. I heard geese fly overhead that day as well. I don't know of what tomorrow holds, for me. Or where I go from today, and I fear, I am scared. I leave it to the Creator. He will take it from here.

———

Finally, the stone walls of the Prison for Women were gone for Yvonne. Within the Healing Lodge's powerful Native atmosphere and natural setting, she found the support to grow stronger in understanding her spiritual longings and heritage; to recognize more fully that the most significant person in her life had been, and still was, her Grandmother Flora. As she writes to me in January 1998:

"Could it be that Grandma did ceremonies on me so I would forget, as a cleansing, and also as a sort of initiation, where I'd be reborn to fulfil my position as Medicine Bear Woman? I had the innocence of a child when those ritual initiations were done. But I left [and] I never actually returned to the rez to stay [. . .]. Grandma waited, I never returned for her to explain the special gifts I was initiated into as a child. Prior to her death [June 1986] she came many times to seek me, yet I was blind, asleep as they say in alcoholism and confusion. My gifts became my unknown burden. Grandma died long before I awoke, she died without advising me. But a few of her final words were STOP YOUR DRINKING. Now I understand that you cannot walk in balance with Medicine in one hand and booze and drugs in the other."

It is at the Healing Lodge that Yvonne begins slowly to explicate her memories of her grandmother.

———

Yvonne: When I was little, I sensed Grandma Flora was a powerful woman. I know now she had power to the extreme in what Whites would sneer and call witchcraft—if they ever thought about it—but Indians call it medicine power. Perhaps she saw gifts in me, but I felt that the mysterious things she did to me came from a deep compassion and love. So I went along in silence. And my heart felt it would burst with love. I had no need to try to understand, I just did anything she said.

Grandma woke me up in darkness, and she'd lead me out to watch the sun come up over the meadow and the far trees. I did not speak Cree, but she taught me by touch, by eye contact, by miming what I should do. So she showed me how to look at the sun rising, and what did I see? She would cry out, wail suddenly, and stop. And I saw things in the coming light. I knew I was doing what my ancestors have done since the time when the earth was first born.

Every day we got up to greet the sun, and every day we watched it sink away to sleep as well. I don't recall what I saw except once, something, in the first rays of its light. An Elder has told me that, just as the sun rises, there may be a small slit in time when you can see spirits there, though I wasn't told what kinds of spirits. I can't speak about myself, then, but I know I didn't think it through. I just accepted whatever I was given as a child deep within myself: the spirits were there.

Grandpa and Grandma Bear lived in an old bus, while Mom and us kids lived on the reserve in their house. Leon was there, I remember walking with him in the trees, and once he led me to a baby deer lying curled almost invisible on the ground. It was so motionless I bent and touched its eye with my finger, but it would not open. On another walk he did something to me, and then gave me a baby duck to play with, splashing in a puddle. I don't know what happened, and I told Grandma nothing about our walks but she showed me I should not walk with Leon any more.

Then everyone was gone. For a time I lived alone with her in the bus, and she had me sit watching the fire for what seemed for ever. One day I ran to her, screaming: there were women and children in the fire, she had to get them out!

Grandma laid me on the ground with my ear pressed against the earth. If I wriggled and tried to get up, she'd pat my hair, not say anything, just reassure me with her hand, turn my head sideways and lay me down again in the sunlight against the earth. I found it soft, comfortable, and it seemed there were voices talking, singing in the earth. I was a little scared because it was something I couldn't understand, and yet under the sounds there was a deep silence that came over me, like peace. Like the lullaby I wanted to hear all my life—no one ever sang to me at bedtime—and I drifted to sleep where my grandmother laid me down. It was as if I could feel the earth's heart beat. I was a baby cuddled on my mother's breast, in her womb, my mother who absorbed every fear and every thought, and she was all around me, I was floating in warmth and dreamless sleep. Heart beat.

Behind the bus and house was a small hill, and over that a slough with the hole dug beside it where we got our drinking water. One day Grandma had some men pile a mound of grass on the hill, and when I went to play in it she chased me away, "Muskeke, muskeke!" I now know that means "medicine," but then I thought, like children do, that she was just mean, never wanting me to have fun. A few days later she set the grass on fire, and it must have been sweetgrass because the smoke didn't rise. It hung low, thick and heavy along the ground.

Grandma told me to bring the water buckets and we went towards the smoke. She stopped there, and signed for me to go through it and get water. The smoke was really dense, I couldn't breathe but I got through fast to the waterhole and into the fresh air. Grandma was waiting, so I filled the pails quickly and went back. I stumbled a bit in the smoke, and spilled a little, but I got through okay. Grandma poured some out on the ground, some into what I now know was a water drum, and immediately sent me back for more.

Again and again. Into the dark smoke, bending down, lifting and carrying that heavy water, I could hardly stay on my feet and finally I fell, trying not to spill any water and choking, because even close to the ground all there was to breathe was smoke. I heard Grandma calling for me but I could hardly gasp a cry, and when she found me she was almost overcome herself. She bent over me and drew out a hunting knife. I thought she was going to kill me, but she pulled me up and where I had fallen she drove the knife into the ground. Then she dragged me away. We barely made it to the edge of the smoke.

We lay together on the ground coughing for air. When I finally felt the burning smoke soften in my lungs I was crying. Grandma turned to me, touched me all over, and then she began to cry too. I don't know why. She rubbed my hair and looked into my eyes—she never did that—I thought: obviously she didn't want to hurt me, and yet she had made me do something so dangerous she was crying. I thought my heart would break, I loved her so much.

On the spot she had marked with a knife, where I fell, my grandmother made a frame with four poles driven into the ground, about a yard square. Other poles were tied across between them, and this frame was covered with blankets. I had animal skins wrapped around my middle, and huge leaves binding me. I was laid in the little structure, it was dark and I heard noises of work, I heard drums and singing.

The darkness was so black you could take it in your hand and feel it, like my dad sometimes said about working a mile inside Butte Mountain, "Now that's darkness." There was no beginning or end to it. And it wasn't close to me, it just seemed part of what I was or could be. And I saw things moving, coming at me out of the darkness inside the little tent, and then lights like round stones of fluorescent swinging, moving quick as an eyeblink and gone, all was quiet and motionless. And I lay still.

Grandma seemed in a panic, she was ripping the binding off me, though one rope stayed on my feet, and I could not move because I felt so completely tired, and Grandma was yelling, but I didn't answer her. After a while she rubbed me, wiping me down, I could see her do this, as if she was walking around inside me looking, it seemed her spirit was mine and she was looking for things I could not hide even if I knew what they were, and I was outside myself, like watching from a distance. She asked what I had seen, and I couldn't say, though I knew in my spirit what had happened. She spoke and spoke as she unwrapped me, and I knew she was saying to me, "Now, look at yourself, see, you are all better."

So I looked. I didn't know what I was looking for. I seemed normal, quite all right, there were no marks or bruises or scratches or scabs or even scars on my body. As if I had been reborn, my skin perfect. And I felt this deep need to find something I now couldn't see: something should be there on my body, but there was nothing.

And I looked at Grandma. With surprise and awe, and I felt her pride about an act well done. She peered at me as if she was walking inside me, looking around to see if all was well, and she saw my spirit was well. Though it seemed to me she did not quite trust my body, or my mind.

———

Yvonne tells me this particular story of ceremony the day in August 1996, when we complete the second four-round sweat on the high glade near Okimaw Ochi. Unlike the cluttered, windowless box inside

P4W, we now talk in the Elder's room on the back curve of the Spirit Lodge; through its large windows we look out between tall, dense aspen, down across the ravines and draws of the Cypress Hills to the prairie. She tells me the story again, in greater detail, in the pages she types for me afterwards, circling around and around with variant facts as if by sheer fore of will she *will* ultimately unwind a meaning my intellectualized mind can, against all odds, fathom. And all I can say is, as usual, is, "Yes . . . yes," and listen.

Her struggle is for her own benefit as well as mine. She tells me, grinning slightly, "I know this makes no sense . . . but in a kind of a way it does."

She says she has talked to Elders about what happened. Even the oldest can — or will — tell her little; one older man said, "It sounds as if she did ceremonies on you" — well, she knew that. He added that it might be better if she acted as if it never happened. Later he did add that it sounded like a shaking-tent ceremony; where bound medicine people are placed inside a tent and when the spirits come they untie them, and they appear free outside the tent again.

"But what was it? Why did she do it to me?" she asked him.

He would not explain. All he would say was, "Maybe she saw something in you, as she worked with you."

So what else did she see in her? And why? The endlessly questioning mind. The Creator gave her a mind, so why?

And as Yvonne puzzles, she remembers that, long ago, her sister Kathy said to her, "Grandma helped you. She did not help me," and that Grandma called Kathy a "White girl" because she did things like a White person. Yvonne is certain Kathy also suffered abuse as a child, but Grandma Flora only helped her. Why?

As I write this, I take out the two pictures of Flora Baptiste Bear which Clarence Johnson gave me. I remember looking for her grave in the cemetery beside the small Roman Catholic church on Red Pheasant Reserve; there was no marker with her name on it protruding from the deep February snow when I was there. Actually, I had driven over the hills from Saskatoon hoping to visit Cecilia, but I couldn't find her either — she was travelling somewhere; as she once answered in a courtroom, "Oh, if I didn't [travel], I'd go crazy" — and looking at Flora's pictures, I remember that, before Yvonne was born, her grandmother had already passed on to her through Cecilia her own manifest gift of a cleft palate.

———

Yvonne: Sometimes I feel flooded with knowledge of the Creator, sometimes even in P4W I smelled flowers in winter, and once in spring, when the Woman who sits in the West visited me as I slept and I woke up afraid to look and I was almost asleep again, I felt someone tap my shoulder. I did not dare ask, was it a good spirit or a bad, but I knew the Woman who smells of all things beautiful, spring, medicine, sweetgrass, was with me and I felt calm. I partly saw this as vision, as I became Bear—and yet, Bear vision is different.

> O Creator, I want to continue the battle of my ancestor, Big Bear, who lived on the prairie free as an eagle but who died in misery when he was caged. I have lived a captive from the day I was born, my children have been torn from me as Big Bear's people were torn from him, his spirit was divided, there was nothing left but to die. I do not know my family, or where they are, they do not know me. O Creator, when will it end? We have survived five hundred years, when will the Native people again thrive in peace?

The sun was high at noon over the Red Pheasant Reserve. I may have been naked or only my chest bare, I was standing on a hide with my hair loose and tangled, hanging down. I was sweating—it may be I had just come out of a sweat—and I faced north, the sun rose on my right and set on my left, and my grandmother blew all over me with a long thin whistle. She was blowing and sucking, mostly circling around my stomach and around to my back while I stared ahead, blowing from the top of my head down my spine to my tailbone.

It was as if she were shaving my skin off. I felt myself opened, as if split down my back, she was reaching inside and I feared to look at what I would see there. I stared ahead while she sang, talked, prayed, answered someone whatever was needful. Then she went away, and came back with a black bear's paw and started to rub it over me. She was speaking Cree, and she went away again and returned with a yellowish paw. She rubbed me with that too, still mumbling to herself, and now she was trying to scratch me—but she still was not satisfied, so she went away again.

When she came back she carried a big bear's paw with five huge curved claws. She began to sing, moving around me, scratching me, and I felt pressure building inside me and I wanted to be clawed, scratched raw by those big claws, I longed for relief to burst open. And it seemed the claws rubbing down my arms cut me to the bone, and it felt so good, like scraping an itch away, and I wasn't scared, I rode with it into—as Jung writes—a "supreme euphoria." A high beyond drugs, a calm and force beyond any force, a fearlessness, as becoming one with all mass and energy.

Grandma did that. Using the bear claw to scrape off the outer layer of my body, she split me open from the back of my skull to the bottom tip of my spine. It seemed she was scraping me clean inside the way she had scraped my arms, drawing the claw from my shoulders to the tips of my fingers as she sang and then shaking whatever she had scraped off with the claw onto a hide lying on the ground. I was opened, cleaned out, circled by love and ceremony.

Then she looked inside my belly, searching, and it sounded like she was following orders. She knelt in front of me and began to suck on my navel. I could feel her reach deeper into me, and she started to draw a cord out of my body. I could feel the cord coming out, she was pulling it and soon I was exhausted, empty, but she kept on doing it and I began to cry. She strained and pulled, groaning as she hauled this rope out of me, and I just wanted it to end, get it out of me! And finally she threw the last part on the ground, and then she blew on my stomach, and stuffed the hole in my skin shut. I cried out in amazement and looked down at the hide, there was something heaped on it but she forbade me to look. She pressed moss on my stomach and bandaged it tight.

And I remember most clearly: she brought a hide funnel and used it like a megaphone to shout all over my body. Against one ear, the other, my nose, mouth, every part of me, in some places she shouted twice, she had me face in the four directions and in every one she called the same Cree words as if she would drive them into my flesh and through to my spirit. And I began to call too, words I couldn't understand coming from inside me, I couldn't recognize the depth of my own voice repeating what she said, she made me shout it four times in each direction, each time louder: call to the ground, then straight ahead, then higher, then straight up into the sky, each time with more strength that seemed to well up from my gut and I still couldn't roar it loud enough. It was my name, my spirit name!

Finally I collapsed on the ground. It was years before I knew again what my name was; after the long waiting and many sweats in P4W when the Elder told me in English, and gave it to me again in Cree. Medicine Bear Woman: Muskeke Muskwa Iskwewos. That was always my name, and I knew it.

I can only pray the Creator will reveal to me why I am what I am.

———

Both the pictures I have seen of Flora Baptiste Bear are black and white snapshots.

The first shows her standing with a hoe among young potato plants in a weedy garden. Her hoe is planted firmly between her feet; she grips it upright with both hands and is looking away to her left. The four posts of a barbed-wire fence enclose the garden, and directly behind her, against the fence, is an ancient hay rake designed to be pulled by horses; its thin steel wheel intersects with the distant shape of a late forties car parked between a white rectangular tent and a small log cabin with two tin stovepipes. The door of the cabin stands open, and beside its window on the longer cabin side, near the car, stands a man. He is barely discernible against the corner of the stacked logs of the cabin and the tall white poplars lifting their leafy tops all along the upper line of the picture. The man's hands are behind his back; it seems he is looking at the camera, but he is too small, too grainy in this old photo to be seen clearly. In the flatness of the picture his half-bent left leg—he may be in the act of walking forward—is precisely on the edge of Flora Bear's black hair in the foreground, level with her ear. She is wearing what is probably a grey blouse buttoned around her neck, its long sleeves pushed up to her elbows, and what seems to be a dark blue skirt that hangs below her knees and is dotted with white strawberry shapes. Her feet are planted in the earth: she looks as if she has grown there with all the other young spring plants, trees, grass, potatoes.

The second picture is head and shoulders only: she is older and seated inside a car with a rounded windshield visor—perhaps it is the same car as in the first picture, the shades of colour seem to be the same—and the rectangle of the car's right front window frames her exactly. Her heavy hair is parted at the centre, and around her forehead into two broad, doubled braids that lie on her shoulders and slant down her checked dress, down out of sight behind the car door.

Her braids frame her striking face. She stares directly into the camera, expressionless, monolithic. The cleft of her lip seems to begin at the top of her head, where the thin white line of the part in her black hair curves over the crown of her head, and continues in a straight line down between her heavy eyebrows and piercing, intense eyes, widens to the flare of her nose, and then gathers below it, broadly scarred, into the fold of her full upper lip. An indelible face.

———

Yvonne writes to me in January 1998:

> *A bear always has a fold in her upper lip. My grandma, I, my eldest child, have the gift and the legacy of the bear so strong, we have the Bear's Lip.*

———

And she has a final story to tell me, of vision and ceremony. She writes, "I do not know how to put it in words," but really she does, circling in long phrases as usual, and without much difficulty I compile it:

Memories of my grandma before I lost her. I don't know if I was in a vision, or vision state, or dream, but I was taken to a place that seemed like a place in the sky. It seemed as if it were happening in the stars, the stars were not above us but with us, and like a full moon, everything was light by itself. I recall suddenly being by my grandmother, she was with a huge circle of women. She stood in the North of the circle and on the ground next to her were baskets filled with food, or possibly medicines. Grandma passed me a basket and moved her left hand, east, as if to tell me, Go this way. I was shy and scared, but I offered each of the women in the circle to take something from the basket. They were all different, ages, dress, even demeanour, some were so intense I shook at the thought of offering them anything, I just stood in front of them, head bowed, offering, and some of them took, some not. One woman's hair hung down whiter than the purest snow, I didn't think anyone could ever look that old. A different older woman said something I could not understand, and would not take, and there was a kind and beautiful girl next to her, she told me to place something by her anyway. I had to go around and around until each basket was emptied. I was so tired and drained when I once again stood by Grandma. She seemed proud of me, and then she talked to the women again. The whole area was filled with light, it seemed as if it had no beginning and no end, and had no need for either one either. It seemed as if it was happening on an island floating in light in the sky.

I don't remember being transported, but the next thing I knew I was out walking with Grandma. As we usually did, it was in the light of ordinary day, it was the real world, not a vision or dream. I watched Grandma go to the centre of the meadow that was encircled by trees, she was talking again to someone, and singing as well. She started to dig in the ground, then she became very excited and called me to her. She pointed to a half-buried rock in the hole she had dug, and spoke Cree again. Then she had me sit on the ground next to the rock and she placed my hand on it, and gestured for me to remain there and stay still. I was scared, and I heard singing, talking, I could not say what I heard, but the rock began to shake. I sat as I was told to do, I *was calling for Grandma who had left me in this open field with this quivering rock. So I closed my eyes and waited, and just let things happen.*

Soon Grandma came back, and she laid down chewing tobacco and then ever so delicately she dug around the rock and lifted it up. She placed it in her apron as tenderly as a precious baby. She used this rock for her ceremonies with me; at night it was always in the room with me.

This all happened in spring, when the world is becoming new. Grandma searched for many rocks, it seemed as if she could actually see them hiding in the ground. I understand now they were the grandmother and grandfather rocks she used in the sweat lodge, and when the spirits began to shake them, they were saying, I give myself to you for a sacrifice. And now I believe that the women I saw in the sky circle were the people I saw in the fire. The Grandmothers.

━━━

Yvonne: I understand the medicines take care of themselves. Ceremonies are gifts given; they are as sacred tools given us so we can bridge the physical and spiritual worlds.

I was in the Shaking Tent ceremony and I was told that my life was hard, and it would remain so. I was told to keep seeking, I was told you do not give your pain to the spirit world, you must give your pain away. Does that mean share it somehow? I do not know how to do this. I ponder how to give birth to myself, in a spiritual sense.

And I recalled what an Elder told me, once as I screamed out in the sweat lodge. She told us we go to the sweat to suffer, and when you cry out like that it is as a scream of a child being born. That first scream at birth, the coming together of both physical and spiritual in the ultimate merging of the Creator's act of life. So, could it be that I too, after more than thirty-five years of existence, I can be reborn under the ceremonies?

My spirit name is Medicine Bear Woman. I ponder this greatly and still endlessly, what is a medicine person?

I know that my great-great-grandfather Big Bear's medicine power bundle rests on a shelf in a museum in New York City. It has been waiting there for sixty-five years. I also remember where my grandmother Flora's medicine bundle is, but I cannot go to that place now. And I have not spoken to the Elders about it yet.

One thing I can say now is this: a medicine person is meant for the people, and not for themselves. This in itself answered a question which I asked myself many times: why it is that my life never seems to be my own?

I have already learned that, though I am deeply sorry for the grievous pain I have caused, I must also reap what I have sown. So I offer berries to Chuck on the sacred fire, I pray for him. I cannot change what has happened, but I believe he is on a journey—may it be safe and secure—to another place, and I can still help him. I feed him when I can. I sing for him, I dance for him, and I beg he forgives us all.

Another thing is that, as the Elders tell me, all that you have experienced you must learn from, and the people who live the hardest lives can have the greatest understandings and teachings to give others. So learn well, for the sake of others.

It seems medicine people suffer in their humanness. They always seem alone, even with everyone as their friends and relatives they have their own existence. They become the unexplainable loner, because of their spiritual challenges. Others see their difference and may call them strange, or try to place a name on the unnameable. Place an earthly name on a spirit.

If this is part of what I am, I must learn how to live. Only the Creator can give destiny and fate.

Epilogue: Where People Are

Chantal, James, Susan, and Taylor: Living with their foster parents and going to school. Since Yvonne has moved to Saskatchewan and the Healing Lodge, they can visit her both in summer and during the Christmas and New Year holidays.

Dwayne Wenger: One year and three months away from serving his full ten-year prison sentence for second-degree murder: in September 1999, he could be released into lifetime parole. He is working through the various prison programs and post–high-school courses, and plans to become a licensed social worker. He and Yvonne visit each other for three days every three months.

Clarence Johnson: Now seventy-three, he remains in his little house in Butte, Montana, and drives north to visit Yvonne regularly. In October

1997 he drove to the Healing Lodge in the ancient family logging truck, and slept under it overnight to make sure he arrived as early as possible in the morning. "He has never cast me aside," Yvonne says, "or given up on me, and whatever happened between us in the past has been confronted, and settled. We tell each other stories, and try to laugh as much as we can."

Perry Johnson: Yvonne's "Little Brother" lives on the Red Pheasant Reserve, but he is, as she explains it, like so many young Indian men, "caught in the revolving-door syndrome of the legal system. The RCMP see a car full of Indians and they stop them — somebody's sure to be doing something wrong — so arrest, give them a less than two-year sentence in a provincial jail, release them home to the rez, and in no time they're arrested again. Jail doesn't scare any of them: it's just a part of who you are, where you live. And, I suppose, a continuing way of keeping the money rolling over in the provincial legal system."

Karen Sinclair: Resides in Winnipeg, but has great difficulties caring for her three children. She has addictions, and "she's still suffering," Yvonne explains. "She has lost control of herself and her children, who mean everything to her, and the whole family played headgames on her, so now she feels pressure, guilt, both for sending Leon to jail, and for not taking a stand for me in my trial against him. Her life is really hard."

Minnie Johnson: In Winnipeg as well, she has adopted two children and, as a licensed child-care worker, also at times provides the foster home for Karen's three children. "You couldn't find anyone, anywhere, who loves children more than Minnie," Yvonne says. "She knows there's something badly wrong with our family, but for her there's no talk, just damage control. She wears, and denies, the pain the best of any of us."

Kathy: Has completed a teacher-training course and lives with her husband and children on a Manitoba reserve. "She wants to remain a shadow," Yvonne says, "anonymous, go on with her life without getting involved with the endless troubles of our family. She insists she'll do her healing in her own way, by herself; she's not responsible for the rest of us."

Leon Johnson: Completed his three-year sentence at Prince Albert Prison in August 1997, and now lives with his wife and children on the Red Pheasant Reserve. Yvonne says, "He's still in heavy-duty denial, he hasn't resolved anything. I want him to say what Dad said to me. Maybe he's feeling guilty about what he did to me, but he hasn't been in touch, not a word, since he got out. Mom says Leon forgives me — but what do I need his forgiveness for?"

Cecilia Knight (*née* Bear): In 1997 she came to the Healing Lodge twice, the first time she visited Yvonne in prison since her sentencing. "Mom lives on Red Pheasant," Yvonne says, "with Perry's little boy, whose mom is dead. Otherwise she's alone, no one helps her; her car is gone, she came here at Christmas with an old clunker she borrowed and she had to pour water into it every few miles. She wants to help me, but she still denies everything. She attends a women's wellness group on the rez, but she doesn't know how to help, she never knew how to deal with me. She wants me to be strong, independent, like she's always been, but I've shamed her. She decided at some point she had to choose whom to support, and she rode that choice, but she's stored me in the back room of her heart. The residential school, I believe, six years of it, damaged her beyond belief.

"She really, really loves me, deeply. At Christmas she was here, and I had music on and was dancing with the kids, all of them, and Mom jumped up and came to me. She lifted up her arms and she danced with me, waltzing around the room."

Ernest Jensen: Continues to serve his second-degree-murder sentence in the federal Edmonton Institution; like Dwayne Wenger, he could be released on permanent parole by September 1999. He has not contacted Yvonne since March 1994, when he wrote that he was doing his "best to get a perjury charge laid against" Shirley Anne Salmon [. . .]. If we just point out that Shirley lied, we should get a new trial." Nothing has come of this suggestion.

Shirley Anne Salmon (*née* Bear): Rumours are she may be in Thunder Bay, or sometimes in Toronto or Wetaskiwin, or Vancouver. Her mother, Auntie Josephine Bear, will say nothing. In seven years Yvonne has not had one contact with her: "She may never face the consequences of her original lies, nor admit she was manipulated by the law to nail me. She must have so much pain, and me, out of my own pitifulness, I have no feelings of revenge. Shirley Anne is her own worst time, she has to put up with herself.

Leonard Charles Skwarok (1953 – 1989): Yvonne continues to pray and lay down tobacco for him.

O Creator, here I am, Medicine Bear Woman. Forgive my pitifulness. I have shared my pain because I know it is also the pain
of my people.

I pray you,
>   remain with my words, I mean no harm;
>   may the existence you have chosen for me
>   enlighten all people to a better understanding;
>   that we learn humility and pitifulness, so that no one needs
>   to suffer alone, but can find spiritual union
>   with all humankind.

A–HO

Yvonne Johnson, 1998

About the Authors

Rudy Wiebe is the author of several short story collections and essays, including *River of Stone*, and eight novels, including *The Temptations of Big Bear* and *A Discovery of Strangers*, both winners of the Governor General's Award for Fiction. He lives in Edmonton.

Yvonne Johnson is a member of the Red Pheasant Cree nation in Saskatchewan, imprisoned for first-degree murder in 1991 in Kingston Federal Prison for Women, and transferred to the minimum security Okimaw Ohci Healing Lodge for Native Women, in Saskatchewan in 1995. Thirty-six years old, she is married with three children.